THE

Cable Car
IN America

REVISED EDITION

GEORGE W. HILTON

THE
Cable Car
IN America

REVISED EDITION

A New Treatise upon Cable or Rope Traction
as Applied to the Working of Street
and Other Railways

CARTOGRAPHY BY
James A. Bier

STANFORD UNIVERSITY PRESS

Stanford 1997

STANFORD UNIVERSITY PRESS
Stanford, California

© 1982 George W. Hilton
Revised edition published in 1982 by Howell–North Books
Reprinted by Stanford University Press, 1997
Printed in the United States of America

Library of Congress Cataloging-in-Publication Data

Hilton, George Woodman.
   The cable car in America: new treatise upon cable
or rope traction as applied to the working of street and
other railways / George W. Hilton: cartography by James
A. Bier.
      p.   cm.
      Originally published: Rev. ed., 2nd ed. San Diego,
Calif.: Howell–North Books, c1982.
      Includes bibliographical references (p.   –   ) and
index.
   ISBN 0-8047-3051-2 (cl.)
   ISBN 0-8047-3052-0 (pbk.)
      1. Railroads, Cable. 2. Street-railroads—United
States.
I. Title.
TF835.H5   1997
388.4'6' 0973—dc21   97-26113
                                                               CIP

∞ This book is printed on acid-free, recycled paper.

Original printing of this edition 1997

Last figure below indicates year of this printing:

06   05   04   03   02   01   00   99   98   97

To the Memory of
FRANK J. SPRAGUE

"It's very rude of him," she said,
"To come and spoil the fun!"
        — Lewis Carroll

Table of Contents

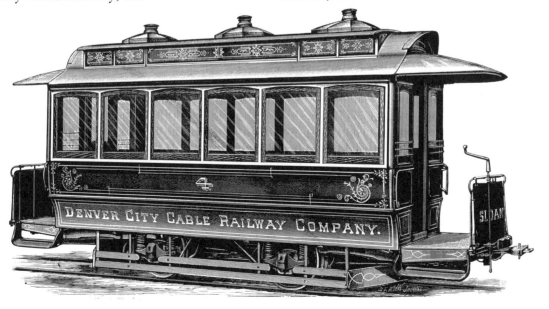

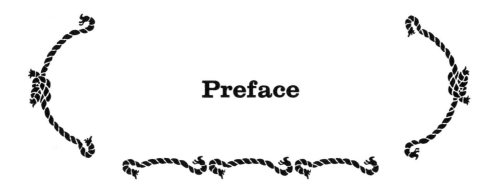

Preface

One of my father's contributions to knowledge is the concept of "gadget value" — the intrinsic interest of machinery unrelated to its use. With all respect to the steam locomotive and the theatre organ, the cable car may be said to have more gadget value than anything else.

Though I was drawn to the cable car by its gadget value, I have endeavored to set forth its economic history straightforwardly, without nostalgia, and without bias; placing the cable car in proper perspective relative to the electric streetcar requires a cold-blooded approach. Lest the reader misunderstand, the inexhaustible character of the cable car's shortcomings increased, not decreased, my affection for the whole institution as the book progressed.

The reader should also be alerted that the book is entirely devoted to cable traction of the San Francisco type, in which cars grip and ungrip an endless cable. The book does not encompass funiculars, such as Angel's Flight in Los Angeles, in which a motor on the sheave reverses the positions of a pair of cars at opposite ends of a finite cable, or counterbalances, such as the former Fillmore Street arrangement in San Francisco, in which electric cars assist one another up and down a hill at opposite ends of a finite cable turning on an unpowered sheave.

For brevity in the text, I have used the following abbreviations:

M&SP — *Mining & Scientific Press*
SRG — *Street Railway Gazette*
SRJ — *Street Railway Journal*
SRR — *Street Railway Review*

My debts to individuals are particularly numerous. Those who assisted me on individual cities I have endeavored to recognize at the close of the cities' histories. On the subject generally, Addison H. Laflin, Jr., tirelessly drew from his remarkable fund of knowledge on cable traction to assist me from my first efforts to arrange an outline in 1964 to the finished manuscript, which he read in 1970. Henry C. Collins and Foster M. Palmer both allowed me to draw upon their research for books on the cable car which they themselves had projected in past decades. Colleagues J. Clayburn La Force and Bruce Herrick read the manuscript, along with Lawrence W. Treiman, George Krambles, Charles Smallwood, Jeff Moreau, Charles J. Murphy and Phyllis B. Hilton. Mr. Murphy was especially helpful in restraining my passion for grips by pointing out that I was writing a history of technology, not a Masonic manual. U.C.L.A. provided funds for cartography. The comments of Professors Donald V. T. Bear, Ross D. Eckert and Jack Hirshleifer on my rope diagrams were invaluable.

Most of the actual writing of the book I accomplished during the 1968-69 academic year when I served as Acting Curator of Rail Transportation at the Museum of History & Technology of the Smithsonian Institution. John H. White, Jr., the Curator, was continually of help in drawing on his own considerable body of knowledge of the subject, in referring me to sources which he found in the course of his own research on car architecture, and in reading the completed manuscript. Robert M. Vogel, Curator of Engineering, served in like fashion, providing me with continual assistance on conduits, cables and engines. Captain Melvin H. Jackson, Curator of Marine Transportation, made splicing operations comprehensible to me, and Donald H. Berkebile provided a great deal of information on the relation of cable traction to horse-drawn vehicles. Betsy Braunagel typed the manuscript with an efficiency that never ceased to impress me. The research facilities of the Smithsonian generally were ideal for a project of this character.

In the course of research for this book, I followed, either on foot, by automobile or on public transportation, every cable line which ever existed in America, and every line shown as seriously projected. At various times I also followed the routes of the installations in London, Birmingham, Matlock, Douglas, Glasgow and Lisbon, along with a portion of the Edinburgh system. I cannot suggest that anyone else undertake a comprehensive tour of this character, but I do recommend that a reader seriously interested in the subject follow a former cable system to see the logic of the rope drops, the use the engineer made of gravity and the method whereby he dealt with curvature. Baltimore, partly because of its undulating terrain, partly because of the survival of five of its six powerhouses, is the most rewarding city for exploration of this character. Kansas City is also recommended for this purpose, particularly since the city's cable network was so large, though only one of its powerhouses has survived.

Finally, there is no substitute for acquaintance with the remaining San Francisco cable installation. My purpose has not been to produce a guide to the surviving San Francisco lines; rather, I hoped that enthusiasm for the San Francisco lines would lead many to enquire into the history of cable traction more generally. Anyone who uses the book in reverse fashion to move from interest in the cable era to enthusiasm for the surviving cable lines is equally meritorious, however.

GEORGE W. HILTON

University of California, Los Angeles

September 26, 1970

Preface to the Second Edition

By 1971, when the first edition of this book appeared, cable traction had virtually ceased being a dynamic subject. Accordingly, most of the changes for the second edition represent correction of errors or reinterpretation of facts. Notably, excavation of a terminal sheave on Paca Street in Baltimore and discovery by Robert A. LeMassena of a photograph of 17th and Larimer Streets in Denver required revision of maps of the two cities. Research by Terrence W. Cassidy confirmed some judgments on Kansas City, allowing removal of the question marks on the maps of that city. One might hope that the maps are now wholly accurate, but given the inherent uncertainties involved in historical reconstruction of this character, one cannot be so optimistic.

In the course of editing J. Bucknall Smith's *A Treatise upon Cable or Rope Traction as Applied to the Working of Street and Other Railways* for republication by Owlswick Press in 1977, I read the preliminary serial version of Smith's text in *Engineering*. This proved to be somewhat richer in historical detail concerning the invention of cable trac-

tion than his book. In particular, Smith demonstrated that Beauregard's grip in New Orleans was of the type later known as the bottom grip, and that it originated the basic idea of jaws closing laterally on the cable that William E. Eppelsheimer adapted as the Hallidie grip. This strengthens the argument of my book that Hallidie was the entrepreneur of the first successful cable railway, rather than a mechanical innovator. The present edition contains a revised treatment of Beauregard's grip and of the development of the grip for the pioneer Clay Street line.

Finally, one statement in the first edition proved accurate. On page 179 it is stated that the shortcomings of cable traction are inexhaustible, and so they have proved to be. To the uncounted number in the book should be added another: cable traction could not be adapted to inter-city service, which is to say that an interurban could enter a city on an electric streetcar line, but not on a cable line.

G. W. H.
March 7, 1981

The Cable Car in America

PART ONE:

Cable Traction

Horsecars came in two basic versions. The standard model, exemplified by the Hartford & Wethersfield Horse Railroad's No. 10, entailed a two-horse team, a two-man crew, and a rear platform. The bob-tail car, shown below running in Washington, D.C., had a single horse, no rear platform, and sometimes a one-man crew. Passengers entered by the single step in the rear, and in one-man operation, paid fares to the driver through a slot at the front of the car. (*Smithsonian Institution*)

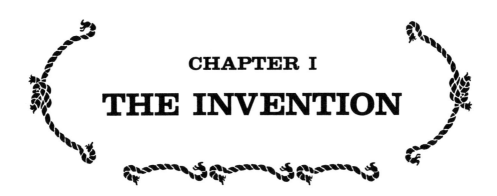

CHAPTER I
THE INVENTION

Like most of the technological advances of the 19th century, cable traction was an effort to adapt James Watt's colossal invention, the stationary steam engine, to a public demand, in this instance street passenger transportation. Urban transportation had lagged far behind intercity, since the adaptation was more difficult in several respects. It was easiest to adapt the steam engine to the hulls of ships, so that steamboats were available by the first decade of the century. Developing a self-moving steam engine was more complicated, but locomotives were economic for railroad use by 1830. The steam locomotive could have served urban transportation, as well, but for running in city streets it suffered from three disabilities — listed in very greatly diminishing order of significance: it frightened horses; its exhaust was offensive to pedestrians and residents alike; and owing to the considerable economies of scale of steam boilers, a steam engine small enough for street use was relatively inefficient. As a result, "steam dummies," as street locomotives were called generically (as a consequence of efforts to mute their exhausts), were mainly limited to suburban use.

Cable traction was an effort to make a purely mechanical connection between a stationary steam engine and the passenger. We now know that the connection should have been made electrically through attaching the engine to a dynamo and transmitting direct current to motors on electric streetcars. This is, of course, the technology perfected by Frank J. Sprague in 1888. Immediately earlier, however, for a short period of six years,

cable traction was the most economic available solution to the urban transportation problem.

It is customary to say that the cable car was invented in San Francisco in 1873 by Andrew Smith Hallidie. This is on a par in accuracy with attributing either the locomotive or the steamboat to an individual; in each instance, several men were endeavoring to bring together existing technological devices to produce an innovation. Cable traction was a highly derivative invention, not only in drawing on a combination of existing technology, but in having abundant precursors. The originality of Hallidie's invention was of more than intellectual interest; the question of the degree of novelty was basic to the legal conflict over the validity of patent rights to cable traction.

Essentially all of the elements of cable street railways had been patented or implemented experimentally before 1873. J. Bucknall Smith studied Hallidie's precursors extensively and concluded that the earliest were W. and E. K. Chapman, who in 1812 proposed moving vehicles along streets by means of a fixed cable with winding devices on the vehicles. About 1824 William James proposed drawing vehicles along highways by a chain in a hollow rail. M. Dick projected an endless-cable system with a stationary power source in 1829, and in 1838 W. H. Curtis applied for a patent on a rope haulage system in which the vehicle clamped and unclamped by vertically moving jaws — the side grip of cable technology. In 1845 E. W. Brandling in Britain proposed the first system based on a cable moving continuously in an open box, reached by a gripping mechanism

Andrew Smith Hallidie *(Smithsonian Institution)*

—in this instance a pronged device—from the car. In 1858 E. S. Gardiner of Philadelphia applied for a patent on a conduit with a narrow slot, including carrying pulleys and other devices for guidance of a cable. Surprisingly, Gardiner made no effort to patent a grip. Later, opponents of Hallidie and the San Francisco patent holders typically argued that Gardiner's patent, though never implemented, contained all the essential novelty in cable street railways.

The steel cable—or more precisely, wire rope—had been available since the period 1829-1841, when it was widely introduced into British mines for underground haulage. Once again this development was the product of several intellects, one of whom was Andrew Smith, the father of Andrew Smith Hallidie, who began experimenting with wire rope in 1828 and took out a British patent in 1835. The leading American figure in the development of steel cable was John Roebling, who established himself in 1831 as an engineer in Pittsburgh and in 1841 began manufacturing wire rope for the Allegheny inclines of the Pennsylvania Main Line of Public Works, which had used endless

hemp hawsers beginning in 1834. Roebling's wire ropes were available commercially from the early 1840s, though steel cable of homogeneous quality capable of operating for the long distances of the street railway systems described in this book waited upon the development of the open hearth process of steelmaking around 1880. Even so, by the mid-1840s all of the essentials of the technology were available, and had cable traction been introduced at that time, it would have had a long and reasonably successful history, rather than a brief flash of popularity on the eve of development of the electric streetcar.

The first successful installation of cable traction for large-scale passenger movements was in fact in the 1840s, on the Blackwall Railway in London. This operation, opened in 1840, was a railway of 5'-0" gauge, 3.75 miles long from the Minories to Blackwall. It was extended to Fenchurch Street in 1841. Initially it was operated by the paying out and reeling in of a hemp rope, but a metallic cable was shortly substituted. The first car was fixed to the cable, and others were picked up or set out at six intermediate stations; the operation appears to have been based on a cable wound alternatively around drums at the two termini. The cars set out at intermediate stations apparently were capable of gripping and ungripping from the rope. In 1844 the line handled over 2.5 million passengers and was turning in favorable financial results. Improvements in locomotives caused it to be replaced with ordinary railway technology in 1848. Cable assistance of locomotives was fairly common in early British railway practice.

Cable traction did not come to America when it was first technologically available simply because the country's urban concentrations did not yet warrant it. Indeed, it was not until the eve of the Civil War that major American cities had installations even of the horsecar. Although New York had a horsecar line in 1832, and New Orleans another in 1835, widespread adoption of horsecars came only after 1856 when a line was built from Boston to Cambridge. By 1859 horsecar lines were operating in Philadelphia, Baltimore, Pittsburgh, Chicago and Cincinnati. The horsecar was unquestionably an improvement in speed and dependability over the horse-drawn omnibus, but its shortcomings were increasingly apparent as American urbanization progressed. Horse traction was capable of about 4 to 6 miles per hour, barely faster than walking, with a standard of comfort which was a continual source of complaint in the press. A car horse cost about $125 to $200 and was good for an average of four years of service before he had to be sold for less difficult duties. In the interim he was likely to have lost most of his value. Mules, which were customary in the South, were cheaper in first cost, stood heat better and were somewhat cheaper to maintain, but they depreciated more rapidly than horses. The ratio of horses to cars varied widely between companies on the basis of terrain and traffic. A line with frequent starts and stops, as in New York, or continual undulation of terrain was likely to need two horses to a car and to have to change horses every few hours. Consequently, operators varied from four to ten times as many horses as cars. Thus, a major street railway necessarily had much of its investment in horses, an asset which depreciated rapidly and was subject to decimation from disease. The Eighth Avenue Railway in New York in 1891 alone reported 1,116 horses. The possibility of destruction of this investment through disease had been widely recognized, and this disaster descended in the form of the Great Epizootic in 1872. A respiratory and lymphatic disease of horses in the nature of influenza, the Great Epizootic descended upon the eastern United States killing 2,250 horses in Philadelphia in only three weeks and either killing or disabling 18,000 horses in New York. The decimation in New York was so bad that gangs of immigrants were hired to haul horsecars through the streets manually. The shortcomings of the horsecar were widely recognized previously, but the Great Epizootic — or more precisely, the fear of its recurrence — greatly increased the incentive of street railway operators to replace horse traction.

The incentive to replace the horsecar varied between communities. By the standards of the typical small town, the horsecar was reasonably satisfactory; it required little capital in track and was cheap and fairly flexible. The incentive to get rid of horse traction was directly proportionate to the frequency of service, frequency of stops, gradients and severity of climate. All of these con-

siderations increased the ratio of horses to cars and made the operation more expensive. Even moderately hilly cities such as Baltimore had markedly higher operating costs than flat cities, and even mild snows seriously interfered with horse traction. Accordingly, the operator of a mule car in a southern town was quiescent, but the heads of street railways in northern cities sought alternatives to the horsecar with increasing avidity as the 1870s and 1880s progressed.

Similarly, city governments had a strong incentive to urge replacement of the street railways. A horse dropped over ten pounds of fecal material a day on the street and periodically drenched the pavement with urine. Not only was this offensive *per se,* but the feces contained the virus of tetanus, such that any skin abrasion on the streets entailed the risk of an absolutely fatal disease. Urination was so frequent that smooth pavements such as asphalt were not practical; either dirt or cobblestones had to be provided to assure traction between a horse's hooves and the street. All forms of economic activity yield external benefits and involve social costs, but the social costs of horse traction were the most offensive in the history of transportation.

Unfortunately, until Sprague's perfection of the electric streetcar in 1888, none of the alternatives to the horsecar was satisfactory. The most that can be said for the cable car is that it was the best of a collection, all the rest of which were also unsatisfactory. Battery cars and compressed-air motors were limited in speed and range; both suffered from very rapid dissipation of their power supply with increase in speed. Various motors which generated heat through chemical processes using ammonia, caustic soda or other compounds never became more than curiosities.

More to the point, until 1888 the electric streetcar was also unsatisfactory and demonstrably inferior to the cable car. Although there were experimental electric locomotives in the first half of the 19th century, the first commercial electric railway, only a mile and a half, was built at Lichterfelde, near Berlin, by Ernst Werner von Siemens in 1881. Two years later Siemens and his brother built a 6-mile electric railway between Portrush and the Devil's Causeway in Ireland. Thomas A. Edison developed an experimental

America's first commercial cable passenger operation was Charles T. Harvey's Greenwich Street elevated of 1868. The line was reported to extend to 30th Street on Ninth Avenue, though the north station, shown above, was at 29th Street. The intermediate station at Dey Street is shown below under construction in 1869. *(New-York Historical Society)*

electric locomotive in 1880, and in 1883 the British-born inventor Leo Daft at Saratoga, New York, demonstrated an electric locomotive capable of hauling a railroad coach. Daft in 1885 electrified the Hampden line of the Baltimore Union Passenger Railway, which proved to be the first American electric line to operate commercially for any extended period. Simultaneously, a Belgian immigrant, Charles J. Van Depoele, developed an electric streetcar system which he exhibited at the Toronto Industrial Exposition in 1884 and 1885. In November 1885 Van Depoele opened a line of four cars in South Bend and by 1886 had several others in service, including the first complete electrification serving any city, in Montgomery, Alabama. Daft used a 120-volt DC system, and Van Depoele, 1400-volt with a motor mounted integrally with the controller on the front platform.

The innovators of the electric car suffered from two dilemmas: either they used a low voltage such as Daft's which was unable to carry far, or they used a high one such as Van Depoele's which arced and otherwise presented safety problems. Either they mounted the motor on the axle, where it shook itself to pieces, or they mounted it on the car body, where it made an imperfect connection to the axle via belts or gears. Sprague's invention was essentially a resolution of both these dilemmas. He developed a workable 500-volt DC motor (later almost universally 600-volt), and mounted it between the axle and a spring so that it made a secure mesh with a gear on the axle, but was cushioned against shocks from the track.

By the test of market choice, the pre-Sprague electric cars were inferior to the cable car. Not a single cable line was removed to be replaced by a pre-Sprague electric, but several cities adopted cable systems after unsatisfactory experience with pre-Sprague electrics. Daft's Hampden electrification in Baltimore poisoned the municipal government against electrics until well into the 1890s. The Los Angeles Cable Railway embarked upon a general cable system after the unsuccessful installation of a Daft line on Pico Street in 1887. The San Diego Cable Railway and the entire Kansas City system were built after highly unsatisfactory installations of a system of John C. Henry, which was similar to Daft's. Experimental

installations of a conduit electric system of Edward M. Bentley and Walter H. Knight preceded cable lines in Cleveland and Pittsburgh, and the Denver Tramway adopted cable only after trying a series electrification by Professor Sydney H. Short of the University of Denver.

Thus, until 1888, a purely mechanical connection between the stationary steam engine and the passenger was the most promising available. Hallidie was no earlier than third among Americans who attempted a solution via the endless cable. The first and more important of Hallidie's predecessors was Charles T. Harvey, who in 1866 patented a system based on gripping forks or claws on rapid-transit cars extending to engage collars or ferrules on an open-running steel cable, carried on small 4-wheel carts called travellers. In 1867 Harvey secured authority from the New York legislature to build an experimental half mile of elevated track on Greenwich Street between Battery Place and Morris Street for installation of his system. He was later allowed to extend track to Cortlandt Street and was reported to have made his experimental trip from Battery Place to Cortlandt Street on July 3, 1868. In April 1870 the line was extended north on Ninth Avenue to serve the Hudson River Railroad station at 30th Street.

Harvey's plant, known as the West Side & Yonkers Patent Railway, consisted of a single track erected above the east curb line of Greenwich Street to Little West 12th Street, and thence along the west curb line of Ninth Avenue to 30th Street. Harvey placed steam engines at intervals of about 1,500 feet in vaults under the sidewalks. The line had an intermediate station at Dey Street and an unspecified number of passing sidings. This simple installation, reportedly the first elevated in the world, was capable of service at 15 miles per hour, but it was not a success. It failed, ceased service and was sold at auction on November 15, 1870, for $960. The rolling stock consisted of three completed cars and six car bodies. The property passed into the hands of the New York Elevated Railroad, which removed the original structure in 1878-79 and built a new Ninth Avenue elevated in 1880.

The former Confederate General George F. Beauregard between June and November 1870 experimented with an overhead cable for his New

Above, Charles T. Harvey himself made the trial trip on the Greenwich Street elevated in 1868. *(George Krambles — except for present-day views, all credits are to collections)*

There are no known photographs of General George Beauregard's overhead cable installation in New Orleans, but after expiration of Beauregard's patent Henry Casebolt rigged an adaptation of the technology in Oakland in an unsuccessful effort to interest the Consolidated Piedmont management. The grip was a pair of jaws closing on the cable laterally, with a roller to lift the cable into the jaws — a primitive version of the arrangement later used by Worcester Haddock in Cincinnati. *(Smithsonian Institution)*

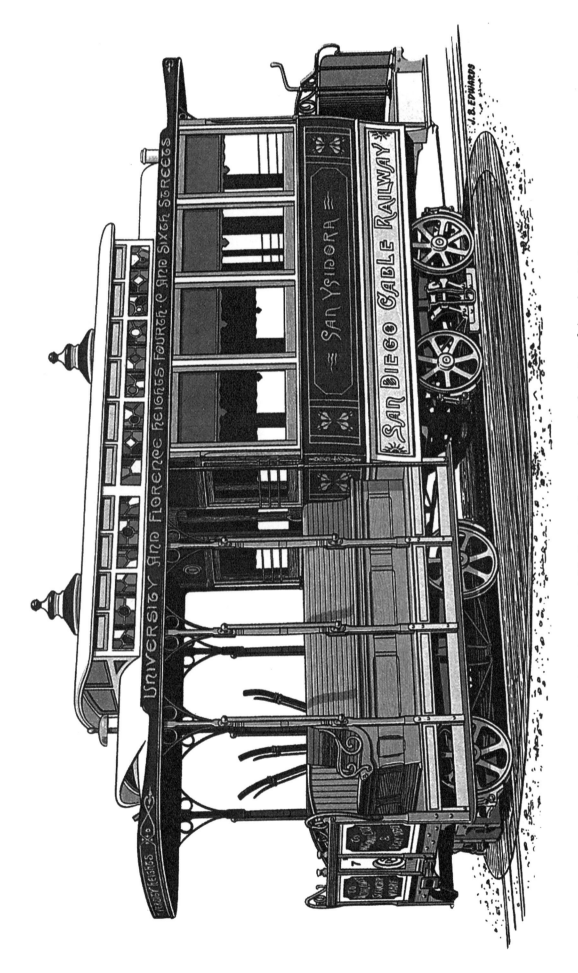

A car of the San Diego Cable Railway, from a series of color prints of American tram-cars by the British firm of Prescott-Pickup & Co. (Copyright, world rights reserved, *Prescott-Pickup & Co., Ltd., Bridgnorth, Salop., England*)

Never pass a "Let go Sheave" at the terminal switches or intermediate points without throwing grip wide open at signal plate "OPEN." Failure to do this will result in cutting the cable, or in otherwise damaging the grip and cable, for which no excuse will be accepted.

Never stop a Grip Car on a curve, except to avoid an accident.

In switching by gravity at terminals, stop before reaching signal plate "OPEN," and do not close grip again until switch is made, and return rope taken at pick up.

Where hand pick-ups are used, let grip pass about 3 feet beyond before stopping to take the cable.

Trains must not pass each other on curves. Those running east have right of way. Those running west must stop 20 feet before entering curves, if necessary to avoid meeting. Pennsylvania Avenue cars have right of way crossing 7th street in both directions.

Never start a gravity run until you see the way is clear to reach the "Pick up" before stopping. If compelled to stop to avoid an accident, the car must be pushed to the "Pick up."

Bell signals between Conductors and Gripmen are as follows:

From Conductor to Gripman:

One stroke — to stop.

Two strokes — to go ahead.

Three strokes — "stop immediately."

From Gripman to Conductor:

One stroke — Come forward.

Two strokes — I am ready to start, or passing a car of this Company, coming in an opposite direction.

Three strokes — Apply the brake immediately.

Caution persons not to get off until the car stops and to beware of passing vehicles. Children must not be allowed to move about the Grip car, and small children must not be allowed to take hold of the car to run with or beside it. Passengers must not be allowed to climb over, or stand upon the seats of cars.

When trail cars are attached for running, the signal for starting must be given by the Conductor of the rear car *first* and promptly repeated by the Conductor of the forward car, each Conductor being careful to know that passengers are safely on and off his car. Gripmen must start only on forward car's signal, but the signal to stop must be promptly obeyed when given from either car. If given from rear car, it must be repeated by Conductor of forward car.

When, from any cause, it becomes necessary to remove a Grip from the conduit, the car must first be run to a Grip hatch. If the Grip should break, immediately push or tow the car to the first Grip hatch ahead, and after removing the Grip from the conduit,

Washington & Georgetown R.R. Co.

WASHINGTON CITY, D. C.

August 1st, 1892.

RULES AND REGULATIONS

FOR

CONDUCTORS AND GRIPMEN.

WASHINGTON:
GIBSON BROS., PRINTERS AND BOOKBINDERS.
1892.

couple the car to a preceding car, or, if that cannot be done, to a following car to be pushed to the terminus. When a car is pushed over any portion of the road, both Gripmen must keep a vigilant watch; and if there is any liability of accident, the forward Gripman must immediately give the signal to stop by one stroke of the rear bell sharply, and at *the same time apply the brake.*

Never pass a let-go pulley with a broken grip. No excuse will be received for failing to close a grip-hatch or pulley-trap, after using.

Cars must be brought to a *full stop* to allow passengers to get on and off. Stop at the further crosswalk of all street-crossings when running in either direction, except at Transfer junctions, with the rear platform occupying one fourth of the crosswalk. When a stop has to be made before crossing a street, the first crosswalk must be left clear in front of the car.

Should the rope stop running, the Grip must be immediately released, and the Gripman be ready to apply it again when the rope resumes running and the preceding car has started. When a car is delayed from this or any other cause, it must not be allowed to obstruct a street-crossing or the tracks of another road.

In the event of an accident rendering it necessary to stop the rope, you will immediately run to the nearest telephone and call up the Central Power Station, No. 630.

Good order must be maintained among passengers, and drunken or disorderly persons, or any in such condition as to make them offensive to others, must not be allowed to ride. Allow no person unable to take proper care of themselves to ride on the Grip car.

Gripmen are not allowed to be seated while the car is in motion, or to lean against the seats or levers. Keep your positions near the levers ready to release the Grip and apply the Brakes *instantly*. When on the stand, or if detained on the road, the Grip must be thrown wide open and Brakes set firm.

Gripmen will not permit any person, not authorized by the Superintendent, to handle the levers or to ride within the space provided to work them.

Whenever the rope is released from the Grip it must be for the purpose of slowing down or stopping, *and in no case to increase speed*, as the speed of the car must never exceed that of the rope. Any Gripman known to run downgrade with the rope loose in the Grip, except in case of a strand, or at places provided for in *rules* and *orders*, will be liable to immediate discharge.

Never attempt to adjust a Grip while the car is in motion.

The utmost care must be used to prevent accidents, or injury to the car and property of the Company. When the car is in motion do not look back for any purpose whatever until you are sure that the way is clear a sufficient distance ahead to insure perfect safety, and under no circumstances must your attention be taken from the running more than a few seconds at a time.

Do not run nearer to a preceding car than one hundred feet, unless ordered to do so. No excuse will be received for collision with a preceding car.

Any Conductor knowing a Gripman to run down grade with the rope loose in the Grip, except when provided for in Rules and Orders, and failing to report the same, will be liable to discharge.

SPECIAL CAUTION: Gripmen and Conductors must *never take it for granted* that passengers will step on or off the car or train quickly enough to avoid an accident, *but stop and wait till all are safely on or off* before giving the signal to start or applying the grip. Also, *never be too sure* that persons on or near the track will see the Car or Train and keep out of your way, but *be prepared to stop instantly* if necessary and especially *when children are near, release your cable* and go slowly past them. *A life saved or accident prevented is worth more than promptness in time or anything else.*

H. HURT
President

(Collection of Robert A. Truax)

Orleans & Carrollton Railroad. Opposite what is now Audubon Park he arranged a route of less than three blocks, with a cable supported on bracket arms above the track and powered by two old locomotives at opposite ends of the line. Beauregard used a grip in which a roller pushed the cable upward into a pair of gripping jaws; the gripping action tended to raise the cars off the track and to derail them while starting. Asa Hovey, in 1888, argued that Beauregard's experiment was of no value, except for development of the first workable grip.

Hallidie claimed to have conceived the idea of cable street railways in 1869 while walking up Jackson Street, San Francisco. The Omnibus line — on a route which, somewhat surprisingly, was never cabled — regularly used two horses per car, but added a further team of three for the grade from Kearny to Stockton. As Hallidie watched the horses being whipped while slipping on the wet cobblestones, he conceived — alike on humanitarian and economic grounds — of applying the cable propulsion to which he was already devoting his life to street railway transportation.

Hallidie had been born in London on March 16, 1836, son of Andrew Smith and Julia Johnstone Smith; he adopted the surname Hallidie in honor of his uncle, Sir Andrew Hallidie, a prominent British physician. After early apprentice training in the mechanical arts, the young man's health deteriorated, so that in 1852, partly in an effort to restore it, his father took him to California. The elder Smith returned to England in 1853, but Hallidie remained in California as a prospector. After indifferent success in seeking gold, he began putting his mechanical training to use. In 1855 he arranged a wire suspension bridge for an open flume, and in 1856 he rigged a wire-rope haulage system for a mine at American Bar. Having now become involved in the family business of steel cable, he went to San Francisco in 1857 and established a small factory for wire rope. He divided his energies between the cable factory and the designing of bridges and haulage systems for mines. In particular, in 1867 he patented the "Hallidie Ropeway," a system of moving ore out of mines by means of an overhead cable. This system involved gripping and ungripping of buckets off an endless cable in the fashion he eventually needed for street cable systems. How much Halli-

die drew upon the earlier unexecuted patents of British and American inventors to adapt his haulage system is impossible to say; an inventor has an incentive to maximize his claim to novelty.

In any case, Hallidie inevitably conceived the application of his mine haulage system to urban transportation, and following 1869 endeavored to finance a project to scale the east escarpment of Nob Hill. With the assistance of Joseph Britton, Henry L. Davis and James Moffitt, associates in the Mechanics' Institute of San Francisco, which Hallidie had helped to found, Hallidie by 1872 had secured financing of the enterprise. He bought the franchises of Benjamin H. Brooks, who had failed to finance a proposal for endless-rope traction in the city. After considering California Street, Hallidie decided upon Clay on the grounds that construction would be cheaper and that the residents were willing to contribute $40,000 to his financing. Only $28,000 of this sum manifested itself, but the line was built as the Clay Street Hill Railroad in 1873, to be opened on August 1. With some difficulty Hallidie had the property ready for trial trips by August 2, and finished the line for revenue service on September 1.

It was this modest Clay Street Hill Railroad, a mere six-tenths of a mile of lightly-built double track, which inseminated the cable movement in American surface transportation. Since this was the first massive movement away from the horse, it was no small achievement. The installation contained every basic element to appear in every later standard cable system: a wire rope running in a conduit with a narrow slot, a stationary power source, a device for maintaining tension in the cable, and a grip on the cars capable of providing a continuum from full release to a full hold at which the car moved at the speed of the cable. Every part of the technology had some degree of evolution in subsequent installations, but the technology was so simple it was not capable of a high degree of improvement.

Apart from the question of the novelty inherent in Hallidie's invention, in light of its precursors, there is a question of the precise degree of responsibility Hallidie had in the design of the plant, relative to his draftsman, William E. Eppelsheimer. In the later history of cable traction, Eppelsheimer bulked considerably larger than

Hallidie's grip car was so obviously a replacement for the horse, given the pure bob-tail architecture of the trailer, that traditionalists doubtless looked upon it as yet another attack of modern technology on the old order. (*Roy D. Graves*)

WM. EPPELSHEIMER.   HENRY CASEBOLT.   ASA E. HOVEY.

Second of San Francisco's cable lines was the Sutter Street Railroad of Henry Casebolt and Asa Hovey. Here 15 of the company's employees line up at the twin turntables at the west end of the route. (*Roy D. Graves*)

Hallidie. Indeed, Hallidie's original Clay Street technology was used in only one subsequent installation — the Presidio & Ferries, in which Hallidie had an interest — whereas Eppelsheimer became one of the most prominent engineers in the industry. It is notable that no one, as far as is known, ever sought out Hallidie as the engineer for an installation in another city, though many engineers engaged in this activity. In a legal action in 1883, the Market Street Cable Railway claimed that Eppelsheimer had actually designed Hallidie's grip. J. Bucknall Smith stated flatly in 1884 that Eppelsheimer had designed the grip, but that the principle was Beauregard's of 1869. Eppelsheimer certainly worked out much of the mechanical detail of the line.

Eppelsheimer was born in Germany in 1842 and educated in engineering at the Polytechnic Institute of Karlsruhe. Hovey reported that Eppelsheimer had considered cable traction in Germany before coming to San Francisco in 1869. Eppelsheimer worked for a year at the Union Iron Works and, after some additional experience in engineering, met Hallidie in February 1872. He supervised construction of the Clay Street Hill Railroad, but resigned in March 1874 to go into private practice of engineering. He remained active in designing cable projects in San Francisco and, after 1880, in Britain.

Regardless of the relative degree of responsibility of Hallidie and Eppelsheimer for the Clay Street Hill Railroad, the pioneer line was a great success. Hallidie hoped the company would handle about 3,300 passengers a day and return 12 per cent on the $85,150 investment, but the line developed the Nob Hill area extremely well and quickly exceeded expectations. At times the company reported as much as a 35 per cent return.

Inevitably, the high return to the Clay Street Hill Railroad attracted other firms. Significantly, San Francisco's second line was not a parallel ascent of Nob Hill, but a route along Sutter Street, an undulating major thoroughfare running west from the central business district, skirting the south escarpment of the hill. The Sutter Street Railway, successor to the Front Street Mission & Ocean Railway, had been in operation since 1873 without notable success; but conversion to cable in January 1877 resulted in the line attracting an

additional 962,375 passengers relative to 1876, and caused the company's stock to appreciate from 24 to 60. Operating costs fell about 30 per cent. The experience indicated that cable traction was economic even without grades such as the 15 per cent and worse on Clay Street which were really impossible for horse traction.

The Sutter Street Railway was operated by Henry Casebolt, proprietor of a major machine works who had become active in street railways. The installation was designed, in collaboration with Casebolt, by Asa Hovey, who became another of the major figures in cable engineering. Hovey had been born in Waterford, Vermont, in 1830 and at the age of twenty became a salesman for the Fairbanks Scale Manufacturing Company. He claimed to have thought first of cable traction as a means of moving the East Boston ferry in 1848. He also purported to have developed his grip as early as 1852, but he may well have been endeavoring to maximize his claim to primacy. He claimed to have studied Cyrus Field's system for maintaining constant tension in paying out the Atlantic cable in 1852 and considered adaptation of the process to cable traction. Hovey's claim to primacy for tension devices is entirely credible; the Sutter Street powerhouse contained the first tension run in which the cable ran to a movable tension carriage, which came to be the standard method of dealing with the stretching of long cables. Hovey, who considered himself one of the four inventors of cable traction, along with Beauregard, Hallidie and Eppelsheimer, endeavored to build the Sutter Street line with an entirely original set of patents so as to avoid infringement on Hallidie's. Hallidie, who had formed the Traction Railway Company in 1875 to hold his patents, brought a legal action initiating the conflict concerning patent rights which characterized the entire cable era.

Third of San Francisco's cable lines was the California Street Cable Railroad, an effort to provide a second ascent of Nob Hill from the east and to penetrate the Western Addition beyond Van Ness Avenue. The company was a promotion of Leland Stanford, marking the entry of the Southern Pacific's interest in the cable network. The line, which was opened in 1878, also marked the entry into the industry of Henry Root, yet another of the principal engineers of cable traction. Root

The inconspicuous intersection of Geary and Larkin Streets in San Francisco established the industry's usual — though not invariable — rule of placing the senior cable on top at a crossing. A Geary Street train stands just west of the crossing. *(Roy D. Graves)*

The photograph of the east terminus of the California Street Cable Railroad in the 1880s, below, shows the surface of Henry Root's iron-and-concrete conduit. The overhead view also demonstrates Root's terminal arrangement. After uncoupling, the trailer rolled across the upper turnouts to the bottom of the track. The grip then also descended by gravity to couple to the trailer in the position shown here. *(Roy D. Graves)*

had been born in Vermont in 1845 and immigrated into California in 1864. He joined the Southern Pacific in 1866 and ten years later was a well-established engineer of the Southern Pacific and its subsidiary horsecar lines in San Francisco. Stanford had directed Root to observe the Clay Street Hill Railroad closely throughout its construction and early operation, and when the decision was made to attempt a cable line on California Street, he deputed Root to design it. Root recognized the inadequacy of the cheap conduits of the earlier lines and devised a heavy-duty conduit of old railroad iron bent into yokes and set in concrete. Although later engineers typically used cast iron for yokes, Root had invented the iron-and-concrete conduit which became standard in the industry. This development was more important than it appeared; only an iron-and-concrete conduit was resistant enough to contraction to make cable traction workable outside of the mild climate of California. Root's other major contribution was his single-jaw side grip which, though similar to Hovey's, proved to be the most widely used in the country, thereby placing Root in a central position to the later patent conflicts in the industry.

San Francisco's fourth installation, the Geary Street Park & Ocean Railroad, was similar to the Sutter Street Railway in being a project to connect the central business district with the Western Addition across terrain that was only hilly. This line, opened in February 1880, was designed by Eppelsheimer, who used the opportunity to create the bottom grip which bears his name — the grip still used on the remaining lines in San Francisco. Since the Sutter Street Railway had built a branch down Larkin Street in 1878, it became necessary to cross two cable lines for the first time. Obviously, one cable had to be passed over the other; the car on the lower cable necessarily was forced to drop the rope and take it again on the opposite side of the intersection. It was clearly preferable to have the top position, since dropping the cable and picking it up entailed wear alike on the cable and on the dies in the grip; the process also involved the risk of hitting the superior rope if the gripman through negligence or malfunction of the grip failed to drop the inferior rope. The Larkin rope was placed over Geary,

Henry Root in Berkeley in 1920. *(Louis L. Stein)*

settling the problem by pure seniority, thereby establishing a tradition which was observed slavishly in San Francisco and a majority of other cities.

As the decade ended in 1880, a fifth line was built in San Francisco, which like the rest made contributions simultaneously to the development of the city and to the technology of cable traction. In an effort to reach the Russian Hill area, the financial interests which had been associated with Hallidie in the Clay Street Hill Railroad promoted the Presidio & Ferries Railroad to run along Union

25

Last of the cable lines built in San Francisco before the spread of the innovation to other cities was the Presidio & Ferries Railroad. This view of grip and trailer, both numbered 17, dates from the 1890s, after the line's extension into the Presidio. (*Louis L. Stein*)

Street, north of Nob Hill. Previously, all of the lines in the city had been straight; cable traction was widely thought incapable of traversing curves at all. Union Street, however, was so far north of the business district that some method had to be found to bring cars south. Happily, at the intersection of Union with Montgomery (now Columbus), the city's one diagonal street in the area, both streets descended as they approached the crossing. Accordingly, the line was rigged so that cars dropped the rope in each direction approaching the 8-foot sheaves on which the cable turned, and picked it up again after rolling around the curve on momentum. Such an arrangement was known as a "let-go curve," in distinction to what came to be known as a "pull curve," in which the car held the cable in its grip while turning the angle. As the year 1880 closed, the pull curve was yet to be developed.

By the end of the decade in 1880, San Francisco had the modest total of 11.2 miles of cable route, but the experience of the period had demonstrated that cable traction was highly profitable, and that all of the major problems in technology except the pull curve had been solved. This was not, of course, lost on the street railway industry as its leaders looked about for an alternative to

the horse. The experience in San Francisco was widely considered a special case, however, because of the city's odd geographical properties. Its streets had been laid out in the usual American grid patterns without regard to the topography, producing on the one hand, its spectacular views down the streets, but on the other, grades such as are rarely found elsewhere. Several streets have grades in excess of 20 per cent, and some, notably on the east and south escarpments of Telegraph Hill, are so steep as to be beyond vehicles of any type. Cable traction was ideal for such circumstances, since almost alone among means of replacing the horse it did not depend on adhesion between the wheel and the surface on which it ran. At the opposite extreme, it was not yet demonstrated that cable traction could be adapted generally to curves. Grip shanks had to be thin enough to run through slots less than an inch wide, and whether they could be subjected to lateral pressure on pull curves was an open question.

Finally, San Francisco enjoyed a mild climate, so that ice and snow did not build up deposits in the conduit. No one doubted that cable lines could be operated in the South, but few southern cities had the population to justify such a capital-intensive system; and for reasons previously mentioned, the humble mule car served the South better than the horsecar served any other part of the country. The incentive to get rid of the horsecar was directly proportional to the severity of the climate of a city, but so was the difficulty of operating a cable system, not only in accumulation of snow in the conduit, but also in protection of the slot from closing. The range of temperatures in San Francisco was small enough that slot closure did not arise, but in a city with an ordinary continental climate, the cold of the winter would contract the entire conduit, and tend to narrow the slot to the point that the grip shank could not pass through it. The colder were the winters, the heavier had to be the ironwork to prevent slot closure, and the deeper had to be the conduit to allow the snow and ice to accumulate without interfering with the free running of the cable.

Thus, the decision to build a cable system in a city with ordinary northern winters was a momentous one; he who made it was an innovator of the cable car not to be ranked behind Hallidie, Eppelsheimer, Hovey and Root — though he might never hold a patent. He proved to be C. B. Holmes, president of the Chicago City Rail-

way. This, the largest transit operator in the most rapidly growing American city, had as great an incentive as any company to replace the horse. Holmes came to San Francisco in 1880 and was greatly impressed with what he saw. Not only did he decide to chance installation of cable traction in a city with really fierce winters, but he helped organize the innovators in San Francisco for the spread of their invention. He assisted them in resolving the dispute over patents between Hallidie and Hovey, so that on April 14, 1881, the officers and directors of the Clay Street and Sutter Street companies formed the Cable Railway Company as a patent trust, which eventually was expanded to encompass all of the patents of the San Francisco innovators and some from other cities. The trust endeavored — as will be seen, with mixed success — to monopolize patents for cable street railways so that no line could be built without infringing one or more of the San Francisco patents. The trust, anticipating world-wide adoption of cable traction, established the Patent Cable Tramway Company of London as licensee of its patents for Britain and the British Empire. As it proved, the next installation and the next advance in technology were to be in the British Empire — and in one of its most remote reaches.

The Presidio & Ferries line gave cable traction its first let-go curve. At the intersection of Montgomery and Union, both streets descended to the crossing. Union descended sharply from the right and Montgomery, now Columbus in this present-day view, came down gently from the left. The angle is obtuse, allowing an easy passage around the curve in full release. (GWH)

27

The cable system Asa Hovey designed for C. B. Holmes' Chicago City Railway went far beyond anything San Francisco had produced in size and complication. Most difficult feature of the installation was the joint terminal loop of the State Street and Wabash Avenue lines. Here, before the arrangement was modified in 1892, a State Street train turns from Madison Street into Wabash, while a Wabash-Cottage Grove Avenue train waits to follow it. *(Chicago Historical Society)*

CHAPTER II
THE EXPANSION

On February 24, 1881, Dunedin, New Zealand, became the first city in the world, apart from San Francisco itself, to open a cable street railway built with the Cable Railway Company's patents. Remote from San Francisco though Dunedin might be, the city's geographical properties called for cable traction as much as any in the world. Located 13 miles up an inlet called Otago Harbour, Dunedin has a flat central business district, built largely on artificial land, surrounded by steep hills on three sides. To the north the hillsides are covered in part by a parkland known as the Town Belt, above which are several residential neighborhoods, including the Borough of Roslyn. To connect Roslyn with downtown Dunedin, George W. Duncan and his associates promoted the Dunedin & Roslyn Tramway Company in 1880 and set forth to design the physical plant. The line left the central area via Rattray Street, which necessarily involved a curve at St. Joseph's Cathedral on a 13 per cent grade. Duncan could arrange for a let-go curve on the order of the Union-Montgomery curve in San Francisco for his downbound cars, but the grade was too heavy for upbound cars to traverse the curve in full release. Consequently, Duncan was forced to solve the one major remaining problem of cable traction: to invent the pull curve. This he did, arranging a set of horizontal pulleys behind a chafing bar. The cable ran on the pulleys, and the chafing bar held the grip shank out from the pulleys to protect it against lateral pressure. Unfortunately, it was necessary to traverse a pull curve at the full speed of the cable since, if the cable were not held with a full grip, the lateral pressure might tear it from the jaws, cut strands on the cable and possibly also damage the grip. Nonetheless, Duncan had made a technological advance which rendered cable traction practical in cities which were not characterized by the straight streets and direct transit routes of San Francisco.

It remained to be shown that cable traction was practical in ordinary American winters. This was to be demonstrated beyond question by C. B. Holmes' installation on the Chicago City Railway. This was a far larger, more capital-intensive and complicated physical plant than any of its predecessors. Although Chicago has an ordinary grid pattern of streets, the Wabash-Cottage Grove line required several curves to follow Lake Michigan to the southeast and involved a joint loop of two lines on streets in the central area. The loop entailed not only pull curves, but two auxiliaries — low speed cables run off reduction gears in vaults under the streets — in an effort to have cars take the pull curves at half the speed of the main line cables. The use of a loop at the north end and ordinary turnouts at the south required Asa Hovey, the designer, to develop the double-jaw side grip, capable of holding the cable from either side of the shank.

When the Chicago City Railway's first cable track on State Street opened on January 28, 1882, the city was in the midst of a typically severe winter; no better time or place could have been chosen to demonstrate the general practicality of

C. B. Holmes' demonstration that cable traction was workable in ice and snow was basically responsible for the spread of cable lines after 1882. Here a crew clears snow from the slot on the 7th Street line in Washington in the 1890s. *(Library of Congress)*

In San Francisco, with no such problems, 1883 saw the opening of the Southern Pacific's Market Street Cable Railway. Here Market Street combination cars run past the old Palace Hotel in the 1890s. *(Roy D. Graves)*

cable traction. Hovey later reported that he had almost refused the commission to design the line. He was walking to the telegraph office to wire his refusal to Holmes on the ground of his dislike of Chicago's climate when he met a friend, F. F. Low, who talked him into accepting. Hovey owed a great debt to Low, since the Chicago City Railway installation proved to be eventually the largest in the country and one of the most influential in the design of systems in other cities. Hovey's grip, in particular, was highly influential in later design.

The Chicago City Railway cable lines proved able to move passengers at half again the speed of horsecars in the central area and at only about half the cost per mile to the carrier. The advantage in speed over the horsecar increased with distance from the terminal loop; the cables ran at successively higher speeds, eventually up to 14 miles per hour, toward the south end of the system. This arrangement, which was a further advance over practice in San Francisco where the companies were limited to 8 miles per hour by municipal regulation, became customary in the industry.

If cable traction had been considered a special case because of San Francisco's heavy grades, absence of curvature and mild climate, Holmes demonstrated that it was economic on absolutely flat terrain, with several pull curves, and in a climate that ranged from −10° to 100° in the ordinary course of a year. The fact that the cars did not depend on adhesion was a positive advantage in winters; cable cars were marvelously superior to horsecars in the snow. The system replaced about 1,000 horses and 200 stablemen with only some 400 horsepower from the powerhouse. Within two years, 150 to 180 cable cars were running on lines which had been served by 60 horsecars, and within five years the company was reported hauling 27 million cable passengers a year. Stock of the firm went from 100 to 300.

The street railway industry could hardly avoid the conclusion that, if the cable car was economic in Chicago, it would be economic in any city of substantial population. Thus, January 28, 1882, marks the opening of the second period in the history of the cable car, the period in which cable traction was the most economic means of public

CHARLES B. HOLMES, PRESIDENT OF THE AMERICAN STREET RAILWAY ASSOCIATION.

urban transportation. The cable car spread, as any other technological improvement would have done, in response to rates of return which justified the investment. In the case of cable traction, the investment was usually argued to be around $100,000 per mile of double track, about two-thirds embodied in the conduit. As will be argued in Chapter VII, this estimate in retrospect appears grossly inadequate relative to the reported investment of cable companies; but in any case, the investment was so heavy that cable traction was justified only on the most major routes or on lines being built into high-lying residential lands inaccessible by other forms of transit. There were plenty of situations of both sorts in the country. The economy was relatively prosperous, our cities were growing rapidly, virtually all street railways were experiencing secular growth in traffic and many cities were expanding toward uplands which horse-drawn vehicles could not serve adequately.

The following year, 1883, saw three dissimilar installations of cable traction. In San Francisco the Southern Pacific interests opened a heavily built system, the Market Street Cable Railway, mainly to serve the flatter areas of the city which had the highest population densities. Previously,

31

The New York Cable Railway, which the patent trust endeavored without success to promote from 1883 to 1890, was to cover Manhattan with 29 lines. The crosstown lines were to be operated with ordinary grip-and-trailer technology, though the main north-south routes were apparently to have more substantial equipment. The reason for the lefthand operation in the engraving is unknown. *(M&SP)*

all of the cable lines had used single-truck open-grip cars, with separate trailers — usually a single trailer, but in the case of the Chicago City Railway, as many as three. Henry Root for the Market Street installation designed double-truck combination cars, combining an open front section for the gripman and those passengers who preferred the out-of-doors with a closed compartment for the rest. Subsequently, cable engineers had a choice of single-truck or double-truck equipment; the majority preferred the traditional single-truck grips and trailers, but a minority, especially on heavily travelled lines, used combination cars. Double-truck cars were also considered more stable on short curves.

The other two installations of 1883 were the first efforts at cable lines built to patents not controlled by the trust of the San Francisco inventors. Since the trust charged about $5,000 per mile for the use of patents, the incentive to avoid it was

considerable. Col. W. H. Paine, assistant engineer of the New York & Brooklyn Bridge, designed a cable rapid transit line, which had been part of the bridge project from the outset. In Philadelphia Peter A. B. Widener attempted a mile and a quarter of street railway using non-trust patents for a lightly built physical plant with a cheap bolted conduit and a top grip in which the jaws held the cable from below.

The prospect of non-trust systems arising, plus the less-than-total effectiveness of the Cable Railway Company in resolving patent disputes between the various San Francisco inventors, caused Hallidie, the Casebolt-Hovey interests and the Southern Pacific-Root interests to begin efforts to reform the trust. In July 1883 the Hallidie interests arranged with William P. Shinn, a Wall Street railroad financier, and patent lawyers John R. Bennett and George Harding to form the National Cable Railway Company, based in New York, to license the trust's patents. Hallidie and the Southern Pacific interests formed the Pacific Cable Railway Company in San Francisco. On October 21, 1885, the two companies executed a market-sharing agreement whereby National Cable was to have rights for the area east of the 106th degree of longitude (which is just west of Denver) with the exception of Chicago, Pittsburgh and Omaha, in which Root had already licensed patents. Pacific Cable was to reserve the West Coast. A patent pool implemented with a market-sharing agreement would be unquestionably illegal under subsequent interpretation of the antitrust laws, but the arrangement antedated the Sherman Act by five years. When the two companies issued their joint prospectus in 1887, it showed 95 patents covering every phase of cable technology, but the most basic were the Hovey, Root and Eppelsheimer grips, and Root's iron-and-concrete conduit. The prospectus shows Hallidie as president of Pacific Cable, with Stanford and Crocker of the Southern Pacific among the directors, and Hallidie's associate on the Clay Street Hill Railroad Henry L. Davis, as president of National Cable Pacific Cable organized a subsidiary, the Pacific Cable Construction Company, which operated a a contractor for several West Coast installation:

The first line built by Pacific Cable after th reorganization of the trust was the Second Stre Cable Railway in what was looked upon as tl small but promising city of Los Angeles. This u obtrusive line was the first effort at single-tra operation of a line with movements in both direc

W. H. PAINE.

tions; it was also notable for the worst grade on any American line, 27.7 per cent. Among the installations of 1885, non-trust lines far outnumbered the Second Street line in mileage. Henry M. Lane, who had a non-trust version of Hovey's Sutter Street technology, built his first line in Cincinnati; most of the Philadelphia system was put in service; and Robert Gillham opened the first line in Kansas City — though he had to arrange with the trust for use of Hovey's Chicago grip when a non-trust grip proved inadequate for his grades. More important, the Third Avenue Railroad in New York in 1885 and 1886 opened about 4.8 miles of cable line on 125th Street and Amsterdam Avenue in New York with the "American system" of D. J. Miller. Like many who became prominent in the industry, Miller had worked under Hovey in designing the Chicago City Railway. He had been a draftsman in Chicago, but in 1883 he went to New York, where he developed an extremely capital-intensive system involving duplicate cables for the Third Avenue Railroad.

Opening day of the Payne Avenue line in Cleveland brought out the Cleveland Grays Orchestra and an impressive show of bunting. Three inaugural trains line up before the fine old Victorian Hollenden Hotel. *(Frank A. Gifford)* Similar festivities greeted the opening of the Downey Avenue line of the Pacific Railway in Los Angeles. *(Security Pacific Bank)*

The New York installation was particularly menacing to the trust, since National Cable had a plan to build a huge system, nearly five times larger than any actually built, covering Manhattan Island. On April 24, 1884, the rapid transit commissioners of New York, appointed by Mayor Edson the previous year, recommended a network of 29 routes, three major lines to run north and south on 1st-2nd Avenue, Lexington and 10th Avenue, partly on embankments with semi-rapid-transit technology, and the rest to operate on other north-south streets or cross-town. National Cable incorporated the New York Cable Railway to build the system of some 72 miles, but the mayor vetoed the franchise on March 16, 1885. The trust continued its efforts to promote this project throughout the 1880s and was not finally defeated until the state senate refused to enfranchise the company in 1890. Accordingly, the trust had maximum incentive to try to put down a rival on Manhattan Island. The Third Avenue Railroad, as its name indicates, intended a route from the Post Office to the Harlem River along Third Avenue, with Miller's technology. National Cable by July 1885 had instituted 27 infringement suits, ten in Philadelphia, three in Cincinnati, six in Kansas City, two against the Brooklyn Bridge and six against the Third Avenue Railroad. As was to become apparent in 1889, the actions against the Third Avenue Railroad were the most important the trust undertook.

The trust had a good year in 1886; all of the installations were made with its patents. James G. Fair's Oakland Cable Railway brought forth a narrow gauge version of the Market Street Railway, and the Temple Street Railway in Los Angeles essentially duplicated the Second Street Cable Railway of the previous year. The St. Louis Cable & Western initiated cable service in the Mississippi Valley, and the North Hudson County Railway used trust patents for a short but heavily-built rapid-transit line in Hoboken and Jersey City.

By 1887 cable traction had proved itself widely enough to have escaped the category of the experimental. At the end of 1886, 62.3 miles were in existence in eleven cities, including an experimental line on the grounds of a mental hospital in Binghamton, New York. The level of business activity was rising, and especially in the Missouri

OAK HILL.

THIS ADDITION of 120 acres, lying adjoining IRVINE PARK on the east, is composed of about six hundred fifty-foot lots, laid out uniform with WYATT PARK, and IRVINE PARK, and GRAND SUMMIT, forming one splendid, large addition of 1,585 lots, with much the same natural features of

SHADY GROVES AND BEAUTIFUL LAWNS,

And Fine Scenery.

This property will be the eastern terminus of

THE CABLE LINE,

With the power house and other buildings of the Cable Company. Here, also, will connect with the Cable the DUMMY LINES to be built to the stock yards and factories to the southwest, and to the asylum and fair grounds to the northeast, affording rapid transit to those points, as well as to the center of the city. The united syndicates will place on all these additions water and gas, when and wherever needed, and a fine school house will be built on a central location. Lots will also be donated to any and all Christian denominations who will build upon them. These lands are high, dry, and undulating; a succession of beautiful hills and fine shady groves. No place presents better advantages for a beautiful home than OAK HILL.

This fine plat of 1,585 fifty-foot lots will be placed on sale in St. Joseph at the office of

W. J. & C. W. Hobson, N. W. cor. Fifth and Francis

AND

Irvine & Cox, Delaware Street, Kansas City, Mo.

The Wyatt Park Railway was counted upon to develop Oak Hill and three other subdivisions in St. Joseph, Missouri. Begun as a cable line, the railway was completed as an early Sprague electrification. *(Library of Congress)*

Valley and the Pacific Northwest, a boom was developing in land on plateaus or in undulating areas behind central business districts. As a consequence, the cable car was to reach its peak in installations almost simultaneously with Sprague's perfection of the electric streetcar, which was shortly to annihilate it.

In 1887, 32.2 miles of cable line were built, nearly double the mileage installed in 1886. The Metropolitan Street Railway and the Grand Avenue Railway in Kansas City opened 11.4 miles of route, built with Root's own technology; and the Cable Tramway Company of Omaha opened a line built with trust patents by Robert Gillham. Lane's second line in Cincinnati, the Vine Street Cable Railway, was the only non-trust installation of the year.

Although cable installations were not to reach their peak until 1889, in an intellectual sense the movement reached its high point in 1887 with the publication of J. Bucknall Smith's *A Treatise upon*

Two opening days in Southern California: above, the Boyle Heights line of the Pacific Railway of Los Angeles, and below, the short-lived and unsuccessful San Diego Cable Railway. *(Security Pacific Bank; Title Insurance & Trust Company)*

Cable or Rope Traction as applied to the Working of Street and Other Railways. Smith, a British civil engineer who had been in charge of construction on the first British endless-cable line built with trust patents, the Highgate Hill Cable Tramway of 1884, produced the only treatise on the cable cars of the entire cable era. Lucid, well-written, copiously illustrated, the book was a serious exposition of cable traction mainly in an effort to interest British tramway operators in the American innovation. He wrote with an engaging honesty in obvious conviction that cable traction was an advance which ought to be disseminated in his country. Smith's timing was superb: he wrote at the only possible time he could have produced the book he did. He lumped the electric streetcar with the compressed air motor at the outset as "expensive or unreliable" and treated it in only cursory fashion later in the volume. Even a year later he would have had to begin qualifying his enthusiasm, admitting electric traction a place on secondary lines or in minor communities. Earlier he would have had to treat cable traction itself as to some degree experimental. In 1887, however, he could produce an unqualified advocacy of the cable car. The book stands without a rival as the literary monument to the cable car, not merely as an historical source, but itself an integral part of the history of cable traction.

Even as Smith did his proofs, Frank J. Sprague was perfecting his electric car. Sprague in 1887 was working on installations in St. Joseph, Missouri and Richmond, Virginia. Although the Richmond line has always been considered Sprague's initial success, he put his installation on the Union Street Railway of St. Joseph in service on September 6, 1887. Though the opening made little impression on the industry, it was locally celebrated as a complete success, and it quickly killed two local projects for cable railways. Sprague had greater difficulty in bringing the Richmond Union Passenger Railway to completion and missed a target date in late 1887. After various problems, mainly in connection with adapting the cars to climb a hill ranging from 4 to 10 per cent, Sprague had the line ready for revenue service on February 2, 1888.

D. J. MILLER.

As has often been recounted by historians of the trolley car, widespread acceptance of Sprague's invention was initiated by Henry M. Whitney's decision to electrify the West End Street Railway in Boston after inspecting the Richmond installation in mid-1888. Since Whitney had announced plans earlier in the year for two cable lines, the decision was a clear indication that one major figure in the industry — indeed, the head of the largest street railway in America — had recognized the superiority of the Sprague electrics to the cable car. It is tempting to argue that the entire industry should have done as Whitney did; certainly, in retrospect, it is obvious that he was right and the operators who continued building cable plants were dreadfully wrong. This is, however, very definitely a retrospective judgment; the issue in historical perspective is a very different thing from what it was to those facing the decision in 1888.

February 2, 1888, initiated a period of about five years in which the cable car and the electric car were in rivalry. During this, the third phase of the cable car's history, a minority of the industry — a rapidly diminishing minority — argued that cable traction was preferable to electric on heavily travelled lines. They were of course wrong, but one must sympathize with their logic. Neither motors nor control mechanisms of electric streetcars had been perfected. In 1888 most electric streetcars were run off rheostats, which were inefficient and wasteful for heavy-duty work, and

One of the major carbuilders during the cable era was the venerable firm of John Stephenson on East 27th Street, New York. The plant was so constricted in yard space that cars, such as the Kansas City Cable Railway trailer on the right, were simply placed on the cobblestones in front of the main gate for their builder's photographs. At left is a car for the Omaha Street Railway, which had become an unenthusiastic cable operator in the year of the photograph, 1889.

Below, workmen bolt together trackwork on New York's vast Broadway cable installation in 1891. (Both, Museum of the City of New York)

the typical motor was only of 25 horsepower. The president of the Third Avenue Railroad visited Richmond in 1888 but, in spite of the grade Sprague had overcome, explicitly rejected electric traction as impractical for anything but absolutely flat operation and continued his plan to lay cable down his main line, which had one modest grade. The Amalgamated Street Railway of Grand Rapids experienced months of difficulty in adapting electric cars to climb the grades of 8 and 10 per cent on its cable line as late as the fall of 1891.

More basically, it was fairly widely felt that the technological properties of cable traction lent themselves to heavy and growing traffic. Since more than half the energy in the system was expended in moving the cable, additional passengers could be handled at relatively low additional cost. A cable line required about seven times the investment of a Sprague electrification, but since by 1890 most of the country's heavily-travelled street railway lines were cable operations, the average cable line had about six times the traffic of the average electric line. Thus, the argument of the superiority of cable on major lines had a superficial attraction. The SRJ, always a voice for conservatism and rationality in the industry, in 1890 severely criticized Theodore P. Bailey for proposing in an address to the Chicago Electric Club that all cable lines be converted to electric. The editorial writer wrote:

> We do not believe that there is an electric company in the country that would undertake to equip with electricity such lines as Broadway and Third Avenue, New York or Pennsylvania Avenue at Washington, if they were to manage the lines and be held responsible for their economical working for the next five years. However much anyone may entertain the hope expressed in the paper named above, that horse, cable or steam power will be numbered with the events of the past and that electricity will claim supremacy, we do not believe that cable railway managers nor those contemplating the building of such systems are giving themselves very much concern over the possibilities of such an event.

Finally, several cities manifested an hostility to the electric car, either because overhead electric wires were thought dangerous, or because

they were considered eyesores. Baltimore, which had an unsatisfactory experience with electric shocks from the third rail on Daft's early installation there, was especially characterized by fears of the electricity in the overhead. Both Washington and New York prohibited overhead wires on esthetic grounds. At least the former objection rapidly dissipated in the five years after 1888. Electric cars proved to have only about half the incidence of accidents of cable, and 600 volt DC in the overhead did not arc long distances or otherwise present major hazards. Indeed, safety considerations became one of the major sources of political pressure to get rid of cable lines.

The greatest force for continuation of building after February 2, 1888, was simply the momentum the cable movement had before Sprague's innovation occurred. Given the ponderous nature of the technology, the lead time between the decision to lay cable and the first day of operation was usually between a year and two years, depending on the size of the system. All of the installations of 1888 had been planned before Sprague's achievement in Richmond. The trust saw its patents used for the first installation in Seattle and also in St. Paul, the most difficult city climatically in which cable traction was ever attempted. Among the trust's rivals, Henry Lane produced a big installation on the Denver Tramway, William Phenix opened the first portion of his system in Grand Rapids and the Widener-Elkins interests opened installations of their characteristic top-grip technology in Pittsburgh and on the north side of Chicago. The year's total installations came to 59.3 miles, including major additions to the mileage in San Francisco (mainly of the new Ferries & Cliff House Railway), Kansas City and St. Louis. A. D. Whitton, the Widener-Elkins syndicate's house engineer, produced a grip for the Pittsburgh Traction Company that was capable of negotiating pull curves in partial release; had this been adopted outside Pittsburgh it might have been considered a major contribution to cable technology. It was assuredly the last important contribution to the technology.

The principal hope of cable advocates lay in systems based on shallow conduits and alternatives to the standard grips. Especially once the electric streetcar had been shown to be economical of capital, cable enthusiasts recognized that they had to reduce the enormous investment of their system, which was mainly embodied in the conduit. To some extent, revision of the grip was integral with this, since the depth and strength of the conduit were required by the nature of the grips; but even apart from the consideration, the grip was responsible for most of the wear on the cables, and insofar as it tangled with loose strands on the cable or lost its hold, for the two worst sorts of accidents the cable lines suffered. There were three major non-grip technologies: the Rasmussen system, in which a sprocket wheel engaged with buttons on the cable; the Johnson ladder-cable system, in which a cog-wheel did the same with cross-bars connecting a pair of cables; and the Fairchild twin-cable system, which operated in the fashion of some of the mechanical cranes of the time. All will be described in the

next chapter, but for present purposes it is enough to say that all were based on the cable actuating a wheel on the car which was stopped with a brake to make the car proceed. The car stopped for a passenger by releasing the brake on the wheel, permitting it to revolve freely. The most important of these, the Rasmussen system, was installed in Newark in the second half of 1887, in expectation of service early in 1888. The promoters were never able to make the system function effectively, and by mid-1888 it was reasonably clear the experiment was a failure. The Fairchild system had been installed experimentally in Binghamton on the grounds of the state hospital in 1885 and was removed in late 1887 or early 1888. The Johnson ladder-cable system had an experimental installation in Brooklyn between March 6 and July 15, 1887, where it proved to have none of the advantages in cable life and saving in power anticipated of it. Thus the years 1887-88 saw not only the demonstration of the practicability of the electric car, but the impracticability of the non-grip shallow-conduit systems which it had been hoped would be competitive with electric cars in capital outlay and possibly also in expenditure of energy.

Even so, cable installations reached their peak in 1889, when the industry opened 66.1 miles of line. The trust's patents were used for the Omnibus Railroad & Cable Company in San Francisco, the Pacific Railway in Los Angeles and the Denver City Cable Railway, all big installations of more than ten miles, plus the Front Street line in Seattle and the Spokane Cable Railway. Charles Vogel and Frank Whalen, of San Francisco, made a pilot installation of a non-trust bottom grip in 1889 on the Butte City Street Railroad, and William Phenix opened his second installation in Sioux City. In Pittsburgh the Citizens Traction Company made an installation of Whitton's technology on one of the country's most heavily-travelled lines.

If 1889 was a good year for the trust in the streets, it was a bad one in the courts. Root's two actions against the Third Avenue Railroad produced decisions in which the trust nominally broke even. The Third Avenue Railroad's Jonson grip, in which the lower jaws were mobile — presumably in an effort to establish novelty — was held to infringe an unused patent of Eppelsheimer (39 Fed. Rep. 281). On the other hand, Root lost his action against the company for infringement of his patent on the iron-and-concrete conduit (37 Fed. Rep. 673). The Federal court, which was upheld by the Supreme Court in 1892 (146 U.S. 210), found that Root's use of the conduit on California Street for more than two years before application for the patent rendered it invalid. Root considered the decision a disaster and clearly showed his bitterness even in his autobiography in 1921. He felt that his use of the conduit before his patent application in 1881 had been experimental and that the courts should have treated it as such.

The net effect of the two decisions was to weaken the trust's position greatly. The trust had made an ostentatious show of confidence in the comprehensiveness of its holdings, arguing that no one could build an endless-cable line without infringement of its patents. It purported to control patents for every phase of the technology, save possibly the slot. If the patent on something as basic as the conduit was invalid, there was no such absolute assurance as the trust claimed that any of its patents were valid. The head of the Metropolitan Street Railway of Kansas City concluded that the patent rights of which he was local licensee were of extremely questionable value and quickly agreed to a franchise which obligated the company to license its holdings.

In general, the trust was successful in actions to protect its patents on grips, but mixed in its success on other hardware of cable technology. By 1893, when the subject lost its interest, the trust had won actions against Philadelphia Traction for infringing Root's grip, Consolidated Piedmont of Oakland for infringing Eppelsheimer's bottom grip and both the Brooklyn Bridge and the Butte City Street Railroad for infringing Hallidie's original grip. Thus, the trust had taken successful actions against bottom and top grips with its patents on side and bottom grips; it could hardly have done better, especially since the basic grip of Beauregard antedated the San Francisco inventors. On the other hand, the actions on conduit fittings were distinctly mixed. The trust won a case against the Sioux City Cable Railway for infringement of Hallidie's slot switch, but lost

on a yoke and tube Phenix had used in the conduit and also on running two cables in a single conduit, which Hallidie had patented. In the action against the Butte line the trust won on infringement of a basic patent of Hallidie on separate grip cars and on a track brake patented by Root, but lost on a shallow tube conduit Vogel and Whelan had used, which the trust claimed had infringed on a patent of T. H. Day in its holdings. The Mount Adams & Eden Park of Cincinnati won an action for use of a cheaply constructed tube as a conduit. Against Consolidated Piedmont the trust proved infringement for the standard system of taking up tension, but lost on use of an iron tube in the conduit. In the same action, the chafing bar in pull curves was held a valid patent, though Consolidated Piedmont was judged not to have infringed it.

There had been, of course, those who argued that the trust's patents had little validity through lack of novelty. A. H. Lighthall, who had his own set of patents similar to California Street technology, issued a pamphlet entitled *The Lighthall Cable Traction Tramway Company* in 1883, in which he made an impressive show of unused patents of earlier inventors to demonstrate that the San Francisco inventors were devoid of novelty. Lighthall, a shady figure who purported to have invented the pull curve on the basis of having worked on the Sutter Street Railway's extension across Market Street in 1882, and who skipped on his hotel bill while showing his system in Cincinnati, never arranged an installation of his own patents; though he endeavored to promote a line in Troy, New York, and was making one of the installations in St. Joseph when the Sprague electric line succeeded there.

The year 1890 was the first to show a diminution in building of cable lines. The year's installations totaled 54.3 miles. The legal disaster of the previous year to the contrary, the trust dominated

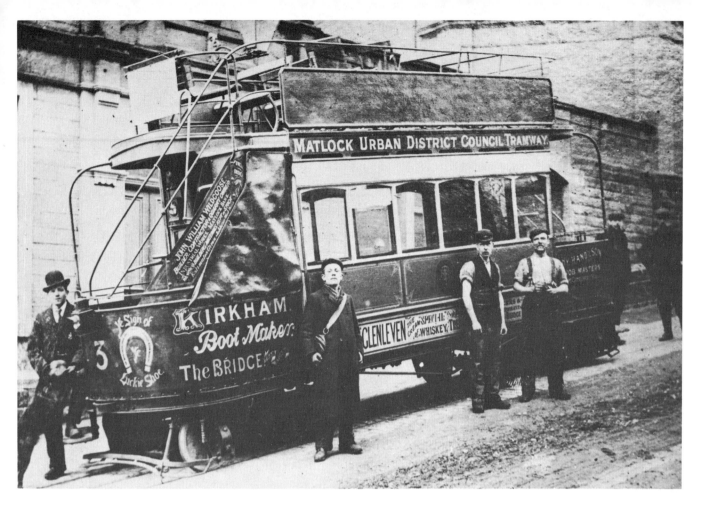

Cable traction was mainly an American technology; only Melbourne and Edinburgh among foreign cities had comprehensive cable networks. The British firm of Dick, Kerr & Co. built several cable lines in the British Isles, including one in the hilly Midland resort town of Matlock, above, and another in Douglas on the Isle of Man, below. The Matlock line climbed a relatively straight heavy grade, but the Douglas tramway had a tortuous route of only moderate gradients. (*J. H. Price; S. R. Keig, Ltd.*)

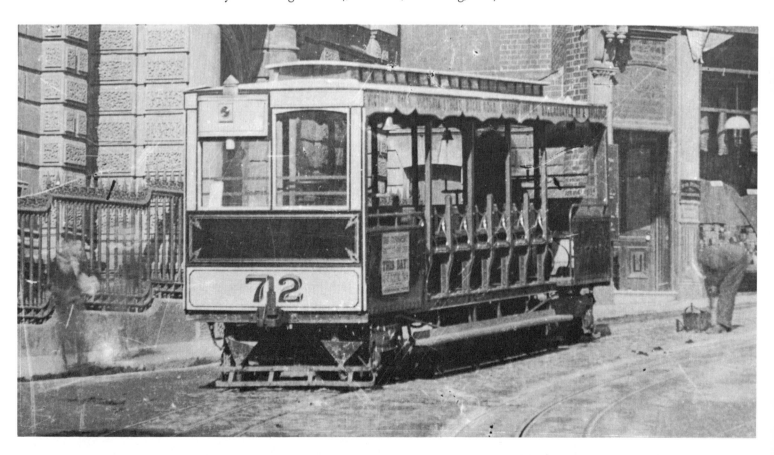

At right, a crew of the big Edinburgh cable system poses beside its characteristic British double-decked tram. The pilot wheel controls W. N. Colam's side grip. Hilly Lisbon had two dissimilar cable lines built by the German firm of Machinenfabrik Esslingen. The tiny grip and trailer ran on the Estrela line and the double-ended single-truck car to Graca. (*J. H. Price*)

the year's installations. Promoters used the trust's patents for the Portland Cable Railway, two new lines in Seattle and two more in St. Louis, the Cleveland City Cable Railway, the Central Traction Company in Pittsburgh and the first portion of the Washington & Georgetown Railroad. Among the intrepid, promoters in Oakland made the only non-trust installation in the San Francisco Bay Area on the Consolidated Piedmont Cable Company, thereby initiating a great deal of litigation. Frank Van Vleck built a short-lived line in San Diego with his own patents, and in Chicago the Widener-Elkins interests opened the first mileage of the second biggest cable operation in the industry, the West Chicago Street Railroad. In Providence Henry Lane made New England's only installation.

H. M. LANE.

As late as 1890 the installations were a representative sample of what the industry had brought forth previously; Sprague's electric cars could easily have run the installations in St. Louis, Cleveland, Washington, San Diego and Chicago. Beginning in 1891 cable installations were special cases, justified either by excessive gradients or hostility of municipal governments to electric wires over the streets. The Union Trunk Line in Seattle and the Tacoma Railway & Motor Company built short cable lines on extreme grades as adjuncts to large electric systems. The Brooklyn Heights Railroad opened a similar short cable connection from the waterfront to downtown Brooklyn. Only one big, new system was built, the Baltimore Traction Company; given Baltimore's geographical properties, it is surprising that the city was among the latest rather than among the earliest to have cable traction. Apparently indicating that the trust's legal reverse of 1889 was not fatal, all but 1.5 miles — an extension of the North Chicago Street Railroad — of the year's total of 21.9 miles were built with trust patents.

There is little question that the decline of cable installations had made itself felt on the trust, however. In 1890 Pacific Cable arranged not only to use its Market Street patents but to participate directly in the financing of the Dallas Cable Railway. Pacific Cable paid its franchise deposit with a bouncing check and was unable to finance the installation. In 1892 there were no entirely new installations in the country. New mileage fell to 22.4, of which the Pennsylvania Avenue lines of the Washington & Georgetown Railroad were the largest, 7.5 miles. Had the District of Columbia been willing to accept overhead wires, this mileage would never have been built.

In 1893, superficially, the cable car made a comeback. Mileage installed rose to 28.2, and mileage in service reached its peak at 305.1. The revival was only superficial, however. Most of the mileage was completion of the long-planned Third Avenue and Broadway lines in New York, which had been delayed for years by legal actions — only some of which were the battles between the trust and the Third Avenue management. The other major installation on the East Coast, the Baltimore City Passenger Railway, was variously reported to be the consequence of the city's hostility to electrification and of the president's adverse reaction to Sprague's Boston electrification. The other important installation of 1893 was the southern pair of lines of the West Chicago Street Railroad, again long-planned but delayed by the difficulty of tunneling the Chicago River. Notably, all four of these installations were non-trust. A. N. Connett designed the Baltimore City Passenger Railway without any reported effort to base the design on an existing patent system, either the trust's or one of the independent sets of patents.

There still was enough interest in cable traction in 1893 that the street railways exhibited a comprehensive set of grips — trust and non-trust, alike — at the World's Columbian Exhibition in Chicago. The exhibit was in fact, though not in intention, a memorial to the cable car, for 1893 was the end of the period in which the cable car had any claim to competition with the electric car. In that year General Electric introduced the Type-K controller and Westinghouse brought forth its Number 3 motor. Together these inventions did what Sprague had left undone. The Type-K controller was a dependable and durable control of power supply, used for decades in successive modifications until the very end of the history of the standard electric streetcar. The Number 3 motor was a substantial and powerful driver, capable of dealing easily with grades of 8 and 10 per cent that had appeared earlier to demand a non-adhesion system.

Only three cable installations were left to come. In 1894 the Metropolitan Street Railway opened a branch of its Broadway line up Columbus Avenue in Manhattan, and in 1895 it built a similar extension up Lexington Avenue. Earlier in 1895 the Columbia Railway in Washington became the last American company to begin cable operation. In demonstrating how weak the trust's hold had become, William B. Upton, who had previously been identified with Daniel Bontecou in trust installations, drew on the non-trust Broadway line for his prototype. All of these installations were made only because New York and Washington persisted in their refusal to have overhead wires on esthetic grounds. Both cities in 1895 also experienced installations of electric conduit. Such little scope as the development of the Type-K controller and the Number 3 motor had left the cable car was now ended, and no more lines were begun. Only a short extension of the Market Street Railway in 1902 to serve an amusement area and a restoration of a portion of the Madison Street line in Seattle in 1913 were ever built thereafter.

The obsolescence of the cable was all but universally recognized. The SRJ in 1895 prefaced a valuable biographical account of the major cable engineers — probably out of deference to the subjects — by saying:

A considerable portion of cable railway mileage has been changed to electric traction,

notably roads in Omaha, Denver, Sioux City, Philadelphia, Grand Rapids, St. Louis and Providence, in some cases because the traffic was not sufficient to warrant cable power, in other cases to unify the method of operating cars, not because of any particular inherent defects in the cable system.

Only a year later, John Young and William Clark, general manager and engineer of Glasgow Corporation Transport, visited the United States and said of the cable in the same journal:

One cannot pass with open eyes and ears through the cities of America without being thoroughly satisfied that it has been superseded. The American street railway men, one and all, speak of it as a "back number."

Somewhat surprisingly, the interpretation that the early conversions were motivated, not by the inherent shortcomings of cable traction, but by a desire for uniformity in power distribution was most popular in Britain. After Eppelsheimer's initial cable line at Highgate, London, in 1884, cable traction had spread to Birmingham and Edinburgh in 1888, Brixton (London) in 1892 and Matlock in 1893. Building continued with the Upper Douglas Cable Tramway on the Isle of Man in 1896 and the Glasgow Subway in 1897. In Dunedin, New Zealand, building continued well into the twentieth century; the Kaikorai Tramway was opened in 1900, and the Elgin Road line in 1906. As far

No. 10. Head Light. As used on Tenth Avenue, New York, Cable Road. Throws a powerful light 100 feet. The best in the market for Cable Roads.

45

Steepest cable grade by a wide margin was the 27.7 per cent being descended by the Second Street Cable Railroad train in Los Angeles, above. In third place was the block adjacent to the YMCA on the Madison Street line in Seattle, at left, 20.88 per cent. (*UCLA Libraries; Washington State Historical Society*)

as is known, only some extensions of the Edinburgh system were built later.

By the end of the cable era, cable traction had spread to every major American city except Boston and Detroit. There was never an installation in the South, though Atlanta had the population and undulating terrain to justify a line, and New Orleans had a large population together with straight streets. Canada, mercifully, never had a cable system.

Boston's near miss is famous, but Detroit's absence of cable lines is strange. If one were to specify the geographical conditions which most facilitated cable traction in the sense of minimizing accidents and maximizing cable life, one would want a radial pattern of streets to avoid curvature, flat terrain to avoid depression pulleys, and broad boulevards for visibility at intersections. Clearly, Detroit satisfies these requirements better than any other city. A single powerhouse could have been put about 2.5 miles out each of its major streets, and an almost ideal line of some five miles could have been run out of the central area in each direction. The superficial attractions of cable traction in Detroit were not lost on local figures. The Detroit *News* was strongly pro-cable, recommending cable systems as permanent, proved and safe. A promoter named Frank X. Cicott in the late 1880s and in 1890 attempted to promote cable lines, apparently in collaboration with the trust, on a variety of routes; and Col. James M. Clark in 1890 endeavored to promote one or more lines on unspecified streets, with the Vogel & Whelan technology. Franchise insecurity had discouraged the city's street railways from any replacement of the horsecar until this time.

A reporter for the Grand Rapids *Eagle* in 1890 interviewed Cameron Currie, secretary of the Detroit City Railway, which operated the radial horsecar lines on Jefferson, Woodward, Michigan and Gratiot, asking him whether he considered the Grand Rapids installation a model for Detroit. Currie expressed a low opinion of cable, partly on safety grounds, partly because he expected to maintain an electric overhead for a quarter the cost of cables, sheaves and pulleys. Remarkably, since his company operated on one-minute headway on Woodward, he considered Detroit not large enough for cable traction. It was, of course, mainly a city of single houses with low population density. The officers of the Fort Wayne & Elmwood Street Railway, after a cost comparison described in Chapter VII, reached the same conclusion for their Fort Street line.

In all, the industry produced 59 cable street railways, two rapid-transit lines (plus the pre-Hallidie line of Harvey in New York) and the facility on the grounds of the Binghamton State Hospital. Two additional lines, the Rasmussen installation in Newark and the Union Cable Railway in Kansas City, were built, but could never be made to function well enough for revenue service. The total American mileage of cable lines was 360.6, not all of which was in service simultaneously. Trust patents were used for 40 lines, representing about 64 per cent of the mileage. Legal action or the threat of it brought several non-trust operators to pay fees to Pacific Cable or National Cable.

San Francisco was never closely approached in mileage with its 52.8 miles. Chicago, which had the two largest lines in mileage, was second with 41.2 miles, but in traffic and roster of equipment it was the largest system in the country. At their peak the three companies had 710 grip cars; in 1892 they handled 237 million passengers by cable. Kansas City was third with 37.8 miles, but it was the most comprehensively covered of any city; only a single line into the central business

district failed to be converted to cable. These were always the "big three" of cable cities. Only Melbourne in Australia rivaled them; it was reported to have 45.5 miles of lines. Among other American cities, St. Louis with 25.9 miles, New York with 25.0 and Denver with 24.3 were virtually the same size in mileage. New York's two companies were probably second only to Chicago in traffic, and Denver had a comprehensiveness in coverage second only to Kansas City.

It is somewhat arbitrary to distinguish between lines that were justified by extreme gradients and those which were brought forth merely by demand for something more economic than the horse. The Metropolitan Street Railway of Kansas City had one major grade of 20 per cent in a city otherwise only continuously undulating. The company of the same name in New York had one grade of 13 per cent which could probably have been modified or avoided if cable traction had not been used on an otherwise flat system simply in response to heavy traffic. Including the former, but in general excluding the latter class of lines, about 29 systems can be said to have been called forth by extreme gradients, the rest by ordinary demands. No grade closely approached the 27.7 per cent on the Second Street Cable Railway in Los Angeles. This was within 1 per cent of the worst in the world, 28.5 per cent of the Maryhill extension of the Mornington Tramway in Dunedin. Three grades virtually tied for second place: 20.93 per cent on the trestle of the Portland Cable Railway, 20.88 on the Madison Street Cable Railway in Seattle and 20.67 per cent on Hyde Street ascending Russian Hill from the north on the California Street Cable Railroad. The last of these is still in service.

As it proved, only a small percentage of the country's cable mileage contained grades so severe that the electric car could not be adapted to climb them. Only some 5.5 per cent of the mileage was able to withstand the superiority of the electric car on the basis of cable traction's one undeniable attraction. Ere we turn to the virtual annihilation of cable traction by Sprague's invention, however, let us enquire at length into cable technology, both for its intrinsic interest, and to see why the electric car was able to vanquish the cable car so completely.

48

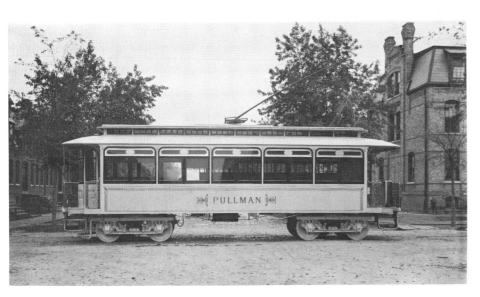

Among the lesser failures of the cable era was this experimental cable car built by Pullman in 1888. Although built along the lines of rapid transit equipment of the time, the car was apparently intended for street railways. The car had no takers among cable operators and was rebuilt as an early interurban. As such, it became Dayton, Springfield & Urbana No. 25 and, later, Ohio Electric No. 284. (*George Krambles*)

Asa Hovey's side grip gave such a firm hold that the Chicago City Railway was able
to haul electric cars into the Loop, as in this view of State Street in 1905. This is one
of a set of superb photographs of downtown Chicago taken in the last two years of
operation of the city's huge cable system. (*Chicago Historical Society*)

CHAPTER III
THE GRIP

"The distinguishing features of the cable system are the *cable* and the *grip*. All the other mechanical and engineering devices are accessory." Quite so — but William D. Henry, author of this statement in 1888, would have been well advised to give the grip primacy. Since the cable had been invented previously, the principal novelty in the system was in the device for taking and holding the cable. The patent rights to the grip were, consequently, the most important in the industry. The principal patent controversies concerned grips, and as we have seen in the previous chapter, the trust was most successful in its infringement actions on grip patents. Finally, the hopes for improvement in the system were centered on the grip, since improving cable life and reducing the investment in the conduit both required some improved or at least different gripping device. On all grounds, the grip was the central element in the system.

The most obvious device for providing a continuum from a full stop to moving at the speed of the cable was a set of rollers which could be stopped to hold the cable and propel the car, or be allowed to rotate when the car was stopped. So obvious was this idea that it occurred to Hallidie, Asa Hovey and W. H. Paine, all of whom endeavored to patent it in 1875. Paine was given the patent and for two years attempted to use it on the New York & Brooklyn Bridge Railway. His patent entailed two horizontal sheaves which held the cable from opposite sides; in service he used four sheaves about 7 inches in diameter. This concentrated the gripping action on two very limited areas, relative to a standard grip. As a consequence, the roller grip was unable to hold the car well enough to start it from a standing stop; Paine had to use steam locomotives at the termini. Worse, the action of the grip was precisely that of a rolling mill, so that the cable stretched and became thinner more rapidly than in a standard system. Thus the difficulty of holding the cable became successively greater as time passed.

Hovey planned to use a roller grip on Sutter Street, San Francisco, and experimented with one in the second half of 1876, paying Paine for the right to do so. Paine's grip was operated off a wheel on the front platform, but Hovey's was lever-actuated, with sheaves placed vertically on the shank. Hovey was able to start a car from a standing stop, since his equipment was lighter than the rapid-transit cars of the Brooklyn Bridge, but he found it impossible to hold a car on a 7 per cent grade with the rollers on a worn cable.

Hallidie experimented with a roller grip of four small horizontal sheaves for the Clay Street Hill Railroad, but concluded it was impractical. Either he or Eppelsheimer turned to Beauregard's original idea of gripping the cable by a pair of jaws closing laterally. The result was the grip which bears Hallidie's name, the first practical bottom grip. Basically it was Hallidie's projected roller grip with the addition of two small jaws of only 3.5 inches in length. They released the cable entirely to stop for a passenger, while the cable ran through the grip on the four small carrying sheaves. The

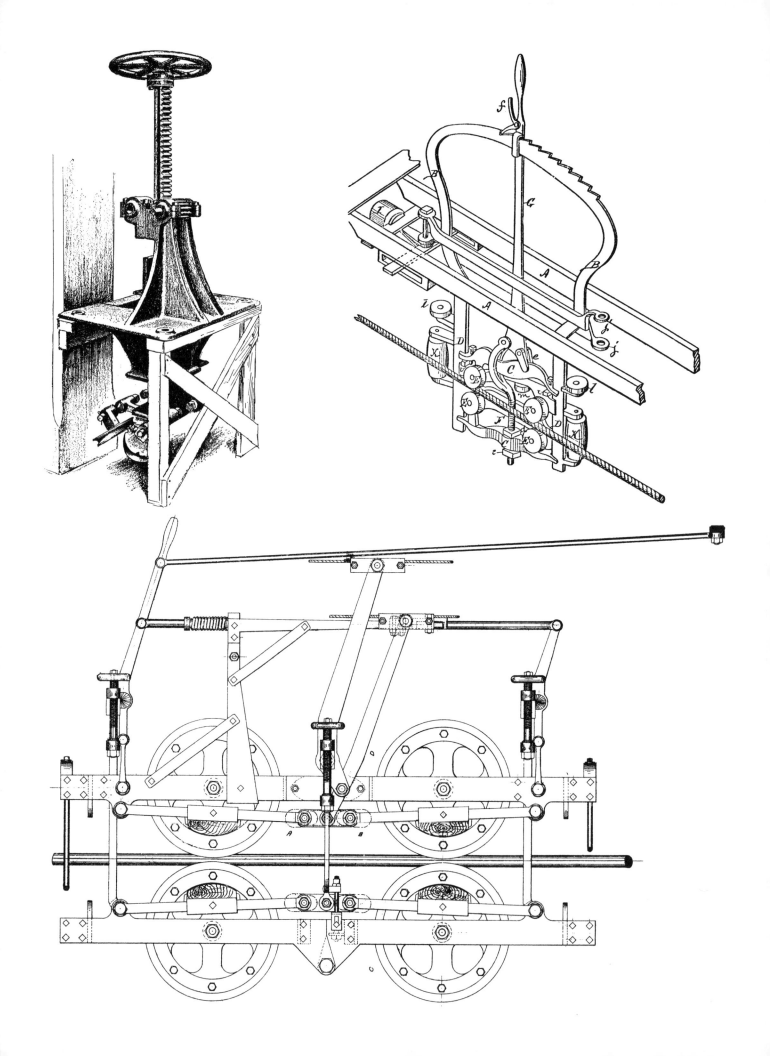

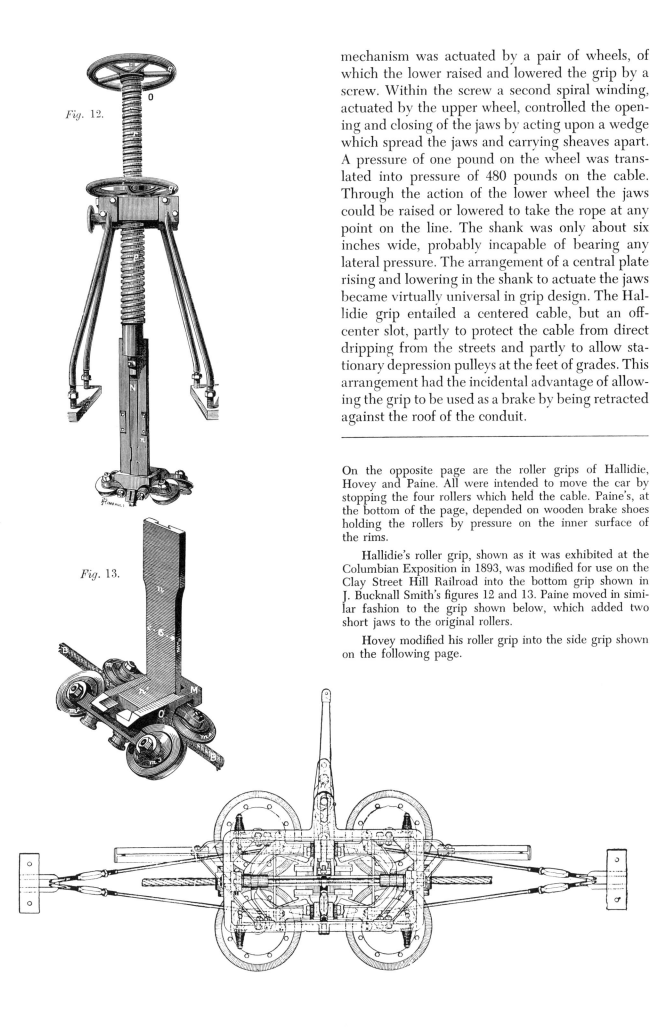

Fig. 12.

Fig. 13.

mechanism was actuated by a pair of wheels, of which the lower raised and lowered the grip by a screw. Within the screw a second spiral winding, actuated by the upper wheel, controlled the opening and closing of the jaws by acting upon a wedge which spread the jaws and carrying sheaves apart. A pressure of one pound on the wheel was translated into pressure of 480 pounds on the cable. Through the action of the lower wheel the jaws could be raised or lowered to take the rope at any point on the line. The shank was only about six inches wide, probably incapable of bearing any lateral pressure. The arrangement of a central plate rising and lowering in the shank to actuate the jaws became virtually universal in grip design. The Hallidie grip entailed a centered cable, but an off-center slot, partly to protect the cable from direct dripping from the streets and partly to allow stationary depression pulleys at the feet of grades. This arrangement had the incidental advantage of allowing the grip to be used as a brake by being retracted against the roof of the conduit.

On the opposite page are the roller grips of Hallidie, Hovey and Paine. All were intended to move the car by stopping the four rollers which held the cable. Paine's, at the bottom of the page, depended on wooden brake shoes holding the rollers by pressure on the inner surface of the rims.

Hallidie's roller grip, shown as it was exhibited at the Columbian Exposition in 1893, was modified for use on the Clay Street Hill Railroad into the bottom grip shown in J. Bucknall Smith's figures 12 and 13. Paine moved in similar fashion to the grip shown below, which added two short jaws to the original rollers.

Hovey modified his roller grip into the side grip shown on the following page.

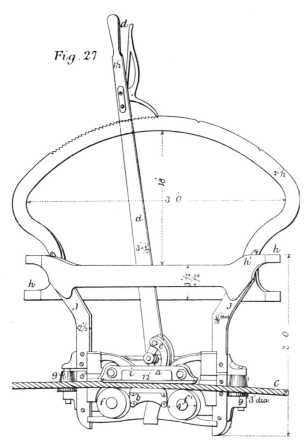

Fig. 27

Hovey's Sutter Street single-jaw side grip.

Asa Hovey upon rejecting the roller grip moved in the opposite direction to develop the first workable side grip for Sutter Street. Using the same general outline he had planned for the roller grip, Hovey arranged a grip that held the cable from above and below. In the accompanying diagram, Figure 27, from J. Bucknall Smith, the grip was attached to the car with the carrying plate h. The grip had two thin shanks j, which held the lower jaw b and the carrying pulleys f at a fixed distance from the carrying plate. To close the grip on the cable the gripman pulled back on the lever d, which was connected with the lower jaw (and thus with the carrying plate) by the link e. This action forced the lever, the quadrant and its connection inside the shanks j, and the upper jaw a downward on the cable. To stop for a passenger the gripman put the lever forward approximately to the position shown in the diagram, raising the upper jaw and allowing the cable to roll through the grip on the carrying pulleys. To eject the cable

from the grip the gripman threw the lever all the way forward, not only raising the upper jaw, but lifting a pair of conical ejection spools g, which moved the cable to the right and out of the grip.

Hovey's Sutter Street grip itself was never used again, except reportedly in Omaha. It was designed for a line without curvature and had such unsubstantial shanks that it would have been inappropriate as it stood for general use. It was, however, the prototype for all later side grips, and in its control device, for lever grips of all types. Henry Root's single-jaw side grip, shown in its formulation for the Market Street Cable Railway (Smith's Figure 50), shows the basically similar nature. Here the carrying plate E is connected to the lower jaw f by means of the shanks F. The lever A and the quadrant act on the upper jaw through the plate G and the link D. The grip is more substantial, but the only real refinement is the screw C for tightening the hold of the jaws, as for example at the top or bottom of a grade. Here the upper jaw, about a foot long, extends over the carrying pulleys h, as in Hovey's grip, to hold them still in a full hold; Root's earlier California Street grip had used upper and lower jaws of the same length. Root did not use ejection spools.

The Root grip was the most widely used in the industry, either as illustrated or with its carrying pulleys removed. In fact, any simple single-jaw side grip built under license with trust patents was likely to be described as a Root or as the "California type." The Seattle grips, which were massive, simple single-jaw side grips, were so described, for example.

Hovey used the basic elements of his Sutter Street grip in Chicago to develop the double-jaw side grip. He designed a solid center plate (M in the accompanying diagram) between two shanks L, rather in the nature of Root's grip, but he also provided conical ejection spools P. This was an excellent grip, which because of exceptional length of the jaws, 26 inches, made a very secure hold on the cable. Experimentally, the Chicago City Railway hauled a ten-car train with it, and in later years the company was able to pull single-truck electric cars into town on the end of cable

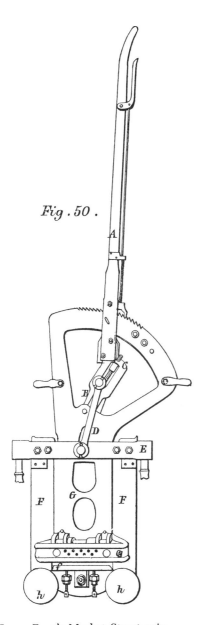

Fig. 50.

A

B

C

D

E

F   G   F

a

h   h

Henry Root's Market Street grip.

chafing bar on a pull curve to minimize the angle of the cable at each end of the jaws on the curve. With the jaws to the chafing bar the cable was pulled only about 1½ inches, but with the shank to the bar, the deflection was about 4½ inches, which did triple the damage. With a double-jaw side grip one had the option of using either set of jaws in the circumstance. Similarly, one could run two cables in one conduit, either in the same direction, as on the Chicago loop and in the New York installations, or in opposite directions, as on the single-track installations in Los Angeles, Spokane, Sioux City and Grand Rapids.

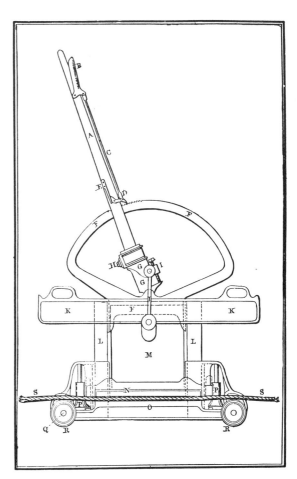

A. Grip Lever. B. Lever Handle. C. Lever Rod. D. Lever Dog. E. Lever Dog Spring. F. Quadrant. Upper G. Adjusting Head. Lower G. Adjusting Shoe. H. Lever Set Screw. I. Adjusting Screw. J. Grip Links. K. Grip Beam. L. Grip Shank. M. Grip Plate. N. Upper Jaw. O. Lower Jaw. P. Spools. Q. Roller Journals. R. Grip Rollers. S. Cable.

Hovey's double-jaw side grip for the Chicago City Railway.

trains. The engineers who studied American cable installations in preparation for the unbuilt Boston lines stated flatly that this was the best grip.

Installations which entailed a loop at one terminus but switches at the other, as the Chicago City Railway did, required a grip which could hold the cable on either side, since the car would present alternate sides of the shank to the cable on successive trips. Even apart from this attraction, double-jaw side grips presented certain advantages. In laying out a cable plant it was desirable to have the jaws of the grip toward the

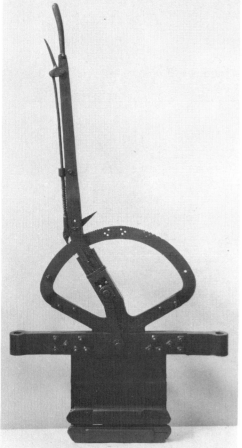

The three grips above were part of the exhibit of grips at the Columbian Exposition of 1893. At the left is Root's single-jaw side grip with its carrying pulleys removed. In the center is Robert Gillham's massive double-jaw side grip lettered for the Denver City Cable Railway. At right is a version of the Jonson grip of the Third Avenue Railroad, also with its carrying pulleys removed. Note that this grip, unlike the others, is arranged with its lower jaws mobile.

Below is the heavy single-jaw side grip designed by Samuel Gibson used, as far as is known, on all of the Seattle lines. At left, the grip is open and at right closed — though not fully. *(All, Smithsonian Institution)*

The trust had an alternative double-jaw side grip in Robert Gillham's grip, essentially identical to Hovey's Chicago grip except for its lack of ejection spools. The non-trust operators had versions of the Root or Hovey grips. Henry Lane had a single-jaw side grip essentially identical to Hovey's, except that it centered the cable under the slot — thereby avoiding one of the principal attractions of side grips. Lighthall's, which he never placed, was essentially a variant of Root's. Most of the independents had designs modelled on Hovey's Chicago grip, if only because so many of them had worked for Hovey on the huge installation. William Phenix's grip was a lightweight version of the Chicago City Railway grip with a foot-operated ejection button. William Noble in designing the St. Louis Cable & Western used a very similar grip, the Snelson & Judge, which proved too light for effective service. D. J. Miller necessarily used a double-jaw side grip on his

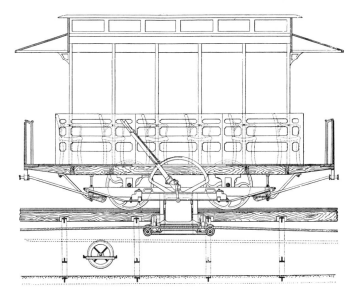

Above, Hovey's grip is shown in place in a Chicago City Railway car. Below, Henry M. Lane's grip was developed for hauling horsecars of the Mount Adams & Eden Park up the Gilbert Avenue grade. The grip was attached ahead of the car, as shown. Later versions were mounted below the car in orthodox fashion.

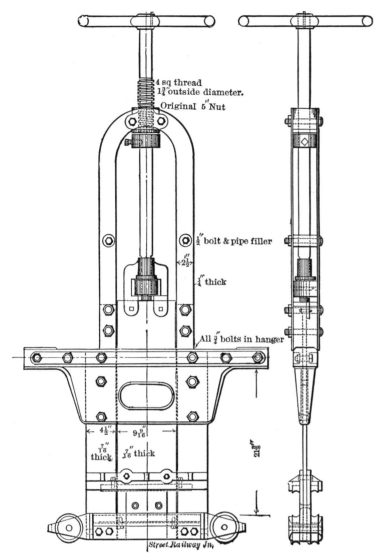

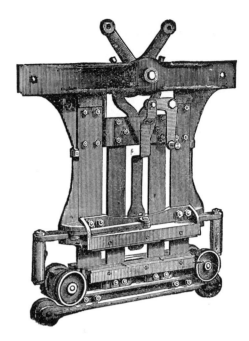

The Jonson grip of the Third Avenue Railroad.

SCREW SPINDLE GRIP—PROVIDENCE, R. I., CABLE LINE.

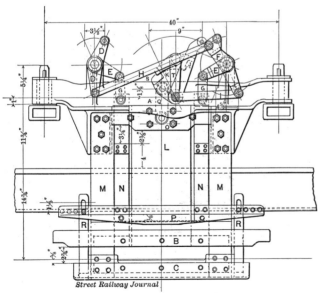

THE NEW BROADWAY CABLE GRIP.

Third Avenue Railroad installation, which entailed a duplicate cable. This grip, invented by Julius Jonson, was notable for having the lower jaws mobile and the upper jaws fixed to the carrying plate. Miller claimed this arrangement reduced wear on the cable, but probably he sought — unsuccessfully, as it proved — to develop novelty in the patent dispute in the industry. The most common British grip, the Colam, was a side grip with the lower jaws mobile, capable of descending to take the rope at any point.

Several operators, including the Grand Avenue Railway and the Third Avenue Railroad, removed the carrying pulleys from side grips. Dirt falling through the slot tended to clog the journals and to stop the pulleys; a stopped pulley added friction without providing any benefit. The later side grips, such as the double-jaw models of A. D. Whitton on the West Chicago and A. N. Connett on the Baltimore City Passenger Railway, were built without carrying pulleys.

The majority of the industry used side grips, but a minority of companies opted for bottom grips. The Hallidie bottom grip itself had a limited history: after its original use on Clay Street, only the Presidio & Ferries ever used it, though

Rope drops were a major incentive to use bottom grips. The Pacific Railway in Los Angeles adopted the Eppelsheimer bottom grip, in part, because of its rope drop for the Second Street Cable Railroad, shown above on the Pacific Railway's opening day of service in 1889. *(Title Insurance & Trust Company)*

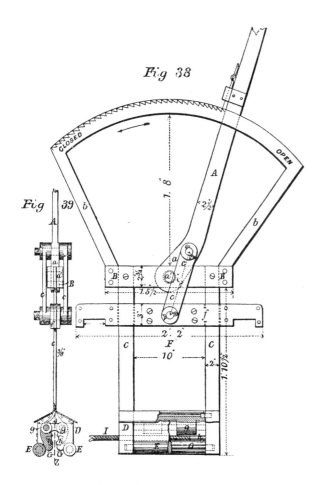

Fig 38

Fig 39

The Eppelsheimer bottom grip.

The trust placed the Eppelsheimer on the Ferries & Cliff House, the Omnibus and the Hyde Street line of the California Street Cable Railroad in San Francisco, the Pacific Railway in Los Angeles, the Citizens' Railway and the St. Louis Railroad in St. Louis, and on the Portland Cable Railway. When the Portland line proved to be troubled with slot closures, the company's own engineer, R. A. McLellan, developed a similar grip with a narrower shank which appears to have been equally satisfactory. Jacob Volk, an employee of the Citizens' Railway of St. Louis developed a bottom grip for his company in 1889; his principal novelty was a set of four carrying pulleys on which the cable rode in partial release. He formed the Volk Cable, Crossing, Grip & Car Brake Company to market the grip, but never placed it beyond his own line.

A special case among bottom grips was the Endres grip, used on the North Hudson County

R. A. McLELLAN.
CABLE GRIP.

No. 501,467.   Patented July 11, 1893.

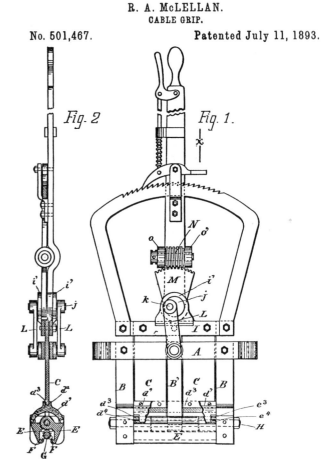

the New York & Brooklyn Bridge in 1885 adopted a grip similar enough to lose an infringement action. Apart from its limitations on curves, the jaws were so short that they were hard on rope. Eppelsheimer, when given the opportunity to design the Geary Street line, developed his own bottom grip, the model still in use in San Francisco. The grip, shown in Smith's Figure 38, had an orthodox action of lever, quadrant and link. To close the jaws, the gripman drew back on the lever, toward the left, thereby lowering the plate F and driving the jaws G against a pair of rollers E, which caused them to close on the cable. The jaws, shaped like a pair of commas, were 10 inches long in the original installation, a foot in current practice. The present model weighs about 325 pounds.

The Eppelsheimer became the trust's standard bottom grip, as the Root became its side grip.

Railway, a licensee of National Cable. J. J. Endres, the chief engineer of the company, needed a grip heavy enough for rapid-transit cars on a trestle with a 5 per cent grade and 9¼ mile per hour speed. He designed a massive bottom grip with two cast iron jaws which moved laterally to hold the cable. The jaws were three feet long and the grip weighed over 1,000 pounds, by far the greatest weight of any grip. Endres put one grip on each truck of his cars, but since the grip was incapable of picking up the rope, he had to provide a pair of pincers called cable-lifters at each end of each grip to bring the cable into the jaws. The lifters chipped the cable, but otherwise the grip served quite well.

Another special case was J. C. H. Stut's bottom grip for the Presidio & Ferries. In redesigning a line built for the original Hallidie grip, to run over a pull curve, Stut was forced to develop an off-center bottom grip, the only bottom grip in which only one jaw moved to hold the cable.

Among the independents, side grips were more popular than bottom. The one of three non-trust lines in Cincinnati to use a bottom grip was the Mount Auburn Cable Railway, which was inferior to the Mount Adams & Eden Park at two intersections. Its engineer, Worcester Haddock, dealt with the problem by designing a bottom grip with an extension arm which reached down to pick up the rope and lift it into the jaws. The grip was apparently quite effective, the one satisfactory part of a cheap and impermanent physical plant.

The Consolidated Piedmont of Oakland used a bottom grip called the McClelle which had its jaws slightly offset to the right to allow the cable to avoid direct dripping through the slot. The grip was fitted with a split link for automatic release at rope drops; a rod in the conduit tripped a hook on the shank which broke the link connection with the lever to open the jaws. Frank Van Vleck's grip at San Diego was almost precisely the Eppelsheimer, modified to hold the cable far enough to the right to permit single-track operation in opposite directions.

The most important of the non-trust bottom grips was the Vogel & Whelan, which was quite different in design and purpose from the Eppelsheimer — notwithstanding the successful infringement action to the contrary. The designers used

The Endres grip of the Hoboken elevated.

a bolted iron conduit only 10 inches deep, with carrying pulleys 7 inches in diameter. The grip, which had a cylindrical outline, dropped the rope at every stop for a passenger. The gripman depressed the grip by a pedal with his left foot until it engaged the cable and then pulled back on his lever in the usual fashion to close the jaws. A pair of springs raised the jaws high enough to clear the carrying pulleys. This arrangement was designed simultaneously to reduce the investment in conduit and to minimize the friction on the cable. The grip's ability to take the rope at any point was argued to be an important safety feature; only the Vogel grip offered any real prospect of retaking the rope after losing the grip on a grade, which was the second worst hazard of accident in the technology. But the Vogel was introduced so late, in Butte in 1889, that it was never widely adopted. The Kansas City Cable Railway converted to it in 1889, and the West Chicago used it for its Halsted-Blue Island lines in 1893. The West Chicago's engineers expressed satisfaction with the Vogel, but said the jaws, which were about 12 inches, should have been longer.

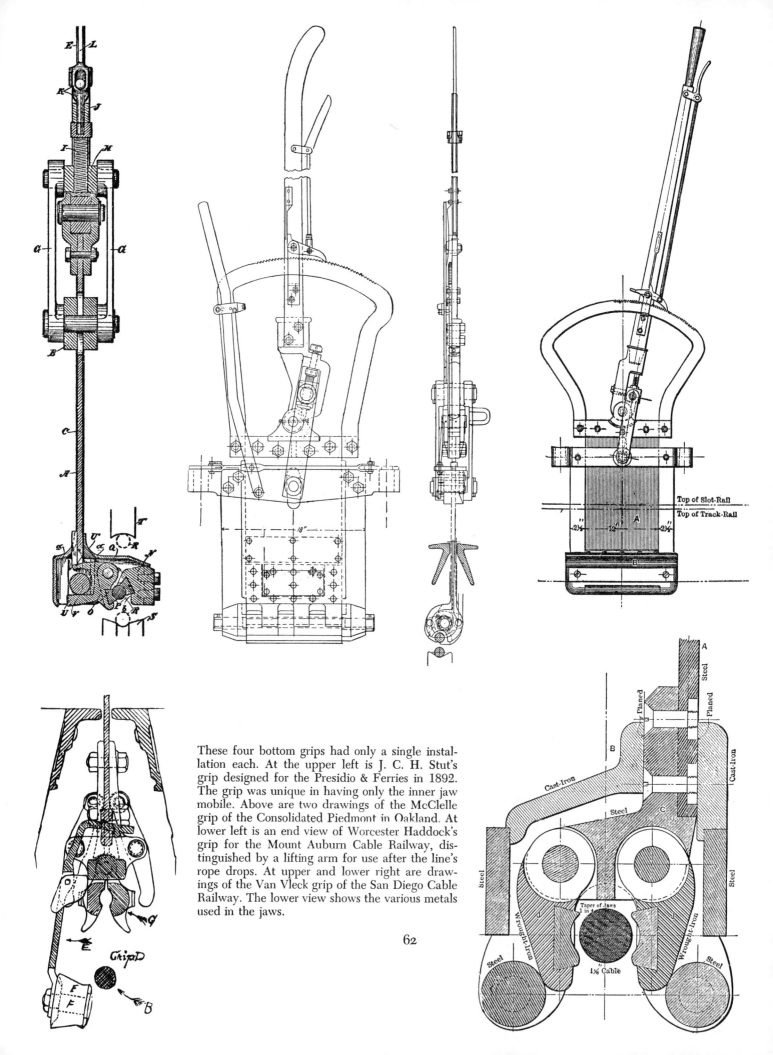

These four bottom grips had only a single installation each. At the upper left is J. C. H. Stut's grip designed for the Presidio & Ferries in 1892. The grip was unique in having only the inner jaw mobile. Above are two drawings of the McClelle grip of the Consolidated Piedmont in Oakland. At lower left is an end view of Worcester Haddock's grip for the Mount Auburn Cable Railway, distinguished by a lifting arm for use after the line's rope drops. At upper and lower right are drawings of the Van Vleck grip of the San Diego Cable Railway. The lower view shows the various metals used in the jaws.

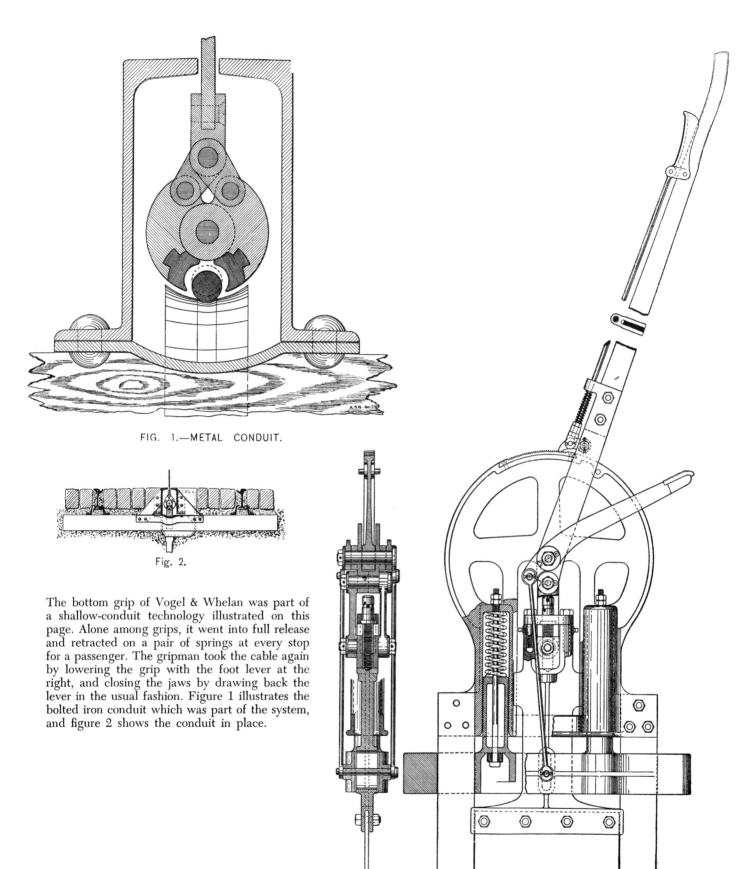

FIG. 1.—METAL CONDUIT.

Fig. 2.

The bottom grip of Vogel & Whelan was part of a shallow-conduit technology illustrated on this page. Alone among grips, it went into full release and retracted on a pair of springs at every stop for a passenger. The gripman took the cable again by lowering the grip with the foot lever at the right, and closing the jaws by drawing back the lever in the usual fashion. Figure 1 illustrates the bolted iron conduit which was part of the system, and figure 2 shows the conduit in place.

63

FIG. 3.—THE VOGEL GRIP.

CONTINENTAL CABLE & GRIP CO.,

Eastern Office, 11 Wall St., New York.

This Company owns all the Terry Patents on the Iron Ties, Shallow Conduit, Terry Grip, and other valuable improvements.

Can be built for LESS THAN HALF THE COST of other successful cable roads, and operated for LESS THAN HALF THE COST of horse power roads.

THE ADVANTAGES OF THIS SYSTEM ARE AS FOLLOWS:

(1st.) The depth of the conduit required being only from seven to twelve inches, the road can be built for **one-half** or **less than one-half** the cost of any other successful cable road.

(2d.) It can be applied to any horse railroad, without disturbing the rails, ties or stringers, or even stopping the running of the cars.

(3d.) No grip car is required. The grip, weighing less than 300 lbs., is attached under the center of the car, and operated by a wheel on either platform, like an ordinary brake wheel, which is much easier worked than the long lever grip, and occupies no passenger room.

(6th.) The gripman cannot exert more pressure on the cable than is necessary to pull the load, so there can be no flattening of the cable. The same wheel which operates the grip, operates the brakes, thus putting the control of the car into the hands of the gripman in the quickest possible time, and it is especially adapted to heavy grades.

(7th.) This system requires no extra men to switch or make up trains at terminal points, as the train is automatically switched and made up under the control of the gripman. It is the only automatic grip for switching and crossing in existence.

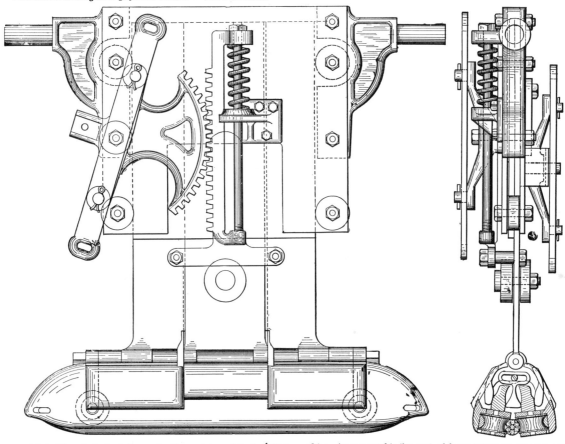

(4th.) The grip is simple in construction, certain and elastic in its action, thus obviating the jerking rebound on starting the cars. It takes hold of the sides of the cable, and not of the top and bottom. The pressure is against rollers, and the car can be run at any speed, from creeping to the full speed of the cable. The motion of the cable when the pressure is applied, moves the rollers forward into a wedge-shaped socket, thus holding tighter as the pull becomes stronger. In crossing another cable line, or meeting any obstruction in the conduit, the grip automatically loosens its hold of the cable.

(5th.) The cable can be dropped at any point, either on curves or straight lines, and picked up at the will of the gripman, thus avoiding any accident at curves or crossings, or stranding of the cable.

(8th.) As compared to the cost of horse-power on street roads running cars every five minutes or oftener, this cable system effects a saving of from fifty to seventy-five per cent. The cost for power does not exceed **eight** to **twelve** cents per car mile; while for horses, it reaches **twenty-five** to **forty** cents.

(9th.) The Terry Patents on the grip, shallow conduit, etc., are the only modern improvements on cable roads, that are tenable in the courts.

(10th.) It is not an experiment; it has been fully tested, and can be seen in actual operation on the Union Cable Railway in Kansas City, Missouri.

Further particulars furnished on application at the Eastern Office of the Company, Room 31, No. 11 Wall Street, New York.

The Terry grip was an unsuccessful effort at a similar shallow-conduit bottom-grip system, installed on the Union Cable Railway of Kansas City. The grip was designed for installation at the center of horsecars, to be run off wheels at each platform by rods and a rack-and-pinion connection. The apparatus added about 300 pounds to the weight of a horsecar. The cable ran through four horizontal wheels in a housing similar to a bobbin which held it in partial release. Tightening the grip caused the cable to push a small pulley overhead in the grip into the front of the bobbin-shaped housing. This it was hoped — vainly — would allow the car a smooth start. Putting the grip into partial release allowed the pulley in the front of the housing to revolve. The grip could drop or pick up rope at any point, and was reported to have an automatic device for release at let-go points. The promoter claimed that the grip cars in some unexplained fashion could switch to make up trains.

Which was preferable, the side grip or the bottom grip? Like many another question, this is insusceptible of a simple answer. There was no significant difference between the two in effect on cable life. The engineer of an uncomplicated system, such as the West Seattle or the Tacoma installation, opted almost automatically for a single-jaw side grip. It was simple, probably cheaper in first cost and maintenance and had certain advantages for design of the conduit. Notably, since all of the side grips except Lane's kept the cable to the side of the slot, it was possible to use a stationary depression pulley in place of a movable depression arm at the foot of a grade. Freedom from direct dripping from the slot was an undeniable advantage, both in preserving the cable and in keeping it dry for a more secure hold in rain or sleet. Further, a long-jawed side grip such as Hovey's in Chicago made an extremely firm hold on the cable, allowing long trains such as would have been inconceivable with bottom grips. All bottom-grip operators, as far as is known, operated either with combination cars or grip cars with single trailers.

On the other hand, bottom grips were preferable both in taking and dropping the cable. To take the cable automatically with a side grip it was necessary to have an elevating sheave in the conduit to bring the cable up to the level of the jaws, and then to move the car laterally with a track deflection to bring the jaws over to the cable. Alternatively, the cable could be taken manually with a lever called a *gypsy*, to be described in chapter V, lifted by the conductor. With a bottom grip, the cable could usually be taken simply by providing a declivity in the track of about three inches to bring the jaws down to the level of the rope.

Most cable cars carried greased hooks for the crew to pick up the cable manually at points where no other method was provided. This was always an emergency measure, but it was fairly common. To do this with a side grip was quite difficult. An incidental disadvantage of a double-jaw side grip was that if the rope were put into the wrong jaws by error, the grip would pull the cable off the deflection pulley at the next let-go point. Taking the cable with a hook into a bottom grip was easy and free of this risk.

The advantage of a bottom grip in dropping the cable was even greater than in taking it. Any of the bottom grips could drop the rope at any point in an emergency, or merely in ordinary service. A side grip could do this only if it were fitted with ejection spools, but these had the usual problem that dirt and horse droppings falling through the slot tended to clog them. If they stuck and the car failed to ungrip at a let-go point, the car could damage the cable, pull it off a sheave, bash into a superior cable or hit whatever else might lie ahead. The alternative method of letting go with a side grip entailed the same risks. If the grip had no ejection spools, the conduit had to be fitted with a deflection sheave which pulled the cable to the side at a point, usually marked LET GO or DROP ROPE. A gripman who had no ejection spools, if he missed a let-go point, had no way to release the cable and sailed straight into whatever awaited him. Since many lines provided a lateral deflection of the slot at rope drops, failure to let go involved a lateral pressure which bent the grip shank. The Grand Avenue Railway suffered a shank wedged in the slot from this cause in 1887. Similarly, in an emergency all a gripman could do was go into partial release; he could not drop the rope completely.

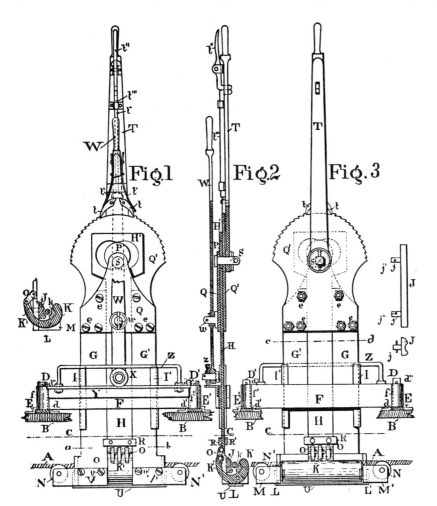

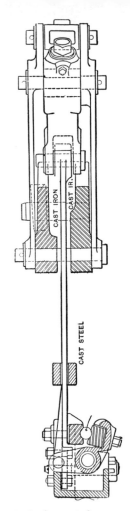

Cable traction had only two top grips. Figures 1 through 3 are the patent drawings of the Low & Grim grip of evil memory in Philadelphia and on the north side of Chicago. The patent shows the grip in open position; it was closed by moving the lever in either direction. As far as is known, this control was never used; all photographs of cars with this grip show orthodox lever control. At the right is the more satisfactory Whitton top grip from Pittsburgh.

In contrast, however, a bottom grip was more likely to become enmeshed in a loose strand and thus be unable to ungrip. Necessarily it had more moving parts and long hinged connections between the jaws and the body of the grip in which a loose strand could be caught. Since this was the worst accident risk inherent in the system, it was a serious objection to bottom grips.

Currently it is common to argue that bottom grips are superior on lines with curves because of the smaller probability of the cable being torn out of the jaws by lateral pressure. This was never, to my knowledge, argued in the trade press during the cable era. The interpretation presumably stems from the decision of the California Street Cable Railroad to use an Eppelsheimer instead of a Root when it built its O'Farrell-Jones-Hyde crosstown line in 1891. Though California Street was straight and O'Farrell-Jones-Hyde an-

gular, the decision was prompted by the large number of rope drops on the newer line. Dropping a rope 22 times and retaking it with a Root grip would have been unbearable. California Street itself was senior to the two lines of other companies it intersected. Similarly, the St. Louis Railroad, which combined a crosstown route with the latest franchise in a city that assigned positions on seniority, had 18 rope drops in a round trip, and thus had little alternative to a bottom grip.

An inconspicuous but important advantage of bottom grips was that they held the cable closer to the carrying pulleys in the conduit than side grips — by an inch to an inch and a half. This reduced the energy of holding the cable and allowed a shallower conduit. The saving of an inch in the depth of the conduit might appear trivial, but the economy in investment over the course of several miles was appreciable.

Nonetheless, a substantial majority of operators opted for side grips. Twenty-two companies used single-jaw side grips, 15, double-jaw side grips and one, the Washington & Georgetown, both single and double. Thirteen used bottom grips exclusively, two used bottom and single-jaw side grips, two more used bottom and double-jaw side grips and another, the New York & Brooklyn Bridge, used a roller grip and a bottom grip. Four companies used a top grip.

This compilation indicates that only a small minority used top grips. J. Bucknall Smith, in a characteristic passage, described the Philadelphia top grip:

> In the types of grippers previously described, the hauling cable is either picked up from below or at about right angles to the nipping jaws, but in the grippers at present referred to, the cable was taken in from the top of the apparatus; the reason of this is, however, not clear, as it appears that it would entail greater difficulties in ejecting the cable.

Eighty-three years have passed, but the attraction of the top grip remains "not clear."

The industry had two top grips, both used by the Widener-Elkins syndicate. For the installation on the Philadelphia Traction Company and again on the North Chicago Street Railroad, the syndicate's engineer A. D. Whitton used a top grip patented by Abraham K. Grim and Joel B. Low. Apparently the choice was dictated by a desire to avoid trust patents, rather than by the intrinsic merits of the device. The grip was arranged so that the usual action of depressing the shank caused the outer jaw to close on the cable by moving in an arc. Hovey expressed a very low opinion of this grip, characterizing it as "unyielding as a vise." He described it as extremely hard on the cable and on the dies in the jaws of the grip alike. He reported that dies on his double-jaw side grip lasted a month or more on the south side, but dies on the Low & Grim on the north side of Chicago required replacement every three or four days.

The worst disadvantage of a top grip was the long distance required for a rope drop. Only in Philadelphia did the problem arise, but to cross two top-grip lines it was necessary to bring the inferior cable up and to the side with an elevation sheave to bring the rope out of the grip, then down under the superior cable with a stationary depression pulley, up again with an elevation sheave, and down into the grip jaws. To accomplish all this required at least 40 feet, more than a car could roll on momentum. The Philadelphia Traction Company used horses and, later, auxiliary cables at 7th and 9th and Market to assist cars across the intersections or around the curves. The grip had no method of expelling the cable except with elevation sheaves, or presumably with a hook.

A. D. Whitton when called upon to design the Pittsburgh Traction Company developed a top grip of his own, in which the outer jaw closed on the cable from a hinge by leverage, rather than by the vise action of the aptly-named Low & Grim. Whitton's top grip was extremely deep, intended to allow the grip to hold the rope on curves in partial release on the line's double reverse curve on Soho Hill. A top grip was suited to this purpose because, unlike a side or bottom grip, it could not drop the rope in partial release. A cable dropped from a side or bottom grip on a pull curve might fall below the curve pulleys and be ruined by abrasion against the conduit wall or the non-revolving fittings of the pulleys. Whitton's grip required a deep and expensive conduit, but it was so well suited to Pittsburgh's topography — which was at the opposite extreme from Detroit's in practicability for cable traction — that it was used again on the city's Citizens Traction Company. Elsewhere, there appears to have been no interest in top grips.

A grip of any standard sort held the cable in a pair of dies set in the edges of the jaws. These dies usually bore friction of the cable in partial release and thus were central to the gripping operation in two respects. The Chicago City Railway used brass; the San Diego Cable Railway, cast steel; the Citizens Traction Company of Pittsburgh, cast iron; the Grand Avenue Railway of Kansas City, an unspecified amalgam; and various others, tooled or rolled steel, phosphor bronze or alloys of some sort. The short jaws of the Brooklyn Bridge's second grip used hard rubber dies. Inevitably, there was a trade-off between durability of the dies and life of the cable. Dies were

The orthodox placing of the gripman in the center of the car entailed a considerable waste of space, as the end view of Washington & Georgetown grip car No. 1, at left, demonstrates. The entire center of the car is out of revenue service. On the Brooklyn Heights Railroad, at right, the gripman controlled his grip with a wheel, and took no more space than a horsecar driver. (*Museum of the City of New York; Edward B. Watson*)

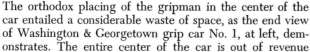

grooved to fit the cable, but the friction in partial release abraided the dies and the rope in some proportion, depending on relative hardness. The Chicago City could get 2,000 miles out of a set of brass dies, but Citizens Traction, only about 12 days' wear out of its soft cast iron. The Vogel grips in Butte had dies of an alloy called "metris metal" which gave 20 to 30 days of service. Steel dies were probably the most popular, being considered on the whole most economical. Cast steel dies were very durable, but hard on the rope surface. They could provide about twice the life of rolled steel, but at least one author, P. Moar, argued that rolled steel was the optimal material for durability and ease on the cable. Presumably no single answer was appropriate for all companies. Depending on the frequency of gripping and the various influences on life of the cable, the companies differed in their needs for durability of dies and longevity of rope. Unsurprisingly, T. C. Nash, one of the industry's most notable

rope experts, preferred dies somewhat softer than the cable.

In addition to replacement of dies, a grip required renewal of the shank because of abrasion against the slot rails. A grip cost about $50 to $100, but required continual maintenance expenses.

Companies differed also in the control mechanism they designed and the location they chose for them. All standard grips operated either off levers on quadrants or wheels on screw spindles. The majority used a lever operating directly on the grip shank. This arrangement had the advantages of simplicity, of a firm hold through the jerking action of pulling back on the lever and of a quick release by pulling up the dog on the quadrant and throwing the lever forward. One pound of pressure on the lever of the Pacific Railway's Eppelsheimer grip put 300 pounds of pressure on the cable. The principal disadvantage of the standard arrangement was the waste of space it entailed. The gripman occupied the middle of the

68

car, but in the ordinary single-trucker a passage had to be left the length of the car for removal of the grip. The total space requirement was as much as a third of what would otherwise have been the entire passenger area. This consideration caused the Denver Tramway, the Third Avenue Railroad and the North Chicago to put the gripman on the front platform, operating the grip by lever through extension rods. The New York Broadway line, the Columbia Railway, the Baltimore City Passenger Railway, the Brooklyn Heights Railroad and the Missouri Railroad in either original or replacement equipment used wheels mounted on the front platform to control the grip. Not only did such arrangements save space, but they gave the gripman an unobstructed view of the track ahead of him. Wheels lent themselves to such placing, since they were compact, and had none of the jerking of levers. It was uncommon to use a wheel mounted at the center of the car, directly on the grip. Hallidie's two installations were so arranged, and so were the independent installations of Henry Lane in Providence and Worcester Haddock on the Mount Auburn Cable Railway in Cincinnati. Both the Lane and Haddock installations entailed double-ended operation of short-grip cars, for which wheel-operation was well suited, since it was neutral with respect to direction. Many lines used lever grips under such circumstances, leaving the gripman to push in one direction and pull in the other to take the rope; but it was always felt preferable to have him pull. A wheel at minimum obviated this problem. A wheel also gave the gripman a continuum of positions, but not the quick release of a lever. On the other hand, it was so difficult to take a firm grip with a wheel that the Mount Auburn gripmen carried heavy bars for leverage against the spokes. Here there is little question that the majority who preferred levers were right.

All grips, incidentally, were placed in the expectation that the gripman was righthanded. Gripmen noticed that their trade produced a differential development of their right shoulders and forearms. Strength, obviously, was a help, but the various grips required only ordinary masculine development.

The gripman's other responsibility was braking. Even as the grips were never felt satisfactory

This drawing from Frank Parker's *Anatomy of the San Francisco Cable Car*, published by James Ladd Delkin in 1946, shows the placing of the grip and three brakes on the surviving Powell Street cars.

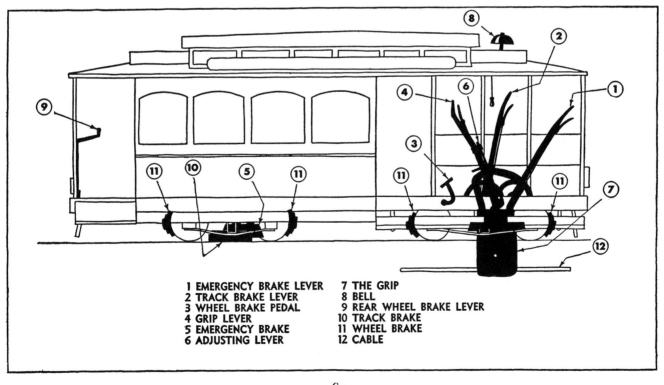

1 EMERGENCY BRAKE LEVER
2 TRACK BRAKE LEVER
3 WHEEL BRAKE PEDAL
4 GRIP LEVER
5 EMERGENCY BRAKE
6 ADJUSTING LEVER
7 THE GRIP
8 BELL
9 REAR WHEEL BRAKE LEVER
10 TRACK BRAKE
11 WHEEL BRAKE
12 CABLE

in the industry, so the brakes were always thought imperfect, at least for the emergencies inherent in the system. The brakes served well enough for routine operation. The typical cable car had at least two braking systems, one operating with brake shoes on the wheels in the usual fashion of railroad brakes, and the other pressing on the tracks. In the San Diego Cable Railway car on the color plate the center lever is the grip, the right lever operates the shoe brake on the front truck and the left lever the track brake on the rear truck. The conductor operated the shoe brakes on the rear truck from the gooseneck on the rear platform. It was more common to operate the shoe brake on the front truck from a foot pedal at the right of the grip. The track brake was typically lined with soft pine, a wood which eroded rough for maximum friction, rather than wearing smooth as almost any other wood would have done.

Braking on grip-and-trailer combinations was necessarily more complicated, but the majority of companies had to deal with the problem. Twenty-eight companies operated grips and trailers exclusively, and 12 others, grips and trailers in conjunction with single-unit equipment; only 20 used single-unit cars exclusively. The Chicago lines all ran brake lines from the grip car to the trailers, actuated by a lever in the hands of the gripmen. The conductor on each trailer had a gooseneck brake on a platform, in addition. The Seattle lines apparently used no brake lines, but relied exclusively on the conductor's gooseneck on each trailer.

The problems which the ordinary braking system could not solve were cable traction's two principal accident risks: getting caught in a loose strand, and losing the grip. The cars, not being dependent on traction between the wheel and the rail, could climb grades far beyond what any ordinary braking system could cope with if the car were to come free of the cable. Thus the cable was itself necessarily a braking device, either on upgrades or downgrades. Similarly, the power being transmitted from the powerhouse in the cable was so enormous, relative to the friction the brakes could generate, that they were impotent to deal with a car caught in a loose strand. To deal with this problem, and to some extent with

losing the grip, George Duncan, who had developed the pull curve, invented an emergency slot brake, a wedge poised rather appropriately like a pair of hands at prayer over the slot. On the Ferries & Cliff House lines, surviving on the San Francisco Municipal Railway, the slot brake is operated from a long, red-painted lever, to the front of the gripman's area. The gripman in an emergency raises the lever and drives the wedge into the slot behind the grip. This will, in general, tear a car free from a loose strand, though usually with damage to both the cable and the grip. It is almost impossible to release the slot brake unaided after such an episode. The Municipal Railway sends out a truck to push the car backward or, failing that, to break out an acetylene torch to cut the wedge free. Most flat systems did not use slot brakes.

Finally, the question arose whether the gripman could be enclosed. Since he evolved from the horsecar driver, who was necessarily stationed on the front platform, placing him out-of-doors was an obvious step, probably made without much thought. In addition, the cable car was developed in a mild climate, where out-of-doors work involved little hardship. The only engineer who systematically endeavored to enclose the gripman was A. D. Whitton, who used a double-truck car with a gripman's compartment in his installations in Philadelphia, Pittsburgh and Baltimore. He did not do so in Chicago, possibly because he preferred not to sacrifice visibility. In yet another of the typical irreconcilable problems of the cable car, the incentive to enclose the gripman for comfort was greatest in harsh climates, but there the general operating problems were most difficult, the clouding of glass in cold weather most extensive, and thus the incentive to leave him open for safety reasons greatest. The Butte City Street Railroad, with one of the most severe climates, enclosed the gripman in a glass compartment at the center of the car, but little of its line was in the streets. The Sioux City Cable Railway provided a diamond-shaped glass housing for the gripman. The Chicago lines made some efforts at protection of the gripman from local winters in the last year of cable operation, when the relative comfort of the front platform of an enclosed electric car was the normal case.

This truck, an adaptation of the Tackaberry truck of electric cars, was built by John Stephenson for the Cable Tramway of Omaha. The upper view shows clearly the arrangement for placing the grip at the center of the truck. *(Smithsonian Institution)*

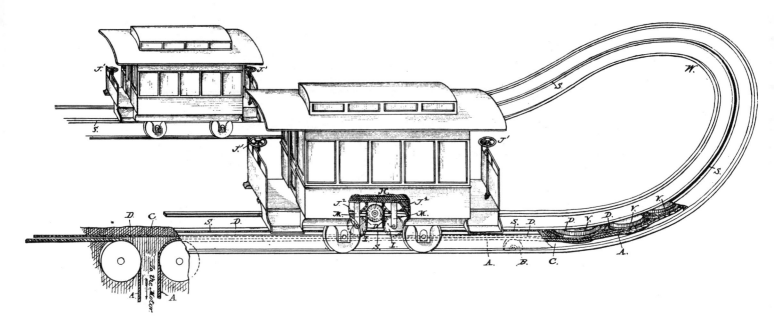

The Fairchild twin cable system, described immediately below.

NON-GRIP SYSTEMS

As mentioned in the previous chapter, one of the hopes of the optimists in cable traction was development of a system that dispensed with the grip entirely, simultaneously reducing the need for investment in the conduit and cutting wear on the cable. Three such systems were tried in 1887-88, all of which were demonstrable failures.

C. B. Fairchild promoted the twin-cable system, wherein the car held not the cable payed out by the powerhouse, but a rope of smaller diameter laid on the carrying pulleys beside the main cable. Friction with the main cable and its carrying pulleys ran the smaller rope, which was about ½-inch in diameter, at the same speed. The half-inch rope was intended to rise through the slot, and run up over a drum connected by a clutch to a set of gears. The drum could be engaged through the clutch to gears which would drive the car forward at the speed of the cable, forward at double the speed of the cable, or backward at half the speed of the cable. The arrangement was apparently adapted from the propulsion of movable cranes of the time. A system which could move faster than the cable and back up had obvious attractions, and Fairchild claimed

the system required only about a fourth of the investment of standard systems. Since the friction was on the clutch, rather than on the cable, ropes were expected to last three to four years. On the other hand, it was necessary to end lines in loops, and there was no apparent way to drop the rope. Whether the rope could have been taken through the slot with guide pulleys, as intended, is doubtful. The only installation was on a private right-of-way on the grounds of the Binghamton State Hospital, where the cables could be laid on pulleys on the ties without a conduit. It operated for two seasons in 1886 and 1887 and was removed. This modest show of feasibility was the greatest success of any of the non-grip systems, but no railway is known to have considered seriously a street installation.

The second, chronologically, of the three systems was the ladder-cable technology, customarily known as the Tom L. Johnson system after the Cleveland traction magnate who financed it, though it was invented by Milton A. Wheaton of San Francisco. The system was based on a pair of steel cables of ¾-inch diameter, connected at 6-inch intervals by steel crossbars. This ladder-cable ran about two inches below the surface in a conduit only 6 inches deep. Wheaton's patent entailed a latch at the end of a lever to engage the crossbars, sprung to allow easy starts; but all accounts of the actual installation report that cars carried cogwheels of 12 spokes to engage the crossbars. The gripman — or more precisely, the non-gripman — tightened a band brake to stop the wheel and start the car. To stop for a passenger he released the band brake to allow the cogwheel to revolve with the ladder-cable. Since the cable was normally horizontal, it had to be turned to a vertical position to round sheaves; thus, any curves had to be let-go curves.

Johnson experimented with the system on an eighth of a mile in Cleveland and then arranged a short non-revenue installation on May Street, Cincinnati, in the summer of 1884. There it was not considered successful, but Johnson arranged a commercial installation under the name of the

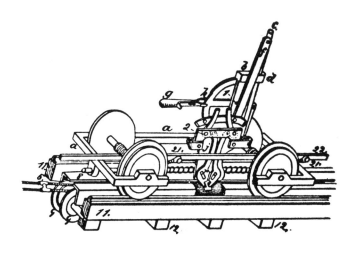

In Milton A. Wheaton's patent for the ladder-cable system, cars gripped the crossbars with the mechanism shown above. As installed in Brooklyn, a cogwheel engaged the crossbars in the conduit, below.

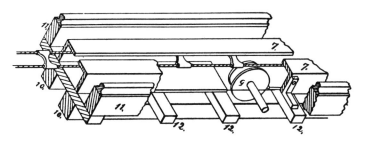

Brooklyn Cable Company on a line of the Atlantic Avenue Railroad. Even though the system was expected to have low energy requirements, it proved to require about double the power of standard cable technology. The shallow conduit filled with dirt more rapidly than standard conduits, and cable wear proved so much above expectations that the ladder-cable had to be replaced after three months. The system managed to operate in Brooklyn from March to July of 1887, but the technology was such an unquestionable failure that no further installations were attempted.

The third non-grip technology, the Rasmussen system, was by all odds the least likely to be successful, but proved to be the one most closely observed by the industry, and the one on which the hopes of enthusiasts for non-grip systems ultimately rested. The system was based on a patent of Lafayette Parker of Davenport, Iowa, of 1880 and a series of patents by Charles W. Rasmussen of Chicago between 1882 and 1885, held by what was first called the Rasmussen Cable Company and later the United States Cable Railway Company of Chicago, of which F. E. Hinckley was president. H. W. McNeill of Oskaloosa supervised installations, and the Iowa Iron Works of Dubuque contracted to provide the hardware.

The Rasmussen system entailed installation on existing horsecars of a thin sprocket wheel of about three feet diameter which reached into a standard-width slot in a shallow conduit to engage with iron buttons attached as collars to the cable. The operator had a single control, a gooseneck which he wound clockwise to tighten a band brake on the sprocket wheel, thereby stopping it and causing the car to move forward in the same fashion as in the Wheaton-Johnson ladder-cable system. To stop for a passenger he moved the gooseneck counterclockwise, releasing the band brake and allowing the wheel, which had eight sprockets, to revolve. The same gooseneck was attached to the wheel brakes, so that a single motion released the band brake on the sprocket wheel and tightened the wheel brakes, or released the wheel brakes and tightened the band brake. To allow the cars to operate on non-cable track, the sprocket wheel could be raised by a floor pedal on the front platform. The installation

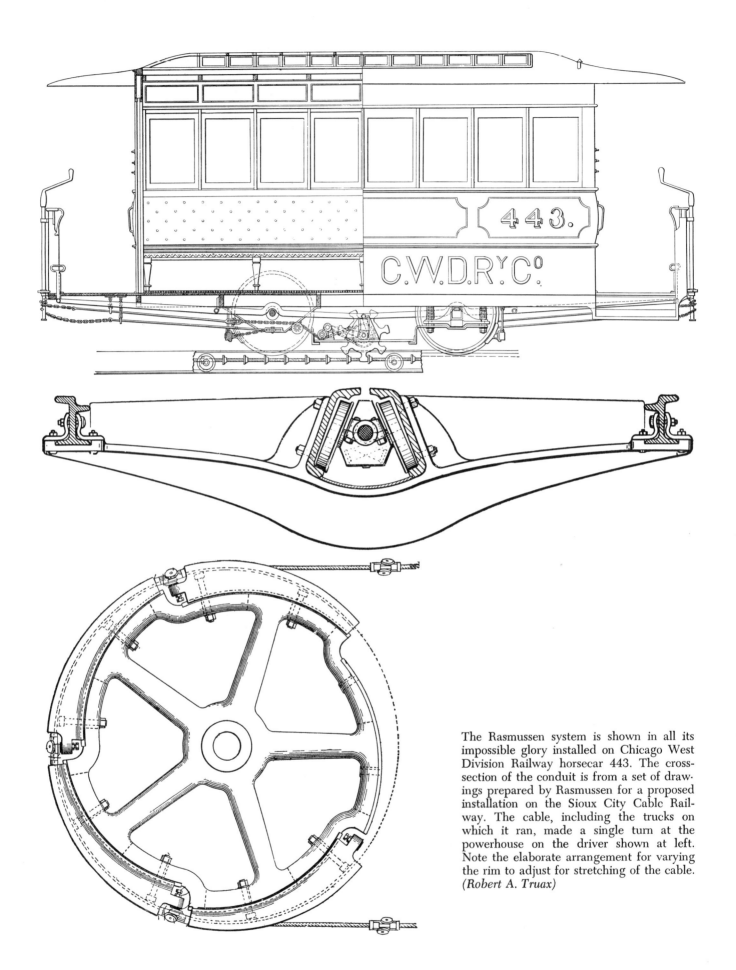

The Rasmussen system is shown in all its impossible glory installed on Chicago West Division Railway horsecar 443. The cross-section of the conduit is from a set of drawings prepared by Rasmussen for a proposed installation on the Sioux City Cable Railway. The cable, including the trucks on which it ran, made a single turn at the powerhouse on the driver shown at left. Note the elaborate arrangement for varying the rim to adjust for stretching of the cable. (*Robert A. Truax*)

added only about 200 pounds to a horsecar, and was intended to cost only $50.

The cable was extremely complicated. To a standard 1-inch Roebling rope Rasmussen attached a series of buttons, 3½ inches in diameter and 1½ inches long, at 8-inch intervals. The buttons were bolted or riveted together and held on the cable by babbit or type metal. At 6-foot intervals was an iron truck of two wheels of 6 inches diameter on which the cable rode on tracks in the conduit. Trucks at 250-foot intervals carried steel brushes to clean the conduit; there were catch holes for dirt and debris at 500-foot intervals. Tracks ran on both the top and bottom of the conduit to deal with declivities, crowns, and flat running. The wheels had a clearance of only ¼-inch between the top and bottom rails, so that they changed from one to another frequently and imperceptibly. Originally, the system was intended to have orthodox pull curves with horizontal pulleys slotted in the same fashion as the sprocket wheels on the cars. Terminal sheaves were slotted to hold the trucks at a right angle to their normal position while turning for the return trip. The conduit was only 6 inches wide and a foot deep between existing horsecar rails. Crews were expected to be able to lay about a mile of the bolted iron conduit per day (though they proved to lay only about 800 feet), and the installation was intended to cost only $10,000 per mile. Cables were expected to last from five to eight years because of the absence of gripping and ungripping. Had it been successful, this would have been an extremely cheap cable system.

The foregoing description is based mainly on Rasmussen's catalog of 1887 in the collection of Robert A. Truax of Washington. In turn, the catalog is based on the system as installed experimentally on 3,000 feet of track on Lake Street west of 40th Avenue on the Chicago West Division Railway in 1886. This demonstration, which proved, at minimum, that a car could be made to move, allowed Hinckley to arrange for an installation at Newark, New Jersey, in the following year. For the Newark installation, the technology was modified in two major respects. In an effort to reduce the capital required, the curve pulleys were replaced by a simple canting of the track in the conduit by 45 degrees to guide the

cable around curves. It had apparently been found in Chicago that the sprocket wheel meshed with the buttons effectively only in the immediate vicinity of the trucks; accordingly, at Newark the cable had at each truck a pair of buttons set eight inches apart. One was a plain disk ¾ inch thick and 2⅝ inches in diameter, designed to engage the driving wheel in the powerhouse. The system was designed to require only a single wrap on the driver; the tension device was on the terminal sheave. The other button was a 3-inch malleable iron collar with a flange of the sort used in Chicago, intended to mesh with the sprocket wheel.

As might easily have been foreseen, the system did not work. The press typically reported simply that stretching of the cable prevented meshing of the buttons with the driver in the powerhouse and with the sprocket wheels on the cars, but the men in charge of the installation denied this. They argued that they had planned on stretching of the cable, and provided adjustments on the driver for it. Rather, they found it impossible to secure the buttons on the cable as it stretched. As the buttons moved back along the cable from the truck, it became successively more difficult to hold them in the sprocket wheel. As recounted in the history of the line in Part II, the system was modified to operate with a four-pronged arm gripping the trucks, in the nature of Harvey's technology on the Greenwich Street elevated, but it still would not function properly. The failure was reasonably clear by mid-1888, even though the efforts to make the line workable persisted into 1889. The failure of the Terry system late in 1889 was less widely noted, but it served to drive home the failure of shallow conduit systems generally.

The only shallow conduit system to succeed — insofar as anything in cable traction can be called a success — was the Vogel & Whelan bottom-grip technology, which managed to reduce the capital in the substructure and to reduce friction on the cable in the manner the innovators of non-grip systems sought. Such attractions as the Vogel & Whelan technology had were trivial in comparison with the economies of Sprague electric cars. Thus, even had the non-grip innovators succeeded, Sprague's electric cars would have spread as inexorably as they did.

CHAPTER IV
THE CABLE

Since the various developers of the cable car took the cable as given, it is superficially surprising that there is more to be said about the cable than anything else in the technology. That is to say, all of the innovators from Hallidie to Rasmussen simply ordered out of the catalogs of the major cable firms; none of their inventions was a new cable *per se*. The inventions from Hallidie's grip through Rasmussen's buttons were ways of making use of existing cables. Since the cable was the method of power transmission and — almost equally important — the source of the worst accidents, it is not actually surprising that engineers thought and wrote a great deal about the cable. Further, with the possible exception of a series of articles on western cable lines which C. B. Fairchild published in the SRJ in 1893 on the basis of an inspection trip of the previous year, the principal firsthand account of cable systems we have is a series of notes and letters of J. B. Stone, a cable salesman for Washburn & Moen, preserved in Baker Library of the Harvard Business School. Stone, inevitably, evaluated cable railways mainly from the point of view of wear on cables. His view of cable traction as a mass of hardware all centered on the cable is at first jarring, especially if one has taken a legal view, which equally inevitably, delineates the technology as a mass of hardware all centered on the grip. And yet, in its way, Stone's view was accurate and consistent; certainly it was a view that let us know a great deal about cables.

Since the cable was extrinsic to the development of technology in the industry, it did not have a chronological development parallel to the grip; street railway engineers were confronted with approximately the same set of alternatives by the cable manufacturers throughout the cable era. Cables differed in diameter, weight, number of strands and direction of winding. As in the case of dies in the grip, no single choice was appropriate for all operators.

The standard street railway cable, as exemplified by the Chicago City Railway's rope, consisted of a hemp core, surrounded by 96 steel wires wound into six strands of 16 wires each. The core was a standard hemp rope impregnated with Stockholm tar, which remained in a semi-liquid state as a lubricant and waterproofing. Since the cable was what is known as an "ordinary lay," the strands were wound to the right around the core, but the wires were wound to the left in each strand. For general industrial use, such an arrangement was most satisfactory for strength, freedom from unwinding, and ease of splicing.

As an alternative, the British firm of George Cradock & Co. in 1881 introduced Lang's Patent Wire Rope, which was commonly known as the "Lang lay" cable. Lang's innovation lay in winding the wires in a strand in the same direction as the winding of the strand about the hemp core. In the ordinary lay, each wire rose to a peak as it reached the surface, thereby presenting itself to the jaws of the grip so that the pressure was concentrated at a single point. As the cable aged in service, wires typically broke at exactly the point where the grip touched them, and thus where they were most likely to come free to be-

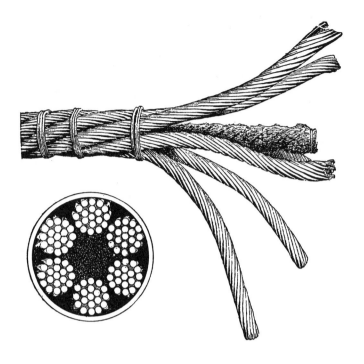

BROADWAY CABLE FULL SIZE

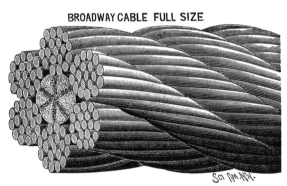

At the top is an ordinary lay cable, separated to show its construction. Note that the six strands are wound around the hemp core to the left, but the wires are wound in each strand to the right around one another. The cross section shows such a rope of six strands of 19 wires each. The Broadway cable is of the same type. Below are Fairchild's illustrations of ordinary lay ropes after long service. At lower right is the locked coil rope used briefly by the Brooklyn Heights Railroad.

AFTER MAKING 71,241 MILES.

AFTER MAKING 65,575 MILES.

come caught in the grip — the worst of the ailments intrinsic to this form of transportation. In the Lang lay rope, the wires presented long continuous surfaces to the grip over which the pressure was evenly distributed. Thus Lang lay ropes tended to wear smooth as they aged, rather than to fragment. This might appear an unmixed benefit, but there were none such in cable traction — and few enough elsewhere. Lang lay ropes were difficult to splice from the outset, and as they aged they became successively more difficult. William D. Henry believed they could not be safely spliced, and recommended against their use. Most of the large companies experimented with both ordinary and Lang lay ropes, but by the time of Fairchild's western trip of 1892, it was obvious they were showing a strong preference for Lang lay ropes in reorders.

On the other hand, the Chicago City Railway was endeavoring to operate its outermost cables at a very high speed, 14.75 miles per hour, and found that the grip action tended to crystalize the outer wires of Lang lay ropes so that they broke quickly. Accordingly, Fairchild found less enthusiasm for Lang lay cables in Chicago than he encountered in the West. Fairchild himself was strongly in favor of them, feeling that their "general adoption would, no doubt, work a large saving in the expense account of cable railways." The surviving San Francisco lines use Lang lay rope.

A third alternative was the "locked coil" rope, in which the wires were grooved to interlock with one another. Such a cable presented a very smooth surface, but it was generally thought impossible for street railway service because it could not be spliced. It was used in mines and elsewhere as a finite cable ending in a coupling socket. Only one company, the Brooklyn Heights Railroad, attempted endless-cable traction with a locked coil rope; it used electrical welding to make the splice. The experiment was unsuccessful, and the com-

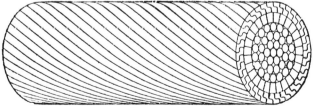

LOCKED WIRE ROPE.

pany shortly turned to ropes of the standard hemp-centered varieties.

Cable producers provided the industry with a variety of windings within the two classes of ordinary lay and Lang lay. It was possible to order cables with either 16 or 19 wires per strand, notably. On some 19-wire strands, seven wires served as the core with the remaining 12 wrapped around them to provide the surface of the strand. The 12 surface wires, which bore all of the friction from the grip in such ropes, were of larger diameter. On the so-called California rope, six of the 19 wires were triangular and the rest round in cross section in an effort to provide a smooth surface to the strand. As in other aspects of the technology, there was a trade-off between strength and flexibility. Ropes with strands of 19 wires were strong and durable, but owing to their inflexibility, were thought inappropriate for lines with large numbers of curves.

The same trade-off applied to choice of materials and diameters. Since a street railway cable had to bear extreme longitudinal stress, steels of high tensile strength were superficially desirable, but such steels are brittle and thus subject to fragmentation on turning at curves or sheaves. Here again, the companies differed in their needs depending on curvature and other considerations, but the orthodox view in the industry was that steels of very high tensile strength lacked the flexibility street railway service required.

Similarly, a company had an incentive to minimize the diameter of its cables. A cable of thin diameter required less energy to move, did less damage to the carrying pulleys and was easier to handle. In particular, thick cables required a disproportionate amount of energy to turn on sheaves and winding machinery. On the other hand, heavy traffic with frequent gripping and ungripping required a durable cable. In general, the industry's cable diameters were directly proportional to the traffic and operating difficulty of the lines. Increasing the diameter of the cable was a standard response to persistent cable troubles. One of the most difficult cables in the industry was the loop cable of the North Chicago Street Railroad, which combined heavy curvature, 7 per cent grades on approaches to a tunnel, exceptionally dense traffic and the obdurate Low & Grim grip. The man-

agement increased the cable from 1¼ to 1½ inches after a few months service in an effort, which was at least partly successful, to increase cable life and reduce failures in operation.

J. B. Stone reported that Washburn & Moen had delivered cables with a range from ⅞ inch to 1½ inches. As far as is known, this is also the range of the industry. Stone wrote that only the Spokane Cable Railway, a very lightly-travelled line, attempted a ⅞-inch rope, and the North Hudson County, a rapid-transit line with extremely heavy equipment, used 1½-inch cable. The two Pittsburgh lines which trailed the cable in partial release with the Whitton grip had an exceptional amount of friction on the rope, and used 1⁵⁄₁₆-inch diameters. The Cable Tramway of Omaha, which also had excessive friction, and the big Metropolitan Street Railway of Kansas City, used 1⁵⁄₁₆-inch rope. Most other systems used either 1⅛ or 1¼-inch cable, which represented a reconciliation of the demands for lightness and durability. The Chicago City Railway cable of 16 wires per strand described at the outset as typical was of 1¼-inch diameter.

How long a cable could be run? There was no single answer, again because of difference between lines in curvature and traffic. The early San Francisco lines all used relatively short cables, partly because most of them ran short distances, partly because they were built before the improvement in cables with the introduction of open hearth steel about 1880 and partly because the technology was still to some extent experimental. As the industry spread, engineers widely argued that the maximum practical length of a cable was about 5 miles. Cables of the length of 22,000 to 27,000 feet are most characteristic of the maps of the large cable systems in Part II of this volume, including the later San Francisco lines. Among the early installations, the cable of 34,600 feet of the St. Louis Cable & Western was considered notable. The unstranding of this cable under a concentration of equipment at the lower end of the line following a parade in October 1887 was widely interpreted as demonstrating the unworkability of ropes of over five miles, at least on lines with serious curvature such as the Cable & Western had. The Troost Avenue cable in Kansas City was almost exactly the same length,

but served adequately owing to a low degree of curvature.

Longer cables were, however, attempted. The Denver City Cable Railway used a rope of over 36,800 feet on its Welton Street line in 1889, and the Metropolitan Street Railway laid duplicate cables of 43,700 feet on Lexington Avenue, New York, in 1895. The Lexington Avenue cables were laid so late that they are generally overlooked, but the ability to run cables of that length without unstranding is remarkable, even under favorable circumstances. The cables had no curvature at all, except between the powerhouse and Lexington Avenue, and only one short sharp grade almost at the far end of the line. Cars ran at the headway of 2 or 3 per minute, but the line operated without reported difficulty solely attributable to the length of the cable.

The Welton cable in Denver was really more remarkable than the longer Lexington Avenue cables, since it traversed five right-angle curves and one milder curve. If the Denver City Cable Railway on Welton Street showed what could be done with a long cable, the Denver Tramway on 18th Avenue showed what could not. The company incomprehensibly attempted a cable of 32,000 feet with two terminal loops and the equivalent of 14 right-angle turns, plus the curvature at the powerhouse. Unsurprisingly, the company gave up the attempt as hopeless in less than six weeks and amputated one of the two loops.

Cable life, even more than length, depended on the conditions of service. In standard practice, again exemplified by the Chicago City Railway, a cable was impregnated with hot tar for flexibility and then coated with linseed oil to prevent the tar's sticking to the dies of the grip. Fairchild reported that some lines, which he did not identify, used a coating of tar, oil, lime and mica; he recommended distilled tar only. He also recommended having heated tanks at the powerhouse to feed a small, constant stream of the rope treatment to the outgoing cable. The rubber dies of the second Brooklyn Bridge grip allowed the Bridge railway, alone in the industry, to dispense with rope treatment. Wet weather tended to take away the rope lubricant through drippage, and a complete inundation of the conduit, as in Grand Rapids in 1891, denuded a cable almost entirely, requiring an expenditure of about $125 to recoat a 25,000 foot rope. Excessive lubrication resulted in the cable's spreading tar and oil on the winding machinery and carrying pulleys, interfering with their free revolution.

Successive impregnation with the rope coating tended to improve a cable; the surface became more nearly smooth, thereby reducing friction with the dies and carrying pulleys. Additional tar also tended to hold down loose strands. Everything else, of course, tended to make the rope deteriorate. Gripping and ungripping tended to lengthen the cable and narrow its diameter. The stretching of a cable was expected to be 1 to 2 per cent of its length. The Chicago City Railway anticipated a stretch in one of its long cables of about 50 feet the first day and 100 feet the first week, but not much thereafter. The variance in reported lengths of cables on other systems — two reports are almost never identical — indicates a greater stretching than this. The Kansas City Cable Railway customarily cut 40 to 50 feet out of a new cable after two days of service, but a cable it inaugurated in June 1887 stretched 90 feet in 12 hours. Like much else about a cable, its stretching could not be predicted with perfect accuracy.

William H. Searles in 1887 estimated that an average cable would run from 85,000 to 100,000 miles over the course of 12 to 14 months, and lose 10 per cent of its weight but 40 per cent of its strength. Since he estimated the breaking strain of a new cable at 39 tons, a cable had a safety factor of three or four even when old. Others estimated the breaking strain as high as 45 tons. The Chicago City estimated a 1¼-inch cable lost about 3/16 inches in diameter over its lifetime. The Vine Street line in Cincinnati found an 18-ton cable lost 1½ tons in weight and 1/16 in diameter in an average life of seven to eight months. Fairchild in 1892 estimated that the average life of cable for the industry was eight

months and that mileage normally ranged from 40,000 to 150,000.

Cable life was a subject to which the industry gave a great deal of attention. Virtually all companies employed a full-time rope superintendent. R. J. McCarty estimated cable renewal and maintenance at 5 to 25 per cent of the cost of operation. The Grand Avenue Railway estimated cable expense, including grip repairs, at 1.21 cents per car mile. The Metropolitan of Kansas City, after it had absorbed almost the entire Kansas City network, spent about $100,000 per year on cable replacement. Thus, measures which increased cable life were a major source of economy. In general, cable life was inversely related to curvature, precipitation, severity of winters, gradients, speed and traffic. Of these factors, curvature was by far the most important. Berl Katz, distinguished historian of St. Louis cable lines, points out that the Missouri Railroad was an ideal demonstration of the effect of curvature on cable life. The east end of the line, which was straight, had an average cable life of nine to 15 months, but the west-end cable, which bore the same traffic, lasted only five to eight months because of two major and two minor curves. Similarly, the Chicago City Railway averaged 280 days life on its two straight cables south of 39th Street on State Street, but managed only 114 out of a cable which entailed two curves between the powerhouse and 39th and Cottage Grove Avenue, and only about 90 out of each of its two loops in the central business district. James A. Seddon, who attempted a mathematical model of cable life (cited in the bibliography) on the basis of experience in the conversion of the St. Louis Cable & Western from one rope to two, considered a typical right-angle curve the equivalent of a half mile of line in cable wear. J. B. Stone believed cable life was inversely proportional to the square of the curvature.

A good example of the costs of excessive curvature was the original loop terminus of the Grand Avenue Railway. The company's north rope cost $4,500 and because of a series of pull curves on the loop required a replacement every three months. By replacing this arrangement with a simple terminal sheave and a loop which cars traversed in full release, the company anticipated saving $16,000 a year through virtually doubling cable life.

The contrast between well-designed and poorly-designed systems in cable costs was striking. The Metropolitan of Kansas City allocated about $100 a day to cable replacement on its original three lines of six cables, and only about $275 a day after it had absorbed the Kansas City Cable Railway and the Grand Avenue Railway. The Valley City Street & Cable Railway of Grand Rapids, which was the most unworkable physical plant of any of the lines which used standard technology, spent about $49 per day for its north cable and over $56 for its south cable, which had four and six right-angle curves, respectively. Both these figures were well over four times the gross receipts of the two lines.

Gradients adversely affected cable life in two fashions. First, although the car was able to ascend any given grade at the speed at which it traversed level terrain, the longitudinal stress on the cable increased more than proportionally to gradient. Second, and more important, grades required depression pulleys at the bottom and crown pulleys at the top, with additional changes in vertical alignment of the cable at cross streets. Cable engineers generally argued that taking a cable around a sheave of 100 times the diameter of the cable did the cable no harm, but the damage of any smaller sheave or pulley was inversely proportional to its diameter. The nature of the sheaves and pulleys in a conduit will be treated in the following chapter, but for present purposes it is sufficient to point out that depression pulleys necessarily were of small diameter, such that they entailed a drastic angle in the cable. Movable depression pulleys were usually of only seven inches diameter, so that the angle they put in a moving cable was the worst of any sheave or pulley.

Cable life was adversely affected by traffic mainly by the action of the grips in thinning the cable and in fracturing wires on its surface. Henry Root estimated that a cable might run for three years without grips, but only eight to 12 months in actual service; thus, he thought the sheaves and pulleys were responsible for about a fourth of the wear and the grips for three-fourths. The action of the grips simultaneously reduced the cable's strength, made it more difficult to hold and

increased the frequency of loose wires rising from the cable. This problem will be treated in detail at the end of this chapter, but since it was the greatest hazard in a system not lacking in hazards, a rope superintendent had an incentive to suggest replacement of a cable as soon as he noticed the incidence of loose strands increasing perceptibly.

Finally, cable life depended in part on speed. The friction of the grip on the surface of the cable increased more than proportionately to speed. Superintendent Chapman of the Grand Rapids system, who probably knew more about trouble firsthand than anyone else in the industry, estimated that the friction from the grip in taking a full hold of the rope after going into partial release for a passenger covered about 20 feet of the cable surface at five miles per hour, but 60 feet at ten. The friction of the dies of the grip placed an effective upper limit on the speed of cable traction. The SRJ in 1892 stated that the Cleveland City Cable Railway was operating the outer portion of its Superior line at 16 miles per hour and in the following year indicated that the Chicago City Railway was attempting to operate its south Cottage Grove Avenue cable at 14.75. All other sources report that both ran their outermost cables at 14 miles per hour, which was generally considered an absolute limit of cable speed because the friction of the dies would set the rope afire at higher speeds. High speeds were also an incentive to traverse curves in partial release, a fruitful source of severed wires.

How long could a cable last? The question is almost a foolish one; the most important observation one can make is that a rope superintendent could not tell how long a given cable could survive when it was put in service. Cables varied in quality of their steel — doubtless more than they would do at present. A siege of wet weather could unpredictably reduce the lives of all a company's active cables by accelerating corrosion; a special event could create a great deal of gripping and ungripping and, worst of all, failures of gripmen to let go promptly could put kinks in the cable unpredictably. The last of these was one of the most difficult problems for a cable operator, since gripmen were reluctant to report their derelictions; a severe cut or kink might operate all day, beginning unraveling or other serious damage to

Above are Fairchild's two illustrations of ordinary lay cables kinked by failure of the gripman to let go promptly at rope drops. Such a kink, when discovered, would be watched carefully until night, and then removed by a splice.

the rope. It was not uncommon for a company to secure over a year's wear out of a cable and then to have only three or four months from its replacement. The first cable from Eutaw to Gay Street on the Baltimore City Passenger Railway lasted four months, which proved to be typical, but its replacement wore only 34 days.

The question, for all its intrinsic shortcomings, stands: how long could a cable last? The longest-lived were probably on the West Seattle Cable Railway, which operated hourly in connection with a ferry, and alone among cable lines shut down the cable between trips. This company regularly secured a cable life of over two years, but this answer reveals the emptiness of the question. The Denver Tramway on its three lines running straight from the powerhouse regularly got 19 to 20 months from a cable. Fairchild in his book illustrated a Lang lay rope which he claimed had run for 826 days, but he unconscionably neglected to identify the company, and thus we cannot know the nature of its duties. The Pacific Railway of Los Angeles secured 1026 days and 163,944 miles out of a 23,400 foot Hazard rope in the early 1890s on its Grand Avenue line; this was widely thought to be a record. As evidence of what the industry considered exceptionally good service, the Metropolitan of Kansas City reported to the SRJ that a Broderick & Bascom rope of 32,300 feet on the west 18th Street line had run 18 months and 24 days, from December 18, 1888 to July 12, 1890, at 9.75 miles per hour. Since the line had considerable curvature, heavy traffic and eleven rope drops, the performance was well worth publishing.

The California Street Cable Railroad was pleased enough to report a rope which ran 79,800 miles in 20 months at 7 miles per hour. In the process it shrank from 1¼ to 1⅛ inches in diameter. It carried about 6 million passengers, who paid $300,000 in fares. The rope was thought to have done the work of 800 horses.

A rope superintendent could predict the demise of a cable with a fair degree of accuracy on the basis of contraction in the diameter, incidence of loose strands, and visual indication of likely ruptures. Consequently, a company knew within two or three weeks when it would have to replace a rope. The large street railways all had cables on hand for replacement, but for small or unsuccessful companies replacement of a cable was a major expense which was procrastinated as long as possible. The San Diego Cable Railway, the Second Street line in Los Angeles and — of course — the Valley City in Grand Rapids all had long suspensions of service while awaiting cable replacement. Procrastinating replacement was unwise, if only because cables were produced to order. The market for street railway cables was thin enough and the requirements of the roads specific enough that cable producers did not typically stock inventories. The receiver of the San Diego Cable Railway had to wait two months for

AFTER RUNNING 826 DAYS.

his replacement cables from Washburn & Moen, though the necessity of a transcontinental shipment probably made this delay somewhat worse than average.

The dominant firms in the cable industry were three: John A. Roebling's Sons Company, Trenton, New Jersey; Washburn & Moen Manufacturing Company, Worcester, Massachusetts; and the Broderick & Bascom Rope Company of St. Louis. Hazard of Wilkes-Barre, Pennsylvania was also a major producer. Each, naturally, considered its product superior. Roebling claimed as much as 60 per cent greater life than its rivals' ropes, but J. B. Stone, on the basis of his correspondence with his superiors, appears honestly convinced that the Washburn & Moen cable he sold had more longevity than the Roebling or Broderick & Bascom ropes he inspected in service. The street railways seem to have shown no strong preference between brands. Stone was a believer in high standards and consistently counseled his customers against endeavoring to save money on cables or adopting

cheap engineering which would result in high cable wear. In general, the street railways seemed satisfied with what the rope companies furnished them; hope for improvement was always sought in the grip or the conduit, never, apparently, in the cable.

Only the Market Street Railway is known to have made its own ropes, but it gave up the practice when it converted to Lang lay, which its machinery could not produce, in the early 1890s.

A new rope was, like most else in cable traction, both expensive and heavy. A cable of 25,000 feet usually cost from $6,000 to $7,500 including shipping charges in the height of the cable era. In 1900 Roebling charged St. Louis transit 9¢ per pound for cable; ropes of the usual 1⅛ or 1¼-inch diameters ran about 2½ pounds per foot. The Mount Adams & Eden Park estimated its cable cost at $1,400 per mile. The Riverview cable of the Inter-State Consolidated Rapid Transit of Kansas City was 18,800 feet long, and weighed 46,779 pounds. The long-lived California Street

84

rope mentioned previously was 17,513 feet in length with a weight of 44,604 pounds. The Kansas City Cable Railway's Troost cable, which was about 34,500 feet long, weighed 80,000 pounds. Moving something of this mass was a major logistic effort, obviously. Typically, cables were wound on shipping reels which were themselves necessarily massive constructions of wood and iron. The accompanying advertisement of Broderick & Bascom indicates that a rope of 35,400 feet wound for shipment weighed 110,000 pounds; presumably it was a thick cable of about three pounds per foot. Roebling owned a four-truck flatcar which it used exclusively for transporting street railway cables, and the Wabash Railway provided a similar car for Broderick & Bascom. Some cables were shipped unwound, laid loosely in gondola cars, but this method, though cheaper, was usually thought undesirable because of the risk of kinking the rope in unloading it. Such shipment was usually practical only if the powerhouse had direct access to a railroad siding, but most were placed with regard to the operating requirements of the line, not to rail connections.

The rail movement of a cable was the easy part. To move the cable from a railroad siding to the powerhouse through city streets with horse-drawn vehicles was far more difficult. Broderick & Bascom used what was said to be the heaviest four-wheel wagon in the world for deliveries around St. Louis. The Cleveland City Cable Railway's cable wagon weighed 9,000 pounds, and had a capacity of 50 tons. The wheels were 44 inches in diameter with a 9-inch tread. The front axle was 1¼ inches narrower than the rear for better weight distribution. The accompanying photograph of a Washburn & Moen cable being trucked into the powerhouse of the Omnibus at Oak and Broderick, San Francisco, illustrates the nature and difficulty of the operation far better than any description. The team is apparently made up of 54 horses with at least ten riders, even though this was not a powerhouse particularly isolated by gradients. The Grand Avenue Railway received some cable unwound and hauled it through the streets over pulleys on wooden frames with a team of 20 horses. Hauling a coiled cable on a wagon over cable track was particularly undesirable, since the slot rails were necessarily weakly supported, relative to the rest of the conduit; the wheel of a cable wagon could easy collapse the slot in passing. In 1897 a wagon loaded with a 21-ton cable for the Holmes Street powerhouse in Kansas City crashed through the rail-

The Omnibus Railroad & Cable Company's first rope is dragged along Golden Gate Avenue by some 54 horses to the powerhouse at Oak and Broderick in San Francisco. (Roy D. Graves)

A cable for an unidentified street railway is about to be hauled out of the Roebling plant at Trenton by a Pennsylvania Railroad switcher. The car is Roebling's own four-truck flatcar reserved for such movements. (*Rennselaer Polytechnic Institute-Smithsonian Institution*)

road bridge at 22nd and Grand when about two-thirds across it. Fortunately, some water and gas mains about three feet below the roadway supported the structure. Some companies rolled shipping reels through the streets on frames, saving the weight of the wagon, but concentrating the load narrowly on limited areas.

If the cable was the first for a company, the installation was the most difficult part of the entire operation; if it was a replacement cable, the job was relatively simple. A line's first cable had to be laid by horse, usually by the expedient of taking firm hold of the end of the rope in a grip and dragging the grip car around the line with a huge team. The newspaper drawing of this operation illustrated here comes from the flat portion of the Portland Cable Railway. The sight of driving a team up grades of over 20 per cent can only be imagined. The loop cable of the Metropolitan of Kansas City, which traversed grades of only 5 to 8 per cent, required 38 mules hitched to three grip cars spaced along the cable. Lines with major gradients below the powerhouse usually brought the cable to the powerhouse on a shipping reel and then laid it down the grade on each track separately, splicing it at the terminal sheave.

Replacing an existing cable was relatively easy. The shipping reel was mounted on an axle behind the winding machinery so that the cable could be spliced to the old cable, which was cut, and then run out over the line. The old cable, after being wound in by the machinery, was drawn off with a winch and either wound on another reel or simply coiled in the yard of the powerhouse, depending on what use was to be made of it. Most old cable was sold for scrap, but some was sold for use on hoists and funiculars, for which in certain respects it was better than new rope, since it was

A grip holding the first cable of the Portland Cable Railway is dragged down 5th Street by a team of eight horses. Presumably, two to four such teams were at work on the rope, since a team of this size could pull out only two or three blocks of cable. *(Oregon Historical Society)*

Broderick & Bascom made its local deliveries to St. Louis cable power-houses with this vehicle, claimed to be the largest four-wheel wagon in the world. *(National Museum of Transport)*

The engine for converting between cables was this modest winch, shown in the main powerhouse of the Pacific Railway in Los Angeles. The new cable at the left was pulled out onto the line at the end of the old by the winding machinery. As the old cable came into the powerhouse, the winch wound it onto the shipping reel at the right. *(Huntington Library)*

already fully stretched and impregnated with tar. As might be expected, sale of used cable for reuse on funiculars was particularly characteristic of Pittsburgh. Scrap cable could be sold for $6 to $8 per ton.

Cable replacement was typically done in the wee hours, when most cable systems provided service with horsecars. The Grand Avenue Railway could cut an old cable of 30,000 feet, splice in the new, run it out, cut off the old and splice together the new in an hour and 45 minutes. Since the normal run of such a cable was between 30 and 45 minutes, this performance was remarkable; most companies probably could not equal it.

Splicing, clearly, was a major activity in cable technology. On most large systems the rope superintendent's immediate subordinate was the splicer; on smaller lines the two positions were unified. Splicing was a highly skilled craft, and as usual the process was heavy and expensive. The tools were a vise, a marlin spike, wire cutters, pliers, a cold chisel, hammers, mallets, tongs, nippers and a special set of tongs, shown in Fairchild's figure 236, for prying the cable apart to insert strands.

Splicing on a street railway was basically what it was in marine practice, but the process required a high degree of precision because of the absolute necessity of producing a splice of the same diameter as the rest of the cable. When grips in partial release hit a portion of the cable of greater diameter than the rest, they tended to push back the enlargement until the process produced an unwinding of about half an inch some ten or fifteen feet back of the original increase in diameter. This enlargement was subject to breakage of the wires and to rupture in the same fashion as a kink.

In the standard methods of splicing, the two cables were unwound or unlaid by separating the strands of each for about 30 feet beyond the point at which the splice was to be made. The hemp core was removed for this distance. To prevent any further unlaying, the cables were bound or "seized" with short pieces of wire at that point. In the "California splice," which Fairchild described as the most common in the industry, the individual strands were not themselves unwound into their 16 or 19 wires; in fact, Fairchild suggested that they be seized with wire or canvas

to prevent their unlaying. The 12 strands were then brought together or "married" at the point of the seizings on the two cables. A strand of one of the two cables was then pulled back or unlaid, creating a vacant space called a "score" into which the corresponding strand from the other cable was laid. When the strand being inserted had an end of about 18 inches projecting, the strand being removed was also cut back to about 18 inches. The process was followed sequentially for each strand on both sides of the marriage, leaving 12 ends of the 18 inches projecting, as in Fairchild's figure 234. In the California splice, with the tong designed for the purpose, the rope was pried open at each of the points where the 12 strands protruded, as shown in Fairchild's figure 235, the hemp core was removed for a short distance, and the two strands, cut back to short lengths, were inserted to replace the core. Since the core was present for flexibility, not for strength, the splice was as strong as the rest of the cable, but less flexible. The splice ran to about 60 feet.

The principal alternative to the California splice was the Nash splice, invented and patented by Thomas C. Nash, splicer of the Chicago City Railway. Nash's splice entailed unlaying the six strands and removing the hemp core in the usual fashion; his novelty lay in his method of reuniting the strands and tucking in the wires. When two strands were brought together after laying one in the score of the other, the outer half of the wires in each strand were themselves unwound from the rest of the strand. The wires allowed to remain together were tied tightly into an overhand knot which was beaten well down into the score, slightly below the regular circumference of the rope. The wires beyond the knot were also unwound, creating a total of four fringes of eight to ten wires each which were tucked in between the strands of the cable as shown in Fairchild's figures 237 through 241. Nash's splices were reportedly far more secure from unraveling than California splices. Fairchild reported that Nash's method could not be used with Lang lay rope; the knotting of the strands in a Lang lay cable unwound the strands, whereas it tightened them in an ordinary lay rope. In any splicing method, the splice was pounded with mallets until it was as close to conformity with the rest of the

FIG. 232.

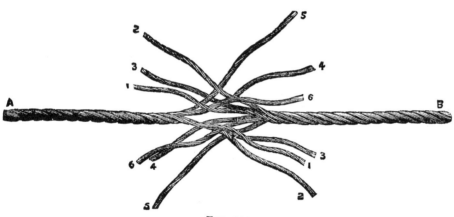

FIG. 233.

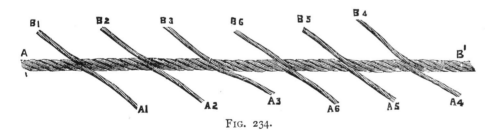

FIG. 234.

FIG. 236.

These figures from Fairchild illustrate the description of splicing on these pages. Figure 232 shows the two cables "married" in a vise at the powerhouse. Figure 233 shows the marriage in detail. Next, strands of one cable were unlaid and replaced by the other for a distance of about 30 feet. When about 18 inches of the strands being put in place remained, the strands being removed were themselves cut back to 18 inches, as shown in figure 234. In the California splice, the splicing gang finished the job as shown in figure 235. The cable is held in the vise at left. The second man from the left unwinds the cable by means of the hemp rope racking and the marlin spike in his hands. The splicer at the left pries the cable open with the special tongs shown in figure 236. The strands will be cut back to a few inches and stuffed into the center of the cable, replacing the hemp core. The gang of four will proceed to the pairs of strands at the center and right.

FIG. 235.

Below, figures 237-241 show the Nash splice, described in the text. Figure 242 illustrates the consequence of a bad splicing job, in which the rope was left thicker at the splice than elsewhere. Grips in partial release have pushed the enlargement back in the cable until the wires ruptured.

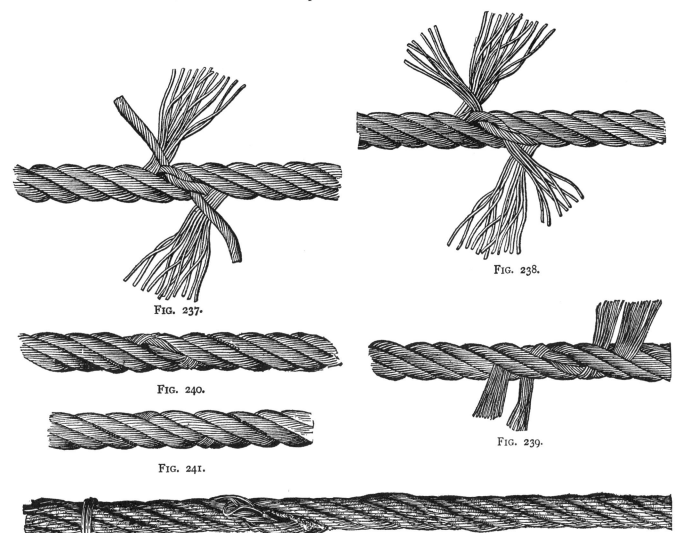

FIG. 237.

FIG. 238.

FIG. 240.

FIG. 239.

FIG. 241.

FIG. 242.

cable in diameter and surface characteristics as it could be made.

Apart from the replacement of cables, it was necessary to splice a rope after a rupture, to remove a kink, to reduce the length or to replace a badly damaged portion. The Kansas City Cable Railway spent about three hours removing the first two days' stretching from one of its cables. Replacement of a damaged portion was difficult, partly because it required two splices, partly because a new segment inserted into an old rope was greater in diameter than the rest, with the attendant problem of the passing grips pushing back the slack in the cable.

Ideally, a company would have sought to avoid gripping and ungripping on a splice because of its inflexibility, but since the rope was out of sight in the conduit, there was no way to arrange this. The Glasgow Subway, which used a high-speed cable without a conduit, painted its splices white and instructed gripmen to wait until the splice had passed before gripping.

*   *   *

At the outset of this chapter it was pointed out that the cable was both the means of transmitting power and the source of the worst accidents in the system. The chapter, naturally, has been concerned mainly with the cable as the transmitter of power; the accident risks inherent in it are also worthy of explicit consideration.

Losing the grip on a grade was essentially a problem of grip design, rather than something inherent in the cable. The accident hazards inherent in the cable stemmed from breaks in the rope and from loose strands.

Breaks in the rope were not a serious safety problem; the Baltimore Traction Company had only one rupture in the first 19 months of operation. Ruptures stemmed principally from mistakes of the gripman, either in failure to let go at a rope drop or in putting a kink in the cable through failure to drop it early enough. Most kinks were discovered only during the low-speed inspection most companies gave their ropes at night. The great majority of kinks were removed by splicing the night of occurrence, before they caused a rupture. It was a cliché of the industry that a cable gave 24 hours notice before it broke. Outright

breaks, contrary to what one might expect, were not particularly characteristic of heavily-trafficked lines, such as the two New York companies or the Chicago City Railway, but rather of lines with a combination of severe curvature and cold climates. The cold made the cable brittle and contracted the slot, binding the grip shank, adding to the friction in the system, and causing the cable to rupture. The misbegotten Grand Rapids system, which had both a severe climate and excessive curvature, had continual ruptures in the cable.

An outright severance of the cable obviously caused the line covered by the cable to stop at once. The loose end occasionally flew up through the slot, but this was not a serious source of accidents. The principal problem arose from inability to stop the engine until the ends of the cable had separated by a considerable distance, usually at least a city block. A team of horses had to be brought out to drag the two ends together so that a temporary splice could be made on the spot; a permanent splice was made at the powerhouse at night. The interruption in service ranged from 90 minutes to six hours. A gripman who was demonstrably responsible for the severance of the cable was fired with no excuses considered on the Washington & Georgetown, and probably had little better luck on other systems.

Loose strands, rather than breaks in the cable, were the principal worry of a rope superintendent — and most others in authority. The term "loose strand" was invariably used in the industry, but it appears to have been applied indiscriminately to strands of 16 or 19 wires, or to single wires, or to several wires. This problem was directly proportional to the traffic on a line; the more frequently cars gripped and ungripped the more rapidly wires fractured and thus the greater was the possibility of loose strands. The New York lines had continual involvements in loose strands, whereas the Grand Rapids system, in spite of its continual cable ruptures, had no recorded accident from a loose strand, presumably because its cars ran at long intervals and gripped infrequently.

The emergence of loose strands was inevitable, and from the Clay Street Hill Railroad, cable lines provided alarms in the form of forks poised over the cable at the powerhouse. When a loose strand was spotted, either by tripping of the alarm or in the nightly inspection of the rope, it was carefully tucked into the cable between the wires. Since the cable invariably went through the grip from back to front, a loose strand, whichever way it arose, was tucked in toward the rear. Consequently, the action of the grips against the cable was rather like combing one's hair; the ordinary gripping action tended to keep loose strands in place.

The danger lay in a gripman, seeking to make up time, going into partial release on a downgrade and moving faster than the cable — an offense known as "skinning the cable." The cable would then pass through the grip from front to rear; the action was like running one's hand from the back of one's head to the front in raising loose strands. The loose strand would stand out from the cable, ready to engage with the next grip ahead. In Grand Rapids grip cars carried bells which rang from a belt connection off an axle; if a gripman skinned the cable, an inspector could spot the speeding up of the bell and identify the offender. The Washington & Georgetown also sacked a gripman for his first offense of this sort without considering extenuating circumstances, and the Metropolitan of Kansas City provided a 30-day suspension.

The horrible examples of this class of accident are indeed horrible. An accident was difficult to avoid because of the close headway of most cable lines. A gripman was instructed to ring a specified signal on his overhead bell — one reason the bell bulked so large in cable traction — to alert the car ahead of him of his plight and to warn its gripman to proceed without stopping. But the leading gripman would shortly approach another car and have to give it the same signal. The probability of the bell signal being transmitted to a series of four or five cars accurately was low, and the probability of that many cars being able to proceed without stopping for a long distance without an accident was lower yet.

In April 1893 a four-car train on the North Chicago Street Railroad entangled its top grip in a loose strand emerging from the south portal of the river tunnel and proceeded uncontrollable at 6 miles per hour around the entire terminal loop in the most congested part of the city. Trains

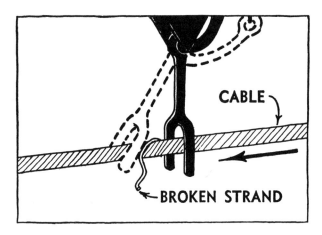

A broken strand alarm from *Anatomy of the San Francisco Cable Car.*

operated at intervals of 15 to 20 seconds. The gripman rang the bell signal, successfully alerting the combination car ahead, which proceeded without stopping, almost succeeding in traversing the loop. Northbound at Randolph Street, however, the combination car hit a horsecar of the West Chicago, knocking its own rear truck off the tracks. Owing to their light weight and shallow flanges, cable cars derailed easily. The car which was fouled in the cable, still unable to stop, hit the derailed combination car, moved it to a right angle to the track and pushed it all the way back to the tunnel portal. The derailed car fouled the southbound track, where an inbound cable train hit it. Even this did not stop the entrapped car, which pushed the entire mass of wreckage of its own train, the combination car, and the southbound cable train to the bottom of the tunnel, where its grip finally broke free. Not even this was the end, for the grip shank proceeded down the conduit, knifing into another four-car train before it was halted. The driver of the horsecar and three cable passengers were seriously injured, and twelve others received cuts and bruises. The loop had to be closed until the following morning.

This class of accident achieved considerable notoriety in October 1887 when it menaced

Grover Cleveland. The president, in Kansas City to lay the cornerstone of a YMCA, had just crossed 9th and Broadway when a Kansas City Cable Railway grip became fouled in a cable scheduled for early replacement. The train plunged into a crowd only ten feet from the president's carriage, injuring a dozen people, two seriously. By 1890, Kansas City's newspapers had phrases such as, "another victim of the cables."

The emergency slot brake described in the previous chapter might be effective against a loose strand of a single wire, or even several wires, but the system had the potential for massive entanglements against which the brake could not possibly have succeeded. The Holmes Street cable in Kansas City unstranded in March 1903, building up a mass of 400 feet of loose wire 4 inches thick and 4 feet long; happily, it was discovered at the powerhouse before it caused an accident. On the Broadway line in New York in 1893, an unstranding built up a mass of 1500 feet of wire over a linear distance of 200 feet.

On at least two occasions, the cable or portions of it looped about the grip jaws. On Sunday evening October 2, 1887, the Mount Adams & Eden Park in Cincinnati was carrying a heavy load of passengers down from its recreational areas in the hills above the city. The cable had been installed only the previous day, and was still stiff. The large number of curves offered considerable resistance and prevented orderly distribution of the slack. At the dinner hour all of the active cars were downbound, with five running on the long grade down Gilbert Avenue. The mixture of conditions caused the cable in front of the bottom car to

unwind into a corkscrew configuration, looping about the jaws of the grip. The loop broke, but two strands — apparently "strands" in the more literal sense of 16 or 19 wires in this instance — became enmeshed in the grip. The car proceeded entrapped to 6th and Main, where it hit the rear of its leading car; the two were carried onward to Sycamore Street, where they collided with a horse-car of another company. The impact derailed not only the three cars involved but the four following grip cars through the shock transmitted in the cable. About 40 people were injured or shaken up by the accident.

On the Metropolitan Street Railway of New York, a southbound Broadway car in August 1893 approaching Bowling Green pushed a stiff cable of six 19-wire strands ahead of it against the resistance of an impending curve. The line was new, and the cable had excessive sag. In this instance, the entire cable looped into a figure eight about the grip jaws. The cable was stopped by telephoning the powerhouse, and the grip was cut off at the shank to free the car.

As mentioned previously, problems of this character were worse in New York than anywhere else, partly because the greater frequency of gripping and ungripping produced more loose strands, partly because there were more vehicles to hit. Both companies — the Metropolitan apparently as a result of the accident just described — used electric alarm systems to deal with the problem. The Third Avenue Railroad placed a signal box, similar to a fire alarm in a shallow housing in the devil strip (the area between double track) at two-block intervals. The conductor of a car caught in

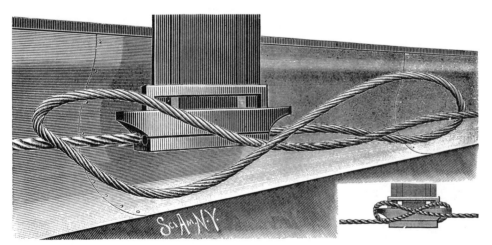

The *Scientific American* illustrates the looping of a cable around a Broadway grip in 1893.

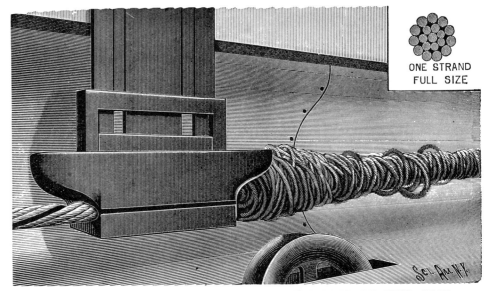

ONE STRAND
FULL SIZE

A BROKEN STRAND PREVENTS THE WORKING OF THE GRIP.

On February 26, 1971, the Powell Street cable unstranded, producing a mass of wire which precipitated this multiple rear end collision on the remaining San Francisco lines. Damage to cars and the terminal facilities ran to $100,000. The engraving is the *Scientific American's* drawing of a similar unstranding on the Broadway line in 1893. *(San Francisco* EXAMINER)

the cable ran to the nearest box, uncovered it by removing a metal hatch, and raised a handle to break a connection. He rang a gong once at the powerhouse and actuated an annunciator reading UP or DOWN to indicate which rope had to be stopped. The company believed the system could stop a car within three blocks, but it is hardly necessary to discuss the damage an uncontrollable vehicle could do on a New York street — and one of restricted visibility, at that — in a three block distance. The company also provided for other signals, although only the "stop" signal was important. Two rings meant "go ahead slow," three "go ahead at full speed," and four "fire." The Broadway line used eight gong signals: one, "stop"; two, "start"; three, "send tool wagon"; four, "fire blocks the line"; five, "release tension"; six, "apply tension"; seven, "telephone"; and eight, "testing." The Metropolitan's gong signals rang not only in the affected powerhouse, but in the president's office at Houston Street — a good indication how seriously involvements in the cable were treated.

The Chicago lines and several others placed telephone call boxes on utility posts along the line for ready access to conductors trying to stop uncontrollable cars. The Market Street Cable Railway, the Vine Street line in Cincinnati and several other heavily-travelled companies attempted continuous inspection of the moving cable as it left the powerhouse; the cable-watcher's job was considered literally maddening, so that employees traded off after short periods.

The melancholy subject of loose strands provides another evidence that the Vogel and Whelan technology was probably the best that cable traction had to offer. The gripman on a Vogel line could go into full release at any point, roll downhill faster than the cable and retake it when he wished. This had its dangers — it could be attempted only on mild gradients — but at least if he avoided retaking the rope when moving faster than the rope moved, he avoided raising loose strands. This observation is further reason to believe that superiority in the context of cable traction was a meager distinction, indeed.

When a grip of the Denver Tramway became caught in the cable, resulting in a broadside collision with a freight train, the rival Denver City Cable Railway began carrying a sign shown here, reading: "Passengers to resorts on City Cable lines cross no steam roads at grade." *(State Historical Society of Colorado)*

VIEW OF MANHOLE AND AUTOMATIC.

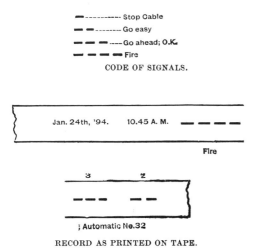

- - - - - - - - Stop Cable
- - - - - - - Go easy
- - - - - Go ahead; O.K.
- - - - Fire

CODE OF SIGNALS.

Jan. 24th, '94.   10.45 A. M.   - - - -

Fire

3   2

- - -   - -

Automatic No. 32

RECORD AS PRINTED ON TAPE.

SIGNAL BOX IN 65TH. STREET POWER HOUSE.

These drawings from the SRG illustrate the Third Avenue Railroad's alarm system. The conductor of a grip caught in the cable opened a hatch and actuated the alarm box at the top of the page. The drawing also shows a portable telephone plugged into the signal box, lying on the pavement. The signal box in the powerhouse included a tape which recorded the gong signals.

97

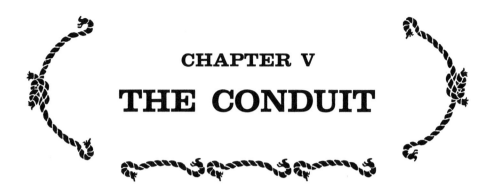

CHAPTER V
THE CONDUIT

An engineer once described cable traction as the summit of the cast iron period of his profession: just give an engineer enough cast iron and the world was his!

The preoccupation of the industry with cast iron grew directly out of unsatisfactory experience with fabricated conduits. As recounted in chapters I and II, cable traction began with conduits fabricated of bar iron, stringers, ties and planks. Such arrangements were tolerable in San Francisco because of the mild climate, but even there they tended to loosen, warp, and otherwise change shape. In cities with ordinary continental climates freezing and thawing accelerated these processes. More important, as water turned to ice in the soil near the tracks, its expansion exerted a pressure on the conduit which tended to close the slot. The Philadelphia Traction Company definitively demonstrated the unworkability of fabricated conduits in harsh climates; its efforts to make a system with a bolted wood-and-iron conduit function properly were never really successful.

Consequently, as cable traction spread beyond San Francisco, it was Henry Root's conduit of iron and concrete which necessarily recommended itself to the industry's engineers; only this construction had the stability and more specifically, the resistance to contraction that the technology required. This situation, in turn, was responsible for the capital-intensive nature of the technology, since about 60 per cent of the investment in a cable system was embodied in the conduit.

Root inaugurated the standard conduit by setting yokes of old iron rail in concrete. His conduit had a depth of 22 inches from the street to the bottom of the tube, approximately the same as the earlier fabricated conduits. C. B. Holmes' installation on the Chicago City Railway necessarily required both more substantial metalwork and a deeper tube because of the harshness of the climate. His engineers worked out a conduit based on two pieces of wrought iron connected with four bolts, supplemented by two tie rods connecting the extremities of the larger (and lower) piece of iron with the Z-section slot rails. As the illustration indicates, this was very much more substantial than any previous conduit. The tube was 36 inches deep to allow for accumulation of ice and snow, and also of dirt, which was probably more of a problem in Chicago than in San Francisco. The inner member of the wrought iron framework crossed the conduit about ten inches above the bottom, rendering it difficult to sweep out debris with a broom pushed down through the slot in the usual fashion. It was partly a desire for a strong unobstructed conduit that caused recourse to cast iron yokes, but more important, cast iron yokes were more resistant alike to contraction in freezing weather and to corrosion. Fairchild recommended that wrought iron yokes be entirely enclosed in concrete to prevent corrosion from moisture in the soil. Wrought iron had the offsetting advantage of taking blows from heavy vehicles without cracking better than cast iron. Beginning with the Kansas City Cable Railway

99

To avoid crossing one another's tracks, the West Chicago Street Railroad and the Chicago City Railway engaged in lefthand operation amid righthand traffic from Madison to Washington on State Street. At left, a Madison Street train has just pulled the curve into State Street amid heavy pedestrian traffic. (*Chicago Historical Society*)

A gang excavated for the Pacific Railway's conduit on 1st Street, Los Angeles, in 1889. (*Security Pacific Bank*)

in 1885, most engineers specified a single-piece cast iron yoke. D. J. Miller on the Harlem installation of the Third Avenue Railroad at the same time used a cast yoke with some bolted wrought connections. Several later engineers used similar connections. Yokes had enormous variety in the industry; representative examples are in accompanying illustrations.

A typical yoke for a 4-foot 8½-inch gauge cable line was slightly over 5 feet wide, about 4 feet deep and 6 to 8 inches thick. The original line of the Kansas City Cable Railway was built with yokes of these approximate dimensions weighing 300 pounds each, set at 5-foot intervals. After several fractured yokes the company concluded this construction was too weak, and for its Troost Avenue line specified yokes of 375 pounds, set at intervals of 4 feet. Yokes ranged from 300 to 400 pounds; the Cleveland City Cable Railway's yoke of 360 pounds was probably representative. H. M.

Kebby estimated that yokes cost $5.30 each, or at the rate of 1,320 to the mile, $6,996 per mile.

Laying the conduit required an excavation, usually about 4 feet deep and 3 feet wide with side bays at 4- to 5-foot intervals for the yokes. If the ground was rock, construction entailed blasting, but the foundation for the yokes was firm. In loose soil it was necessary to lay concrete foundations at intervals for the yokes. In swampy soil, piles had to be driven as a base. In established cities it was necessary to relay gas mains and other utilities to make way for the conduits.

The yokes had to be placed with great precision. Yokes were connected by laying the running rails along the sides and the slot rails at the center. The tube was then formed in either of two ways. Most frequently, a two-part wooden form which could be expanded to the dimensions of the tube was moved into place either by hooks through the slot or by a trolley which ran on the

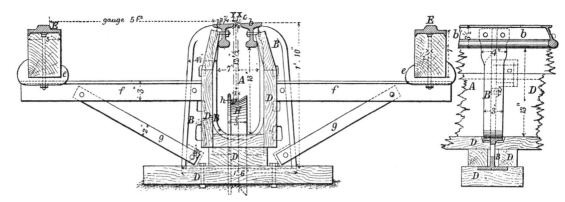

Fabricated wood-and-iron conduits, such as Eppelsheimer's design for the Geary Street line, above, were tolerable in San Francisco, but cities with harsh winters required iron-and-concrete conduits, as shown below. The Chicago City Railway was built with the wrought iron conduit at left. The rail is tram rail laid on wooden stringers. Below are the cast iron conduits of the Kansas City Cable Railway and the West Chicago. D. J. Miller's yokes for the Third Avenue Railroad had cast and wrought elements. Fairchild's figure 166 shows the Third Avenue Railroad's yokes ready for pouring concrete about the folding wooden form used to shape the interior of the conduit. The later conduits are all topped with girder rail.

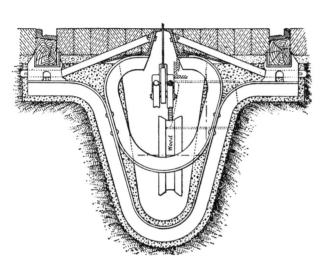

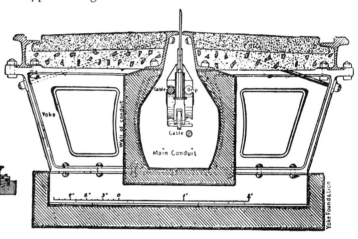

ONE HUNDRED AND TWENTY-FIFTH STREET,
NEW YORK, CABLE LINE.

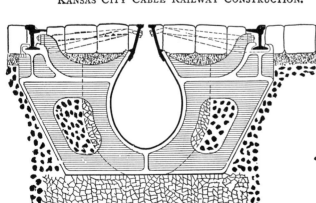

KANSAS CITY CABLE RAILWAY CONSTRUCTION.

WEST CHICAGO CABLE LINE.

FIG. 166.—FOLDING FORM WITH TROLLEY SUPPORT.

The Broadway cable line in New York was so large and conspicuous that its building was widely photographed. These two views show the ironwork being made ready for pouring of concrete at the Post Office and, below, approaching 14th Street. (*Smithsonian Institution*)

slot rail with a center-flanged wheel. Concrete was then carefully poured around the yokes and the wooden form. As it hardened, the form was collapsed on its hinges, as shown in Fairchild's figure 166, and moved on beyond the next yoke where the process was repeated. The alternative, used on the West Chicago and the Metropolitan of New York, was to form the tube of thin steel plating running between the yokes, around which the concrete was poured. The concrete was formed of high grade Portland cement, sand and crushed stone, produced in a mixer on the spot.

Obviously, a finished conduit was an exceedingly heavy, expensive and durable construction. The original 2.9 miles of the Citizens Railway of St. Louis required 130,000 bolts and 16,000 yokes of 370 pounds each. Approximately 20,000 feet of water pipe had to be moved, including the connection to every house and every fireplug along the way. Both gas and sewer pipes required similar relocation. The Kansas City, Kansas, line of the Metropolitan Street Railway was set with 340-pound yokes at 4-foot intervals, a total of 2,019,600 pounds for yokes alone on the original 4.5 miles. The concrete on this line was six to 12 inches thick, depending on the solidity of the substructure; the excavation amounted to removal of 4,055 cubic yards of earth per mile of track. The 3.75 miles of the projected Dallas Cable Railway would have required over 6,000 barrels of imported cement, 8,000 iron yokes weighing over two million pounds, 780,000 pounds of rail and approximately the same amount of tie rods, bolts and other iron.

In part, the standard conduits were so capital-intensive because of the necessity of providing drainage under the carrying pulleys. If this was not done, snow, ice and water would interfere with the movement of the pulleys. The alternative, used by H. M. Lane, was placing the pulleys in recesses in the bottom of the conduit, but this required a drain under every pulley, with a separate sewer paralleling the entire line. A drainage arrangement of this sort entailed an investment of about $12,000 per mile, greater than the entire investment in a horsecar right-of-way. Lane, however, was able to use a conduit only about 24 inches deep in ordinary northern climates, about two-thirds the depth of standard systems. Fair-

child reported the deepest conduit known to him was 42 inches, probably on the two top-grip lines in Pittsburgh. Standard conduits had drains into city sewers at irregular intervals; this method was less likely to produce clogging from solid matter than Lane's separate drain pattern. Lines built into lightly populated areas without sewers required cesspools from which water was pumped periodically.

The conduit was so massive and so expensive — between $60,000 and $100,000 per mile in standard installations — that engineers sought alternatives. The Mount Auburn Cable Railway in Cincinnati used an iron conduit without concrete, which, as might have been predicted, shifted rapidly, producing irregularity in the slot and in rail alignments. At the opposite extreme, John Isaacs used an all-concrete conduit without yokes on the Consolidated Piedmont Cable Company in Oakland. This approach was more successful, though it remained an open question whether it would have been practicable in a climate with freezing weather. Lane used heavy planks to wall his conduits, and Howard C. Holmes used brick extensively in the conduits of the Ferries & Cliff House. Both New York systems had a great deal of brick in the conduits.

The surface of the conduit had to serve simultaneously the requirements of operation of the

Henry M. Lane's method of a separate sewer to drain the conduit is shown here from his Providence installation.

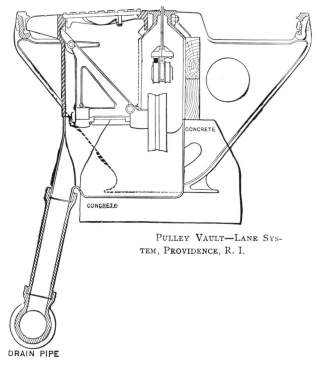

PULLEY VAULT—LANE SYSTEM, PROVIDENCE, R. I.

Crossing a cable line and a steam railroad required essentially a small truss bridge sunk in concrete, as in the West Chicago's plan of a crossing with the Milwaukee Road, below. The alternative was a trestle, such as the Denver City Cable Railway, above, built to take its Sloan's Lake line over the South Platte River and the extensive railroad tracks to the east. *(Smithsonian Institution-Chicago Transit Authority; Library of Congress)*

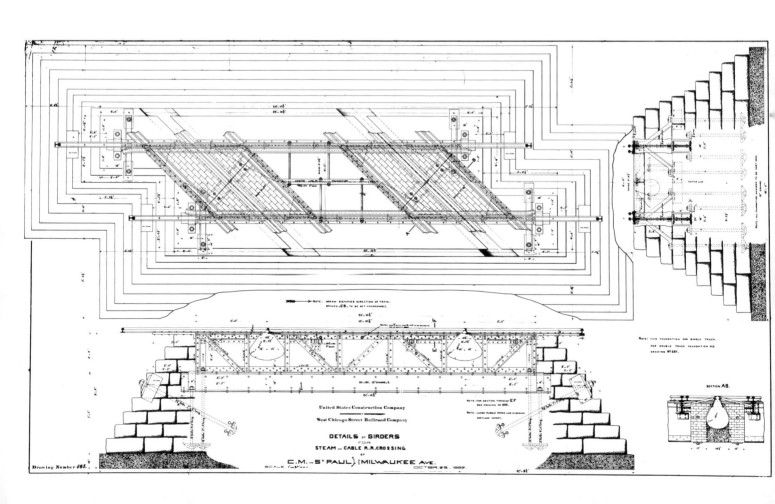

cable line and of the flow of traffic of horsedrawn vehicles on the street. Once again, these requirements were conflicting, and had to be reconciled. A pavement of wooden blocks, for example, was easy on horses' feet, but expanded when wet or frozen. Such a pavement was tolerable over the conduit itself, but not in the devil strip between the tracks, where it added to the pressures for slot closure in freezing weather. Granite blocks, bricks or asphalt were not open to objection on this ground, but paving stones or brick had to be completely set in cement or some other waterproof material to prevent seepage and ice formation which, once again, might close the slot. A solid pavement of this sort had the disadvantage that it prevented easy access to the tie rods which in most conduits connected the slot rails with the extremities of the yokes. Regularization of the width of the slot required occasional tightening or loosening of the tie rods in most conduit designs.

The slot itself presented the major conflicts between the requirements of the cable line and the horsedrawn vehicles on the street. To minimize dripping into the slot, it was preferable to have the slot as high as possible above the rails, about two inches, but if horsecars used the same track, this arrangement made the footing difficult for the car horses, along with any other horses that had to use the area. Most companies compromised on an elevation of ½ inch to an inch. To minimize friction between the slot rails and the grip shank, as well as to deal with slot closure, it was desirable to have as wide a slot as possible, but the wider it was the more likely horses were to catch the calks of their shoes in it. Since a grip shank was about ½ inch thick, a slot could hardly be narrower than ¾ inch, but this was about the size of the typical rear calk on a horseshoe. Having a shoe torn off was painful and damaging, undesirable alike on humane and economic grounds. The Omaha *World-Herald*, when the city's system was under a month old, described a horse which lost a shoe as "one of the latest victims of the deadly grip car slot." The wheel of the typical buggy was only ¾ to 1 inch wide, presenting the imminent prospect of sinking into a slot and wrenching itself off the axle. Accordingly, a ¾-inch slot was all but universal in the industry.

The shape of the slot rail presented a similar problem. A rounded edge minimized abrasion on the shank, but it facilitated entry of calks into the slot. Most municipalities demanded not only a narrow slot, but one with a sharp angle at the surface; obviously, a sharp edge cut into the shank acutely at a single line, increasing the expense of grip maintenance.

As the accompanying illustrations indicate, most companies used Z-rail, so called because of its cross-section, for slot rail. Such rail weighed about 40 pounds per yard, a weight which may seem excessive for rail which did not bear cars. As usual in cable traction, the weight of the rail vehicles was a trivial consideration. In this instance, the slot rail had to be strong enough to prevent the slot's caving in under the weight of road vehicles. The company's own cable wagon was likely to be the worst offender, but the slot in Grand Rapids caved in under a circus wagon. Railroad crossings were particularly difficult, since the drivers of a locomotive bore the greatest weight of any vehicle. A cable engineer had to provide either an elaborate underground construction to deal with the weight, or an overpass. Overpasses were far preferable; the Pacific Railway in Los Angeles and the Denver City Cable Railway had long overpasses over railroad yards in which the continual passing of switch engines would have ruined the slots and presented a safety hazard. A Denver Tramway car, caught in a loose strand, hit a Rio Grande freight train broadside with considerable injury to passengers. Finally, some railroads were able to prevent cable lines from notching their rails for the cable flangeways, though not, of course, for the slot. Cable lines had to bolt wedges on their rails to assist cars up to the level of the railroad rails, which they crossed on their flanges, producing both derailments and cracked flanges.

The relative insignificance of the weight of the cars in cable traction was most evident in the design of running rails. In the early installations the most common was tram rail, a flat strip about five inches wide with a flangeway ¾ inch deep, laid on a wooden stringer about 5 inches square. The Sutter Street Railroad used rail of this character, though the pioneer Clay Street Hill Railroad used light T-rail of the ordinary railroad outline. Tram rail, which served horsecar lines tolerably, was inappropriate for heavy-duty operations of any sort and was superseded by what came to be the typical rail of streetcars of all types, girder rail. Originated in San Francisco in 1877, girder rail was rolled into the standard railroad pattern of a base and web supporting a head, but the flangeway was made integral with the rail. Some girder rail had a bolted connection to buttress the web. Most companies which began with tram rail replaced it with girder rail. The Philadelphia Traction Company relaid its lines from tram rail weighing 40 pounds per yard to girder rail weighing 78 in 1890. Particularly characteristic of cable lines was center-bearing rail, which had a flangeway on each side of the head. The line in Butte was mainly laid with three rails, the middle being center-bearing for use in both directions, and the remaining San Francisco system has center-bearing rail extensively in the vicinity of the powerhouse.

*   *   *

Within the conduit the cable ran on a variety of sheaves and pulleys, all designed to hold it at the optimal position for moving the cars. Most cable engineers sought to center the cable between the rails, with the slot to one side, if necessary, because of a grip that held the cable off center.

The largest and in certain respects the most important of the wheels on which the cable ran was the terminal sheave on which the rope reversed itself at the opposite extreme from the powerhouse. This was a horizontal wheel of a diameter exactly equal to the distance between the slots on a double-track line, usually 10 to 12 feet. This sheave had to bear the entire pull of the engines and thus had to be firmly anchored with a heavy bearing in its own vault. Strikers in Grand Rapids, realizing that failure of the terminal sheave brought the entire operation to a halt, endeavored to bomb the terminal vault during a labor dispute.

Being over the diameter of 100 times the diameter of the cable thought critical, the terminal sheave was believed to do no damage to the cable. Similar considerations applied to the sheaves which brought the cable into and out

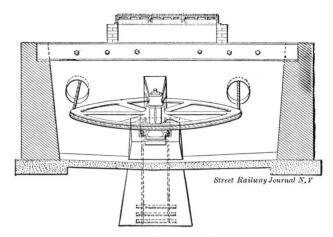

Street Railway Journal N.Y

TERMINAL SHEAVE.

of the powerhouse. As the diagram of a powerhouse in the following chapter indicates, it was customary to bring the cable around a sheave of as large a diameter as possible to turn the right-angle at the track. Preferably, this sheave was also of 10 to 12 feet diameter, but the physical limitations of the plant, including the necessity of raising the cable to a level where the grip could take it, often required smaller sheaves. The Chicago City Railway used sheaves of about 6 feet diameter for this purpose and ran some ropes off two such wheels to produce two angles of 45 degrees instead of one of 90.

The basic wheel in the conduit was the carrying pulley. The frequency of carrying pulleys varied from 30 to 40 feet, but the Chicago City Railway, the Philadelphia Traction Company and most other operators found 32 feet the optimal interval. It was generally felt that ideally a moving cable should be absolutely horizontal, but this was impossible; a 32-foot interval of carrying pulleys was optimal for reconciliation of minimization of investment in facilities and minimization

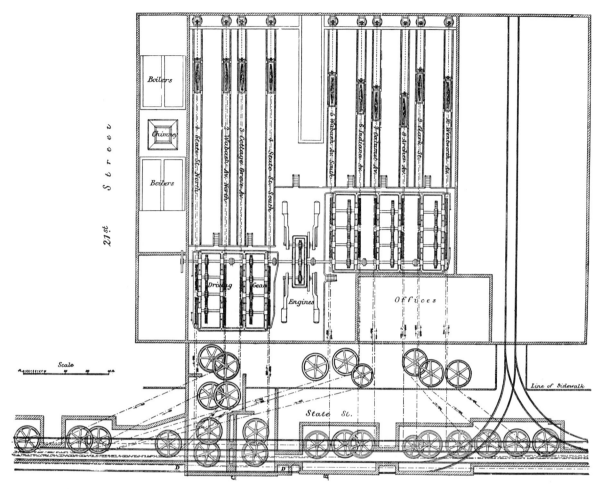

J. Bucknall Smith's plan of the Chicago City Railway's powerhouse at 21st and State Streets shows a variety of sheaves, mainly of 6 to 8 feet in diameter, used to take cables from the winding machinery to the conduits. The plan shows the powerhouse as designed to issue ten cables; the five tension runs at the right were intended for lines which were never built.

of the catenary of the cable. The pulley itself was a broad-faced wheel of 9 to 24 inches in diameter, depending on the space available and on resistance to revolution of the pulley. Augustine Wright stated that, with a given 1-inch journal, a 12-inch wheel required two pounds of force to turn it, but a 24-inch wheel required only one pound. On the other hand, with a pound's pressure of mud or ice against the wheel, a 12-inch pulley would turn, but a 24-inch would not. In 1887 the Chicago City Railway out of this consideration shifted from 16-inch to 12-inch pulleys. The face of the pulley was three or four inches wide, depressed in the center to hold the cable. Since the cable lay lightly on the pulley, most roads used ordinary cast iron, though a minority used a harder facing

such as chilled steel. Some engineers, however, sought to cushion the cable. The Chicago City Railway experimented with a babbitt facing on the pulleys, and the Brooklyn Bridge line, because of its uncoated cable, faced the pulleys with leather or rubber.

The ordinary carrying pulley was inappropriate for the summit of a hill because its small diameter put too severe an angle into the cable. There it was customary to use a similar pulley of larger diameter, about 40 inches, called a crown pulley. At the summit of a major grade more than one such pulley might be used.

The opposite problem of depressing a cable was more difficult. At the bottom of a grade it was necessary to prevent the cable from rising out of the slot, but the method depended on the type of grip the company had adopted. An engineer whose company used a grip which held the cable to one side of the slot usually arranged a series of about five pulleys of extremely small diameter, two or three inches, immediately below the slot rail to guide the cable with as gentle an angle as possible. A grip which held the rope directly under the slot required a movable depression pulley, usually a pair of 7-inch pulleys on a sprung arm which normally lay centered on the slot. A passing car batted the arm to the side, but the spring returned the arm to its position before the cable rose after the car had passed. Such arrangements suffered, first, from the necessity of putting the cable through the sharpest angle of anything in the entire system, and second, from the risk of the arm's not returning to its position. In the latter event, the cable rose out of

the slot, possibly by several feet, converting the force of the engines from a horizontal to a vertical vector on the car. In 1903 a cable failed to return to a depression device on the Metropolitan's 12th Street line in Kansas City, rose out of the slot, raised the passing grip car off the track, and tipped it over onto the opposite track, where it hit a train coming down the grade. Out of such considerations, some engineers specified permanent depression pulleys on the order of crown pulleys at the foot of major grades. The Metropolitan had a permanent depression pulley at the foot of its 20 per cent grade on the 12th Street viaduct, for example, at which cars had to drop rope when passing.

Permanent depression pulleys were most common at crossings of cable lines. Nowhere did the pervasive inflexibility of cable traction manifest itself more obviously than in the difficulty of cross-

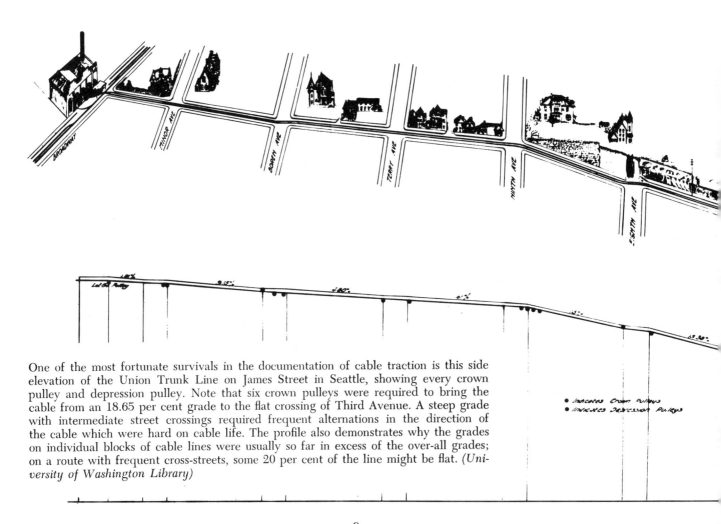

One of the most fortunate survivals in the documentation of cable traction is this side elevation of the Union Trunk Line on James Street in Seattle, showing every crown pulley and depression pulley. Note that six crown pulleys were required to bring the cable from an 18.65 per cent grade to the flat crossing of Third Avenue. A steep grade with intermediate street crossings required frequent alternations in the direction of the cable which were hard on cable life. The profile also demonstrates why the grades on individual blocks of cable lines were usually so far in excess of the over-all grades; on a route with frequent cross-streets, some 20 per cent of the line might be flat. (University of Washington Library)

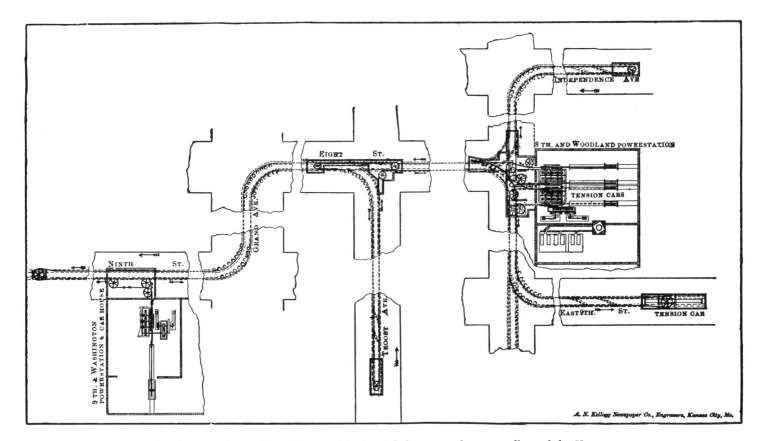

This diagram shows the entire set of horizontal sheaves and curve pulleys of the Kansas City Cable Railway, along with detail of terminals and powerhouses. The diagram corresponds to the 1889 layout on the map of the company in Part II of this volume.

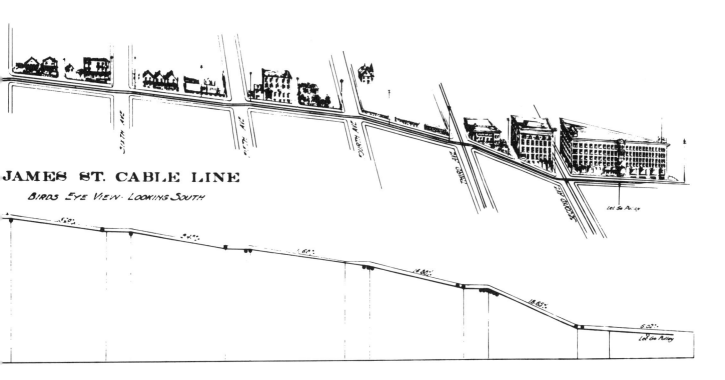

JAMES ST. CABLE LINE

BIRDS EYE VIEW· LOOKING SOUTH

109

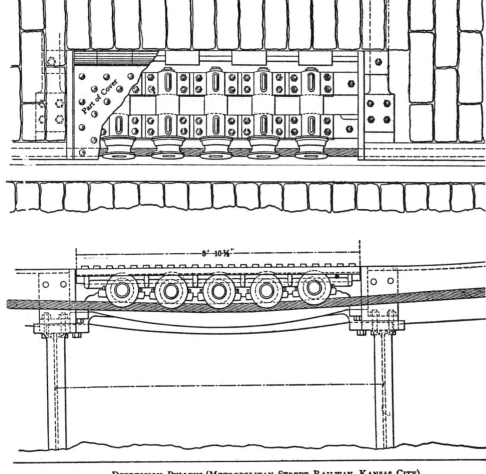

DEPRESSION PULLEYS (METROPOLITAN STREET RAILWAY, KANSAS CITY).

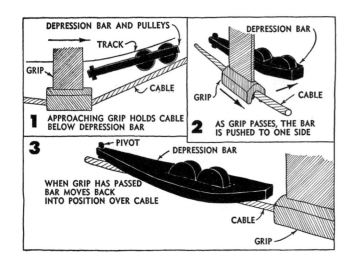

DEPRESSION BAR AND PULLEYS
TRACK
GRIP
CABLE

1 APPROACHING GRIP HOLDS CABLE BELOW DEPRESSION BAR

DEPRESSION BAR
GRIP
CABLE

2 AS GRIP PASSES, THE BAR IS PUSHED TO ONE SIDE

3 PIVOT
DEPRESSION BAR

WHEN GRIP HAS PASSED BAR MOVES BACK INTO POSITION OVER CABLE

CABLE
GRIP

A line which used a grip that held the cable to the right or left of the slot could use at the bottom of a grade a stationary depression device such as the five small pulleys of the Metropolitan of Kansas City, shown here. A design that centered the cable under the slot required a movable depression device such as the depression bar in the drawing from *Anatomy of the San Francisco Cable Car*, at left.

At the bottom of the page is a grip trap for removal of grips in emergencies, also from the Metropolitan of Kansas City.

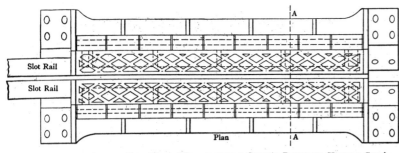

Slot Rail

Slot Rail

Plan

GRIP TRAP (METROPOLITAN STREET RAILWAY, KANSAS CITY).

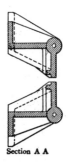

Section A A

110

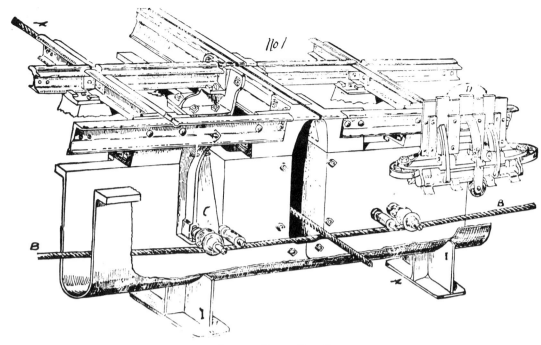

SECTIONAL VIEW OF CABLE CROSSING.

Above is one of the crossings which Worcester Haddock designed to bring the cable of his Mount Auburn Cable Railway under the superior rope of the Mount Adams & Eden Park. Haddock's grip is at the upper right in full release.

Below, the first crossing of them all at Geary and Larkin Streets, San Francisco, was denuded in the process of removing the Larkin line after the earthquake of 1906. *(Roy D. Graves)*

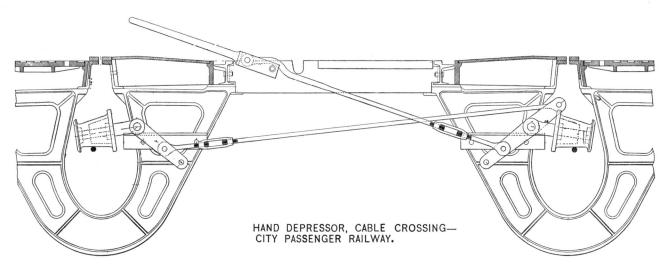

HAND DEPRESSOR, CABLE CROSSING—
CITY PASSENGER RAILWAY.

ing two lines. One cable had to be brought under the other and then elevated in such fashion that the car, which necessarily had to drop rope approaching the superior cable, could retake it on the opposite side. All of this required a construction which, as usual, was heavy, expensive, and difficult. Since the crossing had to allow for an unobstructed passage of the grip in each of four directions, plus provide vaultwork for the depression pulleys and other fittings, the special work of yokes and stringers was necessarily complex. In particular, an ordinary crossing of double-track lines created an island isolated by the four slots which had to be self-supporting.

To some extent, the nature of a crossing depended on the grip the company employed. A top-grip line required an elevation sheave to bring the rope up from the jaws at the rope drop. A side-grip line required a lateral deflection unless the grip had ejection spools, but a bottom-grip line required nothing beyond the usual plate reading LET GO in the street. To depress the inferior cable, an engineer might provide either a single depression pulley immediately under the superior cable or, more commonly, a pair of depression pulleys, one on each side of the crossing. The latter arrangement was preferable since it required less depth of the vaultwork at the crossing; the inferior cable then had to be only low enough to avoid fouling the grips on the superior line. Conversely, the superior cable had to be low enough not to foul the grips of cars on the inferior line crossing in full release. This was not always easy, since the crossing might lie at an intersection from which the superior line rose mildly in both directions. If so, the cable was pulled to the top

of the conduit, so that the engineer had to provide some means of depressing it. The customary method was a conical spool on an extension arm which the conductor of the train on the inferior line actuated with a lever. An accompanying illustration shows an ingenious depression device designed by A. N. Connett, whereby a conductor of his Baltimore City Passenger Railway could depress the superior cable of the Baltimore Traction Company at Fayette and Eutaw in both directions with a single lever.

Avoidance of hitting the superior cable was, to put it mildly, desirable. A car which failed to let go of the inferior rope typically knifed into the superior cable, severing it, kinking the inferior cable and injuring the gripman along with some of the passengers. A Holmes Street car on the Grand Avenue Railway hit the 9th Street cable of the Kansas City Cable Railway in 1889. The car rebounded eight feet, seriously injured the gripman about the right arm and shoulder and inflicted minor injuries on several passengers. The Kansas City Cable Railway estimated every instance cost the company $1,000 in repair costs and lost revenue.

Several companies provided protection of some sort to prevent the lower cable from being held until the grip hit the upper. The West Chicago placed a heavy iron bar called a "dead man" above its cable at the intersections where it was inferior to the North Chicago. The Mount Auburn used a roller which engaged the cable and tore it down from the company's bottom grip before the car could hit the Mount Adams & Eden Park's superior rope. The San Francisco Municipal Railway uses a bar over the cable which, when lifted by

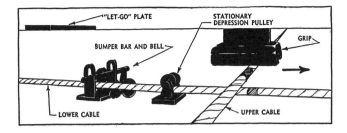

a car that has failed to let go the rope, trips a gong as a final reminder to the gripman to go into full release. Until a maintenance man resets the gong, the motion of the cable against the loose bar rings the gong, alerting subsequent gripmen that someone failed to let go. If the first following gripman reports it, the culprit can be identified. The California Street Cable Railroad used a smashboard in the conduit covered with fish-oil-based red paint, which splattered over the grip of a car that failed to let go before hitting it.

Retaking the cable on the far side of a crossing entailed various processes, depending on the style of grip. With a bottom grip, the car could be brought down about three inches by a declivity just beyond the first carrying pulley, where the gripman could simply close on the rope. A car with a side grip could take the rope by means of a declivity and a lateral deflection; the Denver City Cable Railway was arranged in this fashion.

Below is a gypsy of the California Street Cable Railroad from *Anatomy of the San Francisco Cable Car.* At the top of the page, from the same source is the Municipal Railway's bumper bell at crossings. At right is a Chicago City Railway notice on the proper use of gypsies.

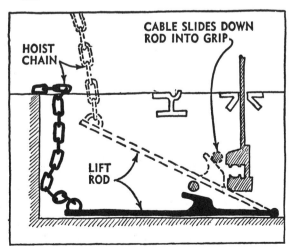

Most side grip lines took rope by means of a gypsy, a second class lever actuated by a chain or rod, which moved the cable laterally into the jaws. A gypsy entailed the risk of fouling the grip of a moving car. A conductor was directed to lift the gypsy behind the grip, never in front of it, to minimize the risk of the car's hitting the lever. There was, however, the risk that the gypsy would not return to its horizontal position upon release; a Grand Rapids grip hit a gypsy in 1890, shooting the headlight 15 feet ahead of it, and pitching the passengers out of the open seats. D. J. Miller on the Third Avenue Railroad used an elevation sheave which could be shifted about two inches to move the cable laterally into the jaws as soon as the grip had passed.

A bottom-grip line at points where it was impractical to place a declivity could install a lever-actuated cable lifter, similar to a gypsy, but properly never called by that name. A cable lifter consisted merely of a small pulley at the end of a lever arm which was elevated behind the bot-

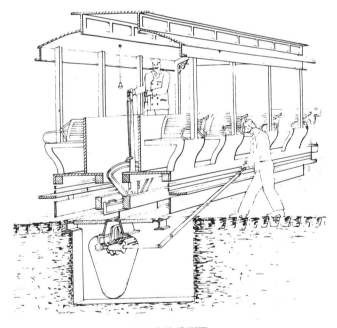

- BULLETIN TO TRAINMEN -

The accompanying sketch shows a case of a gripman breaking a hand pick-up, which can be avoided if the pick-up is used behind the grip. Gripmen must be careful not to start car immediately or until the Conductor has lowered the hand lever if it is raised in front of the grip.

Chicago, October 14th, 1893.

M.K. Bowen
Superintendent.

113

THE VOLK

CABLE CROSSING, GRIP & CAR BRAKE CO. ST. LOUIS, MO.

Dr. K. MORGNER, President.   J. W. GARRETT, Secretary.

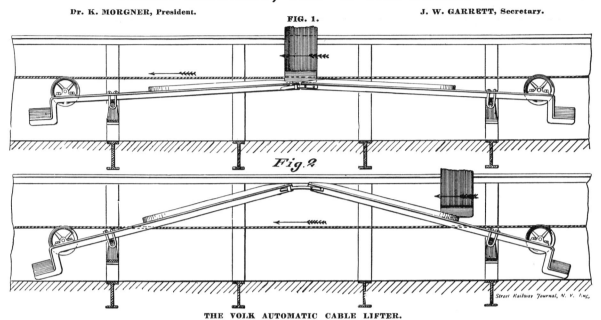

FIG. 1.

Fig. 2

THE VOLK AUTOMATIC CABLE LIFTER.

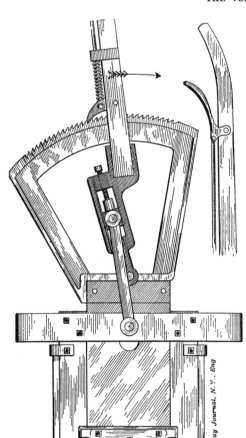

THIS is the celebrated Volk Bottom Grip, which every cable road must have when other cables are to be crossed, and all cable roads should use it, as it will save them thousands of dollars. We guarantee a cable to last twelve months longer to any road which will use our Bottom Grip and the brass dies furnished by our company, which can be proved by affidavits from employes of the Citizens' Cable Railway as to the length of time which the dies last.

PROPRIETORS OF THE

Patent Grip, Grip Carriage,
Automatic Cable Lifter,
Track and Car Brake.

Invented by JACOB VOLK, Master Mechanic of the Citizens' R. R. Co. of St. Louis, and for eighteen years in the service of that company.

ALSO PROPRIETORS OF THE

Chapman Grip and Quadrant,
Of Kansas City, Mo.

We are prepared to make Satisfactory Arrangements with any

STREET CAR BUILDERS

Wishing to Equip their Grip Cars with the Latest Improvements, to use our Grip Carriage and Track Brake. We also solicit

CABLE RAILWAY COMPANIES

To inspect our Grip and Cable Lifter, and we refer all to CAPT. ROBERT McCULLOUGH, General Manager of the Citizens' R. R. Co. of St. Louis, who have Adopted all of our Patents.

ADDRESS ALL COMMUNICATIONS TO

Dr. K. MORGNER
OFFICE IN

Pope's Theatre Drug Store, 901 Olive Street,
ST. LOUIS, MO.

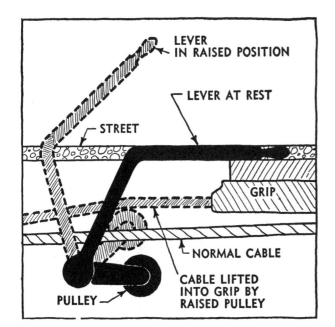

LEVER
IN RAISED POSITION

LEVER AT REST

STREET

GRIP

NORMAL CABLE

CABLE LIFTED
INTO GRIP BY
RAISED PULLEY

PULLEY

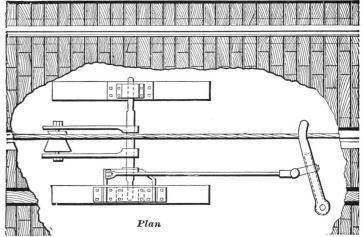

Plan

FIG. 200.—AUTOMATIC ROPE LIFTING GEAR.

At left is an advertisement for Jacob Volk's bottom grip and elevation device. The advertisement reverses the proper position of figures 1 and 2, unfortunately. The grip, striking the elevation device as in figure 2, depresses the center portion, raising the sheaves at the opposite ends of the levers to the position in figure 1, thereby elevating the cable into the grip jaws.

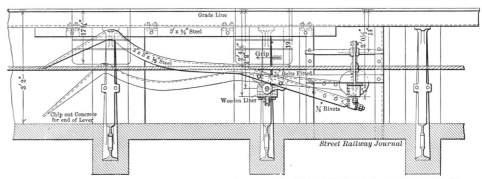

SIDE ELEVATION OF AUTOMATIC PICK-UP—WASHINGTON & GEORGETOWN
RAILROAD.

On this page are more orthodox devices for taking the cable. At left, above, is a manual cable lifter for bottom grips from *Anatomy of the San Francisco Cable Car*. In Fairchild's figure 200 is an automatic lifter for bottom grips from an unidentified line. The lifter is actuated by a grip shank passing from left to right tripping the arm across the cable. At right are side and end views of an automatic gypsy for the side grips of the Washington & Georgetown. At bottom is a simplified diagram of taking rope into the Chicago City Railway's side grip by means of an elevation sheave and lateral track deflections.

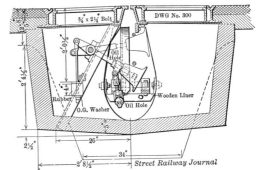

CROSS SECTION OF AUTOMATIC PICK-UP—WASHINGTON.

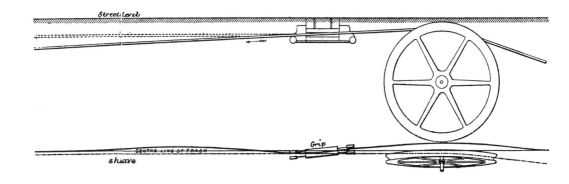

Madison and Front Streets, Seattle, was a good place to violate seniority in positions at a cable crossing. The Front Street line, running across the photograph in the foreground, was senior, but putting a rope drop in the Madison Street line's ascent out of the business district would have presented a safety hazard. Consequently, Madison was made superior, even though junior. (*University of Washington Library*)

The advertisement below is a fine indication of the vast sets of carrying pulleys cable systems required.

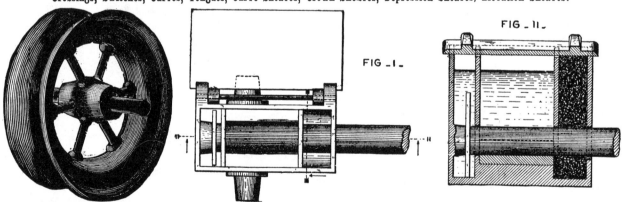

tom grip to draw the cable up into the jaws. This operation was so simple that it could be done automatically; in fact, the ability to take the rope automatically was one of the incidental attractions of bottom grips. Jacob Volk of the Citizens Railway of St. Louis developed an automatic cable lifter in the form of a pair of balanced arms loosely connected at the unweighted ends which, when depressed by the passing bottom grip, raised the carrying pulleys before and behind the grip, thereby lifting the cable into the jaws. For the Pacific Railway, Augustine Wright used a simple balanced arm which pushed the cable upward into the jaws.

When these devices for retaking the cable failed, there always remained the hook carried on every grip car on most lines, by which the conductor could fish for the cable through the slot behind the grip. Undershooting a pick-up point entailed pushing the car forward. Overshooting it was a more serious matter if, as on Powell Street southbound at California in the remaining San Francisco lines, the pick-up point was at the top of a grade so steep that cars could not safely descend without a full grip on the rope. San Francisco seems never to have considered this problem seriously and always assigned rope positions by seniority, regardless of topography. St. Louis, of the cities with a large number of crossings, did the same. Kansas City, Seattle and — somewhat surprisingly — Denver, required rope positions between companies to be assigned on the basis of relative gradients, with the steeper line superior. Kansas City empowered the City Engineer to assign positions by this criterion, if the companies were unable to agree. Denver required this criterion where its two companies crossed one another, but left either company free to assign positions at crossings of its own lines.

One final observation should be made on the difficulty of crossings: the slot rail had to be anchored very securely, since it was a potential source of accident. The friction from the grip shank tended to make the slot rail creep forward. In 1897 the slot rail of the 5th Street line of the Metropolitan of Kansas City crept far enough that a Main Street grip hit it, catapulting the gripman over the dash into the street and, as usual, throwing the passengers from their seats.

Given the various disadvantages and hazards of crossings, companies had a considerable incentive to avoid them. The 18th Avenue line of the Denver Tramway was removed partly to avoid a crossing with a line of the Denver City Cable Railway which was abuilding. In particular, it was so important to avoid crossings that, where two terminal loops of righthand-operated cable lines were run on the same street, the companies resorted to short distances of lefthand running. As the map of Chicago in Part II indicates, LaSalle, State and Wabash had lefthand operation at various times, because two lines were occupying the same street with their terminal loops. A mixture of lefthand cable operation with the characteristic traversing of pull curves at top speed on heavily utilized streets with righthand traffic in the center of the second largest city in the country was one of the worst hazards cable traction ever presented.

Of the two problems, pull curves were on the whole worse than crossings. Fairchild wrote:

Curves are the bane of cable construction. Their first cost is enormous; they consume power, materially shorten the life of the rope, and are a source of endless care and anxiety to the management.

Basically, a pull curve was a series of horizontal pulleys set behind a chafing bar which bore the jaws of the grip of a moving car so as to prevent lateral pressure on the shank. Implementation of this simple idea was — yet again — heavy, expensive and cumbersome. The curve pulleys had to be set in small vaults, which required specially designed yokes and incidental ironwork. The diameter and frequency of the pulleys depended on the length and severity of the curve. Fairchild reported that diameters ranged from 15 to 48 inches; the Chicago City Railway's early lines used 18-inch pulleys at 24-inch intervals. Pulleys of 24-inch diameter at 30-inch intervals were particularly common. A series of large pulleys not only dissipated less energy in friction than the same curve set with small, but also lasted longer, and were easier on rope; a sharp curve required small pulleys at frequent intervals, however. Curve pulleys had to be set with great precision for two reasons. First, since they bore 600 to 800 pounds lateral pressure, they had to be placed so

117

The Market Street Railway's drawing of a pull curve, below, delineates the basic elements of the design. *(Charles Smallwood)* Above, the slot and hatches on the Pacific Railway's pull curve at Spring and Temple Streets, Los Angeles, show the deflection of the grip for the chafing bar, and the continuous line of pulleys between the slot and the inner rail. *(Title Insurance & Trust Company)*

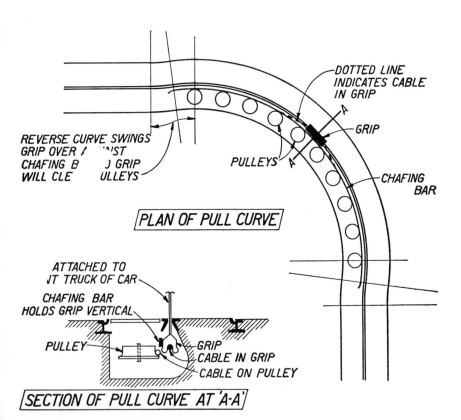

DOTTED LINE
INDICATES CABLE
IN GRIP

GRIP

REVERSE CURVE SWINGS
GRIP OVER AGAINST
CHAFING BAR, GRIP
WILL CLEAR PULLEYS

PULLEYS

CHAFING
BAR

PLAN OF PULL CURVE

ATTACHED TO
JT TRUCK OF CAR

CHAFING BAR
HOLDS GRIP VERTICAL

PULLEY

GRIP
CABLE IN GRIP
CABLE ON PULLEY

SECTION OF PULL CURVE AT 'A-A'

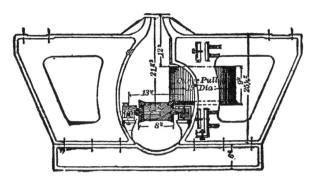

FIG. 187.—CURVE AND CARRYING PULLEY
COMBINED.

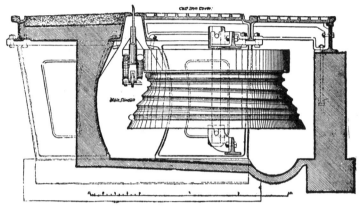

FIG. 191.—SPIRAL GROOVE CURVE PULLEY—TENTH AVENUE,
NEW YORK, LINE.

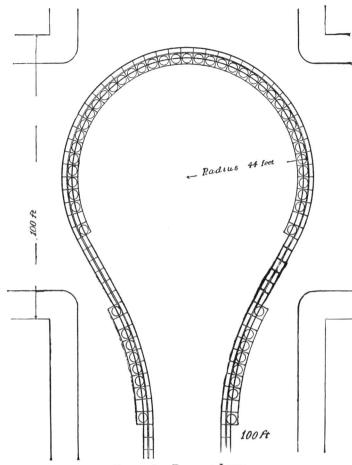

FIG. 198.—BALOON LOOP.

Above are two efforts of D. J. Miller to deal with the danger of dropping the rope from a grip on a pull curve. In Fairchild's figure 187, Miller placed a carrying pulley immediately under the curve pulley, and in figure 191 he gave the curve pulley a spiral winding extending to a point under the outer jaw of the grip. Figure 198 shows a virtuoso performance in pull curves, Henry M. Lane's original terminus of the Broadway line of the Denver Tramway.

Below are a string of curve pulleys, three with hatches removed, from Miller's 125th Street line in New York, and a photograph of the pull curve at Market and Haight Streets, San Francisco, during construction in 1883. Why the young lady chose to pose for a photograph in a denuded pull curve is unknown. (Roy D. Graves)

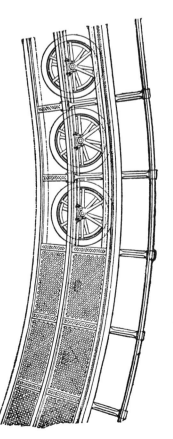

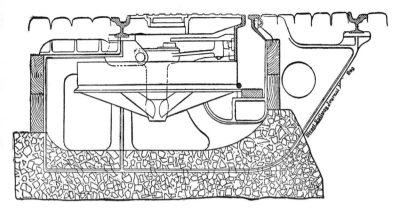

CURVE PULLEY MOUNTED FROM THE TOP—PROVIDENCE, R. I., LINE.

H. M. Lane in Providence sought to minimize the danger of ruining a rope by dropping it on a pull curve by bringing the fir lining of his conduit up to the lip of his curve pulleys, and mounting his journal above, where the rope could not abraid it.

The extension of the Presidio & Ferries line to the Presidio in 1892 entailed a curve at Union and Baker Streets on a 10 per cent grade. J. C. H. Stut rigged the curve as half pull, half let-go. Cars upbound from Baker into Union pulled the cable on the outer track, but downbound cars went around the inner track in full release.

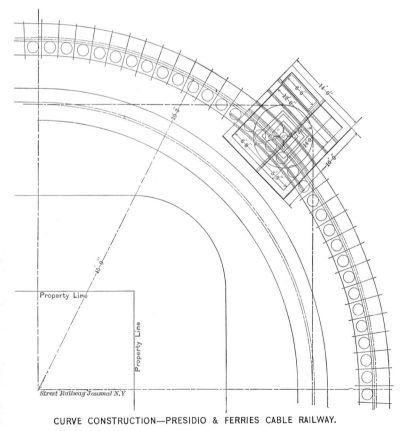

CURVE CONSTRUCTION—PRESIDIO & FERRIES CABLE RAILWAY.

as to distribute the pressure equitably. A curve pulley that bore excessive pressure, or was made of a soft material, developed a groove which tended to denude the cable of its oil and tar. If the groove became more than half as deep as the cable, the jerking motion of the grip began to damage the cable. To minimize this problem, a hard chilled steel was preferable for curve pulleys.

The second reason why curve pulleys had to be set with such precision was the risk that a car going into partial release on the curve — in avoidance of an accident, for example — would drop the rope. The cable at a pull curve necessarily had a degree of slack to allow the passing grips to draw it off the pulleys. The necessary slack could be provided by avoiding one carrying pulley approaching the curve; this slack, however, created a risk if the rope were dropped. If the cable fell below the pulleys, it abraided against the bearings of the pulleys, the wall of the conduit, an exposed surface of a yoke, or whatever else might protrude. Nothing could ruin a cable as quickly or as completely as this, for unlike kinking or even unraveling, the abrasion could go on for thousands of feet before it was detected. The typical curve pulley, consequently, was cone shaped, tapering outward, but with a lip at the bottom of the face. The cable, when released, flew back against the tapering sides and slid down against the lip. D. J. Miller on one curve used a carrying pulley immediately under the curve pulley to deal wtih the risk of the cable falling free, and at another point used a large pulley of about 45 inches diameter with a spiral grooving, tapering inward. A cable dropped on the curve fell directly onto the lower grooves and was raised to the upper level, just below the jaws of Miller's side grip, by the screw action. Henry M. Lane brought the board lining of his conduit directly up to the lip of the curve pulley and at least in Providence used an overhead journal for the pulley's bearing.

The other component of a pull curve, the chafing bar, also had to be set with great precision. The lateral pressure on the grip shank had to be minimized, and the bar itself had to be mounted so that the pressure of passing grips did not loosen it. A loose chafing bar had the potential of creating an intermediate degree of havoc if it came out so far that the grip went behind it. A grip in Grand Rapids went behind the chafing bar on the pull curve at Bridge and Canal Streets in 1889 and tore out 64 feet of the bar, with incidental damage to the pulleys and vaultwork.

One engineer managed to avoid the chafing bar entirely. Worcester Haddock arranged his Mount Auburn Cable Railway in Cincinnati with two large horizontal wheels on each grip shank which ran on the iron wall of the conduit above the curve pulleys. The arrangement served the function of the chafing bars with one less fitting in the conduit.

The problem of lateral pressure on the grip shank, which was so basic to curve design, was also inherent in the layout of switches. It was necessary to have a single tongue which closed one slot and directed the shank into the other at a switch. Malfunction of this, which alas was also particularly characteristic of Grand Rapids, bent or fractured the shank, tying up the system until the car could be removed.

Any pulley or other fitting in the conduit, such as a slot switch or a safety latch, which San Francisco presently uses at the top of the Hyde Street grade, required an access hatch for service. A pull curve necessarily was surfaced by a continuous series of access plates with handles for removal. It was also necessary to provide hatches for removal of the grip through the slot rails in emergencies.

The complex construction below was a switch on the West Chicago. A small vault had to be provided for machinery to move points on both rails and the slot. In few respects was the greater simplicity and cheapness of electric traction more obvious. At right is the signal tower at another of the West Chicago's major intersections.

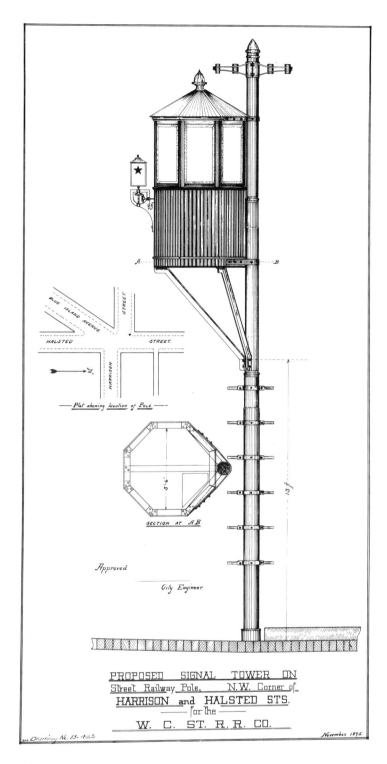

BLUE ISLAND AVENUE

HALSTED STREET

HARRISON STREET

— Plat showing location of Pole —

SECTION AT A B

Approved

City Engineer

PROPOSED SIGNAL TOWER ON
Street Railway Pole, N.W. Corner of
HARRISON and HALSTED STS.
— for the —
W. C. ST. R. R. CO.

Drawing No. B-422   November 1895.

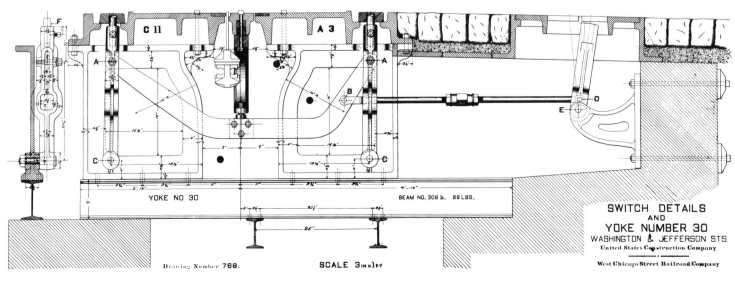

YOKE NO 30   BEAM NO. 308 b. 22 LBS.

SWITCH DETAILS
AND
YOKE NUMBER 30
WASHINGTON & JEFFERSON STS.
United States Construction Company.
West Chicago Street Railroad Company

Drawing Number 768.   SCALE 3 in=1ft

Above is the machinery for running the Cleveland City Cable Railway's auxiliary cable described in the text on the opposite page. Below is the Washington & Georgetown's layout just west of the Capitol, where horizontally-set reduction gears ran the auxiliary cable to the B&O station.

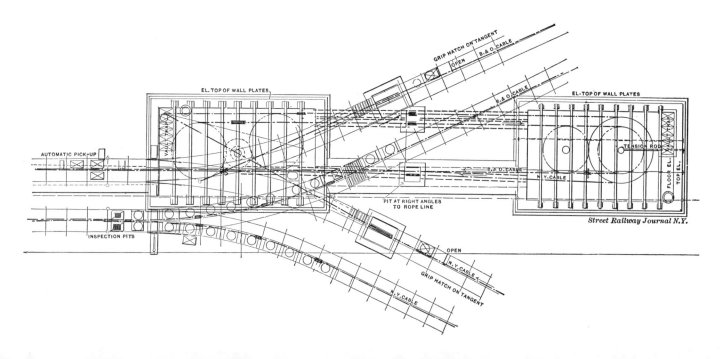

Any enlargement of the conduit to house curve pulleys, terminal sheaves or special machinery was known generically as a vault. Most of these were of brick or concrete. The largest vaults were provided for reduction gears, by which the companies ran auxiliaries off the main cable. Adjacent is Fairchild's illustration of the brick vault in Public Square, Cleveland, along with the reduction gears used for driving the Cleveland City Cable Railway's low-speed cable to Union Depot. As usual, the purpose of the arrangement was to allow the cars to traverse a pull curve at low speed. In this instance, the company's Superior Avenue cable entered from the left conduit in the background, went on two wraps of the sheaves at the left, turned on a 12-foot terminal sheave in the portion of the vault toward the artist but out of the drawing. The cable then returned to the power-house through the conduit to the right. The reduction gears, like most in the industry, were in a 2:1 ratio. The two sheaves at the right ran the cable at 6 miles per hour from Public Square to Union Depot. The horizontal sheave at the far end of the vault rested on a truck on a 20 per cent grade, so as to maintain tension on a cable which necessarily had no tension machinery at the power-house.

Reduction gears unquestionably did the job of providing half-speed operation, but they did so at a very considerable cost in additional friction. They also introduced another "dead spot" between a rope drop and pick-up point in each direction. The heavy drain on power caused the Philadelphia Traction Company to give up reduction gears for two terminal loops about 1889. The Chicago City Railway removed its three sets of reduction gears between 1892 and 1894, and the Cleveland City Cable Railway removed the illustrated set in the same period.

All of the foregoing descriptions are of standard systems in which the conduit contained a single cable, but two arrangements each required two cables in a single conduit. One of these was D. J. Miller's duplicate system, in which two cables lay parallel in the conduit. Miller, one of the many cable engineers who learned his trade under Asa Hovey on the Chicago City Railway, essentially adapted Hovey's use of two cables moving in the same direction in a single conduit on the Chicago terminal loop to general application. Miller reasoned that the incidence of breakdowns to a single cable was high enough that for contingencies a second would be desirable, either of which could be taken with a double-jaw side grip with equal facility. The system particularly lent itself to 24-hour operation, since the service could be provided with one cable while the other underwent the nightly low-speed inspection, replacement of the cable, or maintenance of the pulleys.

The system, as its name indicated, required a complete set of duplicate facilities: engines, winding machinery, carrying pulleys, curve pulleys, terminal sheaves and elevating devices. Miller used an elevation sheave to lift the cable into position to be taken by the grip; to change from one cable to the other, he merely shifted elevation sheaves, and kept both cables running until all of the cars were on one rope. Miller claimed a gripman would not even know which cable and which jaws of his grip he was using. The system was most capital-intensive on pull curves; it was necessary to have two full banks of curve pulleys, set step-fashion one below the other. Miller, like most cable engineers, grossly understated the cost of installing his system while propagating its attractions. He argued that the duplicate system could be installed for $221,000 per mile, somewhat more than double what was considered (erroneously) to be standard. Actually, both installations of the duplicate system involved investment of over $1 million per mile, about triple the actual average investment of American cable systems. Unsurprisingly, both installations of duplicate cables were in New York, where traffic density was so great that breakdowns were particularly undesirable and where 24-hour operation was demanded.

Elsewhere, only the Kansas City Cable Railway attempted the duplicate system, but the company was highly dissatisfied with the experience. Robert Gillham found changing between duplicate cables in an emergency required more time than repairing the damaged rope. He also argued that the idle rope was so cut and chafed by the running cable that it was likely to be useless when most needed. Unless the idle cable was moved at low

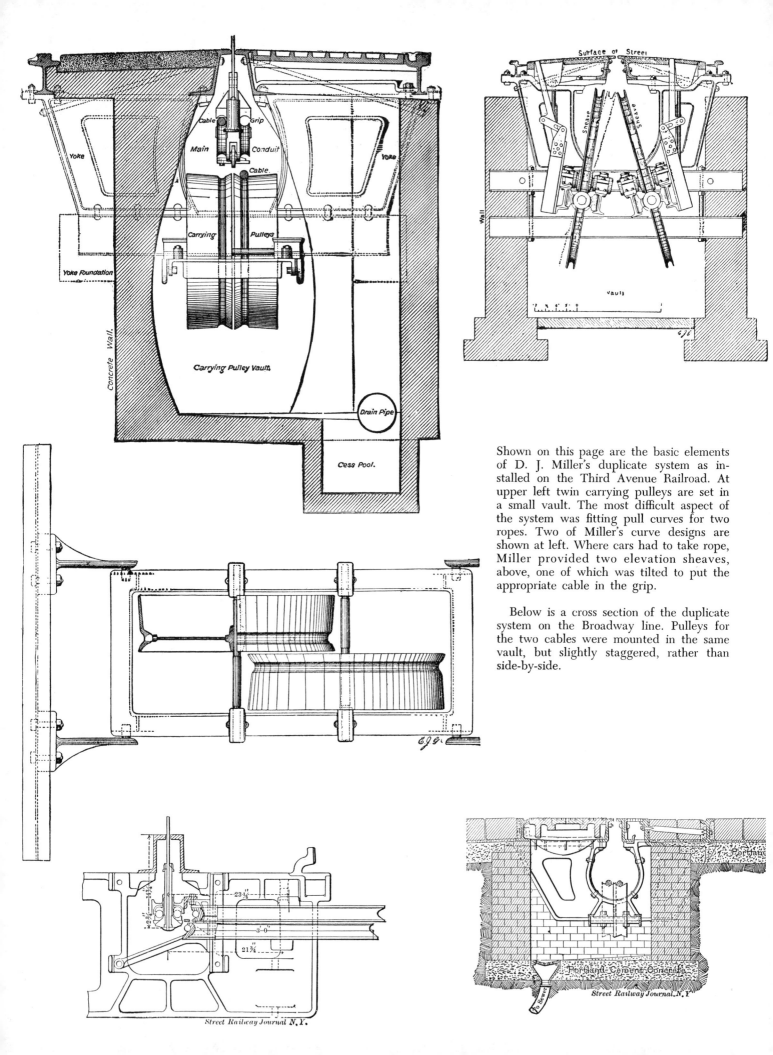

Shown on this page are the basic elements of D. J. Miller's duplicate system as installed on the Third Avenue Railroad. At upper left twin carrying pulleys are set in a small vault. The most difficult aspect of the system was fitting pull curves for two ropes. Two of Miller's curve designs are shown at left. Where cars had to take rope, Miller provided two elevation sheaves, above, one of which was tilted to put the appropriate cable in the grip.

Below is a cross section of the duplicate system on the Broadway line. Pulleys for the two cables were mounted in the same vault, but slightly staggered, rather than side-by-side.

speed, it quickly became caked with dirt and grit. This, obviously, entailed expense, but far worse, Gillham argued, was the cost of capital and labor for which there was no direct return. He removed the duplicate cable after only four months in 1885.

The other and, to some extent, the opposite use of two cables in a conduit was single track operation. The investment in conduit was so great that the incentive to minimize it by operating in both directions was considerable. The incentive was greatest on the lines built for real estate promotion, which usually operated only at 15 to 30-minute intervals; most of the single-track lines were of this character. Single-track operation was standard and straightforward on either horse or electric lines — not to mention steam dummies or virtually any other conceivable rail technology — but the reader will not be surprised to learn that with cable traction single-track operation involved problems, expense and danger. As in the duplicate system, a single-track line required carrying pulleys set in pairs at normal intervals. Obviously, there was no need for a second set of engines, but curve design was extremely difficult. It was necessary to have a cable which was on the same horizontal plane on both sides of the conduit traverse a pull curve in opposite directions. Frank Van Vleck dealt with the problem by arranging the San Diego Cable Railway with sidings set into each pull curve; the tracks separated approaching the curve, and the inner cable traversed a longer radius than the outer. William Phenix in Sioux City and in downtown Grand Rapids went to double track immediately before his curves. He did not do so on the outer portions of the Grand Rapids system, and how he managed the problem is unknown. Van Vleck, taking advantage of his bottom grip, arranged sidings so that the downbound car went into full release, coasted and picked up the rope on returning to the single track. The two single track lines in Los Angeles, though they used side grips, were also arranged in this fashion, but Phenix apparently rigged his two lines so that grips held the cable through sidings.

The worst hazard of single-track operation was head-on collisions. Although one might think that the North Chicago Street Railroad's involvement in a loose strand in the previous chapter could not

have been worse, it was a series of rear-end and broadside collisions; a head-on collision would undoubtedly have created more serious personal injuries. This was precisely the prospect that single-track operation presented. In 1894 a downbound car in Sioux City became caught in a loose strand and descended the Jackson Street hill out of control. The upbound gripman, fortunately, was waiting at the end of double track; the company counted itself lucky to have avoided a serious accident. Van Vleck's San Diego cars carried a red light at the forward bulkhead and a green light at the rear to alert oncoming gripmen of their direction in the dark. Fortunately, all the single-track lines were low-density operations on which the incidence of loose strands was not high.

Little need be said of blind conduits. Many companies found it necessary to run cables down streets on which they had no desire — or no franchise — to operate. The Brooklyn Heights Railroad had to locate its powerhouse so far off line that about 40 per cent of its cable ran through a blind conduit. The largest blind conduit in the industry was the Denver City Cable Railway's tunnel under 18th and Arapahoe Streets, through which five of its seven cables issued from the powerhouse. A blind conduit was a simple construction, having no slot, and thus needing no protection against slot closure. Access hatches could be placed directly over the carrying pulleys. The lack of a slot added to the difficulty of cleaning but also prevented the direct dirtfall through the slot of ordinary conduits. The absence of a slot was most a problem in running a new cable through a blind conduit. To install its 17th Street cable the Denver City had a small boy crawl through the Arapahoe Street conduit with a hemp rope, with which the cable was then drawn into place.

Maintenance of a conduit, obviously, was a continuing operation. A non-revolving pulley abraided the cable, wore a flat spot on its own surface, and increased the demand for power from the engine. An accumulation of dirt dropping through the slot might build up to the level of the bottom of the carrying pulleys to exert enough friction on them to stop them. Alternatively, falling dirt might enter the bearings of the pulleys to add to the friction. In addition, much of what fell through the slot was fecal material and urine

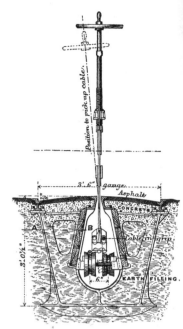

CONDUIT AND GRIP—
TEMPLE STREET CABLE RAIL-
WAY, LOS ANGELES.

Single-track cable operation, as usual, was difficult but not impossible. Above and below are a grip car on the single-track portion of William Phenix's Grand Rapids installation. *(Mrs. L. Charles Rowley)* At upper right is the typical design of single track with a double-jaw side grip from the Temple Street line in Los Angeles. At center right is Frank Van Vleck's design for single-track operation with a bottom grip in San Diego. At right bottom is Van Vleck's handling of pull curves on single track.

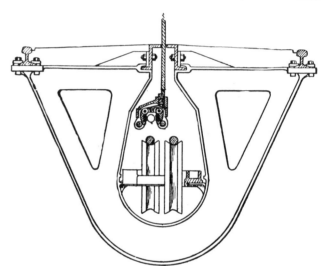

SINGLE TRACK CABLE CONSTRUCTION.

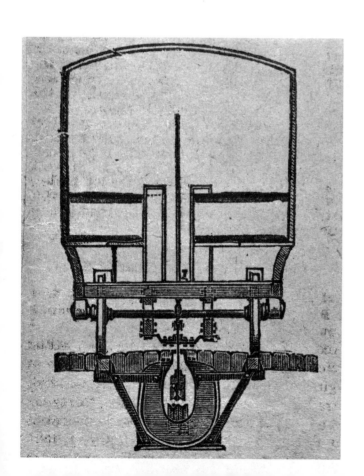

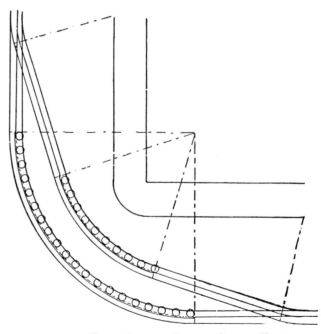

TURN OUT ON CURVE—SINGLE TRACK
CONSTRUCTION.

from horses; an accumulation of this combination was malodorous, but it also attracted and bred insects, who in turn could spread whatever disease hazards the accumulation incubated. Thus, maintenance was not only a facilitation of the operation of a cable system, but also a means of holding down the social cost of the enterprise.

Ideally, the bearings of all the pulleys and sheaves in the system were lubricated daily. John Walker, the producer of driving machinery, observed, "In the ordinary way of oiling a cable road, it takes four men, and an oil refinery to keep them going." The Chicago City Railway averaged 330 carrying pulleys per mile of double track; each was oiled by raising the access plate and applying the oil can to the bearing. Any mechanical lubrication device for the entire system would have been impossibly expensive.

Cleaning the conduit was also necessarily a manual process. Typically, a crew pushed a broom through the slot during non-running hours, and scooped out the accumulated material at access hatches for removal in a wagon. The frequency with which this was necessary varied considerably between companies on the basis of climate, density of horse-drawn traffic and nature of the road surface. Many cable lines ran on streets which were unpaved except for the conduits themselves. Deposit of material in the conduit was worst in the winter weather; the Chicago City Railway anticipated a deposit of mud of 1½ to 2½ inches per month in winter, less during the rest of the year. Accordingly, the conduit had to be scraped about monthly in harsh weather, perhaps once in three months in the milder seasons. The Baltimore Traction Company provided the service with gangs of 4 to 14 men, called the "mud brigade." In general they could work through the slot with a scraper, but at pull curves a man frequently had to climb into the vaultwork to clean out the conduit and service the lower surface of the pulleys.

The size of the labor force necessary for maintenance of the conduit also depended on the severity of the climate. For a heavy-duty, double-track line of the Chicago-Kansas City sort, a company could plan on one man for every half mile of route. Tending Miller's duplicate system in New York required much more, and the typical promotional line far less. Engineers planning the

Passing sidings on single track were usually arranged so that the downbound car dropped and retook rope. Dick, Kerr & Company's design for the single-track line at Matlock, England, included this adeptly-designed passing siding in which both cars held the cable. (*A. Winstan Bond*)

unbuilt Boston lines projected maintenance costs of $32 per day per mile of track by analogy to other heavy-duty installations.

The worst single maintenance problem was inundation of the conduit. A flood or downpour that filled the conduit not only denuded the cable of its dressing, but deluged the bearings of the pulleys with dirt and other abrasive material. The pulleys all had to be removed, cleaned and oiled before they could be allowed to turn. James Clifton Robinson was fired from general managership of the Pacific Railway for neglecting this in his haste to restore the system to operation after a downpour on Christmas Eve, 1889.

The same downpour demonstrated an even worse property of conduits in heavy rains: on a steep grade a conduit served as a storm sewer, carrying off the water at high speed and with terrific force. The Second Street Cable Railroad, which climbed Los Angeles' Bunker Hill, suffered a torrent down its conduit which wiped out most of the fittings, and brought an end to the operation. This company was the only line to be wiped out in this fashion, though economic forces in 1889 were poised to do to the rest of American cable traction what the downpour had done to the Second Street line.

127

CABLE DRIVING PLANT.
DESIGNED AND CONSTRUCTED BY
POOLE & HUNT.- BALTIMORE. MD. U.S.A.

For an advertisement Poole & Hunt had commercial artist P. F. Goist delineate a typical powerhouse issuing two ropes. Goist did a fine job, presenting one of the best encapsulations of cable traction ever attempted. The powerhouse has two horizontal single-cylinder engines, either of which could power both cables. The cable being held by the car in the foreground feeds in under a powered idler, and makes two wraps around the driver and idler before going on the tension run to the sheave in the right background. As on most tension runs, the cable feeds from below and returns to the conduit from the top of the sheave. As far as is known, the lithograph shows a hypothetical representative powerhouse, rather than any actual structure. (*Smithsonian Institution*)

CHAPTER VI
THE POWERHOUSE

Presumably a cable engineer began his considerations of the powerhouse with the question where to put it. All engineering involves trade-offs between strength and flexibility, or longevity and initial cost such as the three previous chapters have described, but the special characteristic of cable technology was a choice in which both alternatives were so impossible that the question could be resolved only by giving up cable traction. The greatest of these questions was where to put the powerhouse. Assume that the typical cable line ran up one side of a hill and down the other in the fashion of the Presidio & Ferries in San Francisco or the Yesler Way line in Seattle. Should the powerhouse be put near the highest point? Presumably so, since then the engines could draw the cars up the grade — preferably in each direction, if two ropes were used. The alternative of putting the powerhouse at the bottom of the hill in either direction required the engines to draw the closest cars down toward the powerhouse, thereby maximizing the stress at the terminal sheave at the opposite end of the line. But if the powerhouse were put at the highest point on the line, it almost certainly would not be near a railroad, and thus the coiled cable, coal, and supplies would have to be dragged up laboriously with horsedrawn vehicles. Unsurprisingly, engineers divided about evenly on this problem; on the Presidio & Ferries, the powerhouse was put near the highest point, but on the Yesler Way line it was placed at water level at the east end. Among lines which climbed a single grade, the powerhouse on the Union Trunk Line in Seattle was at the top,

and on the Tacoma Railway & Motor Company at the bottom.

If the powerhouse were on a grade, the terrain had to be modified so that cars could roll across a rope drop. On a double-track line this could prove quite difficult. The entire Providence Cable Tramway had to be lefthand-operated because otherwise the cars could not have rolled past the powerhouse.

On a flat system, location of a powerhouse was still difficult. The problem was simplest with a physical plant such as the Sioux City or San Diego installations, where the powerhouse could be put at approximately the mid-point of a long, if not entirely straight line. The map of St. Louis illustrates the typical placement of powerhouses about two and a half miles out of the central area on major lines. A system of three cables, two on the main line and one on a branch, such as the Citizens' Railway in St. Louis, had a powerful incentive to place its powerhouse at the junction of the two lines. The Citizens' Railway did not quite make it and had to resort to a blind conduit, but the Grand Avenue Railway in Kansas City was widely cited as ideal in this respect. The powerhouse was exactly at the junction of the main line on Grand Avenue and the 15th Street branch, so that cables issued straight in three directions. The subsidiary Holmes Street Railway had its own powerhouse at the end of the line. Except for the necessity of a lateral movement of a block from Grand to Walnut on the downtown cable and a long series of gentle pull curves on the south cable, the system was essentially ideal. At the opposite

The two big 24″ x 48″ engines of the New York & Brooklyn Bridge Railway were the most widely photographed in cable traction. They operated the rapid transit line on the great bridge from the Brooklyn side. *(Edward T. Francis)*

extreme was the Cable Tramway of Omaha, where placing the powerhouse three blocks south of the main intersection on the system required five right-angle pull curves on a physical plant that could have been designed with only two.

If a system with a radial pattern was to be run from a single powerhouse, the structure had to be put in the central business district, where land values were highest. Both Denver companies chose this course; the Denver City Cable Railway ran the largest powerhouse in the industry (by the measure of length of output) with over 30 miles of cable in seven ropes. The projected powerhouse of the unbuilt Minneapolis cable system would have been of the same character.

Placing a powerhouse halfway out the line in the San Diego-Sioux City fashion may have been the best solution available, but there was no presumption such a powerhouse would be near a railroad. There was no way to resolve the problem; a system which demanded this rigid relation between the line and the source of power was so inflexible as to drive operators to seek an alternative without this disability — which, of course, Sprague provided.

The central element in the powerhouse was, obviously, the engines. As in the case of the cable, the inventors of cable traction invented no engines; they took as given what the developers of the stationary steam engine had done. Fortunately, by the 1880s the stationary steam engine had been developed to a high degree of perfection; it had been the prime mover of economic activity for most of the nineteenth century, subject to a continual effort at perfection by engineers in Britain, America and elsewhere.

A cable engineer's needs for a stationary steam engine were extremely simple, such that he could easily find what he wanted in the catalog of a major producer. In general, he wanted a low-speed simple engine of intermediate horsepower, which presented no problem to any producer. Most cable engines ranged from 200 to 1,500 horsepower, depending on the needs of the system. Fairchild suggested, as a rule of thumb, computing the power requirements of a cable system by assuming every 1,000 feet of cable required four horsepower, corrected for curvature by treating a right-angle curve as the equivalent

of 1,500 feet of cable. The Chicago City Railway presumed such a curve required 28 horsepower. Fairchild suggested adding three horsepower for each car of ordinary size, and 60 horsepower for the winding machinery. The 43,700-foot Lexington Avenue cable required an 1,800-horsepower engine, but otherwise even the New York systems required no more than 1,500 horsepower engines. Fairchild estimated that major American systems averaged 25 horsepower per car. Doane and Plimpton, two engineers who studied all of the large American cable systems, except the San Francisco lines, in preparation for designing the projected West End Street Railway cable installation in Boston, reported that horsepower per mile of cable ranged from 60 on the well-designed Grand Avenue Railway and 64 on the underpowered Philadelphia Traction Company to 200 on some of the Chicago lines.

Cable engineers were confronted with the usual choice between simple and compound engines. As in other power generation, compounds offered the advantages of greater economy of fuel and water inputs, at the cost of greater initial investment. A minority of cable engineers felt that these advantages — which made compounds virtually universal in marine applications, for example — also made compounds appropriate for cable powerhouses. F. W. Wood of the Temple Street Cable Railway of Los Angeles believed that if power amounted to 20 per cent of the costs of a cable railway (he estimated power at 6 to 25 per cent of costs for cable operations generally), compounding would save 1.2 per cent of total cost. He believed that heavily-trafficked lines with a cost of coal over $3 per ton should use compound engines. A. N. Connett of the Baltimore City Passenger Railway, the industry's most vocal enthusiast for compound engines, estimated that he could save five pounds of water per horsepower per hour by compounding.

Set off against these advantages was the problem that the unique properties of cable traction, in the opinion of most engineers, required a compound engine to be condensing. Gripping and ungripping of cars was random, so that the engine had to produce a continuously variable output of power to provide an approximately constant speed of the cable. Those who have ridden the remain-

THE LANE & BODLEY CO.

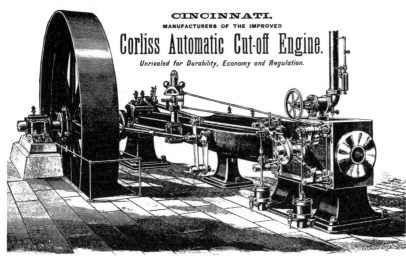

At left is an advertisement for a typical cable engine, a Corliss from Henry M. Lane's firm in Cincinnati. Below is a Wetherill Corliss with its crew in the North Chicago Street Railroad's Lincoln Avenue power station. (*Chicago Historical Society*)

ing San Francisco lines will presumably remember the lurching quality of the movement which stems from the gripping of other cars. The governor on the engine automatically regulated its speed, but under the circumstances, the admission of steam varied greatly, and in particular, the pressure in the cylinder varied unpredictably. In a compound engine, the pressure in the low-pressure cylinder is likely to be close to atmospheric pressure; consequently, given the variability of the demands on a cable engine, the pressure in a low-pressure cylinder was likely to dip periodically below atmospheric pressure, so that the engine could not exhaust unless it had a condenser to produce a vacuum. Most cable engineers preferred the economy in first cost of non-condensing engines, and thus opted necessarily for simple engines. Consequently, the standard cable power plant was a high-pressure, automatic cut-off, horizontal single-cylinder engine, usually a Corliss. Such an engine had a price of $11,000 to $13,000.

Connett, who designed three compound non-condensing power stations for his company, argued that the logic of the foregoing paragraph was based on the experience of the New York & Brooklyn Bridge Railway, where the short distance and heavy weight of the rapid transit equipment caused the demand for power to be more variable than on street railways. Both of the big New York installations opened in 1893 were powered with simple non-condensing engines; these decisions at the end of the cable period were widely looked upon as a definitive judgment in favor of the traditional power of cable plants.

As far as is known, only one company ever switched from simple to compound engines, but this was very much a special case. After the World's Columbian Exposition in Chicago in 1893, the Kansas City Cable Railway bought a quadruple-expansion engine exhibited by E. P. Allis & Company for the powerhouse at 8th and Woodland. This was by far the largest engine ever put into cable service. Although the system was modified to run every line except one from this engine, the company had the engine altered before delivery to produce 1,400 horsepower, rather than the 3,000 which had been advertised for it at the Exposition. Dependence of this sort on a single engine was usually thought undesirable; most major companies had spare engines in powerhouses. Doane and Plimpton reported that most companies had double to quadruple the engine power needed for normal service.

Low revolutions per minute were characteristic of all cable engines. The Pittsburgh Traction Company's engines, for example, ran at 72 and 78 RPM on 90 pounds pressure, paying out cables at 6 and 12 miles per hour. Citizens Traction in the same city ran its engines at 62, 66 and 72 RPM, also at 90 pounds pressure. Equally characteristic of cable engines were large flywheels. Mainly in an effort to regulate the output of the engine in the face of the varying demands on it as cars gripped and ungripped, a cable engine typically was built with a heavy flywheel, the momentum of which was the major immediate force in driving the cable. The Chicago City Railway in its first powerhouse used flywheels of 65 tons. Diameters of 18 to 25 feet were most common. In general, a company with a mixture of heavy grades and relatively flat track, such as any of the Seattle lines, except James Street, was most in need of a large flywheel. The uncertainty of the ratio of cars on grades and flat terrain added an additional source of variability in the demands on the engine, and made it more difficult to regulate the speed of the cable. Thus, the role of the flywheel was most important for such companies.

The spread of the electric streetcar about American cities coincided with a spread of electrification more generally. By the mid-1890s it was possible to substitute electric motors for stationary steam engines. The first company to do so was the Chicago City Railway, which replaced steam engines with a 600 horsepower electric motor in its powerhouse at 52nd and State Streets in 1895. Electric motors produced a smoother torque which was more gentle both to cables and to grips. It hardly need be said that, even if the change was economic, the use of an electric motor to run the cable was a way to harness electricity while retaining the massive loss of energy in moving the rope and turning the sheaves and pulleys. Obviously, using an electric motor mounted on the car was far superior. All of the cable lines which survived to run on grades beyond the ability of electric streetcars were converted to electric motors,

3,000 HORSE-POWER QUADRUPLE-EXPANSION ENGINES.

EXHIBITED BY THE E. P. ALLIS COMPANY, MILWAUKEE, WISCONSIN, U.S.A.

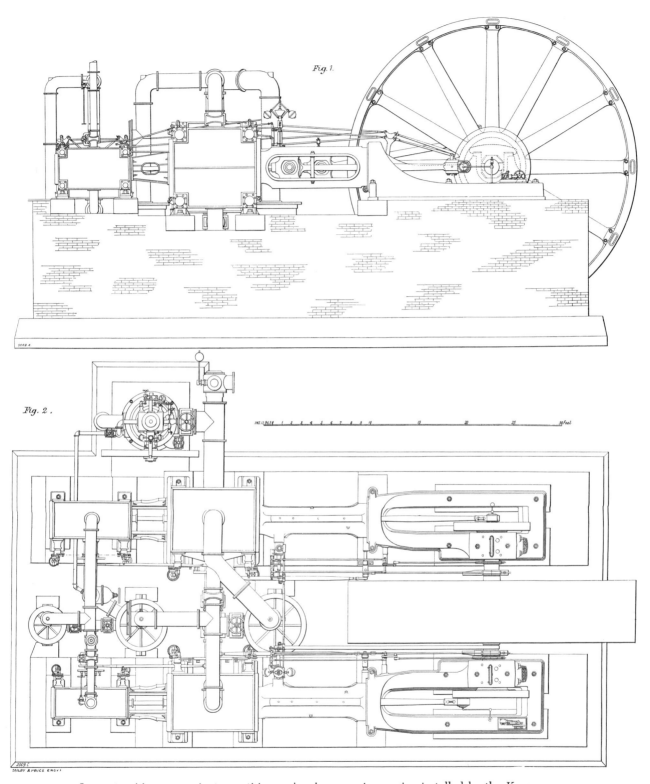

Largest cable power plant was this quadruple-expansion engine installed by the Kansas City Cable Railway in its powerhouse at 8th and Woodland. The engine is shown in an illustration from James Dredge's catalogue of transportation exhibits at the World's Columbian Exposition in Chicago in 1893. Figure 2 is an overhead view, showing the rigging of the four cylinders.

135

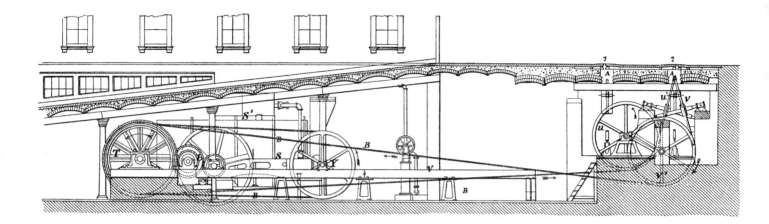

On this page are J. Bucknall Smith's illustrations of the original Clay Street power-house. The driver is connected to the engine by a train of gears and the idler is un-powered. Figure 17 illustrates the clips by which Hallidie held the cable on the face of the driver.

On the opposite page, the California Street Cable Railroad's figure-8 driving and tension devices are at the top and Asa Hovey's multi-wrapped driver and idler for the Sutter Street line at the bottom.

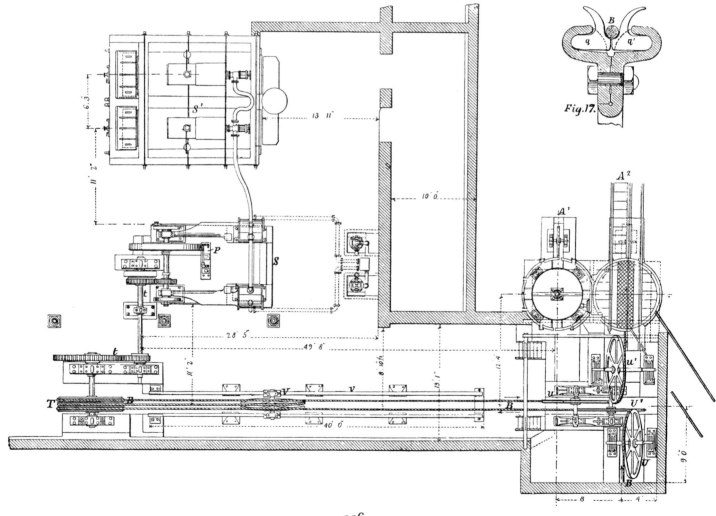

Fig. 17.

however. The remaining San Francisco lines were powered in this fashion, with reduction gears to run the driving machinery at the cable speed of 9 miles per hour. An incidental advantage of conversion of cable powerhouses to electricity was reduction of atmospheric pollution; the Metropolitan was forced to convert the former Kansas City Cable Railway powerhouse at 9th and Washington to electricity in 1897 as part of a comprehensive municipal campaign against air pollution. Powerhouse operating expense fell from $1,025 in July 1896 to $368 in July 1897.

Only one company ever had anything but steam or electric power. The Spokane Cable Railway used water-powered turbines at the falls of the Spokane River, actuating the cable through a geared connection. The company estimated it secured its power for only about $3.00 per day, as compared with $35.00 for a steam plant.

Although production of power in cable powerhouses was simply an adaptation of generation technology in the economy generally, the winding machinery was part of such novelty as cable traction had. Hallidie arranged his Clay Street powerhouse so that the cable entered, turned on a driver which was faced with clips to hold the cable, then ran to an idler of slightly smaller diameter, returned to the driver, and finally payed out into the vault and onto the line. The idler could be moved over a distance of about 60 feet to take up slack as the rope stretched. In addition, the terminal sheave at Kearny Street was mounted on a small cart fitted with a weight hung over a pulley into a pit at the extreme end of the line; this arrangement maintained tension in the face of varying resistance as cars gripped and ungripped. The clips on the driver were also an effort to deal with varying resistance; the greater the drag from cars on the line, the more tightly the cable was drawn into the clips. This arrangement did prevent slippage but the clips abraided the cable and tended to take off the rope dressing. Hallidie connected the engine to the driver by a train of gears.

Later arrangements were efforts to deal with the same set of problems in somewhat different and generally more advanced fashions. The California Street Cable Railroad originally used a method whereby the cable was wound only once

around the driver and idler in figure-8 fashion before going to a sheave mounted on a tension carriage on a steep grade. This method dispensed

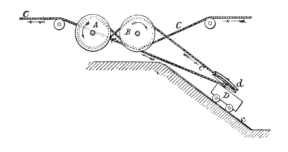

with the clips on the face of the driver, but subjected the cable to a great deal of curvature. Such windings, in figure-8 or S-shape configurations, were never entirely abandoned; the powerhouses established to run the Castro Street and Pacific Avenue remnants in San Francisco after the 1906 earthquake were arranged with figure-8 drive.

Asa Hovey developed what came to be the standard method of winding the cable on the Sutter Street Railway. He used a driver and an idler of the same size, on which the cable was wound directly three times, without either clips or a figure-8 pattern, before it ran to a sheave on a tension carriage set on horizontal rails. Hovey's Sutter Street idler could also be adjusted to take up slack as the cable stretched; most later sets of drivers and idlers did not have this characteristic. Hovey did, however, inaugurate the standard arrangement wherein both drums were faced with parallel grooves, as distinct from spirals, to hold the cable. Spiral windings were impractical because the cable tended to move off the face of the drum in the direction in which it was being wound. Hovey canted the idler about an inch so that the rope would come straight off the first

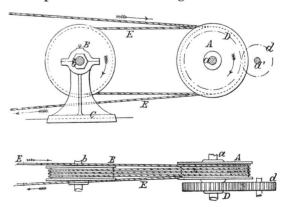

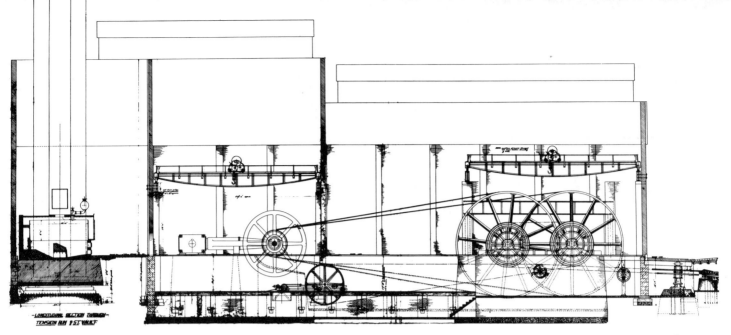

These two views show the West Chicago Street Railroad's Madison Street powerhouse equipped with cotton-rope drive of both the driver and idler. In the longitudinal view, above, the cotton ropes run from the main shaft, identified by the flywheel just left of center, to the large sheaves at right. These, in turn, are on the same shafts as the smaller driver and idler. The cable, a dashed line, enters from the vault at right and turns the driver and idler before proceeding to the tension carriage at lower center. The cross-section, below, shows the powerhouse at the main shaft. The engines are at the extremes of the shaft, outside the flywheels. The drums for driving the cotton ropes to the driver and idler are at center. Note that the tension sheaves at bottom are slightly canted so as to feed out the cable at a vertical plane different from that at which it comes from the driving machinery. (*Chicago Transit Authority-Smithsonian Institution*)

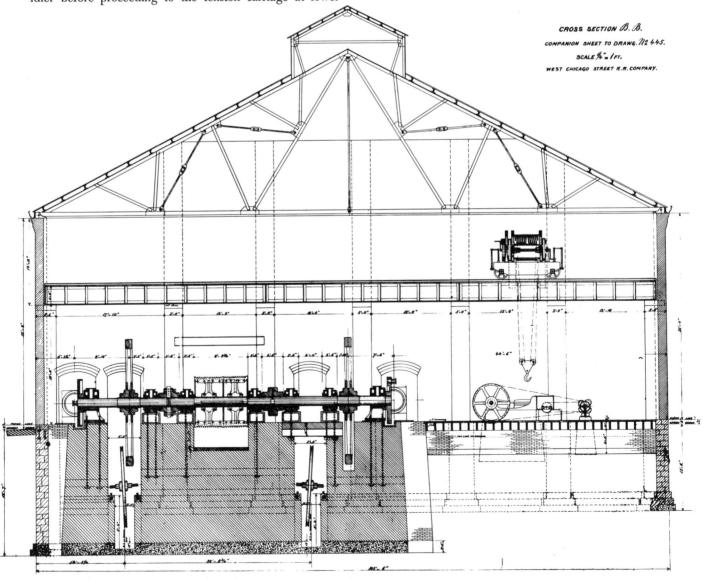

CROSS SECTION B.B.
COMPANION SHEET TO DRAWG. № 445.
SCALE ⅛" = 1 FT.
WEST CHICAGO STREET R.R. COMPANY.

groove of the idler onto the second groove of the driver, and so on, until the cable finally went off one or the other for its tension run.

Hovey's arrangement of a driver and idler involved two problems: first, each successive groove on which the cable turned bore successively less pressure and suffered successively less wear than the previous; second, if something happened on the line to stop the cable, the force of the engine would either unstrand the cable or damage the drums. Both these problems were dealt with by

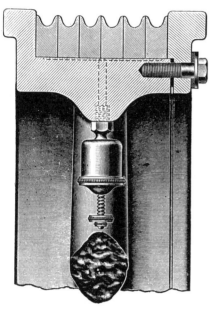

SECTION OF DIFFERENTIAL
RING DRUM.

what was looked upon with some justice as one of the major inventions of cable traction: Walker's differential driving drums. John Walker of Cleveland developed a facing for both driver and idler on which the grooves were independent rings of chilled iron, held in place by bolts. If an accident stopped the cable, its resistance was greater than that of the bolts so that the rings simply revolved until the engine was stopped. Rings which bore the cable on entering were replaced more frequently to deal with their differential wear. In Providence, H. M. Lane sought to accomplish much of what Walker did with differential drums by providing a solid driver but a separate sheave as idler for each of the four wraps he gave his cable.

The standard arrangement of driver and single idler was subject to a wide variety of adaptations in number of windings, gearing and other respects. Companies varied in number of wraps around the drums on the basis of the length and resistance of the cable. The Denver City Cable Railway wrapped its 36,800-foot Welton Street cable on the driving machinery four times, but its six shorter cables only three times each. The Denver Tramway wrapped a new rope three times, but as it grew older, longer, thinner and smoother, the company gave it a fourth wrap. No company is known to have used more than four wraps, but the Pacific Railway and some other flat operators without exceptional cable lengths managed with only two wraps. Most drivers and idlers in the standard system were about 12 feet in diameter; this was itself an important advantage, since in the methods wherein the cable received a single wrap in figure-8 or S-shape on the driver and idler, both drums had to be only about eight feet in diameter, below the critical size for inflicting wear on the cable. Where a single engine was required to run several ropes at different speeds, it was customary to mount the drivers on a single shaft, but to vary their diameters so as to produce the desired speeds. For example, at the Eutaw Street powerhouse the Baltimore City Passenger Railway drove the West Baltimore and Madison Avenue ropes at 11 miles per hour off 14-foot drums and the downtown cable at 6 miles per hour off a 10-foot drum, all off the same shaft from a single engine.

The physical connection of the engine to the drivers was capable of several arrangements. Lane on the Denver Tramway put the drivers directly on the main shaft between the two engines. Such an arrangement required a clutch connection at each end of the shaft, since it was expected that only one engine would normally operate. More common was a direct geared connection from the shaft off the engine to the shaft of the driver. Most companies used this system, again providing a clutch so that either of two engines could be cut in. A geared connection provided the obvious advantage of allowing the engine to operate at an optimal speed, even if this differed from the optimal rate of revolution of the shaft of the driver.

ROPE DRIVE—SPLIT IDLER—PROVIDENCE TRAMWAY.

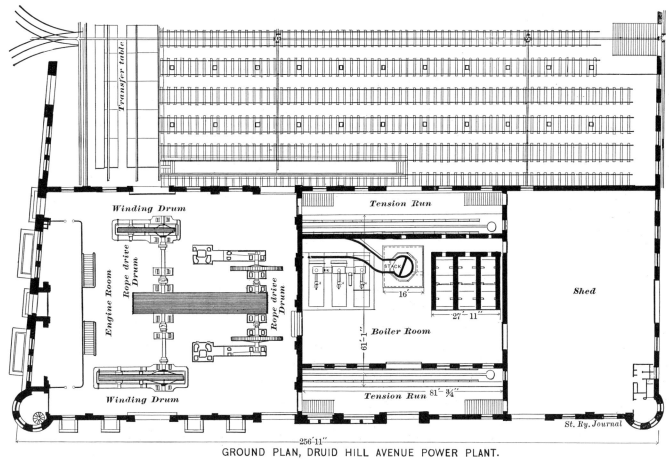

GROUND PLAN, DRUID HILL AVENUE POWER PLANT.

On these pages are representative arrangements of winding machinery. At upper left is Henry Lane's rope-driven driver with four sheaves as an unpowered idler. At lower left is Augustine Wright's rope drive on the Pacific Railway. (*Security Pacific Bank*) Above is the floor plan of a powerhouse with rope drive and an unpowered idler on the Baltimore Traction Company. Below is the St. Louis Railroad's arrangement of driver and idler powered by an intermediate gear on the main shaft.

An alternative to gearing which Lane installed in Providence and which Augustine Wright used on the Pacific Railway in Los Angeles was connecting the shaft off the engine with the driver by two or more short endless cotton ropes. This method entailed less loss of energy in friction and greatly reduced the noise level in the powerhouse.

A question which was never really settled — one of many — was whether to power the idler as well as the driver. Such an arrangement had the advantage of distributing the driving force over two drums, thereby distributing wear somewhat more evenly over the grooves of both. It remained true, however, that the wear on the grooves decreased steadily from the first to the last. As the wear on grooves became appreciably different and as dirt and rope dressing caked in the grooves differentially, a highly undesirable vibration developed if both drums were powered. This consideration caused most cable engineers to power only the driver. Wright, Meysenberg & Co. on the St. Louis Railroad used two powered drums, both run off a gear on the main shaft which was laid between the two. More common was having a continuous set of gears running from the shaft to the first drum to the second; the machinery of the Poole & Hunt powerhouse illustrated in this chapter is arranged in this fashion.

The remaining major element in the powerhouse was the tension machinery. A slack cable was undesirable, partly because the various means for taking rope all presumed a taut cable in a predictable position, partly because slack presented the risk of accidents such as those described in chapter IV in Cincinnati and New York, in which a car pushed the slack in a cable into a corkscrew configuration which entrapped the grip. Maintenance of tension entailed dealing with two problems: first, the stretching of the cable as it aged, which might run to 500 feet; second, the short-run variation, which was usually about three to 12 feet, as a consequence of gripping and ungripping, or expansion and contraction from changes in temperature. The challenge was developing some mechanism that could deal with both simultaneously.

As mentioned earlier, Hallidie on Clay Street dealt with stretching by moving the idler and with short run variation by putting his terminal

sheave on a small carriage, subject to tension from a weight over a pit. This was a method of dealing with the two problems separately; the majority of engineers sought to deal with them jointly. The Chicago City Railway and most later operators used fixed drivers and idlers, with a single sheave of 10 to 12 feet diameter on a tension carriage free to move a short distance. The tension carriage was set on rails on the sides of a pit, usually 75 to 200 feet long, depending on the length of the cable. As the cable stretched, the carriage moved back automatically. A windlass on the carriage was tightened to shorten the chain to the weight which hung over a pit to maintain the tension. If the cable stretched beyond the length of the tension run, it had to be shortened by splicing or wrapped once more on the winding machinery. The Chicago City Railway on long cables of 20,000 feet or more used weights of about three tons to maintain tension. A hanging weight, as might be expected, gave a quicker response than a tension carriage on an incline, such as Root had used on California Street, but a hanging weight presented the prospect of descending to the floor of the pit like a wreckers' ball if the cable broke. In addition, it was usually impossible to build an incline long enough for a tension run of anything but a very short rope. Thus, tension carriages on inclines were characteristic not of powerhouses, but of auxiliary cables run off geared devices, or of terminal sheaves at points where for some reason it was thought desirable to have tension in addition to what was provided by the tension run at the powerhouse.

The menace of the wreckers'-ball effect caused engineers to seek an alternative to a hanging weight. One alternative was suspending the weight below the rails from four rods, two forward and two aft. The aft rods connected the weight to a crossbar, secured to the rails by bolts at the end of the tension run. The forward arms ran from the weight to a four wheel truck which was free to move on the rails in response to the short-run variation in the cable. This truck was connected to the larger truck on which the sheave rode by ropes which could be wound up with a windlass to deal with the long-run stretching of the cable. D. J. Miller in New York used a mixture of this arrangement with a hanging weight

Above is a tension carriage at the original 21st Street powerhouse of the Chicago City Railway. Tension was maintained by the hanging weight at right. On the Pacific Railway Augustine Wright used a double tension carriage, below. The entire carriage was moved away from the winding machinery as the cable stretched, whereas the upper cart which held the sheave moved short distances to deal with the short-run variation of the cable. (*Title Insurance & Trust Company*)

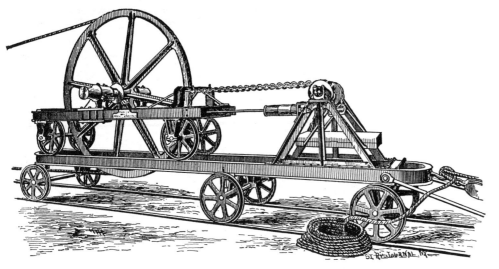

DOUBLE TENSION CARRIAGE—SAN DIEGO CABLE TRAMWAY.

At the top is Frank Van Vleck's double tension carriage, described on the opposite page. At center is D. J. Miller's use of an intermediate weight and pulley to reduce his hanging weight for the tension carriage.

Below is the boiler room of the Baltimore Traction Company's Druid Hill Avenue powerhouse.

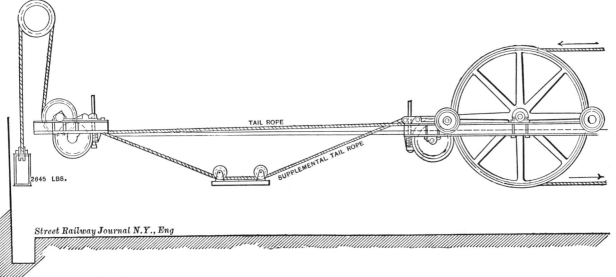

TAIL ROPE

SUPPLEMENTAL TAIL ROPE

2645 LBS.

Street Railway Journal N.Y., Eng

TENSION DEVICE—TENTH AVENUE LINE.

BOILER EQUIPMENT, DRUID HILL AVENUE POWER HOUSE.

on a pulley, and managed to hold the hanging weight down to 2645 pounds.

Frank Van Vleck in San Diego, consistent with his effort to produce a cheap physical plant, avoided the pit characteristic of tension runs by mounting his sheave on a small truck which ran on rails set on a larger truck which in turn ran on ordinary rails laid on the floor of the powerhouse. The smaller truck dealt with the short-run variation and the larger truck with stretching; the larger truck was made fast to the rails with dogs and periodically moved by the powerhouse crew as the cable stretched.

An alternative means of maintaining tension was a sheave which descended vertically on the cable as it left the winding machinery. The California Street Cable Railroad in its second powerhouse used an 8-foot sheave which maintained tension on the rope by gravity. This method was capable of dealing only with the short-run variation of the cable, and some other method had to be used for stretching.

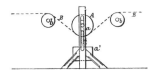

The needs of a cable system were ordinary enough that the standard boiler technology of the late 19th century was perfectly adequate. Somewhat surprisingly, none of the major cable engineers, as far as is known, left a recorded opinion that any specific type of boiler was particularly appropriate to cable service. Coal burning boilers were all but universal, and powerhouses were typically built with tall chimneys for the rising hot gases to create a draft. Several of these chimneys, notably that of the Denver City Cable Railway, remain conspicuous on urban skylines. Doane and Plimpton found the ratio of boiler horsepower to engine horsepower in cable plants typically between 1.5 and 2.0.

Powerhouses were frequently integral with central offices of the company and with car barn facilities. The Chicago City Railway maintained its headquarters at the 21st Street powerhouse, and the Cleveland City Cable Railway had its offices in its only powerhouse. Most of the small companies, such as the Sioux City and Butte operators, did the same. The Sioux City Cable Railway and many others integrated the powerhouse with shops and car-barn facilities. The inability of cable cars to switch themselves was a problem, but moving them was no more difficult than in the case of horsecars. Conduit had to be provided on storage tracks and on transfer tables if the grips were not to be removed, but the cars were generally handled by horse. The West Chicago Street Railroad used a low speed cable for movements in its Madison Street powerhouse and barn, and many car barns were built with gravity assistance in entering or leaving. The necessity of horses for switching movements meant that conversion from horse to cable did not entirely end the need for horses on a street railway. In addition, horses were usually needed for owl-car operation. The stabling entailed the usual problems, including risk of fire from stockpiles of hay; fire from this source destroyed the Washington & Georgetown's powerhouse in 1897.

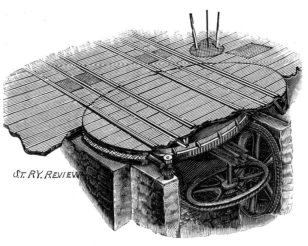

TURN TABLE SHOWING MAIN CABLE.

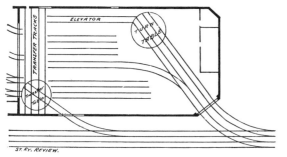

LOCATION OF TURN TABLES IN CAR HOUSE.

The North Chicago Street Railroad turned cars and moved them about the Clybourne Avenue car house by means of the powered turntable at upper left. The Washington & Georgetown used the transfer table at upper right. (*LeRoy O. King*) Below, this tiny tractor shunts cars at the present San Francisco powerhouse, doing what mules did in the cable era. (*Lawrence Treiman*)

Over-all, the powerhouse was an island of safety in an inherently unsafe system. Indeed, a powerhouse must have looked to the employees like a haven: warm, clean, well-maintained and well-ordered. Its hazards were no greater than in operation of heavy machinery generally. An oiler was killed by falling on a cable as it went under the tension sheave in Sioux City, and there were occasional examples of blown cylinder heads, broken flywheels, failed bearings, or slipped cables from the winding machinery. Even in the power-house, accidents were highly concentrated on what was unique to cable traction, the winding machinery, rather than what was a general appli-cation of Victorian industrial technology, the en-gines and boilers. The worst single hazard was the prospect, mentioned previously, that some-thing would stop the cable and damage bearings on the winding machinery before the engine could be stopped. Even apart from giving a street rail-way freedom in placing its powerhouse, Sprague presented the company the opportunity to get rid of the most hazardous aspects of powerhouse op-eration; a generator functioned in its metal hous-ing without serious hazard to anyone. Turn where one would in cable traction, Sprague had found a way to do the job more cheaply, more easily, more safely.

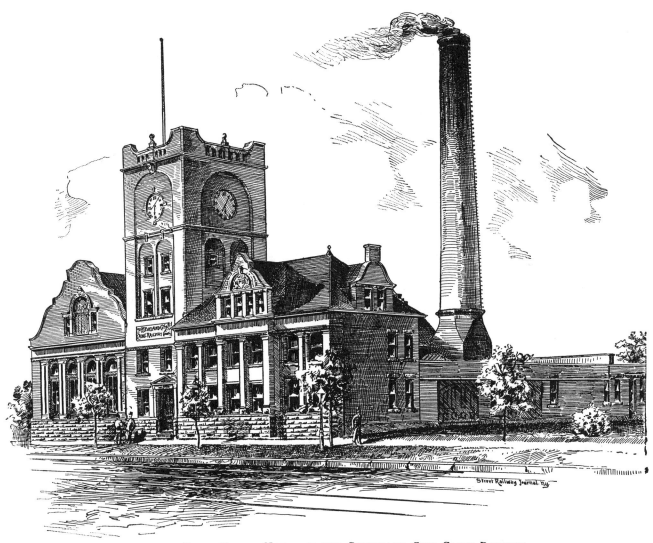

CABLE POWER HOUSE OF THE CLEVELAND CITY CABLE RAILWAY.

After 1888 cable traction was best able to compete with electric streetcars on heavily-travelled lines such as Broadway in New York, shown here in 1895. Unfortunately, the safety hazards of such operations were also the most severe. *(Museum of the City of New York)*

CHAPTER VII
CABLE ECONOMICS

To use a Victorian literary device which seems particularly appropriate: "Surely," I fancy I hear the reader say, "this author is inconsistent, for he has argued in his first two chapters that cable traction was economic for a period of six years and five days, but assuredly the technology he has described in his next four chapters cannot have been economic for the briefest instant."

No, gentle reader, cable traction, for all its inflexibility, accident-proneness, and expense, was in fact the most economic form of urban street transportation from C. B. Holmes' demonstration of its practicality in a continental climate in Chicago on January 28, 1882, to Frank J. Sprague's innovation of the electric streetcar in Richmond on February 2, 1888.

It was, of course, economic earlier, though the industry considered cable traction's early successes unique to San Francisco. The Clay Street Hill Railroad after its extension and rebuilding in 1877 was reported to represent an investment of $241,778.55. Operating at 6 miles per hour at 2½ minute intervals, its operating costs (exclusive of administration) in 1880 were $88,246.71. A horsecar line could have operated on the same headway at 4½ miles per hour at a cost of about $138,880. Cable traction, relative to horse, resulted not only in increased capacity, but in a saving of at least $50,633 per year, a rate of return in excess of 20 per cent. William D. Henry reported that the first six lines in San Francisco paid returns ranging from 8 to 24 per cent on their investment.

The common statement that Holmes' cable installation in Chicago transported passengers at half again the speed of horsecars at only half the cost was, if anything, an understatement. As the system was extended south of the central area, the average speed became twice that of horsecars and the cost advantage was more than double. In 1887 the Chicago City Railway reported costs of 23.16 cents per mile for horsecars and 10.57 cents for cable cars. Daniel Bonticou reported that the Grand Avenue Railway operated cable cars for variable costs of 6.9 cents per mile and average total cost of 11.02 cents. The Sutter Street line in San Francisco had a saving of 30 per cent in operating costs and William H. Searles reported that other lines, which he did not identify, saved up to 36 per cent, relative to horsecars. By 1888 the SRJ could report that only two cable lines (presumably the Philadelphia Traction Company and the Second Street line in Los Angeles) had failed to pay dividends. As late as 1893, when cable traction was losing any general claim to economy, Bonticou reported that his Grand Avenue Railway was still capable of returning 3.5 per cent on its investment.

Owing to the heavy investment required by cable systems, the savings of the technology could not be realized without a relatively dense traffic. What was the minimum density to justify installing a cable line? Bonticou thought that 4,000 passengers per mile per day warranted cabling a horsecar line. The management of the Minneapolis Street Railway, which bought most of the hardware for a cable system before turning to electri-

HE WILL TAKE A REST.

A newspaper cartoon for the opening of the Grand Rapids system. *(Mrs. L. Charles Rowley)*

---

fication, estimated that 3,000 to 4,000 passengers per day were required. D. J. Miller, somewhat surprisingly, believed that only 2,000 passengers per mile per day justified investment in his expensive duplicate system. H. H. Windsor, general manager of the Chicago City Railway, thought the minimum justifiable frequency was a car every ten minutes. William D. Henry estimated that 10,000 passengers per day on a 2½ mile double-track line justified conversion to cable.

If such traffic densities could bring forth the savings which the early cable operators realized, there is no problem of explaining the spread of cable traction during the period in which it was economic. The problem, rather, is explaining why cable traction did not spread more widely than it did. The 1890 census reported that about 6 per cent of American street railway mileage was cable, and there is little question that the foregoing criteria would have brought forth more mileage if a substantial minority of the industry had not held what proved to be a well-grounded skepticism of this form of transit. In 1889 Tom Johnson of Cleveland thought 10 per cent of American street railway mileage would justify cable. Fortunately, at least a few of the skeptics left records of their calculations.

President Brown of the Fort Wayne & Elmwood Street Railway in Detroit estimated in 1889 that a cable installation on his line out Fort Street from Mount Elliott Avenue to Clark Avenue would cost $750,000, on which the interest of $45,000 per year would absorb the entire net earnings of the railroad. He believed that cable traction was economic only in cities of 400,000 to 500,000, or as adjuncts of real estate promotion in smaller cities. He shared the view of the Detroit City Railway's management that Detroit was too small or too lightly populated for cable, and stated, "As a charitable institution, cable roads are an admirable institution, but street railways ought not to be run on that principle." John Kilgour of Cincinnati believed no cable line could cover its operating costs in a city of less than 75,000 to 80,000 population.

In 1887 W. W. Hays, president of the Eighth Avenue Railroad in New York, directed an engineer to study a cable installation for his system. This was a very major operator, one of the most important in the country, and the engineer inevitably concluded that laying cable would be economic. He proposed a system of 9.47 miles of four ropes, graduated from 5 miles per hour at the Battery to 12 in upper Manhattan. The system was to have two powerhouses, one at Abingdon Square and the other at 100th Street, and just seven curves. The investment was projected at only $1,252,072, which was almost surely too low for Manhattan, and operating costs were estimated at $294,373 per year. Including interest, the cable line was estimated to operate for $487,500 per year, as compared with $618,009 for the existing horse operation; the saving in operating costs of $130,500 per year would yield a return of over 10 per cent. Superintendent H. B. Wilson vetoed the investment and made a brilliant evaluation of cable traction:

> If they would surrender entire streets to us, so that we could run on without interference from trucks and danger to pedestrians, it might be all right. But I shouldn't consider it at all safe under present circumstances. It has been suggested that we might put a flag-

man at every corner. That wouldn't do any good. We would be obliged to have a flagman every two feet if we wanted to be safe. In Chicago they used to kill somebody on the cable line nearly every day, and Chicago streets are three times as wide as New York streets and not half as crowded. Then, look at the expense. It would require an investment larger than the whole capital stock of the road, and when we got done we couldn't tell whether the line would be allowed to work or not. I don't think any road in the country would be in a hurry to make a change under the circumstances. I haven't much faith in cable roads or electric motors as yet. I guess we'll stick to plain everyday horses for a while.

In retrospect, it is obvious that Wilson was perfectly right; his view was exactly what a street railway executive should have thought in 1887. Even apart from the accident hazards and huge investment of cable traction which Wilson stressed, the expenditure of energy on moving the cable was a consideration that discouraged some men in the industry. This subject is one of the best documented in cable traction's historical record because of the indefatigable research into it by W. W. Hanscom, a prominent San Francisco engineer who specialized in powerhouses. In a paper delivered to the Technical Society of the Pacific Coast in 1884, Hanscom estimated that 68 per cent of the power generated by the San Francisco companies was expended on moving the cable, 28 per cent on the cars, and only 4 per cent on the passengers. He made his calculation on the basis of the actual average frequency in the city of a car every 1,716 feet. He estimated that with an increase in frequency to a car every 1,000 feet, the percentage distribution would be 57-39-4. The Geary Street line, which had the most favorable figures in the city, approximated this with 60-38-2. The worst, because of its grades, was California Street, with 80-18.6-1.4. By 1888 Hanscom estimated that the power distribution had fallen to the 57-39-4 he had projected with growth of traffic in the city, and stated that the Geary Street line was down to 51-46-3. The Missouri Railroad's Olive Street line in St. Louis, which was an almost ideal mixture of heavy traffic and low incidence of curvature, was thought to have the most favorable distribution in the industry, 48.23-35.90-15.87. Even on the heavily trafficked Chicago lines, 75 per cent of the energy was reportedly expended on the cable and machinery.

A common estimate was that, for individual companies, 55 to 75 per cent of the energy was typically devoted to moving the cable. One engineer who studied the question, T. W. Rae, came to an even more adverse conclusion. In a paper delivered to the Electrical Section of the American Institute of New York in 1887, Rae estimated that for the industry as a whole 84 per cent of the energy was expended on moving the cable and 16 per cent on moving the cars and passengers, as compared with 70 per cent available for moving the cars and passengers on an electric streetcar line. Even though he spoke a year before Sprague's success in Richmond, he concluded:

> How, in view of this showing, any sane man can advocate the system of cable traction, seems incredible, but there are those who will not be persuaded though one rose from the dead.

Sprague himself, naturally, arrived at the same conclusion. In describing the various alternatives for urban transit before the American Institute of Electrical Engineers in 1888, he argued that, since the motive power expense of a horsecar was around $4 per day, essentially anything that could make use of a stationary steam engine to move passengers would look preferable. He recognized that a cable line could operate for 50 to 70 per cent of the operating costs of a horsecar line, but owing to the dissipation of most of the energy in moving the cable, the attractions of cable traction were illusory:

> The chief advantages of a cable are the cheapness, as compared with horse power, of operating a heavily patronized road at a comparatively fixed rate of speed with no regard whatever to grade or gravity; but this cheapness is not inherent to the cable system, but due rather to the fact that steam has such a tremendous advantage over horses.

Sprague's advance was about evenly divided between avoidance of the waste of energy on friction in the cable, pulleys and sheaves, and escap-

The Missouri Railroad on Olive Street in St. Louis was thought to be the most efficient in the country in the sense that it expended a lower percentage of its energy on moving the cable than any other. The company's long trains and straight street are evident in this photograph of the 1890s. *(National Museum of Transport)*

ing the enormous investment in conduit of cable systems. This was no small achievement; most technological advances entail savings on variable expenses at the cost of increased investment. The Diesel locomotive, centralized traffic control, and virtually all applications of the computer were of this character. Sprague's electric systems were usually said to require only about one-seventh of the investment of cable systems, but then the cars operated for only about half the cost per mile of cable cars.

Thomas C. Barr in a paper delivered to the American Street Railway Association in 1889 made the following estimates of investment for a line of ten miles with 15 cars:

Cable:
Conduit	$700,000
Power plant	125,000
Cars	15,000
	$840,000

Electric:
Road-bed	70,000
Wiring	30,000
Cars	60,000
Power plant	30,000
	$190,000

This estimate probably understates the advantage in capital cost of electric systems through grossly underestimating the investment of cable systems. Even the usual estimate of $100,000 per mile advanced by cable proponents in the mid-1880s appears in retrospect an indefensible underestimate. Reported investment for 208.1 miles of the 360.6 miles built, including the entire Chicago and Kansas City systems, is $72,924,709. This sample of 58 per cent, if valid, implies that investment in all American cable systems was about $125 million. This estimate is probably credible, since the sample includes one of the two New York companies, the Third Avenue Railroad, but not the other. The two New York installations involved about a million dollars a mile, some 20 per cent of the total investment in only about 7 per cent of the mileage.

The capital-intensiveness of the New York installations is also a bias in the average investment figure per mile. A simple average indicates that the investment in American cable lines was about $347,000 per mile. Actually, this figure coincides almost perfectly with the estimate of $350,000 per mile which the Census Bureau produced on the basis of the 1890 census. When this average was made public in 1891, such cable enthusiasts as remained were outraged. Daniel Bonticou denounced it, and argued before the American Society of Civil Engineers that cable systems typically ranged from $150,000 to $250,000 per mile. Apart from New York, Bonticou was approximately correct. Only the single-track systems in San Diego, Spokane, and Los Angeles managed to be built for less than $100,000 per mile. Even Phenix's single-track Sioux City Cable Railway involved $440,000 for 3.4 miles, and Lane's Providence Cable Tramway entailed $250,000 for a loop the equivalent of 1.7 miles of double track; both were considered cut-rate installations. Of standard installations, double-track, with orthodox grips and iron-and-concrete conduits, the Denver Tramway is typical with investment of $2 million for 9.3 miles. The Pacific Railway in Los Angeles with a milder climate and a bottom grip, both of which tended to produce a cheaper conduit, had an investment of $1,715,000 for 10.5 miles. Possibly the best single example is the Columbia Railway, for which we know the length to the foot and the investment to the dollar. The installation was a simple one of a single powerhouse with a single cable and very mild curvature. The 2.8-mile line represented an investment of $483,709, or about $172,750 per mile. It should be remembered, however, that the Columbia Railway was not built until 1893-95, when the price level was lower than during the peak years of cable-laying in the late 1880s.

In contrast to the inaccuracy of casual estimates of investment in the cable era, the usual statement that Sprague electric cars could be operated for about half what cable cars required squares extremely well with the historical evidence. In 1890 Robert Gillham stated that the Denver City Cable Railway operated for 8.6 cents per car mile, but the Cincinnati Street Railway reported that its electric cars operated in a city with far more difficult terrain for 4.4 cents per mile.

The Metropolitan Street Railway of New York in 1898 produced an extensive study of compara-

153

The only grades on the Chicago cable lines were the entrances to the tunnels under the Chicago River which wouldn't have been necessary except for cable traction's inability to cross a bridge that opened. Here two North Chicago trains traverse the south approach to the LaSalle Street tunnel. (*Chicago Historical Society*)

tive costs of its cable, electric and horsecar lines which was somewhat more favorable to cable, presumably because of the exceptionally heavy utilization of its cable lines. Approximately 11 per cent of the company's mileage was cable, but this earned 28 per cent of the revenue. The 28 per cent of mileage electrified produced 32 per cent of the revenue, but the 61 per cent remaining under horse produced only 30 per cent of receipts. Operating costs per car mile were 16.42 cents for cable, 17.87 cents for horse, and 10.23 for electric. Operating ratios were: cable, 47.7 per cent; electric, 37.9 per cent; horse, 65.3 per cent. In a homogenous electric system, the company estimated that it would have a saving from conversion of 6.75 cents per car mile, divided as follows: maintenance of way, 3.5 cents; power, 1.25 cents; transportation, 1.5 cents; general expenses, 0.5 cents. The only offsetting factor was a slightly greater expense for maintenance of cars. An electric car involved maintenance of electrical equipment of which a cable was free, but the jerking characteristic of the gripping operation caused cable cars to require more body repairs; the net advantage was slightly in favor of the cable car. Included in the cost calculation was an estimate that renewal of cable, together with wages of splicers or others entirely concerned with the cable at the powerhouse, amounted to 2.1 cents per car mile; this figure alone was in excess of the entire anticipated power cost of the lines when electrified. The Broadway line was thought to be the most densely utilized in the country, with the exception of State Street, Chicago, but the company anticipated a saving on power cost of 30 per cent from electrification. The company found its accident expense of 1.25 cents per cable car mile, which amounted to 3.6 per cent of gross revenue, was about double the accident cost of its electric cars.

The cost calculations of other companies, though less detailed, are consistent with these data. The Third Avenue Railroad in 1896 reported an operating ratio of 54 per cent in 1896; Oden Bowie's hope of securing a lower operating ratio for his Baltimore City Passenger Railway with cable than electric in 1891 is incomprehensible. The Metropolitan of Kansas City also anticipated cutting its accident costs in half by electrifying.

The capitalized benefit of converting the Denver City Cable Railway system was estimated by a municipal official at $480,000.

Apart from the avoidance of friction in moving the cable and the reduction in the accident rate, electric operation promised several important benefits, most of which can be summarized as greater flexibility. An electric car could back up; a cable car could not. An electric car could switch itself at the car barn, and it could go into or out of a powered siding. An electric car could traverse a bridge that opened; in Chicago at least $1.5 million had been sunk in three tunnels because of the impossibility of bringing cable across the city's characteristic double bascule bridges. There was no problem at all in crossing two electric lines. The auxiliaries — heating, carlighting, headlights, air brakes — could all be run electrically; on cable cars, the lights were run by oil, or later off batteries, heat came from a stove, and air compressors working off an axle had too little power to be successful. An electric car could make up lost time; a cable car could not. There were no long dead spots or gravity runs with electric cars. No single failure, such as malfunction of a curve pulley or terminal sheave, could tie up an entire electric system. Electric cars could be raised over

---

The Philadelphia system — admittedly the worst example — was so undependable that conductors carried a transfer for issuance when the operation broke down. (*Joseph M. Canfield*)

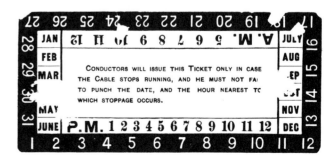

155

fire hoses; cable cars could not. Service could be provided 24 hours a day without reverting to horsecars for owl runs. Cable systems, because of the excessive weight of moving parts, deteriorated more rapidly than electric. A recurrent theme in studies of urban transit systems in the 1890s is that the cable installation, though fairly recent, is highly deteriorated.

The level of strength, skill and coordination required of an electric motorman was far lower than what was demanded of a gripman. The gain in comfort for operators and passengers was a major benefit of conversion. The Kansas City *Times* in January 1890 described winter riding on an open grip car:

> The man who desires a fair idea of the intensity of the cold arctic regions need not take a trip to the north pole to satisfy his curiosity. A 5-cent ride on the grip car of the cable car line on a moderately cold day will give him all the information on that score he will want, plus a pair of feet so cold that they will make his head ache. The world's cold charity will seem red hot in comparison.

More important, an electric powerhouse could be placed with less regard to operating requirements of the individual car line. A powerhouse could be some distance from the line it operated, and in a large city a given line could take power from any one of several powerhouses, depending on the needs of the system at any given hour. This fact, plus the economies of scale of electric gen-

No. 10.—Two-light Car Lamp as used on Tenth Avenue (N. Y.) Cable Road.

erating stations, was a powerful force for concentration in the street railway industry. Most, though not all, major cities experienced a quick movement to consolidation of all street railways under a single company as soon as the electric car was introduced. Since it was economic to replace *any* horsecar line with an electric line, cable lines were quickly surrounded by networks of electric lines, in which they were incompatible, inflexible and dangerous survivals. The Denver Tramway and several other companies at least professed no particular dissatisfaction with cable, but wanted compatibility of their entire systems.

Thomas C. Barr ended his paper of 1889:

> In closing I would say it has been stated that electricity as a motive power is as far ahead of the cable as the cable was an advance over the horse.

For a statement that purported to be no more than a casual generalization, that one proved to be extremely accurate; in retrospect, the cable car was approximately intermediate between the horsecar and the electric car in economy. As in Chapter II, it must be stressed that this is a retrospective view and that the expositors of the argument that cable was superior on heavily-travelled lines deserve more respect than hindsight, at least superficially, gives them. The cost advantage of the early 25-horsepower, rheostat-controlled electric cars over cable was much less than for the 50-horsepower, controller-operated cars of the years after 1893. Andrew Bryson in 1889 argued that cable was more economic on flat terrain at headways of less than four minutes, electric for headways of four to eight or nine minutes, and horse most economic for lighter densities. Gradients moved the ratio in favor of cable. As the title of his pamphlet, *The Return of Power in Electric and Cable Traction* indicates, he stressed cable traction's ability to let downbound cars help haul upbound cars on grades.

The cable car had a further attraction in its simplicity and familiarity. Whatever might be said in favor of cable traction's rival, the cable car indisputably did work. The technology was so simple that its properties were immediately obvious to the managers of horsecar lines, who were not, in general, men of much engineering knowledge;

an electric motor was yet a thing of some mystery to a man who had devoted his mature lifetime to the horsecar. The feeling that cable traction was proved, whereas the electric car was not, cannot be considered entirely a product of ignorance, however. At least until 1890, this point was argued continually by C. B. Holmes, a figure of absolute first rank in the street railway industry. Holmes spoke frequently at industry meetings, obviously with style, effectiveness and persuasiveness. In retrospect, his speeches show an almost theological identification with cable traction, a view that it was not only a technological advance, but even a means of moral uplift. In 1886 he had said:

> A cable road does not eat anything when it is tied up . . . A car has no will of its own to thwart the will and efforts of its faithful driver . . . Since this improvement in means of locomotion has been adopted in Chicago, we find that our car conductors have become superior men, mentally and morally. Compare a car conductor . . . with a car conductor on a horse railroad. Behold how one is clothed, as it were, with a sort of official dignity and importance.

He argued in 1888:

> When an electric motor will draw trains of three or four cars, carrying 200 people, at intervals of 40 seconds, for 15 hours in the day, year in and year out, starting from the very heart of the city, and ending away out in the country, in heat or cold, wet or dry, snow or dust, for 11¾ cents per car mile, at the rate of 10 to 14 miles per hour, then, and not till then, can it ever claim to equal or approach the cable system as motive power.

In 1890 Holmes reported he was experimenting with electricity on his lines in St. Louis, but "was not yet satisfied as to its merits."

Holmes was not alone in his opinions. The M&SP as late as November 1889 reported approvingly of the decision to adopt cable on Broadway, New York:

> Our experience with electric railroads in California has not been favorable; the San Jose, Los Angeles, San Diego and Sacramento roads, on different systems, having all been failures in one way or another, and none of

James Clifton Robinson, from a print by Sir Leslie Ward. (*Title Insurance & Trust Company*)

them are now in operation . . . We have no electric roads in San Francisco or in California. The cable system has proven perfect with us. In addition to the older lines in San Francisco, new ones are being built, and more are projected. The builders are men of experience and wealth, who have investigated all the systems, and they continue constructing new roads in the cable transmission plan.

James Clifton Robinson, the British general manager of the Pacific Railway in Los Angeles, was almost as consistent an enthusiast for cable as Holmes. In 1888 he said:

> Given a busy town, as most of our towns are, a prevalence of steep streets, such as all our chief towns display, an uncertain climate, except for the certainty in winter such as we possess, and the street railway man finds the cable system, and in it alone a mode of traction which meets every need.

In 1891 Robinson delivered an extensive report on cable traction to the American Street Railway Association, which he concluded:

> Remembering that no system of tramway traction is capable of universal application . . . generally, it can be alleged of cable trac-

MILEAGE OF AMERICAN STREET AND RAPID TRANSIT CABLE RAILWAYS 1873-1913			
Year	Miles built	Miles in service	Miles converted or abandoned
1873	0.6	0.6	...
1874	...	0.6	...
1875	...	0.6	...
1876	...	0.6	...
1877	1.5	2.1	...
1878	2.5	4.6	...
1879	2.4	7.0	...
1880	4.2	11.2	...
1881	...	11.2	...
1882	9.1	20.3	...
1883	10.8	31.1	...
1884	...	31.1	...
1885	15.4	46.5	...
1886	15.8	62.3	...
1887	32.2	93.0	1.5
1888	59.3	151.4	0.9
1889	66.1	213.8	3.7
1890	54.3	266.4	1.7
1891	21.9	272.3	16.0
1892	22.4	287.6	7.1
1893	28.2	305.1	10.7
1894	6.8	302.3	9.6
1895	7.5	289.5	20.3
1896	...	255.7	33.8
1897	...	241.7	14.0
1898	...	220.2	21.5
1899	...	183.8	36.4
1900	...	147.9	35.9
1901	...	120.3	27.6
1902	0.4	108.4	12.3
1903	...	101.4	7.0
1904	...	95.3	6.1
1905	...	95.3	...
1906	...	29.3	66.0
1907	...	29.3	...
1908	...	28.2	1.1
1909	...	27.7	0.5
1910	...	25.9	1.8
1911	...	25.0	0.9
1912	...	21.0	4.0
1913	0.3	20.0	1.3

Mileages are miles of double track or equivalent. A single-track line with traffic in both directions is treated as double track, but a single track in one direction only is treated as half of double track.

Source: Corporate histories in Part II.

tion that no condition, demand or requirement in city traffic can be made that it cannot fulfill, demonstrating it to be well in the lead of all modes of affording internal transit to our busy cities.

The question arises how rapidly the industry became disabused of such views. Obviously, early electric cars could easily provide the standard of service Holmes attributed to the cable car in 1888. The idea that electric cars were more hazardous than cable because of their overhead wires was one of the most perfectly wrong ideas ever held, and could not have survived. As early as 1888 there was organized opposition to further cable building in Kansas City on grounds of danger.

The reported opinions of leading figures in the cable movement documents the ebb of their enthusiasm. Asa Hovey, interviewed in September 1888, stated that electric cars, in his opinion, could never supersede cable entirely. He felt their undependability on grades or in snow or ice counteracted their cheapness. Robert Gillham in 1890 argued in similar fashion:

I look upon electric motors as equal to all other motors such as steam and compressed air, which depend on adhesion for power. There is room for electric traction on suburban lines and in small towns where travel is light, but it cannot be operated with the degree of economy that is ofttimes credited to the system . . . because the work done by an electric motor depends on the maximum grade in the system. In order to ascend an eight per cent grade, it requires very much more weight in the motors to secure sufficient adhesion to overcome gravity. The remaining part of the entire system may not have any grades over two per cent. Yet this entire excessive weight in each individual motor, necessary to overcome the maximum grade, must be carried over the entire system each day in the year.

Gillham actually expected more cable track to be laid in the first half of the 1890s than in the second half of the 1880s. His old associate in Kansas City, Clift Wise, announced in the same year that he had been converted to electric, however.

An early convert was John Kilgour of Cincinnati, who in an address to the Ohio Tramway

Association in 1888 treated the cable as outmoded. He particularly attacked the current view that cable traction was superior on heavily-travelled lines, arguing that loose strands and other problems in the rope itself increased more than proportionately to traffic, cancelling out the low marginal cost in energy of additional traffic. Overstating the objections to the financial performance of cable lines, he concluded:

> Cable railways may be considered a blessing in disguise — a blessing to the travelling public, a disguise to the stockholders who expect large dividends from their investment.

Frank Van Vleck, describing his newly-opened San Diego Cable Railway to the American Society of Mechanical Engineers in November 1890, defended it only as a means of climbing moderate grades, and admitted:

> The writer, although connected with the development of the cable system, cannot but conclude that the day of usefulness for the cable on the level is forever gone, and that the electric road stands the champion of the field.

As the electric car demonstrated its ability to climb grades of 8, 10 and, if equipped with magnetic track brakes and pneumatic sanders, even 14 per cent, this judgment became successively more comprehensive as an epitaph of the cable car.

An even more perfect epitaph for cable traction was the bland closing sentence of Daniel Bonticou's paper, "Notes on the Cost of Operating Cable Railways," delivered to the American Society of Civil Engineers in April 1893:

> There has now been enough experience to take the consideration of cable roads as business propositions out of the region of conjecture, and enable the engineer to reasonably forecast their cost, the expense of their operation, and the probable returns.

Quite so, and the economy responded by ceasing to build cable railways.

Typical of the early electrics was this car of Los Angeles Railway, which managed to traverse some of the undulating terrain west of Bunker Hill where the Second Street Cable Railroad had run. (*Title Insurance & Trust Company*)

A superlative example of the titans that did in the cable car is this early electric of the West Side Street Railway in Milwaukee. This company considered cable for its Wells Street line, but opted for electrics, and demonstrated the practicality of Sprague's innovation to the satisfaction of the other Milwaukee operators. *(State Historical Society of Wisconsin)*

CHAPTER VIII
THE DECLINE

The street car cable, the buffalo, the three-toed horse, the mastodon and the ichtheosaurus all have had their day. The latter three are found in fossil form in museums; the second is seen in a few parks and public exhibitions and is rapidly approaching the museum; the first exists simply because it is not easy to dispose of.

Once again, quite so. The author of these words from the Kansas City *Times* of November 18, 1900, pointed out the obvious fact that the technology of cable traction was such as to make getting rid of it almost as arduous as installing it, and a great deal more time-consuming. Economic adjustments are never instantaneous, but this one proved to be quite a bit longer than the period in which investment was made in cable traction. The great majority of investment in cable traction, probably over 85 per cent, was concentrated in a period of only 12 years, 1882-1893. The analogous period of disinvestment proved to be 16 years, 1891-1906. In one respect, this is surprising, since, as the economist W. Stanley Jevons pointed out, sunk costs are only interesting historical facts, not relevant to present calculations. That is to say, even though cable systems entailed an investment of some $125 million, it was mainly embodied — "sunk" in the most literal sense — in conduits which, aside from New York and Washington, were capable of no alternative use. The existence of this investment was essentially irrelevant; all that entered the calculations of street railway operators was that the electric car could provide the service for about half the variable costs of cable and was thus worth the investment in electrical facilities.

Since this logic implies that street railway operators should have attempted to get rid of their cable systems instantaneously, if possible, why the period of disinvestment was so long is a question worth considering. Mainly, disinvestment took so long because of the greater urgency of converting horsecar lines. Almost exactly two-thirds of street railway mileage in 1890 was horse or mule-powered. Cable traction's property of relatively low marginal cost with increases in traffic was not, as so widely argued between 1888 and 1893, a reason to build cable lines on heavily-travelled routes, but rather a reason to retain cable lines in preference to horsecar lines during the conversion process. In addition, the 1890s were a period of general depression, in which some companies found it difficult to raise capital for conversion.

Apart from the experimental non-grip installations in Brooklyn and Binghamton, no cable lines had been converted by 1888. The first entire company to go was the Second Street Cable Railway in Los Angeles late in 1889. A short and lightly-built line, it had been projected integrally with a real estate promotion which had not populated the tributary area enough to justify reconstruction when a downpour wiped out much of the physical plant. In the same year the Inter-State Consolidated gave up on its Riverview line in Kansas City, Kansas, which was also integral with real estate development. These two early conversions (the latter to steam dummy) were prophetic. Lines which were built to open real estate in high-lying

161

areas were the least viable of any cable operations, since the land boom of the 1880s, which they had been designed to further, collapsed toward the end of the decade. This left them running into semi-filled subdivisions that, at worst, did not warrant even horsecar lines. By coincidence, the business cycle acted in such fashion as to reinforce the effect of the innovations in electric traction; the land boom collapsed hot upon Sprague's invention of 1888, and deep depression prevailed by 1893 when the Type K controller and the Number 3 motor ended any claim to general economy of cable traction. This phenomenon manifested itself mainly in the wiping out of the promotional lines in the early or middle 1890s.

No mileage was converted in 1890 except one of the two lines of the Cable Tramway of Omaha, but in 1891 the pattern of general replacement of cable lines could first be discerned. The north end of the Spokane Cable Railway, one line of the Denver Tramway and all of the St. Louis Cable & Western were converted. The pioneer Clay Street Hill Railroad was removed, but for replacement by a longer cable line of the Ferries & Cliff House Railway. More important, 1891 saw the conversion of the first big system — unsurprisingly, the Valley City Street & Cable Railway of Grand Rapids. Conversion of this installation of 6.9 miles and a million dollars of investment should have been more important than it was. The company's history had been a parade of shortcomings of the cable car: ruptured ropes, slot closures, inundated conduits, denuded cables, collisions with horse-drawn vehicles. Everything about its failure was intrinsic to cable technology, but the conversion was barely noticed in the industry. Fairchild apparently never visited Grand Rapids, and none of the trade journals ever devoted an article to the system, either on its completion or its conversion. Thus, a history which should have indicated the hopelessness of cable traction to the industry lay unread in local newspapers, and the conversion was dismissed as merely another example of a desire for uniformity in power supply throughout a street railway system.

The San Diego Cable Railway, an ideal example of a promotional line, ended in 1892 in a bankruptcy action. The remaining portion of the Inter-State Consolidated Rapid Transit Railway in Kansas City was converted, along with the Hoboken Elevated. In 1893 the second big system went, as the Denver Tramway converted. This, too, should have been recognized as prophetic, but for the opposite reason from Grand Rapids; the Tramway was a well designed system with a favorable history. The trade journals duly noted the conversion, but the company's spokesman went to some length not to denigrate cable traction generally. One of the two lines in St. Paul was converted in 1893, but because of the two big New York installations, mileage laid was still greater than withdrawals.

Since 1893 ended the third period of cable history and initiated the fourth, in which cable traction had no attractions save the ability to climb grades beyond the ability of adhesion vehicles, it was inevitable that withdrawals would exceed installations, and so they did for the first time in 1894. The remaining south line of the Spokane Cable Railway, which ran to some point in the woods which the local newspaper could not even define precisely, was simply abandoned. The Sioux City Cable Railway, an equally unsuccessful promotional line, ended in bankruptcy in the same year, although it was electrified and incorporated into the city system. The Citizens Railway was the second of the St. Louis lines to be converted.

The top-grip system of the Philadelphia Traction Company, which might have been expected to vie with the Valley City for first place in the race for conversion, lasted until 1895. The same year saw the end of the lines in Providence and Omaha and the first big conversion in San Francisco, about half of the Omnibus system.

The following year, 1896, saw the heaviest volume of conversions to date, 33.8 miles. The Pacific Railway of Los Angeles, 10.5 miles, was the largest company yet to convert. Before the year was out the Consolidated Piedmont in Oakland converted, as did the Portland Cable Railway, with the exception of the ascent of its 20.93 per cent grade. In the East, Baltimore Traction completed a conversion begun in the previous year, and by agreement with the city the Pittsburgh lines converted the entire cable network, although a portion of the Citizens Traction Company survived into 1897. Otherwise, 1897 saw the end only of the short lines in Butte and West

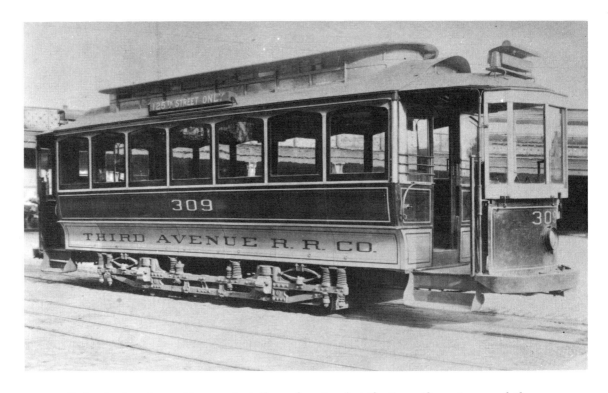

Only the heaviest cable cars lent themselves to electrification. Above is one of the single-truckers of the Third Avenue Railroad after electrification. *(Edward B. Watson)* Below is one of A. D. Whitton's characteristic double-truckers converted into a box motor for suburban runs of the Philadelphia Rapid Transit. Baker Bowl, the Phillies' ball park, is in the background. *(Harold E. Cox)*

The street railways in St. Paul and Providence resorted to counterbalances to get rid of cable lines with short heavy grades. Below, a former St. Paul cable car assists a Twin Cities Rapid Transit car up the Selby Avenue cable line's 16 per cent grade after electrification. *(Minnesota Historical Society)* Above, one of the former cable cars, electrified and equipped to latch onto the counterbalance, sits in Twin Cities Rapid Transit's yard. *(Russell L. Olson)*

Seattle. A fire which gutted the powerhouse of the Washington & Georgetown in September 1897 brought an unplanned end to most of the Washington mileage, and the company wound up the remainder in 1898. In the same year, the Cincinnati Street Railway converted its own Vine Street line and the Mount Adams & Eden Park, which it had acquired. In St. Paul, where the incentive to get rid of cable traction was simply overpowering, 1898 also saw the end of the system. The big Metropolitan of Kansas City had its first major conversion, the tortuous line to Kansas City, Kansas. By the end of the year, mileage was down to 220.2, somewhat less than two-thirds of the total. All of the Chicago system remained, and the withdrawals in San Francisco and Kansas City had been minor.

In 1899, however, the remaining line of the Omnibus in San Francisco and the People's Cable Railway, weakest of the Kansas City lines, were converted. The People's was the last of the lines built for real estate promotion to survive. Elsewhere, the year saw the end of cable operation on the Oakland Cable Railway, the Baltimore City Passenger Railway, the Columbia Railway in Washington — only four years after it was begun — and, most important, on the entire Third Avenue Railroad. Nineteen hundred, the last year of the century, saw the end of the St. Louis Railroad, the Front Street Cable Railway in Seattle and, after three years of acrimony, the entire network of the former Denver City Cable Railway. Denver, alone among American cities, sought to levy a fee for conversion of the remaining cable lines, thereby extracting some of the gains of the Denver Tramway, which had succeeded to the property. The Tramway finally yielded to this pressure, agreed to pay $102,000 and promptly set a record for conversion, getting rid of a 15-mile network in an 8-day period, winding up the whole system only 11 days after securing permission.

By the end of the century, remaining cable mileage was only 147.9, less than half of the peak of 1893. Somewhat surprisingly, the first four years of the new century reduced this figure by only about another third; by the end of 1904, about 95 miles remained. The largest mileage converted in this period was the Metropolitan of Kansas City, which had acquired all the remain-

ing cable mileage of the city and was converting it to electricity as rapidly as its resources permitted. By the end of 1904 the Metropolitan had reduced the Kansas City system to the 12th Street line, which entailed a 20 per cent grade which the company could not yet deal with in other fashions. Elsewhere, the Missouri Railroad, which had re-equipped itself with heavier cable cars as recently as 1896 and the People's Railway both converted in 1901, ending cable traction in St. Louis. The Cleveland City Cable Railway and the Metropolitan of New York converted in the same year. The Temple Street Cable Railway in Los Angeles and, more remarkably, the cheap and unsatisfactory Mount Auburn Cable Railway in Cincinnati lasted until 1902. The one remaining line in Portland was replaced in 1904.

The year 1906 was the height of the great Edwardian prosperity, a year particularly characterized by heavy investment in transport facilities of all sorts. A mixture of events, which were essentially coincidental, combined to get rid of more than two-thirds of the remaining cable mileage in that single year. There had been no conversions at all in 1905, but 1906 produced almost double the mileage of conversions of any previous year. The Metropolitan reduced its 12th Street line to the ascent of the 20 per cent grade, cutting the Kansas City mileage to a meager 1.3. The San Francisco earthquake of April 1906 brought a quick and unintended end to the Sutter Street Railway, the Presidio & Ferries, all of the Market Street Cable Railway except the ascents of Castro Hill, and much of the Ferries & Cliff House. After years of uncertainty concerning franchise rights which had inhibited investment in Chicago street railways, the municipal government and the companies in 1905 arranged a franchise extension entailing the conversion of all three cable systems; the entire network went in 1906. Remarkably, State Street, Chicago, had cable traction earlier and kept it later than Market Street, San Francisco.

By the end of 1906 there was little left to go. Mileage was down to 29.3, a trivial sum in the national mileage, now almost all of electric lines. The electric car was carrying some 90 per cent of urban passengers. The last cable rapid-transit operation, the New York & Brooklyn Bridge Rail-

Eleventh Street, Tacoma, exemplifies perfectly the few transit routes the cable car was able to hold after the onslaught of the electrics. Here a car climbs out of downtown Tacoma in the 1920s. *(Washington State Historical Society)*

way, survived until 1908, and the neighboring Brooklyn Heights Railroad was converted in the following year. The Geary Street line in San Francisco was electrified in 1912, and the Metropolitan modified its 12th Street descent into the West Bottoms to get rid of the last remnant of the Kansas City system in 1913. With those conversions, any claim of cable traction to serving a general transportation function in American cities had disappeared. There remained only 20 miles, all in San Francisco, Tacoma and Seattle, serving grades for which ingenuity provided no alternative. Previously, the operators in Providence and St. Paul had resorted to counterbalances, and later both provided tunnels to hold the gradients down to what an electric car could manage unaided. Portland avoided its 20.93 per cent grade with a circuitous line over an entirely different route.

None of the remaining lines had ruling grades under 13 per cent. Somewhat more than half of the former Ferries & Cliff House survived, with grades up to 18.7 per cent. The California Street Cable Railroad had 18.2 per cent on the main line and 20.67 on Hyde Street. The south ascent of Castro Hill on the short survivor of the Market Street line had an 18.4 per cent grade and the remnant of the Sutter Street Railway on Pacific Avenue had a block of 13 per cent. The Tacoma line had a ruling grade of 14 per cent upbound and 14.29 downbound. Of the three Seattle lines, Yesler Way had an 18 per cent ascent from Lake Washington, James Street a block of 18.65 and Madison Street one of 20.88. The Seattle and Tacoma lines were useful adjuncts to comprehensive city streetcar systems, and the California Street and ex-Ferries & Cliff House lines in San Francisco were major connections between the central business district and densely populated residential areas on the hills above. The only survivor not entirely justified by its traffic and gradients was the Pacific Avenue remnant in San Francisco, which was carried mainly by hostility to overhead wires in an opulent residential area. It was withdrawn in 1929, but the other survivors lasted until the introduction of the trolley bus and gasoline or diesel buses, more powerful than the early models. It is almost ludicrous to ascribe a fifth period to the history of the cable car, but since trolley buses and the later internal-combustion buses could climb any grades a cable car could, the year 1938 marks the beginning of a final period in which cable traction had no attraction except its antiquity and curiosity value.

In Tacoma the cable line was a short and well-designed installation intended to connect the central area with a network of streetcar lines running on cross streets high above. Cable operation was discontinued in 1938 as part of the general conversion of rail transit to bus. The same could be said of Seattle, where the James Street line and the Madison Street remnant served mainly to connect with electric cars on high-lying land; the Yesler Way line was more self-contained and was the source of such enthusiasm as cable traction had in Seattle. Remarkably, cable traction at this late date was still looked upon merely as a method of urban transit by the great majority of the population and had little of the nostalgic enthusiasm it currently evokes. Accordingly, efforts to preserve the Seattle lines were meager and unsuccessful. The city ended all three in 1940, as in Tacoma, integrally with general conversion from streetcar to bus transportation. In San Francisco 1941 saw the end of the Market Street Railway's remnant on Castro Hill, and 1942 its Sacramento-Clay line of the former Ferries & Cliff House. Undoubtedly, except for the War, the remainder of the F&CH would have succumbed not long afterward; but the Powell Street lines passed into the hands of the Municipal Railway in 1944, where political efforts to preserve them were likely to be more successful. In the post-war period, enthusiasm for the cable cars increased enormously; the Powell Street lines survived an effort at conversion to buses in 1947 which was, as Wellington said of Waterloo, "a near thing." The electorate approved a drastic reduction in mileage in 1954, incidental to consolidation of operations of the former California Street and Powell Street lines. The present mileage of 4.7 is only some 9 per cent of the city's peak mileage, but what is remarkable is that it has survived at all. What remains of the California Street line has operated from 1878 to the present, a history of 92 years; the representative cable line was probably the Pacific Railway of Los Angeles: in, in 1889, out, in 1896.

*   *   *

These surviving powerhouses demonstrate the wide variety of uses to which old power-houses were put once the cable era ended. On this page, the Thorndike garage once powered the Cable Tramway of Omaha. The Drake Hotel in St. Louis, below, is a modification of the Missouri Railroad's powerhouse, the only one in the city to survive.

168

The Denver City Cable Railway's powerhouse, which led the industry in mileage of rope, survives, above, as a garage in downtown Denver. Kansas City's sole survivor, which once issued the rope of the Holmes Street Railway, now puts out linen for the Superior Laundry. Consolidated Piedmont's powerhouse in Oakland is resplendent as a Cadillac agency. Cadillacs are serviced in the old car house to the rear. *(All, GWH)*

The North Chicago Street Railroad's Clark Street powerhouse, formerly a swimming pool, is one of several to survive as a garage. The West Chicago's Madison Street plant, center, divided its space between a roller rink and a used-car showroom. The same company's handsome powerhouse for the loop of its Halsted-Blue Island lines, at bottom, is finely preserved as a substation for Commonwealth Edison. The North Chicago's counterpart, which issued the troublesome northside loop cable, is Ireland's on the opposite page, Chicago's premier seafood restaurant. *(GWH)*

Two of Cincinnati's powerhouses have survived, the Mount Auburn Cable Railway's plant as Beck's Studio, a warehouse for theatrical equipment, and the Mount Adams & Eden Park's as Fenton Cleaners.

(Herbert A. Pence, Jr.)

171

Brooklyn Rapid Transit's No. 4, a former cable car of the Brooklyn Heights Railroad, exemplifies the type of car that could be electrified. *(Edward B. Watson)* The ordinary grips and trailers of the Denver City Cable Railway equally well exemplify what could not be electrified in satisfactory fashion. Most such equipment was burned to free its scrap metal, as a crew of the Denver Tramway, below, is doing in 1900. *(State Historical Society of Colorado)*

The question arises, in view of the short life of the typical cable line, how much of the $125 million invested in American cable systems was recovered. There appears to be no way of making a valid estimate of this. Even given the sloppy depreciation accounting of the industry prior to the Panic of 1907, relatively little of the investment was fully depreciated by usual industrial standards. Bion J. Arnold in his study of Kansas City street railways published in 1913 estimated that the one remaining line in the city was 90 per cent depreciated; it was at that time 25 years old, and little cable mileage even approached that longevity. The mileage in Kansas City, which was among the most thoroughly justified in the industry, lasted about 14 years on the average. Apart from lines that didn't work at all, the worst performance was the San Diego Cable Railway, which operated only from June 7, 1890, to October 15, 1892. Grand Rapids had the worst record of any large system, running out its sorry history from April 13, 1888, to November 12, 1891. Of the systems built for general transportation purposes, as distinct from service on grades, the longest-lived was the Chicago City Railway, the central portions of which operated from January 28, 1882, to October 21, 1906 — just under 25 years.

Of all the investment in the cable systems the powerhouses lent themselves most readily to conversion to other purposes. Many remained as generating stations or car barns for streetcar lines. The engines did not lend themselves particularly well to conversion, since electric generation required a higher-speed engine than the typical low-RPM cable plant. Various powerhouses became auditoriums, swimming pools, automobile showrooms, ice plants, garages and a variety of other enterprises, representative examples of which are shown in photographs nearby. There was, at minimum, room for a great deal in a former cable powerhouse.

Experience at adapting cable cars to electric traction was mixed. The heavy single-truck cars used in New York and Brooklyn and on the Baltimore City Passenger Railway and the Columbia Railway in Washington lent themselves well to electric operation, but the typical grip car or double-truck combination car was too flimsy for conversion, and the jerking action to which it had been subjected usually had damaged its joiner work. Some such cars were converted, including the combination cars in San Diego and some of the cars in Philadelphia. Some cable cars were used as trailers behind early electrics, but most were simply scrapped, including almost new equipment in Grand Rapids and Denver.

The conduit lent itself to conversion to electric operation less than any other element in cable technology. Superficially, cable track structure might appear a superlative right-of-way for electric cars, being heavy and stable, but the investment in the conduit was directed toward preventing the slot from closing, not to supporting the cars. Thus, the iron and concrete was highly concentrated toward the center of yokes, and the rails themselves were given little support. A standard four-wheel grip car weighed about 5,000 pounds, but the early electric cars weighed from 8,000 to 11,000 pounds. Double-truck electric cars weighing between 20,000 and 24,000 pounds were in service by the turn of the century. Neither the rails nor the yokes were suited to such weights. Even if the rails were replaced with heavier ones, the yokes tended to fracture under the weight, causing the rail to sink. The street railway in St. Louis complained in 1895 that yokes were breaking continually on newly electrified cable track, entailing a cost of $20 for each fracture. Similarly, cable track was inappropriate for electric operation because the typical flangeway was only ¾ inch deep, too shallow for cars of the weight of the early electrics. Finally, a disproportionate mileage

No. 2. Center Car Lamp, 14 in. Nickel Reflector. In general use throughout the United States and Canada.

173

Los Angeles inherited the cable cars' gauge of 3'-6" and, as these two California-type electrics demonstrate, some of the old cable destinations. *(UCLA Libraries)*

of cable track was narrow gauge, which was less than optimal even for the early electrics. Denver and Los Angeles were cursed with the old cable gauge of 3'-6" to the end of electric operation.

Even for companies which electrified with underground pick-up, cable conduit was unsatisfactory. An electric conduit required an access hatch over every insulator supporting the underground electric rails, but normal practice was to have insulators at triple or more the 32-foot frequency of the access hatches over carrying pulleys. Cable conduit was about twice as deep as electric lines required. Consequently, even though cable conduit was used for the electrifications in New York and Washington, it was subsequently replaced with heavier but shallower conduit specifically designed for the purpose.

Any street railway had an incentive to remove the cable conduit, but the expense of doing so was so great that the companies differed on the question whether it was worth doing. The Pittsburgh lines undertook to remove it immediately (though some was found in place at East Liberty as recently as 1968), but Chicago left it in place and never did make a systematic effort to remove it. In Baltimore the companies left the conduit and its fittings in place until 1906, when the street railway removed them — a process the company likened to converting the city streets into a quarry without blasting. Several other companies removed conduit at that time partly because of the prosperity of the industry, partly because of the proliferation of heavy double-truck cars after 1903.

In the cities in which conduit was simply paved over or filled in with concrete, it became a major impediment to work on the streets. Worse, its location was frequently unknown, since the cable car was typically forgotten quickly in our cities and thought of, if at all, as a single-purpose hill climber, unique to San Francisco, Tacoma and Seattle. Many a guileless sewer contractor, upon making a low bid on a project, discovered to his horror that the street was underlaid with some incomprehensible and all but impenetrable mass of concrete interlaced with cast iron, worse than stone, worse than anything in his entire experience. A contractor in San Diego lost a substantial sum upon encountering the long-forgotten conduit

of the San Diego Cable Railway. Another dug into the Dallas Cable Railway; one can picture his feelings on encountering a cable conduit in a city that never did have cable traction. Conduit is frequently unearthed in Chicago; a great deal of it was removed from Michigan Avenue during excavation for the Grant Park garage in 1953.

This intractable memorial lurking beneath the streets was an important social cost of the cable experience. An attorney who studied Grand Rapids' street railway in 1916 described the investment in conduits as "worse than useless" and characterized the whole cable investment as "an almost total loss." He was, of course, right. Such recovery of the original investment as there was from the powerhouse and cars was counteracted by the costs of dealing with the conduit, and that cost is not entirely ended even today. Which was greater, the recovery of capital for other purposes

Some unintended archeology at East Liberty, Pittsburgh, in 1968 unearthed the conduit of the Citizens Traction Company in the course of some underground construction work. (*Kenneth L. Douglas*)

Why many companies were content merely to pave over their conduits is evident in these illustrations of removal of the conduits of the two Oakland cable operators. On this page and at the top of the next a crew tears out conduit of the Consolidated Piedmont in the vicinity of Broadway and Piedmont Avenue. The two lower views at right show a gang breaking up and removing the conduit of the Oakland Cable Railway on lower Broadway. (All, Louis L. Stein)

One of the final menaces to the cable car was the one-way street; the technology is so inflexible that lines could not readily be rerouted when cities converted to one-way traffic. The O'Farrell-Jones-Hyde line in San Francisco operated against the current of traffic for a block on Pine Street with the aid of an overhead neon sign which the car actuated before turning the corner. *(Roy D. Graves)* Below, a Powell Street car crosses California Street in the last days of the Washington-Jackson line. *(Lawrence Treiman)*

from the powerhouses and other parts of the technology which were capable of alternative uses, or the costs from the survival of the conduit is impossible to say; the answer must differ between cities.

Naturally, when cable lines had been opened, they were expected to be permanent, or at least durable for many decades. The conduit must have seemed a guarantee of this. On the opening of the Denver Tramway in 1888, the Denver *Times* had written of its promoters:

> To them all honor is due; the road will be, when they are no more, an everlasting indication of their enterprise and perseverance.

The Tramway's cable lines were gone in five years, but many a municipal department of streets still has an everlasting indication of the enterprise and perseverance of the local cable promoters.

The promoters and the engineers themselves came off fairly well. Because the street railways were experiencing a continual increase in traffic, they were able to suffer a large unsuccessful investment better than a less dynamic industry could have done. The engineers had training general enough that most switched readily into electric technology. A. N. Connett designed the successful electric conduit in Washington. Phenix became superintendent of track construction for the street railway in New Orleans. Hallidie and Root remained active in engineering in San Francisco. Eppelsheimer went to England in 1880 to design the Highgate Hill Cable Tramway in London and, after working on the Edinburgh Northern in 1885, returned to Kaiserslautern. Henry M. Lane remained active in Lane & Bodley in Cincinnati. Robert Gillham went into steam railroading and died as general manager of the Kansas City Southern. Three major cable engineers failed to live out the cable era; D. J. Miller died in 1889, W. H. Paine in 1890 and W. B. Knight in a train wreck in the same year. Casebolt died in 1892. His old associate Hovey overcame his dislike of the Chicago climate and retired to the city's south side.

The fact that cable traction was not an industry, as the interurbans were, but rather a technology within an industry, was fortunate in several respects. Men did not commit their lives to cable traction in the sense they did to the interurbans. Street railway managements in evaluating their cable systems were free of the characteristic bias of declining industries that loyalty to one's employer implies a show of confidence that the decline will be reversed. This bias typically results in some grossly misguided investments in declining industries. The obligation of street railway managers was only to make an objective evaluation of the alternatives; this undoubtedly hastened the decline of the cable car and spared society some wasteful efforts at updating cable plants.

❊   ❊   ❊

Cable traction has three basic memorials: the remaining powerhouses and conduits; the surviving lines in San Francisco; and the historical source material the movement generated. Of the three, the remaining San Francisco lines are the most conspicuous and in a sense the most important. To close a book of this character with the question, "What of the future?" seems a bit absurd, but it must be done, and seriously at that.

This book has been a parade of the shortcomings of cable traction, but there is no novelty in this, and my purpose has not been to argue for conversion of the remaining lines in San Francisco. All these shortcomings, and doubtless a few others to boot—no one could exhaust them—were well known by 1893, if not by 1888. No one, apparently, argues for perpetuation of the San Francisco cable cars out of a belief that they are the most economic means of providing a transportation service. The necessity of a two-man crew alone assures their unprofitability. They survive simply as a museum piece and as a tourist attraction, and there is little doubt that they serve well as both. As a museum piece, there is no question that the San Francisco cable system delineates the technology far better than placing a San Francisco combination car beside the Seattle Yesler Way car already in the Smithsonian. There is nothing more irrational in the City of San Francisco's running its cable system than in operating its several museums. The system is not in the private sector of the economy, and the San Francisco Municipal Railway is not even a public body required to make a profit, if possible, such as the Chicago Transit Authority; but it is rather a municipal department on the order of departments of streets or sanitation in most cities. Similarly, the cable system is thought, admittedly casually, to be the greatest single tourist attraction in a city in which the tourist trade is of primary importance in the local economy. The cable cars have long since become the symbols of the city; as Herb Caen of the San Francisco *Chronicle* once put it in a Thanksgiving column, without them San Francisco would be only a lumpy Los Angeles.

Rational as it may be for San Francisco to perpetuate the system, cable traction remains as dangerous a form of transportation as it ever was. The cable cars typically turn in about 4 per cent of miles on the Municipal Railway, but 20 per cent of the accident claims. The principal risk to the perpetuation of the cable lines is having a large-scale fatal accident intrinsic to the technology which will create a quick wave of revulsion to the system and sweep it away at the ballot box. Accordingly, from the point of view either of the safety of passengers and motorists or of perpetuation of the system, making the system as safe as possible is of first importance.

Fortunately, since the first edition of this book appeared in 1971, the City of San Francisco has made several alterations in the operating arangements of the cable system in recognition of the hazards of the technology. Notably, the track has been cleared of road traffic on the south ascent of Nob Hill, and parking has been prohibited on Powell Street. The crossings at Bush and Pine remain hazardous, however. Only a single car is allowed to descend the Hyde Street grade at any given time. Standees have been limited.

More important, the City has applied for funds from the Urban Mass Transportation Administration for a comprehensive rebuilding of the entire cable system. As one would expect, metal fatigue is widespread. The rails are so worn that cars frequently run on their flanges, causing derailments and wheel fractures. Malfunction of movable depression devices is particularly dangerous. If the arm does not swing aside as the grip reaches it, the car comes to a stonewall stop. Since the depression devices are out of sight, neither the crew nor the passengers can prepare themselves for the impact. Standees, in particular, are liable to be pitched into the streets. Chin & Hensolt, the engineers in charge of redesign, are considering moving to an offset grip such as the Van Vleck to allow use of stationary depression devices.

Since the demise of the last line in Dunedin, New Zealand, in 1957, the San Francisco lines have been alone in the world in active operation; all other systems live only in the historical record. This, happily, is particularly rich. The SRJ, thanks largely to Fairchild, was an excellent trade journal which followed cable traction closely, at least as long as it was economic. Unfortunately, most street railways destroyed their plans of the cable installations — doubtless with relief — upon conversion. The Smithsonian holds the plans of the West Chicago Street Railroad, deposited by the Chicago Transit Authority. This is an awesome demonstration of what a major cable system really was. As one leafs through the plans, he wonders if it could ever have existed — the hundreds upon hundreds of yokes, the thousands of tons of concrete, the millions of bricks — surely no one ever really built it. The eminent electric railway engineer, George Krambles, pointed out that the mere designing of it would be inconceivable today; no firm could bear the engineering expense of designing the special work a cable system required. The engineering of the nineteenth century was adapted to massive projects of this sort, whereas much of the precision work of the present day would have been beyond it. Exist the system did, and we are fortunate to have the record of it.

The technology of the industry was such as to keep a cable system in the newspapers continually. The local pages of newspapers delineate the day-to-day troubles of cable systems marvelously — unfortunately, somewhat better in the smaller cities than in the large. It was William Phenix's misfortune that his two systems were in medium-sized cities, Grand Rapids and Sioux City, where the comings and goings of local steamboats and the troubles of the street railway, which might have been ignored in Chicago or St. Louis, were the standard items of news pages. Fittingly, Phenix's Grand Rapids installation produced another ideal epitaph for the cable car. In January 1891 one of Phenix's grip cars hit the buggy of H. B. Clark which, as buggies were wont to do, immediately collapsed. A reporter for the Grand Rapids *Eagle* asked Clark if he intended to sue the company, but he responded that he did not. He said, "I can stand it if they can."

For the last time, quite so. But, except in dear San Francisco, nobody could stand it; nobody did.

The cable car is represented in the Pantheon of such things, the railroad hall of the Smithsonian, by this Yesler Way grip car from Seattle. The car, a standard Stockton catalog model, is an ideal choice. The same model was used in Spokane, Tacoma, Los Angeles, and elsewhere. (*Smithsonian Institution*)

The Cable Car in America

PART TWO:

The Individual Cable Lines

American cable traction consisted of 62 firms in 28 cities. In an effort to present an approximately chronological account, but also to provide a unified narrative of each city's individual experience, I have classified the lines by city, listed in the order of the city's first operation. Within each city, lines are presented in the order of their opening dates. The one exception to this classification is New York, which is listed in the order of its first street railway operation, rather than the Brooklyn Bridge Railway's opening. The Union Cable Railway in Kansas City and the Rasmussen installation in Newark are listed on the basis of the one known date of operation of each. Readers who undertake to read all of the corporate histories are advised to deviate from the order in which they are presented here by reading the Philadelphia Traction Company before the North Chicago Street Railroad.

The maps are intended to convey as much information as possible for brevity in the text. With the exception of Sioux City and San Diego, the maps show cables, not track. Track is shown for Sioux City and San Diego, since both companies were simple installations of two cables, interesting mainly for the placement of sidings and turnouts for single-track operation.

On the rope diagrams, an arrow on the cable indicates its direction of travel if the line was lefthand operated, or otherwise divergent from normal practice. Arrows beside the cable indicate major grades, pointing upward. In general, I have endeavored to note all grades over 10 per cent. Where a line had a long, major grade of less than 10 per cent, I have also noted that. For example, the 7th Street line in St. Paul was designed mainly to climb a long grade of about 5 per cent, which is noted on the map; identifying 5 per cent grades in Kansas City would be impractical, since they abound over the entire city.

At intersections the superior cable is shown as solid and the inferior cable as discontinuous. Question marks indicate uncertainty on relative positions. I have used these freely, though at the present writing none remains highly doubtful. The systems in San Francisco and Kansas City were too large and complicated to present on single rope diagrams. Each company's history is accompanied with its own diagram, and maps of the two cities appear on the endpapers.

Cable lengths, unless prefaced by "c.", are actual, as reported in the SRJ, local newspapers or elsewhere. It should be remembered that cables were subject to stretching, as described in Chapter IV, so that the reported figure represents a single observation; at another time the length might be different by as much as 500 feet. Figures preceded by "c." are my own estimates on the basis of the length of the route, with approximately 500 feet additional for the winding machinery.

Speeds are shown if known, except for San Francisco, where a municipal regulation caused all companies to operate just below 8 miles per hour.

A circle indicates a turntable, and a spoked wheel a reduction gear or other device for running an auxiliary cable.

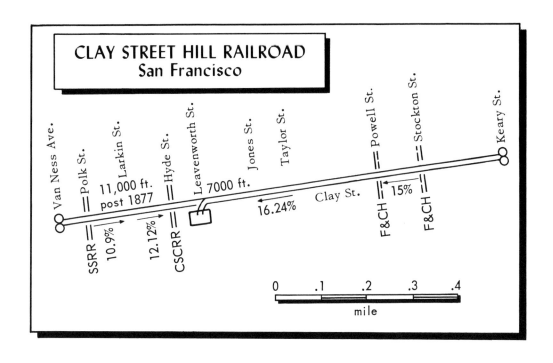

CLAY STREET HILL RAILROAD
San Francisco

Van Ness Ave.

Polk St.

SSRR
10.9%

11,000 ft.
post 1877

Larkin St.

12.12%

Hyde St.

CSCRR

Leavenworth St.

7000 ft.

16.24%

Jones St.

Taylor St.

Clay St.

Powell St.

F&CH

15%

F&CH

Stockton St.

Keary St.

0   .1   .2   .3   .4
mile

Small and unsubstantial by later standards, Hallidie's original Clay Street equipment pioneered the arrangement of a grip car with a single trailer which most companies adopted. *(Smithsonian Institution)*

SAN FRANCISCO

Population in 1890: 298,997

CLAY STREET HILL RAILROAD

Hallidie bottom grip   *Gauge: 3'-6"*

As mentioned in Chapter I, Andrew S. Hallidie conceived of cable street traction in 1869 as a means of climbing the eastern ascent of Nob Hill from the business district below. He first considered laying cable on California Street, but finally determined on building the line on Clay Street. Jointly with Henry L. Davis, James Moffitt and Joseph Britton, he undertook the Clay Street Hill Railroad in May 1873 with $60,000, augmented with $28,000 from property owners along the street and $30,000 from sale of bonds. He designed the line in collaboration with William E. Eppelsheimer and then contracted for construction with William H. Martin and J. Ballard, who built it in six months. On August 2, 1873, actually the day following what was required under his franchise, Hallidie made a trial round trip from Jones Street to Kearny. Apparently out of a desire that a failure be as inconspicuous as possible, he brought Eppelsheimer, his three partners, Superintendent P. H. Campbell and bookkeeper Thomas P. Burns out at 4:00 a.m. and made the trip shortly afterward with all of them as passengers. The trip was successful and an official opening trip was made in the afternoon. The line, after the conduit was completed between Jones and the powerhouse at Leavenworth, was put in revenue service on September 1, 1873.

As might be expected of the first cable line, it was an extremely simple installation. It was double-tracked, 2,791 feet long, terminating at a pair of turntables at Kearny Street. Each turntable was capable of turning 90 degrees — they could not revolve because the cable ran through them — so that a single-ended grip car was turned half on the first and half on the second for the return trip. The first rope was a product of Hallidie's California Wire Works, $\frac{15}{16}$ inch in diameter, which proved to have a life of 64,200 miles over the course of two years and four months. Initially the line operated at 4 miles per hour, later at 6. The original conduit was based on iron yokes, 24" x 18", lined with planks and topped with 30-pound T-rail. J. Bucknall Smith estimated the investment at $85,150. A one-way trip required only 11 minutes.

This small and unpretentious installation was successful enough to engender the investment in cable lines elsewhere in San Francisco and eventually in the nation. In February 1874 it handled 76,500 passengers. Like the later lines in the city, it had a strong predominance of upbound movements, reportedly about 3:1; many who would pay a nickel to avoid a 17 per cent grade up Nob Hill would walk down. As Hallidie and his associates had hoped, the installation developed Nob Hill very well, so that by 1876 the line handled 150,000 passengers per month. In 1877 the company extended the track about 2,000 feet west of the powerhouse to San Francisco's major north-south street, Van Ness Avenue. Previously,

FIG.7

CLAY STREET HILL

VERTICAL SCALE.

HORIZONTAL SCALE.

185

horses had hauled trailers over this distance. This time a more capital-intensive conduit of cast iron yokes and concrete was employed. The line had been equipped with a single turntable at the powerhouse, but at Van Ness Avenue it was given another pair of small turntables. The total length of the line was just under a mile.

As cable lines spread about the city, the Clay Street Hill Railroad became successively less important. The building of the California Street Cable Railroad in 1878 created an alternative route on a more important street with a better physical plant. Smith reported that the Clay Street line operated at five minute intervals in base service and every three minutes in the evening rush hour. The company remained an independent operation until September 8, 1888, when it was sold to the Ferries & Cliff House, which coveted the route as part of its Sacramento-Clay line into the Western Addition beyond Van Ness Avenue. The F&CH built a single track in the devil strip of the Clay Street line from Kearny to Larkin and discontinued the line's own operation on September 9, 1891. A bottle of champagne was broken over the last grip, rather as a token of affection for the pioneer line.

POWERHOUSE EQUIPMENT: Two horizontal engines, 12″ x 24″, Delamater Iron Works, N. Y., about 30HP each; replaced probably in 1877, with two 14″ x 28″ engines.

This view from Van Ness Avenue depicts the Clay Street line after the extension of 1877. The off-center placing of the slot is particularly conspicuous. *(Roy D. Graves)*

SUTTER STREET RAILWAY

Hovey single-jaw side grip   *Gauge: 5'-0"*

San Francisco's second cable installation was the Sutter Street Railway, an established but generally unprofitable horsecar operator traversing the city just south of Nob Hill. In this instance, cable traction was not designed to climb a steep escarpment, but only to run across moderate grades rising to three separate summits.

Henry Casebolt, owner of the line, decided upon conversion to cable in the mid-1870s upon seeing the success of the Clay Street Hill Railroad. Together with Asa Hovey, a foreman in his Casebolt & Van Gulpin machine works, he designed the physical plant. The two men designed a powerhouse at Larkin and Bush north of Sutter, notable for the first tension run of the orthodox sort. The line was opened from Larkin to the intersection of Sutter, Sansome and Market Streets on January 27, 1877. In the following year, the company initiated the first crosstown line in the city, running straight south from the powerhouse on Larkin to Hayes Street. When the Larkin branch was opened late in 1878, the company began to push the main line westward, completing it to Central (Presidio) Avenue in October 1879 and bringing its tracks into the Western Addition beyond Van Ness Avenue. There it terminated in a pair of small turntables in the fashion of the Clay Street road, but in this instance the direction of cars was not reversed. Because the line had only turnouts at the east end and a single-jaw side grip, cars had a permanent east and west end. That is to say, at Central Avenue a grip car was pushed onto the north turntable, turned

90 degrees, pushed onto the second turntable and turned back to its original position. Casebolt and Hovey arranged the line so that gripmen pulled back on the lever eastbound and pushed forward on it westbound on the ground that the grade was predominantly ascending westbound, and that a firm hold was more important downbound.

The company had managed to develop a fairly extensive system, by the standards of the 1870s, with straight routes, but the enterprise was proving successful enough to warrant extension routes that could not possibly be arranged in straight lines. The development of the pull curve in Dunedin, New Zealand, in 1881 caused the company to attempt a major revision of the physical plant including pull curves. In 1883, after the company passed into the hands of Robert Morrow and his associates, the entire operation was consolidated into a new powerhouse built at Sutter and Polk. Previously, the main line from Buchanan to Central had been run from a separate powerhouse, apparently because the cables available before 1880 were incapable of extended distances. The Larkin line was pushed southward to Mission Street in 1883, hurriedly being put across Market Street in advance of the Market Street Railway in hopes of securing the superior rope position. The Market Street line won a legal action for the superior position on the basis of an earlier franchise, but the long crosstown line was superior to all six other cables it crossed. Rerouting the line from the new powerhouse into Larkin via Polk and Post entailed two pull curves, and the

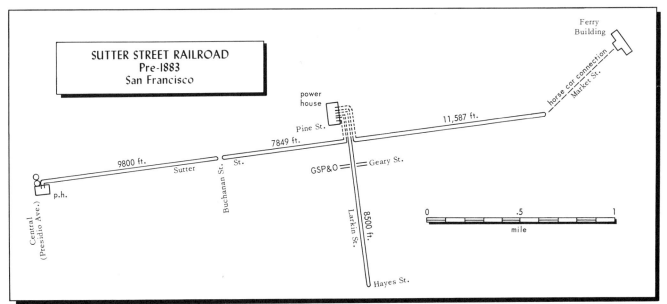

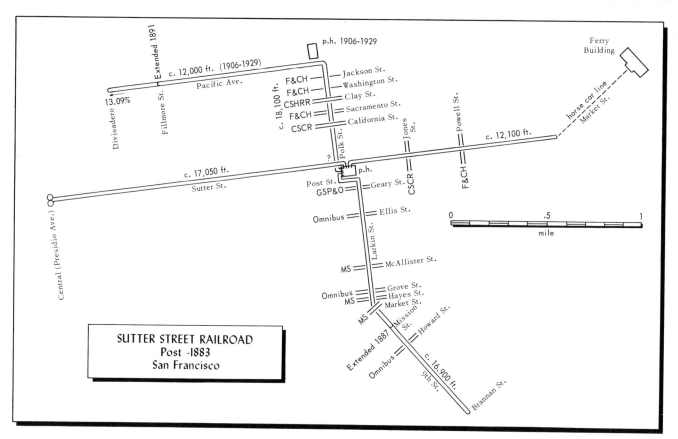

SUTTER STREET RAILROAD
Post -1883
San Francisco

mild curve between Hayes and Market, another. The company planned to extend the crosstown line up Potrero Hill, but stopped with an extension to Brannan Street in 1887. Subsequently the crosstown line was pushed north on Polk to Pacific Avenue and Fillmore Street in 1888 and out Pacific to Divisadero in 1891. The system's track was extensively rebuilt in 1890-91. The completed system had about 6 miles of line, plus a mile of horsecar connection on Market Street from the east end of Sutter to the Ferry Building — a relic the company was never able to convert.

The company survived in relative prosperity until 1902, when it was absorbed into the United Railroads of San Francisco along with the Market Street Cable Railway and two electric lines. This company, to be treated more fully in connection with the Market Street Cable Railway, continued to operate the Sutter Street cable lines until the earthquake of April 18, 1906. The powerhouse was demolished, most of the

rolling stock was burned and the conduit was ruined at several points. Since none of the grades on the line, save the last block on Pacific Avenue, was beyond the traction of an electric car, the company converted the entire system with the exception of Pacific Avenue. It built a new powerhouse at Polk and Pacific and operated the Pacific Avenue segment as an isolated line of limited traffic. This survived, more out of the hostility of residents to overhead wires than because of the short grade at the end, until November 29, 1929, when the Market Street Railway, the successor company, discontinued it.

POWERHOUSES AND EQUIPMENT: Larkin and Bush: Four engines, 12″ x 24″.
Sutter and Central: Two engines, 12″ x 24″.
Sutter and Polk: Two compound engines, 20″ + 36″ x 48″ and 20½″ + 30″ x 48″, 500 HP each.
Polk and Pacific: General Electric Equipment.

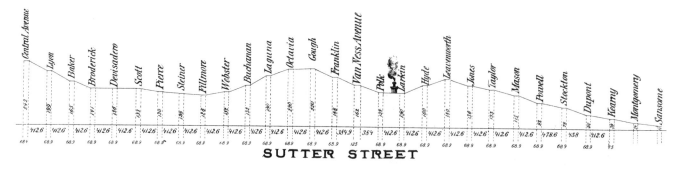

SUTTER STREET

The officers of the Sutter Street line flank Superintendent Johnson Reynolds (front row, center) before the powerhouse. The company was then in the hands of receivers J. B. McGilvery (front, right) and J. A. Fannyhill (second from right, second row). Reorganization changed the company's name from "Railroad" to "Railway" about 1887. Below, a train of the company at Central Avenue. *(Both, Roy D. Graves)*

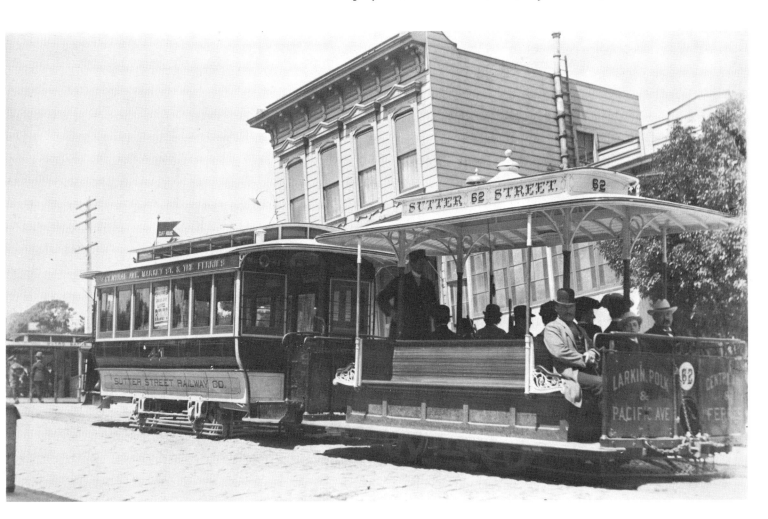

At left are two Sutter Street trains, the upper at Powell Street and the lower at the powerhouse, both in the livery of United Railroads. The earthquake and fire of 1906 reduced the powerhouse to the ruin shown here, and left much of the rolling stock as in the upper right photograph. Nothing of the Sutter Street system was restored but the Pacific Avenue segment, shown below in 1927. (All, Roy D. Graves)

These two early views show the California Street Cable Railroad's ascent of Nob Hill from the east. Both show the company's original equipment. The train above is on the 16 per cent grade approaching Powell Street. *(Roy D. Graves)*

CALIFORNIA STREET CABLE RAILROAD

California Street: Gauge: 3'-6"
Root single-jaw side grip; converted to Eppelsheimer bottom grip, 1957

O'Farrell, Jones and Hyde Streets:
Eppelsheimer bottom grip

California Street, the principal ascent of Nob Hill from the east, was a more promising route than Clay Street, so that upon Hallidie's success, Leland Stanford in 1874 set out to promote the California Street Cable Railroad. In collaboration with several associates in the Central Pacific Railroad, he secured a franchise in 1876, and in the following year entrusted design of the property to Henry Root, who was instructed to produce a high-quality piece of engineering. Stanford was forced to pay Hallidie $30,000 for patent rights.

The line was built beginning July 5, 1877, between Kearny Street at the foot of Nob Hill to Fillmore Street in the Western Addition, about 1.7 miles. The powerhouse, designed by W. W. Hanscom, was put at Larkin Street, with the machinery mainly in a vault under California Street. Initially, the line was operated with 25 grip cars and trailers, built by the Kimball Manufacturing Company and the Central Pacific shops. Service was initiated on April 10, 1878, at a particularly large ceremony, attended by some six thousand people. The route duplicated the Clay Street Hill Railroad on its ascent of Nob Hill, but the western reaches were the first cable service into the Western Addition. Running time was 19 minutes.

In the spring of 1879 the track was pushed west about 0.8 miles from Fillmore to Central (Presidio) Avenue. The extension was cheaply built of wood framing and planks in an effort to finance the project out of earnings. The new trackage was ready for service on May 30, 1879, but the right-of-way proved so unsatisfactory it had to be rebuilt with standard conduit in 1884.

Stanford sold out his interest in the company in 1884 to Antoine Borel, a Swiss-born San Francisco banker, who was to be in financial control of the property for 30 years. In 1889 Borel and President James B. Stetson initiated an expansion of the property entailing a new powerhouse at California and Hyde Streets, an extension of about a half mile east to Market Street in 1890 and finally a new crosstown route on O'Farrell, Jones and Hyde Streets which opened February 9, 1891. This line of about 2.5 miles was intended to provide a direct connection between the Russian Hill area and the shopping district south of Union Square. A shuttle on Jones Street served the Tenderloin district. Howard C. Holmes was in charge of track construction. The new mileage was a useful addition to the city's cable network, but it suffered the obvious disadvantage of running at a right angle to the dominant pattern of cables and being the last line built in the city. As a result, it was inferior to every other cable and, as the "Ballad of the Hyde Street Grip" of Gelette Burgess correctly points out, had 22 rope drops on every round trip. For this reason John C. H. Stut, who was then mechanical engineer of the company, adopted a bottom grip for the new installation. The general rebuilding of the physical plant around 1890 had involved re-equipping it with double-ended combination cars in the sort which became known as the "California type." O'Farrell-Jones-Hyde cars carried an Eppelsheimer grip at the south end, whereas mainline cars carried a Root grip at the west end; in both instances the gripman operated the car from the opposite end with a duplicate lever through a set of extension rods.

FIG. 8

CALIFORNIA STREET

193

In the rebuilding of 1890-91, Cal Cable re-equipped itself with some of the most hand-some cable cars. On the opposite page, car 18 stands at the east terminus of the main line, while car 49 traverses O'Farrell on the O'Farrell-Jones-Hyde line. Car 51, above, the only single-trucker on the system, ran on the Jones Street shuttle. *(Roy D. Graves)*

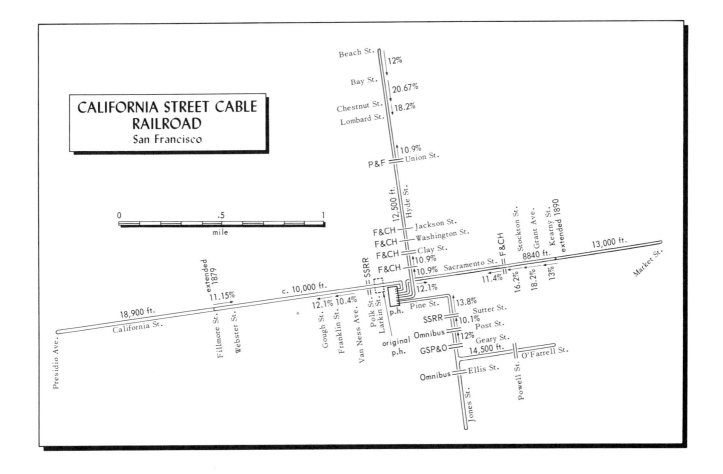

The company was quite successful, rather a blue chip of cable car operators. The main line had a grade of 18.2 per cent on the ascent of Nob Hill from the east, and Hyde Street had one of the worst grades in the industry, 20.67 per cent on the ascent of Russian Hill from the north terminus. Both of these made replacement by electric cars impossible, and thus the three lines of the company survived essentially unchanged into the 1950s. Like the rest of the city's cable operators, the company suffered terrible damage in the earthquake and fire of 1906, enough so that the directors seriously questioned their ability to continue. The Fireman's Fund Insurance Company, with which the company had some common owner-

ship, was so hard hit by the disaster that the company settled for 50 per cent of its claims. The management had the system back in operation by August 1906, but partly because of a labor dispute, full restoration of the physical plant was not finished until July 1908.

The company maintained its independence of the Market Street Railway and of the Municipal Railway, somewhat remarkably, throughout the first half of the century. The Market Street Railway owned a thousand shares of the company's stock from 1907 to 1917, but then liquidated the holding. The city government requested an offer from the company for sale of its properties in 1913, but the directors showed no in-

J. W. Harris, second from left among the four men in the front, below, brought the entire work force of Cal Cable out for a photograph at the Hyde Street powerhouse in 1895. *(Roy D. Graves)*

The Jones Street shuttle was operated with miniature versions of the company's double-enders. Below, O'Farrell-Jones-Hyde car 54 turns the let-go curve from Jones into O'Farrell while the Jones Street shuttle car waits in the background. *(Roy D. Graves)*

J, W. HARRIS.

terest. In anticipation of expiration of the company's franchise in 1929, the city made another enquiry into purchase in 1925, but again the effort came to naught, and the company secured an extension of 25 years. In 1940 President James W. Harris, who had begun working for the company on the extension of 1879, stated with some pride that the firm had paid $600 in dividends over the years on stock of original value of only $60 per share, adhered to a nickel fare through that late date and retired $960,000 in debt incurred to make the expansion of 1889-91.

The forces acting against the transit industry generally began to afflict the company seriously in the late 1940s. Traffic held up fairly well, but costs rose disproportionately. A measure for municipal purchase for $200,000 received a majority of the vote in 1948, but less than the two-thirds required. An unfortunate legal judgment, in which the company was held liable for injuries to a passenger when a truck backed into a car on O'Farrell Street in 1949, caused Lloyd's of London to cancel the company's insurance contract and brought operation to an end on July 31, 1951. The City and County of San Francisco bought the company for a mere $138,000 and restored operation on January 13, 1952. The former Cal Cable lines quickly proved more unprofitable than the Municipal Railway's own cable lines, so that the city sought some arrangement to cut its losses. The city was also eager to convert O'Farrell Street to one-way traffic. As a consequence, the Municipal Railway cut back the California Street line from Presidio Avenue to Van Ness and discontinued the O'Farrell-Jones-Hyde line entirely on May 15, 1954.

The city proposed to discontinue operation out of the Cal Cable powerhouse, reroute the remainder of the California Street line from the Municipal Railway powerhouse at Washington and Mason, and amalgamate the former Washington-Jackson line with the portion of the Hyde line north of Washington. It was necessary to retain the segment of Hyde from California to Washington to provide access for the California Street cars to the Mason Street powerhouse. In addition, it was necessary to convert California Street to the Eppelsheimer bottom grip for conformity with the rest of the system. A measure for this conversion was passed on the 1954 ballot, defeating a countermeasure for retention of the full Cal Cable network and the Washington-Jackson line. The conversion required complete rebuilding of the California Street conduit with a centered slot and construction of a new turntable at Hyde and Beach for the single-ended Powell Street cars. The California Street line was closed from December 29, 1956 to December 27, 1957, and the new Powell-Hyde line opened on April 7, 1957. Since the foot of Hyde has been developed as a tourist area, the new line has proved successful; the view descending the Hyde Street grade is one of the most spectacular in San Francisco. The truncated California line, however, had most of its population amputated, and has had respectable traffic densities only in rush hours. Service has usually been provided by three to seven cars on infrequent headway, often with very small loads. The characteristic California-type cars are currently fitted with an Eppelsheimer grip at each end. Given the heavy labor expense of two-man crews and the cost of moving the lightly-utilized cable, the line is the most unprofitable of the Municipal Railway. In addition, the line was designed with a lateral deflection up Hyde Street, almost back to the powerhouse, which gives it a high degree of curvature, with a large amount of friction. Withal, the line's future appears reasonably secure, since any further changes in the cable network would require action by the electorate on the ballot, and it is most unlikely that a majority would vote for the abandonment.

POWERHOUSES AND EQUIPMENT: California and Larkin Streets: Vertical marine type engine, two cylinders (?) 22″ x 36″. California and Hyde Streets: Triple expansion condensing engine, 14″ + 20″ + 30″ x 54″, 500 HP.

The Municipal Railway painted car 8, above, in the green and white livery of the Powell Street line after acquiring Cal Cable, but shortly decided to retain the company's traditional deep red. At left, a car in Cal Cable's livery but the Muni's lettering descends past Grant Avenue. (*Lawrence Treiman; San Francisco Convention & Visitors Bureau*)

Throughout the Geary Street line's history it terminated at Lotta's Fountain, a San Francisco landmark in the triangle of Geary, Kearny and Market Streets. Above is an early view. Below, a train crosses Dupont Street, currently Grant Avenue, shortly before the rebuilding of 1892. The cable track turning into Dupont is part of a wye for turning combination cars. (*Roy D. Graves*)

GEARY STREET PARK & OCEAN RAILROAD

Eppelsheimer bottom grip:
converted to Root single-jaw
side grip, 1892

Gauge: 5'-0",
converted to
4'-8½", 1892

Geary Street, San Francisco's principal east-west thoroughfare through the central business district, shared the characteristic of Sutter Street, two blocks to the north, of having no serious gradients, but of undulating for its entire length. The project of a cable line on the street was conceived by Charles F. Crocker, son of Charles Crocker, one of the four founders of the Central Pacific Railroad, who incorporated the Geary Street Park & Ocean Railroad on November 8, 1878. After providing service with horsecars from August 23, 1879, the company opened as a cable operation on February 16, 1880. Initially, the line ran from Kearny to the powerhouse at Buchanan Street and to Central (Presidio) Avenue, about 2.1 miles.

The property was designed by William E. Eppelsheimer, who presumably developed his successful bottom grip for ease of taking and dropping the rope at the powerhouse and at Larkin Street, where the company was inferior to the Sutter Street Railway. In other respects, the physical plant was an inferior one. The yokes were mainly of bolted iron construction, with wood-lined conduit and centerbearing tram rail on wooden stringers. Strangely, the slot rails were ordinary T-rail, inverted to put flat faces upward. No grade was worse than 9.2 per cent between Baker and Lyon Streets, and the conduit required no depression pulleys. Alone among the San Francisco lines the company shared track with horsecar lines; the cars were equipped with wheels with centered flanges and treads on either side. Normally, the flanges ran on the inside flangeways of the rail. At junctions, the track was arranged to send the cable cars to the outside flangeways and the horsecars, which had wheels of the usual sort, to the inside. In this fashion horse-

cars could be directed on or off Geary Street without throwing of switches.

Like most of the San Francisco cable lines, the company was a success from the outset. In 1887 the Market Street Railway bought control of the company, but operated it separately from its own lines. In 1892 the Market Street management decided to extend the line 1.9 miles to Golden Gate Park at 5th Avenue and Fulton Street and simultaneously to adapt it to Market Street technology so as to run cars directly from the Ferry Building out Geary Street. The change required converting the track to 4'-8½" and replacing the Eppelsheimer with the Market Street's Root grip. The line was out of service for the entire summer of 1892 while the changes were made. On its reopening, the line was operated with its former equipment plus ten combination cars of the Market Street type, but the plan of running cars on Market Street to the Ferry Building was never implemented. Cars continued to terminate at a turntable at Lotta's Fountain at Geary, Kearny and Market, but whereas the single-truck grip cars with bottom grips had been turned only 30 degrees from the eastbound to the westbound track without reversing ends, the equipment was now entirely reversed.

The Geary Street line was still being operated in this fashion in 1906. The physical plant suffered less destruction than any other from the disaster and was still operable after the earthquake; the ensuing fire caused the company to suspend operations, however. Accordingly, the company was able to continue operations as before after a short period.

The city government had shown especial interest in acquiring this line as the nucleus of a municipal street railway system, using the existing conduits for

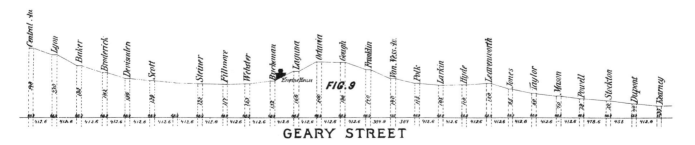

FIG. 9

GEARY STREET

underground electrical pickup. A bond issue for $700,000, the estimated cost of the conversion, had been put on the ballot in 1902, but had been defeated, and again was rejected in 1903. In that year the company's charter expired, but it was allowed to continue operation for a fee of 5 per cent of its receipts. The Board of Supervisors in 1905 appropriated $325,000 toward acquiring and converting the property; negotiation toward this end was progressing at the time of the earthquake. The unexpended funds were used in clearing the damage after the disaster. The courts required that acquisition be submitted to the electorate, and in 1909 two bond issues, one for $1.9 million for a municipal railway from Kearny to

the ocean and the other for $120,000 for an extension to the Ferry Building, were placed on the ballot and approved. Work on erecting the overhead began in June 1911, and on May 5, 1912, the Geary Street cable line was closed for reconstruction. Electric service began on December 28, 1912, and was extended to the Ferry Building in the following year on the route of the Sutter Street line's horsecar, which was finally discontinued on June 3, 1913. The Geary Street line became the main route straight west of the San Francisco Municipal Railway.

POWERHOUSE EQUIPMENT: Two horizontal engines, 18″ x 48″.

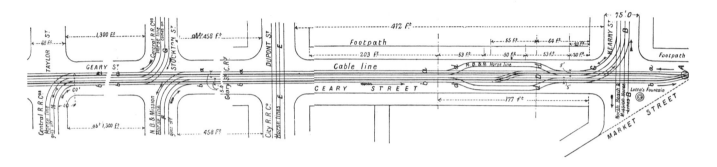

J. Bucknall Smith's map of the east terminal of the Geary Street line illustrates the extensive joint use of track with horsecar lines characteristic of the company.

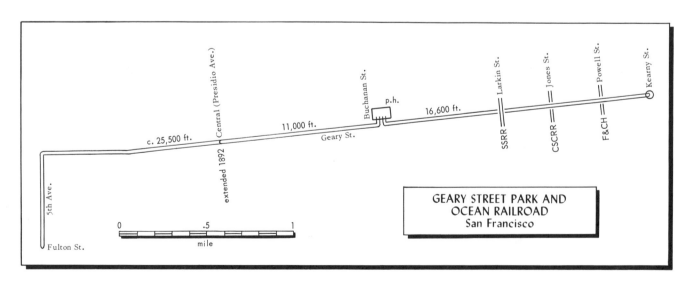

One of the former Market Street combination cars put in service on Geary Street after the reconstruction of 1892 is turned at Lotta's Fountain. If the plan to bring Geary Street cars to the Ferry Building had been implemented, a track connection would have been made to Market Street Cable Railway tracks in the foreground. *(Roy D. Graves)*

Above, a Presidio & Ferries train descends Russian Hill near Polk Street. Below, cable operations terminated at Montgomery and Washington Streets, where passengers proceeded to the Ferry Building by the horsecar shown at lower right. *(Roy D. Graves)*

PRESIDIO & FERRIES RAILROAD

Hallidie bottom grip;   *Gauge: 5'-0"*
converted to Stut bottom grip, 1892

The cable installations on Clay and California Streets had been designed to climb Nob Hill, and the Sutter and Geary Street lines had been built to penetrate the Western Addition. None of the mileage built in the 1870s ascended Russian Hill, immediately to the north of Nob Hill. For this purpose some of the same financial interests who had promoted the Clay Street Hill Railroad conceived a line on Union Street, traversing Russian Hill from east to west. The line was opened on October 23, 1880.

Mechanically, the installation was somewhat reactionary; the physical plant was a broad-gauge adaptation of Hallidie's Clay Street technology, with a strengthened version of his original bottom grip. The plant's advance in cable technology was the first let-go curve ever attempted, installed at Montgomery (Columbus) and Union to move cars onto a diagonal street for approach to the central business district. The line never penetrated closer than the present intersection of Columbus and Montgomery; it reached the Ferry Building by a horsecar line running east on Washington and west on Jackson. Initially the west terminus of the cable was at Steiner, with a steam dummy connection into the Presidio. The powerhouse was put almost equidistant between the termini of the 2.1 mile cable portion of the triple-technology system, at a point near Leavenworth Street which coincided almost perfectly with the highest point on the line. Thus, this was the most extreme example of a company which chose the option of a powerhouse at the highest point with a single cable in each direction, thereby minimizing strain on the terminal sheaves and maximizing the inaccessibility of the

powerhouse for cable replacement and fuel delivery. The original physical plant represented an investment of $190,000.

In the early nineties the company was sold to George A. Newhall and his associates, who set out to extend and improve the physical plant. In particular, cable track was to be extended about a mile from Steiner to the Presidio, via Baker and Lombard Streets on a route different from the steam dummy connection, which had taken advantage of easier grades on Greenwich Street. The extension was to include a curve at Union and Baker which had to be pulled eastbound, being on a grade of 10 per cent. John C. H. Stut was engaged to design the extension and

J. C. H. STUT.

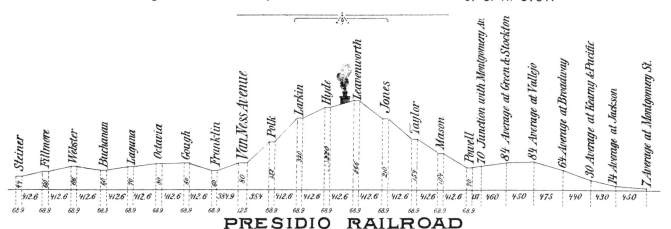

PRESIDIO RAILROAD

205

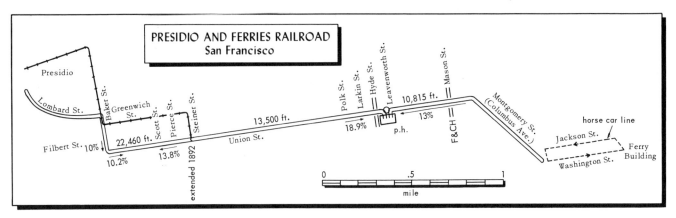

PRESIDIO AND FERRIES RAILROAD
San Francisco

to modify the rest of the physical plant to allow operation on a pull curve. Stut felt the Hallidie grip, which had a very narrow shank, was impossible to adapt to a pull curve, but for reasons of economy, he did not want to change either Hallidie's off-center slot or the placing of the cable far north of the slot. He dealt with this difficult problem by designing an off-center bottom grip with only the inner jaw mobile, an arrangement never attempted elsewhere. The powerhouse was converted from Hallidie's clip-faced driving equipment to orthodox multiple-winding drivers and idlers. The line was closed for about two weeks in 1892 for the change. Like the Sutter Street Railroad, the company was never able to convert its horse-car line to the Ferry Building to cable.

The company was successful, both technologically and financially. It paid dividends regularly and in 1906 was reported to have 63 cars. The devastation of the physical plant from the earthquake of April 18, 1906, was possibly the most complete of any of the San Francisco cable lines. The management decided against any effort to rebuild the cable plant and instead substituted an electric line. This it continued in independent operation until 1913, when it was sold to the newly established Municipal Railway.

POWERHOUSE EQUIPMENT: One cross-compound Corliss engine, 18″ + 24″ x 36″, built by Hinckley, Spiers & Hayes, San Francisco, 300 HP.

With a powerhouse in this condition, the decision not to restore cable operations was not difficult. (Roy D. Graves)

MARKET STREET CABLE RAILWAY

Root single-jaw side grip   *Gauge: 4'-8½"*

Like the Chicago City Railway, the Market Street Cable Railway was designed to serve its city's major shopping street and radiate into the residential area. It was by far San Francisco's largest cable railway, approximately tied with the Metropolitan of Kansas City as fourth largest in the industry in mileage. From the outset, the company was a promotion of Charles Crocker, Henry E. Huntington and others identified with the Southern Pacific Company; indeed, the cable operation was popularly known as the Southern Pacific line.

Henry Root designed the physical plant in the early 1880s in the expectation of producing a higher-capacity installation than any previously attempted. The city's geographical pattern lent itself to a radial pattern fanning out from Market Street into tributary area untouched by the previous companies. Root developed the combination car for this installation. The cars were double-truck, 34 feet long, with capacities of 130 passengers. In 1893 the company was reported to have had 153 built in the Southern Pacific's Sacramento shops, 25 built by Carter Brothers, Newark, and 40 converted in the company's own shops from Stephenson horsecars of the 1870s.

The company's first cable operation, replacing a horsecar line of 16 years, ran from the Ferry Building down Market and out Valencia Street through the Mission District to Mission Street. It opened on August 22, 1883, and later in the same year the company began service on McAllister and Haight Streets. Both of the branches reached Golden Gate Park, the city's major recreational area. The company opened a third line to the Park along Hayes Street on May 26, 1886. The company's fifth and last line was run from the central powerhouse at Market, Haight and Valencia out Market and Castro Streets in 1887 to climb Castro Hill with the only major gradients on the system. The only subsequent additions to the system were two short extensions of the McAllister line, from Stanyan

to a turntable between 7th and 8th Avenues in 1892, and then to another in the vicinity of 12th Avenue in 1902 to serve an amusement facility called the Chutes.

The company had one of the highest traffic densities of any street railway; it regularly ran cars at 40 second intervals from the Ferry Building, with headway as low as 15 seconds in rush hours. The whole installation was very much the pride and joy of the patent trust. Pacific Cable's catalog dwelt longest on its physical plant, and the trust endeavored to use the installation as the prototype for projected railways in Dallas and elsewhere. The branch lines had been arranged to run virtually straight from Market, with rope drops at the junctions. Only in the vicinity of the principal powerhouse and at Market and Castro was there serious curvature.

The company's main powerhouse was particularly considered a model of its kind. Located at the intersection of the Market-Valencia main line with the Haight Street branch, it issued four cables, plus a short half-speed auxiliary to draw northbound cars around the long pull curve from Valencia into Market. The auxiliary was run without tension devices off a 6-foot sheave on the Market Street driver. The powerhouse was 250 feet by 85 feet, with a chimney 151 feet high and 16 feet square at the base. The building had 6 Babcock & Wilcox boilers, which burned $120 in coal per day.

The Market Street rope was nearly 24,000 feet, which by San Francisco standards was a long cable. Utilization was so intensive that the company used a 1⅜ inch Roebling rope, which it removed at six-month intervals to replace on Valencia for another eight to ten months' use.

The other widely praised feature of the physical plant was the switch at Market and Hayes, which cost some $15,000. The company managed to bring the Hayes cable close enough to Market at a difficult angle to allow cars to pass over the rope drop

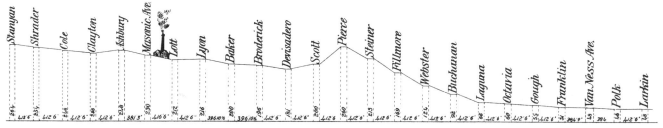

HAYES STREET

208

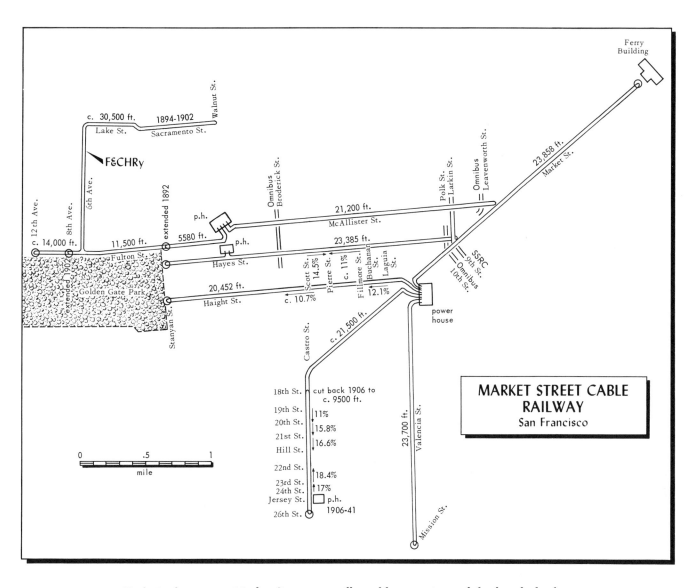

Walnut St.

c. 30,500 ft. 1894-1902

Lake St. Sacramento St.

6th Ave.

F&CHRy

8th Ave.

extended 1892

c. 12th Ave.

c. 14,000 ft.

11,500 ft.

5580 ft.

p.h.

Omnibus Broderick St.

Polk St.

Larkin St.

Omnibus Leavenworth St.

Ferry Building

23,858 ft.

Market St.

21,200 ft.

McAllister St.

extended 1902

Fulton St.

Golden Gate Park

Hayes St.

p.h.

23,385 ft.

Scott St. 14.5%

Pierre St.

c. 11%

Fillmore St.

Buchanan St.

Laguia St.

SSRC

9th St.

Omnibus

10th St.

Stanyan St.

20,452 ft.

Haight St.

c. 10.7%

12.1%

power house

Castro St.

c. 21,500 ft.

18th St.   cut back 1906 to
           c. 9500 ft.

19th St.

20th St.   11%

21st St.   15.8%

Hill St.   16.6%

22nd St.

23rd St.   18.4%

24th St.   17%

Jersey St. p.h.

26th St.   1906-41

Valencia St.

23,700 ft.

Mission St.

0   .5   1
mile

**MARKET STREET CABLE
RAILWAY**
San Francisco

Early in the century Market Street was still a cable operation, at left, though the former Omnibus cable line on Post Street had been electrified. *(George Krambles)* Below, a car passes 21st and Valencia en route to the Ferry Building. *(Roy D. Graves)*

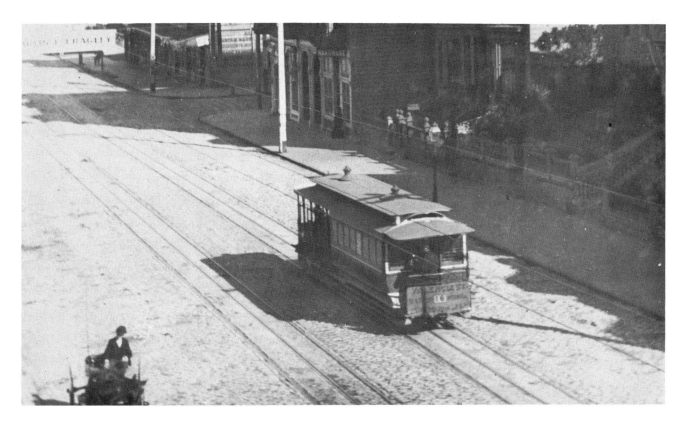

unaided. The company pioneered the use of double-track powered turntables, run off the cable by clutches on the terminal sheaves.

In addition to the five cable lines, the company had one horsecar line on 5th Street from Market to the Southern Pacific station at Townsend, served customarily by a single bob-tail car.

In 1893 the Southern Pacific arranged a merger of the Market Street Cable Railway, the Omnibus Railroad & Cable Company, the Ferries & Cliff House Railway and two horsecar operators into the Market Street Railway. In 1902 this company was merged with the Sutter Street Railway and two electric lines into the United Railroads of San Francisco. By 1906 euthanasia had been committed on the Omnibus, but the United Railroads was operating the former Market Street, F&CH, and Sutter Street lines. The destruction from the earthquake and fire of April 18 was so pervasive that the management was confronted with comprehensive reconstruction of the cable lines or conversion. It sensibly restored only the portions with extreme gradients: the major lines of the former Ferries & Cliff House, the Pacific Avenue extension of the Sutter Street Railway and the Castro Street line of the former Market Street Cable Railway from 18th to 26th Street. This segment climbed and descended Castro Hill with grades ranging from 11 to 18.42 per cent. The reconstruction was a cheap and simple one. Several combination cars were rebuilt as double-ended equipment of the California type, carrying Root grips at the 18th Street end. The turntable at 26th Street was retained, but cars were turned only about 15 degrees between the outbound and inbound tracks, without reversing ends. A remote and inconspicuous part of the city's transportation system, this line served the Castro Hill area unobtrusively without becoming a tourist attraction in the fashion of the company's Powell Street lines.

The United Railroads had inherited debts of $2 million from the Omnibus and $1.7 million from the Ferries & Cliff House. The coincidence of a heavy incidence of debt maturities in 1918 with the worst year the street railway industry had suffered in its history drove the company bankrupt. It was reorganized in 1921 as the second Market Street Railway — really the third use of the Market Street name. The Market Street Railway, though it gave up the Pacific Avenue cable line in 1929, continued the Castro Street segment until the development of more powerful buses, which swept away the Seattle-Tacoma mileage in the late 1930s. Regular operation required only three cars on weekdays and two on Sundays. The arrival of diesel buses allowed discontinuance of the Castro Street remnant on April 6, 1941, ending the last 0.9 mile of what had once been the 13.3-mile Market Street Cable Railway. Only the former Ferries & Cliff House cable lines on Powell Street survived until the Market Street Railway's absorption into the Municipal Railway in 1944.

POWERHOUSES: Market, Haight and Valencia Streets: EQUIPMENT: Two pairs of cross-compound non-condensing O'Neill-type engines, 24″ + 34″ x 48″, 800 HP per pair.

Hayes Street: Two Corliss engines, 20″ x 48″.
McAllister Street: Two high-pressure O'Neill engines, 18″ x 48″.

Castro and Jersey Streets: General Electric equipment.

As far as is known, the big 130-passenger combination cars of the Market Street Cable Railway had the largest capacities of any cable streetcars. Below, two are turned on one of the company's characteristic double-track, powered turntables at the Ferry Building. At lower left, a car stands on the turntable at 12th and Fulton, westernmost point of the San Francisco cable system. *(Roy D. Graves)*

The photographer came out to shoot the Odd Fellows' Band welcoming some national officers to The City, but he incidentally illustrated the Market Street Cable Railway's terminal arrangements at the old Ferry Building. Note the open version of the company's combination cars at left, below.

At upper right is the company's transitional terminal before the present Ferry Building was built. The car starting out is one of the former Omnibus combination cars, converted to standard gauge. At lower right is the terminal arrangement in front of the present Ferry Building during the last years of cable operation. The track at far right was used for loading the company's railway post office. An ex-Omnibus car in the livery of United Railroads loads for McAllister Street on the turntable. (All, Roy D. Graves)

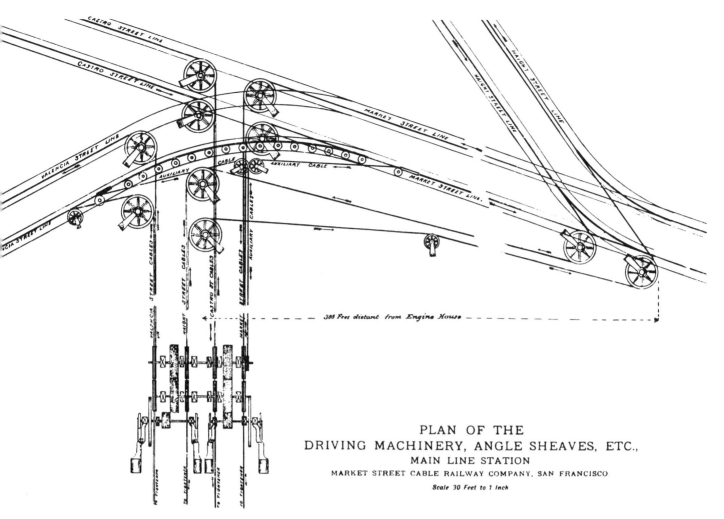

PLAN OF THE
DRIVING MACHINERY, ANGLE SHEAVES, ETC.,
MAIN LINE STATION
MARKET STREET CABLE RAILWAY COMPANY, SAN FRANCISCO
Scale 30 Feet to 1 Inch

The Market Street Cable Railway connected for Cliff House via its Haight Street line and the Park & Ocean Railroad, the steam dummy line shown at upper left. The P&O was built in 1883, and became part of the Market Street Railway in 1894. Steam operation ceased in 1900.

The only portion of the Market Street Cable Railway to survive 1906 as a cable operation was the line over Castro Hill. Below, two of the combination cars, converted to "California" configuration, are shown at the termini. At lower left, a car goes onto the turntable, which had to be extended for double-enders, at 26th Street. Below, car 3 of United Railroads arrives at the switch at 18th Street. (All, Roy D. Graves)

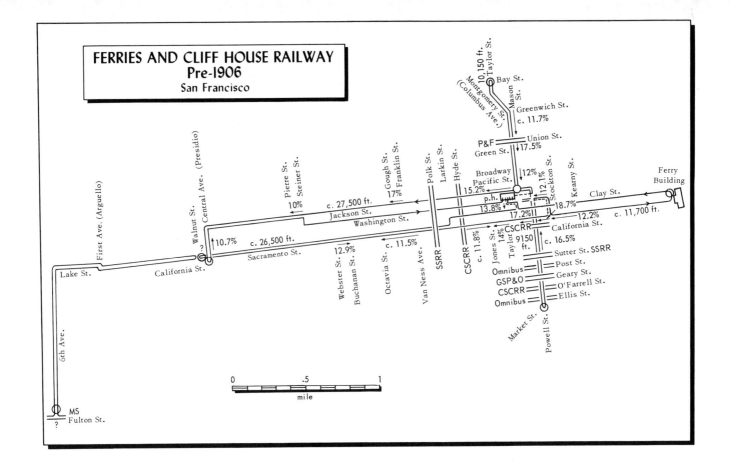

FERRIES AND CLIFF HOUSE RAILWAY
Pre-1906
San Francisco

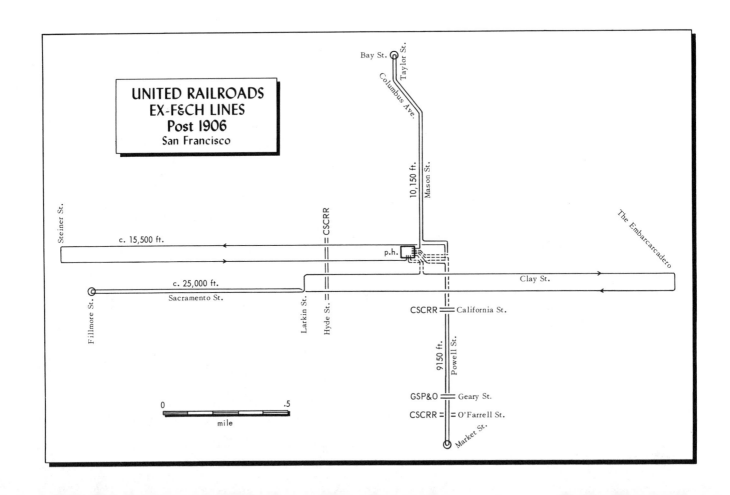

UNITED RAILROADS
EX-F&CH LINES
Post 1906
San Francisco

This company was the amalgamation of two projects of the mid-1880s, one a line across Nob Hill from the central business district on the south to Bay and Taylor near Fisherman's Wharf on the north, and the other to connect the Ferry Building on the east with the Cliff House recreational area on the Pacific by a mixture of cable traction and a steam dummy line. The north-south line, the Powell Street Railway, was projected by W. J. Adams and associates, and the east-west line, the Park & Cliff House Railway, by Gustav Sutro, presumably with the financial backing of Adolph Sutro, the principal promoter of the Cliff House area. Before either project was far advanced, the Sutros sold out to Adams, who merged the two companies to form the Ferries & Cliff House Railway. Though the corporate title described the east-west line, Adams, as might be expected, preferred to stress his entry into the central area south of Nob Hill by painting his cars with "Powell Street Railway."

The effort to run these two dissimilar lines out of a single powerhouse produced the most complicated system, with the possible exception of the Denver City Cable Railway, ever to run from a single station. The design was entrusted to Howard C. Holmes, who had a background in steam railroading, but had previously designed the powerhouse for the Oakland Cable Railway. When Holmes undertook the project most of the city's east-west mileage was built, so that a Powell Street car was expected to drop rope at 14 points, including a let-go curve at Mason and Jackson; accordingly, Holmes had little alternative to a bottom grip. Holmes used wrought iron yokes and a brick conduit. The powerhouse (the present station of the Municipal Railway at Mason, Washington and Jackson Streets) was so constricted in space relative to the extensive demands on it that Holmes adopted the diagonal placing of tension runs feeding cables out to the southeast still in effect. The cables fed one block east on Washington, whence the cables north and west went around the block east of the powerhouse — "around the horn" in the jargon of employees.

The initial system of the F&CH consisted of the present Powell and Mason line from a turntable at Powell and Market to another at Bay and Taylor, and a line west from the powerhouse on Washington and Jackson Streets to a turntable at Central (Presidio) and California. Holmes undertook construction in December 1886 and hoped to have the system operable

by January 1, 1888, but the complication was so extreme that he could not do so. The Powell Street cable was tested on March 27, 1888, and put in revenue service the following day. The entire Powell Street system, including the Mason Street line and the Washington-Jackson route, was in service by April 5, 1888.

The company next undertook the approach to the Ferry Building which had been part of the plan from the outset. The promoters purchased the Clay Street Hill Railroad in 1888 for this purpose, setting aside an earlier plan to build east via Washington and Jackson, streets already occupied by the horsecar line of the Presidio & Ferries. After considering simply extending the Clay Street line east and west, the company decided to build east on Sacramento and west on Clay, with a turntable at the Ferry Building. The line ran west on Clay to Larkin, but thence to Walnut Street in both directions on Sacramento. The Clay Street line was closed in 1891, and its devil strip used for the new single track on Clay. Holmes built the entire 3.4 miles of route of the new line in only 70 days in 1892, including six cable crossings and some extremely complicated trackwork in approaches to the powerhouse. The east cable issued out Washington to Sacramento via Stockton and returned to Mason. The west cable issued blind southbound on Mason and returned blind on Stockton. This arrangement, apart from allowing Clay-Sacramento cars to reach the line from the powerhouse, permitted a route, run

HOWARD C. HOLMES.

The Ferries & Cliff House made its connection to the Cliff House by means of the narrow gauge steam dummy shown above. The line ran out California Street from the company's turntable at Central Avenue, then around Land's End, where the train was photographed, to Cliff House station. The dummy ran from March 29, 1888 until shortly before the 1906 earthquake, when it was replaced by the number 1 car line. Below is the pull curve at Jackson and Central. Note how little developed was western San Francisco at the time. Note also the local custom of lettering cars with any major point that could be reached, however tortuously, by connections. The car shown did not serve directly the Ferries, Cliff House, the Park, or North Beach. At left are three views at the foot of the Powell Street grade in the early years. (*All, Roy D. Graves*)

The Telegraph Hill Railroad, though a funicular, was operated with combination cars of the San Francisco type. The line was built in 1884 by Frederick O. Layman to serve a German castle which he operated at the summit. The funicular was closed and dismantled early in 1887 after a fatal accident and a disappointing traffic volume. (*Roy D. Graves*)

in daylight hours only, from the Ferry Building out Washington and Jackson via Mason outbound and Stockton inbound. Holmes, after creating this model of complication resigned in September 1892 to become chief engineer for the Board of State Harbor Commissioners.

The company, which had incurred a debt of $1.7 million in building the system, was probably not viable as a separate entity. The management on October 13, 1893, merged the firm into the Southern Pacific's Market Street Railway. The merger facilitated the one extension made in the former F&CH system. The announcement of the Midwinter Fair of 1894 in the fall of 1893 caused the Market Street management to decide to extend the Sacramento Street line to Golden Gate Park, site of the Fair, via Lake Street and 6th Avenue. The extension of 1.9 miles was too long and too remote to run from the Mason-and-Washington powerhouse. Accordingly, the company arranged to operate the extension from the McAllister Street powerhouse of the Market Street Railway, reportedly by a long lateral deflection. The resulting

cable of about 30,500 feet with a high degree of curvature and a clutch-operated turntable at 8th and Fulton must have been barely workable. One old employee, who is no longer living, reported on the basis of his recollection that the extension was an auxiliary run off a geared device at 6th and Fulton, but there is no evidence of this in accounts of the line's opening. Regular service on the extension began on February 15, 1894, bringing the former F&CH's mileage to the equivalent of 9.4 miles of double track.

In 1902, along with the rest of the Market Street Railway lines, the F&CH mileage came into the hands of the United Railroads. Also in 1902 the Sacramento line was cut back to Walnut; Turk-Eddy electric cars replaced cable on the route to the Park. The disaster of 1906 demolished the powerhouse and burned much of the equipment, though some of the road's characteristic single-end combination cars escaped through being in the barn at Sacramento and Walnut, which was outside the area of worst destruction. All three lines of the former F&CH had grades beyond the ability of electric cars to climb, and all three were restored in whole or in part. The Powell-Mason line was restored fully, but Washington-Jackson was cut back to Steiner, and Clay-Sacramento to Fillmore Street. Simultaneously, the latter was revised to run eastbound on Clay and westbound on Sacramento, apparently because the management wanted to avoid a walk uphill of a block from Clay Street for patrons going from the Ferry Building to the Fairmont Hotel, which was being completed after being gutted by the fire during its construction. The change also eliminated operation against the current of traffic at the east terminus. The turntable at the Ferry Building was discontinued, and the line was arranged to run from a single cable.

The former F&CH lines survived the United Railroads' bankruptcy of 1918 and reorganization of 1921 into the Market Street Railway. The Sacramento Street line lost much of its traffic when the Eastbay commutation trains were brought into San Francisco and the commuter ferries discontinued. This consideration, plus the introduction of more powerful buses, caused the Market Street Railway to replace the line on February 15, 1942.

The Powell-Mason and Washington-Jackson lines passed into the hands of the Municipal Railway with the rest of the Market Street Railway in 1944. The two lines were by now major tourist attractions and objects of sentimental affection by the population, but there was widespread pessimism concerning their survival. Mayor Roger Lapham, a steamship owner who had been elected on a platform of businesslike gov-

About all that could be said for the Mason-Washington powerhouse after the 1906 disaster was that the remains were identifiable. It was rebuilt into the familiar structure still at the heart of the San Francisco system. A unique feature of the Ferries & Cliff House was the turntable at Mason and Jackson. In order to bring cars north on Mason and then west on Jackson, which is to say from right to left in the photograph below, it was necessary to have a turntable to turn them 90 degrees. Cars from Powell Street going out Jackson ran straight across the turntable. (*Roy D. Graves*)

In 1941 the Market Street Railway installed the present turntable at Bay and Taylor, denuding the conduit in the foreground in the photograph at left. Below, in the same year one of the double-enders of the Sacramento Street line descends Clay Street across Grant Avenue. *(Roy D. Graves)*

These two views show the Sacramento-Clay line's terminal arrangements at the Ferry Building before and after the holocaust of 1906. Before the fire, cars descended Sacramento Street, turned about 90 degrees on the turntable, above, and headed west on Clay directly toward the camera. Afterward, cars simply went down Clay and looped back on Sacramento, as shown below. In the photograph of 1941, the conductor is raising the rope with a cable-lifter in preparation for departure. (*Roy D. Graves*)

A Washington-Jackson car descends Washington toward the powerhouse in the United Railroads era. The photograph is a good demonstration how timeless is the operation. *(Roy D. Graves)*

ernment, announced in January 1947 his intention to get rid of the entire remaining cable mileage, both of the Municipal Railway and the California Street Cable Railroad. A Citizens' Committee to Save the Cable Cars, founded and led by Frieda Klussmann, prevented the conversion throughout the year — even though dual-engine Fageol Twin Coaches were already on order as replacements — and secured a charter amendment on the ballot of November 1947 which entailed retention of the cables incidental to a bond issue of $20 million for rehabilitation of the Municipal Railway. The bond issue carried by 170,000 to 50,000, and Lapham, who did not seek re-election, was replaced by Elmer E. Robinson, who favored retention of the cable lines.

Thereafter, political support for preservation of the cable lines was carried on continually, but the cars, mainly because of their two-man crews, continued to be a financial drain on the Municipal Railway. The Western Pacific, which considered the cable cars the city's greatest single tourist attraction, sent car 524 to the Chicago Railroad Fair of 1948–49, where it carried 416,000 passengers and generated interest in the cable system among many who had never seen the Bay Area. Mrs. Klussmann and her committee continued to advocate retention of the city's entire network of five lines. The Municipal Railway operated the California Street Cable Railroad beginning January 13, 1952, and found the newly acquired mileage more uneconomic than its own. The city, seeking a compromise between retention of the basic system and cutting its deficits, conceived the idea of cutting back the California Street line and the Washington-Jackson line, getting rid of the O'Farrell-Jones-Hyde line, except for the portion from Washington to the north terminus, which was to be joined to the retained trackage of the Washington-Jackson route. Powell-Mason, which bore most of the tourist traffic, was unaffected. Though opposed by the Citizens' Committee to Save the Cable Cars, this measure passed at the election of June 8, 1954, by a majority of only 10,000. Efforts to undo the decision on the November ballot failed.

The last Washington-Jackson car ran on September 1, 1956, and the new Powell-Hyde line was put into service on April 7, 1957. Construction of a turntable at the foot of Hyde was the main source of delay. The changes reduced the city's cable mileage from 8.7 to 4.7, all operated out of the old F&CH powerhouse. The winding machinery was replaced in April 1965, and in 1967 the city began an effort to make the powerhouse a tourist attraction, with observation galleries and restoration of a Victorian atmosphere. The system, including the California Street line, carries about 10 million passengers per year at an average deficit of $920,000. Traffic is currently so heavy as to require additional equipment,

and an extension from Bay and Taylor to Fisherman's Wharf is projected. The cable system has been declared a National Historical Landmark and, as is well known, is one of the principal tourist attractions of the country.

POWERHOUSE EQUIPMENT: Four Corliss engines, two vertical and two horizontal, 22″ x 48″, variously reported between 450 and 600 HP each. Currently, one 750 HP General Electric and one 700 HP Fairbanks-Morse three-phase motor.

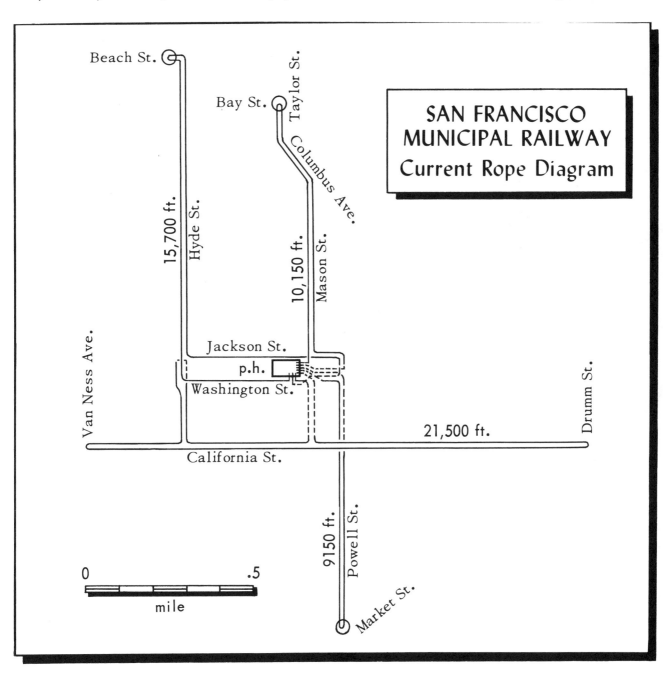

Powell Street cars mix with recent automobiles in the present-day view at the left. Below, a Hyde Street car drops the rope at the power-house. *(Both, San Francisco Convention and Visitors Bureau)* At right, the interior of a Powell Street car, as experienced by millions of visitors to the City over the years. *(Roy D. Graves)*

Two of the Omnibus' combination cars ride the turntable at 26th and Howard Streets. In the grand tradition of San Francisco street railways, the cars carry "Golden Gate Park" on the rear, though the Howard Street line ran away from the Park at a 90-degree angle. *(Roy D. Graves)*

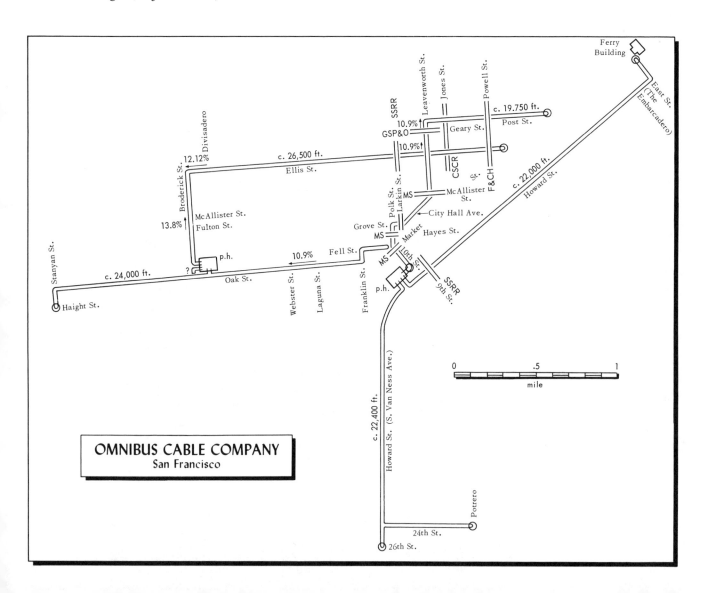

OMNIBUS CABLE COMPANY
San Francisco

OMNIBUS RAILROAD & CABLE COMPANY

Eppelsheimer bottom grip Gauge: 3'-6"

San Francisco's last and least successful cable railway was the Omnibus Railroad & Cable Company, a reformation of the Omnibus Railroad, a 5-foot gauge horsecar operation which dated from 1861. In the 1880s the Omnibus was under the control of Gustav Sutro and his associates, who made a study of about two years' duration of electric and cable systems and misguidedly opted for cable. The system had no grades which demanded cable traction, and the company's main line on Howard Street was two blocks in the wrong direction (south) from Market Street where it was unable to attract a large part of the traffic to the south and west. The entire system was largely redundant upon the Market Street Cable Railway, the management of which particularly loathed it as an interloper. The Omnibus had 11.3 miles of cable line, the second largest mileage in the city.

The system was a difficult one, run from two powerhouses with five cables and a short auxiliary. The main line on Howard was opened on August 26, 1889, and the remainder of the system later in the year. The company operated five lines: two on Howard, one each to 26th and Howard and 24th and Potrero; one on Post from Market and Montgomery to 10th and Howard; one on Ellis from Market Street to Golden Gate Park at Stanyan and Haight; and the last on Oak from 10th and Howard to Stanyan and Haight. Only the Ellis cable had serious gradients, but the Post cable was the most tortuous in the city. Since the company was inferior to everything except Jones Street, the company used an Eppelsheimer grip. The technology was almost identical to the Ferries & Cliff House, with which there was a community of financial interest. The company had 143 combination cars, built by J. Hammond & Company of San Francisco. They were 30'6" over-all and were distinguished by a double clerestory. The company used powered double-track turntables in the fashion of the Market Street Railway.

Somewhat more than half of the Omnibus system remained horse-operated and broad gauge. One of the company's strongest lines, a crosstown line on Third and Montgomery, was one of the most obvious cable routes in the city, even though flat. The company planned to convert it to the 3'-6" of the cable mileage and to operate it from a separate powerhouse in North Beach, but never did so. Planned but unexecuted projects, as might be expected, were abundant in San Francisco. Most major streets had lines projected at one time or another, some, notably Broadway on the east escarpment of Russian Hill, several times over. Remarkably, Mission Street, between Market and Howard, and a far more promising route than Howard, never had a cable installation.

Since Howard was, then as now, an undistinguished secondary business street, the main line traffic of the Omnibus proved disappointing. The cars to 26th and Howard (the company's blue line) were discontinued in August 1893 and reassigned to Ellis Street. On October 13 of the same year the company was absorbed by the Market Street Railway, which could hardly expect to treat it gently. At the end of 1895 the Oak and Ellis cables out of the Oak and Broderick powerhouse were killed. The main line was continued in operation until December 31, 1899 when, along with the Post Street line, it was discontinued. The Oak and Broderick powerhouse became a Market Street Railway facility and the main powerhouse, an overall factory. The Omnibus' roster was so large that the cars spread widely about the industry. Most went to the Market Street lines, where some became railway post offices. Several went to Seattle, where at least one was converted to 4'-8½" for Front Street, back to 3'-6" for Madison Street and finally to 3'-0" for Yesler Way. At the end of Seattle operation, one Omnibus car was in service on Madison and another out of service on Yesler. One electrified Omnibus car was active as a sand car on the Municipal Railway in San Francisco until 1947.

POWERHOUSES AND EQUIPMENT: 10th and Howard: Two pairs of O'Neill cross-compound engines, 29" + 44" x 60", 750 HP each.

Oak and Broderick: Reported as two engines of same type as in main powerhouse, but 500 HP each.

San Francisco references: Edgar M. Kahn, *Cable Car Days in San Francisco* (Stanford University Press, 1940); SRJ, IX (1893), 378-396. Collections of Roy Graves and Henry C. Collins.

The Omnibus reached Golden Gate Park via Oak and Stanyan Streets. At upper left, Oak Street cars approach the turntable at Stanyan and Haight, as food vendors zero in on the passengers. At lower left, the Omnibus' Post Street line ran diagonally in front of the old City Hall and across the Market Street Railway's McAllister line in the foreground. The earthquake of 1906 did a particularly thorough job on the City Hall complex, but the Omnibus cable line was gone by the end of 1899.

The Omnibus' main line terminated at the turntable just south of the old Ferry Building, below. This familiar photograph well illustrates the relative traffic of the Omnibus and the Market Street Cable Railway, four of whose cars are immediately above the Omnibus turntable. (*All, Roy D. Graves*)

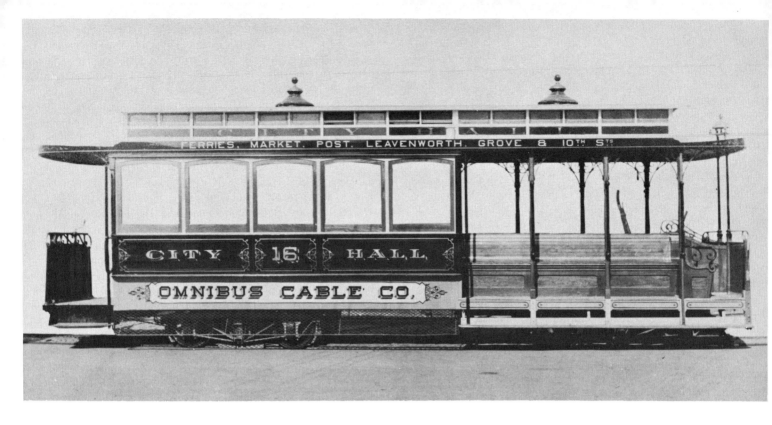

The Hammond combination cars of the Omnibus cost $1900 apiece, reportedly the most expensive in the City. Above is Hammond's builder's photograph of car 16, lettered for the Post Street line. *(California Historical Society)* The Omnibus cable lines lasted a short enough period that the cars circulated secondhand more widely than those of any other company. Below is an Omnibus car, slightly modified and lettered for the Madison Street line in Seattle. *(Lawton Gowey)*

Some of the cars which the Market Street Railway inherited from the Omnibus were rebuilt as railway post offices, one of which loads at the Ferry Building, above. Below, the Omnibus' powerhouse at Oak and Broderick became a barn of the Market Street Railway in the electric era. *(Both, Roy D. Graves)*

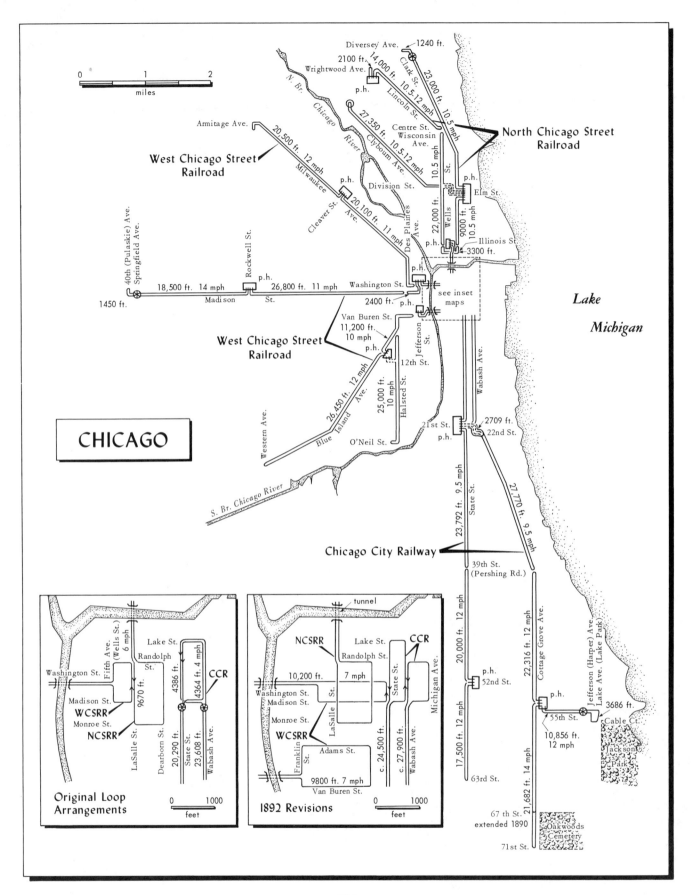

CHICAGO

West Chicago Street Railroad

North Chicago Street Railroad

West Chicago Street Railroad

Chicago City Railway

Lake Michigan

Diversey Ave. — 1240 ft.
Wrightwood Ave. 2100 ft.
14,000 ft.
p.h.
Clark St.
23,000 ft. 10.5-12 mph
Lincoln St. 10.5
Centre St.
Wisconsin Ave.
27,350 ft. 10.5-12 mph
10.5 mph
St.
N. Br. Chicago River
Armitage Ave.
20,500 ft. 12 mph
Milwaukee Ave.
Clybourn Ave.
Division St.
Cleaver St.
20,100 ft. 11 mph
Des Plaines Ave.
p.h.
Elm St.
p.h.
Wells
22,000 ft.
9000 ft. 10.5 mph
p.h.
Illinois St.
3300 ft.
40th (Pulaskie) Ave.
Springfield Ave.
Rockwell St.
p.h.
18,500 ft. 14 mph
26,800 ft. 11 mph
Washington St.
p.h.
see inset maps
1450 ft.
Madison St.
2400 ft.
p.h.
Van Buren St.
11,200 ft. 10 mph
Jefferson St.
p.h.
12th St.
Western Ave.
26,450 ft. 12 mph
Blue Island Ave.
25,000 ft. 10 mph
Halsted St.
O'Neil St.
21st St.
p.h.
2709 ft.
22nd St.
Wabash Ave.
S. Br. Chicago River
23,792 ft. 9.5 mph
State St.
21,770 ft. 9.5 mph
39th St. (Pershing Rd.)
20,000 ft. 12 mph
p.h.
52nd St.
17,500 ft. 12 mph
Cottage Grove Ave.
22,316 ft. 12 mph
p.h.
55th St.
10,856 ft. 12 mph
Jefferson (Harper) Ave.
Lake Ave. (Lake Park)
3686 ft.
Cable Ct.
Jackson Park
63rd St.
21,682 ft. 14 mph
67th St. extended 1890
Oakwoods Cemetery
71st St.

Original Loop Arrangements
Fifth Ave. (Wells St.) 6 mph
Lake St.
Randolph St.
4386 ft.
4364 ft. 4 mph
CCR
Washington St.
9670 ft.
Madison St.
WCSRR
Monroe St.
NCSRR
LaSalle St.
Dearborn St.
State St.
Wabash Ave.
20,290 ft.
23,608 ft.
0 — 1000 feet

1892 Revisions
tunnel
NCSRR
Lake St.
Randolph St.
CCR
10,200 ft.
7 mph
State St.
Michigan Ave.
Washington St.
Madison St.
LaSalle St.
Monroe St.
WCSRR
Franklin St.
Adams St.
c. 24,500 ft.
c. 27,900 ft.
Wabash Ave.
9800 ft. 7 mph
Van Buren St.
0 — 1000 feet

0 1 2 miles

234

CHICAGO

Population in 1890: 1,099,850

CHICAGO CITY RAILWAY

Hovey double-jaw side grip   *Gauge: 4′-8½″*

The largest and, on the whole, the most important American cable system was the Chicago City Railway. The city was growing very rapidly — so rapidly that "to grow Chicago style" became the Russian term for exceptional growth of cities — so that replacement of the horsecar was exceptionally urgent. In particular, the city was spreading southward, with densely populated areas developing straight south of the central business district and along Lake Michigan. This area was served by the Chicago City Railway, of which C. B. Holmes was president. The company, which dated from 1859, had become one of the largest carriers in American urban transportation. On the recommendation of one of his directors, G. W. Allerton, Holmes visited San Francisco in 1880 and was greatly impressed with the cable system. He arranged to license the trust's patents and set out to produce the first American cable installation outside San Francisco. He received his franchise on January 17, 1881, broke ground on June 27 and actually undertook construction on August 12, 1881. The project was entrusted to Asa Hovey and N. P. Fox of San Francisco, who produced the largest and in some respects the most difficult cable plant yet attempted.

The installation consisted of two lines, State Street, running straight south from the central area to 39th Street, then the city limit, and Wabash-Cottage Grove, following the lake to the southeast to the same cross-street. The Cottage Grove Avenue line presented the principal problems, since it required pull curves in and out of 22nd Street. Hovey dealt with this by providing a low-speed cable to traverse both curves. As a downtown terminal, Hovey provided a joint single-track loop about Madison, Wabash, Lake and State for both lines, powered by auxiliary cables (apparently the first attempted) off reduction gears just south of Madison on both State and Wabash. Since both cables were to use the same slot, Hovey had to develop a double-jaw side grip, essentially an adaptation of the Sutter Street grip, and the prototype of most

later double-jaw side grips. Hovey and Fox had the State Street line ready for service between the powerhouse and Madison Street on January 28, 1882. The remainder of the system north of 39th Street was opened during the year.

The system was, of course, one of the great successes of the industry. It worked in very satisfactory fashion in Chicago's harsh climate — opening it in January was psychologically extremely effective — and it returned over 20 per cent on its investment. The area between the Cottage Grove line and the lake, in particular, developed into the city's most desirable neighborhood. By 1887, when J. Bucknall Smith described the system, it was carrying 70,000 to 100,000 passengers per day on the original lines, and the value of the company's stock had tripled. Regular operation required about 150 trains of a grip and two trailers. In the 1880s and early 1890s the city permitted a third trailer, but it later prohibited the practice on safety grounds.

In 1885 Holmes decided on extension of the City Railway system to serve the suburban communities of Englewood, Hyde Park and Woodlawn, which were being absorbed into the growing city. The State Street line was extended to 63rd Street in the Englewood neighborhood in the spring of 1887, and the Cottage Grove line pushed south and east to 55th and Lake Avenue in Hyde Park on November 22 of the same year. Cable was laid on Cottage Grove to the Oakwoods Cemetery at 67th Street in 1888, and pushed to the south gate of the cemetery at 71st Street in 1890. This line was 8.7 miles, by a wide margin the longest cable route in America, and as far as is known, in the world. A trip required about 63 minutes. The State Street line, which probably had the heaviest traffic density in the industry, was 7.4 miles. In 1888 the company was reported to operate 263 trains simultaneously in rush hours, and by 1892 the number had risen to 300. State Street trains hauled Archer Avenue horsecars into the central area, and Cottage Grove

235

grips picked up Indiana Avenue trailers at 18th and Wabash. The company's cable operations reached their peak in 1893, the year of the Columbian Exposition in Jackson Park at the terminus of the 55th Street line. On Chicago Day, October 9, 1893, the company carried 700,000 people to the Exposition, mainly on cable trains. The opening of the south side elevated in 1892 and the spread of electric cars on the south side after 1893 cut into traffic, so that by 1902 the management regularly assigned only 94 cars to Wabash and 89 to State.

At the outset, Holmes expected to lay cables on Calumet, Indiana, Clark, Archer and Wentworth, and even provided space for tension runs in the 21st Street powerhouse. Cars would have entered the central area over the existing cable lines, or on Clark Street, which Holmes intended to convert to cable as far north as Madison Street. Even though Holmes was the street railways' most persistent advocate of cable traction, he never undertook laying cable on any of these lines; with the exception of Calumet Avenue, which was never built, all of these routes remained horsecar lines until converted to electricity. Hovey remained as chief engineer until 1889, when he went to Grand Rapids to supervise revisions — which were never undertaken — in the unsatisfactory Grand Rapids system.

One of cable traction's few redeeming features was an excellent ability to adapt to heavy peaks of traffic. Since most of the energy went into moving the cable, adding people, even by the thousands, was not difficult. Here the Chicago City Railway moves the load to Buffalo Bill's Wild West Show in 1903. (*Chicago Historical Society*)

The City Railway's cable system was modified in the early 1890s, partly to increase its capacity, and partly to simplify it. The joint loop of the two lines was subject to the usual objections to auxiliaries, and also amounted to a bottleneck with respect to traffic which was expected to continue increasing. In 1892 the company put into effect an agreement with the West Chicago Street Railroad whereby the City Railway was permitted to lay track on Michigan Avenue and the West Chicago was allowed to run its downtown loop along State Street. In June 1892 the company opened a separate loop for the Wabash-Cottage Grove line around Madison, Michigan, Randolph and Wabash, and removed the reduction gears at Madison and Wabash. With the new loop the Cottage Grove lines totalled almost exactly ten miles. In April 1894 the reduction gears at State and Madison were removed and the north State Street cable was run around the original terminal loop, which remained in use for State Street trains. In the same period, apparently before February 1894, the auxiliary was removed from the terminal loop of the 55th Street line. Finally, in 1895, the low-speed cable was taken out of 22nd Street; thereafter, grips held the Cottage Grove cable from the 21st Street powerhouse to 39th Street. After these changes the company directed gripmen to run curves at less than full speed, even though the grip was poorly suited to such operation.

The electric car came remarkably late to Chicago; the City Railway did not build its first electric line until 1893, and general electrification of horsecar lines in the city occurred only in the middle of the decade. The cablecar survived so long in the city for four reasons: the huge mileage of horsecar lines to be con-

verted, to which all the companies gave higher priority; the financial problems of the companies; uncertainty of franchise extension; and the city's prohibition of overhead wires on major streets in the central area until well into the 20th century. Indeed, the City Railway's cable trains regularly hauled electric cars from Indiana and Archer Avenues into the terminal loops because of the city's adamancy on overhead wires. The City Railway handled so many passengers (95,238,915 in 1896 on horse, cable and electric cars) that the argument for superiority of cable on heavily-travelled lines was better based here than almost anywhere else. Holmes advanced this argument more avidly than any figure in the industry, but he left the company in 1891. Remarkably, the cable lines survived until 1906. As late as 1905, the company reported 13,816,646 cable car-miles, as compared with 21,891,114 electric. By this time, every other flat cable system in the country had been swept away, leaving only the three Chicago companies.

The uncertainty of the Chicago companies concerning their franchise rights acted as an inhibitor to major changes in their physical plants. The companies' franchises were to expire in 1903, and there was considerable interest in municipal ownership. Instead, the long controversy was resolved by a pair of enactments, the "Settlement Ordinance" of December 4, 1905, and an extension of franchises on February 11, 1907. The former required conversion of the remaining cable and horse mileage, and the companies responded in 1906. State Street was converted on July 22, and Wabash on October 21. The Wabash-Cottage Grove conversion was the last in the city; the 21st Street powerhouse, the first in the city, also proved to be the last to operate.

In spite of the long survival of the Chicago cable system, the cable cars did not last until the city's street railways were unified. Chicago was late in unification, as in other aspects of its street-railway history; the Chicago Surface Lines brought together the city's complete mileage only in 1914.

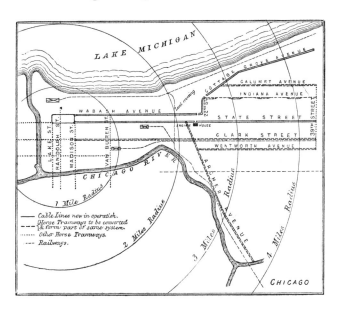

POWERHOUSES: 21st and State. EQUIPMENT: Three 24″ x 48″ Wheelock engines, removed to powerhouse at 52nd and State 1887, replaced by four 30″ x 60″ and two 36″ x 72″ Wheelock engines.

52nd and State. EQUIPMENT: Three 24″ x 48″ Wheelock engines, replaced in 1895 by 600 HP Westinghouse electric motor.

55th and Cottage Grove. EQUIPMENT: Two 38″ x 72″ Wheelock engines.

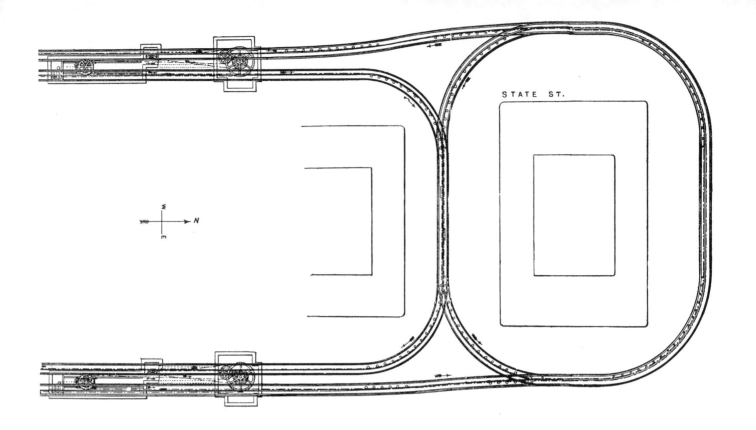

Most spectacular engineering feature of the Chicago City Railway was the joint loop of the State and Wabash lines in the center of the city. At left, above, is J. Bucknall Smith's drawing of the complicated installation, which included two sets of reduction gears. At lower left is the State Street portion of the loop in 1890. On this page are a State Street train, with an Archer Avenue electric car in tow, approaching the elevated station at Van Buren Street, and, below, a Wabash Avenue train in the last days of operation. Electric wires for the replacement are already in place. (*Chicago Historical Society*)

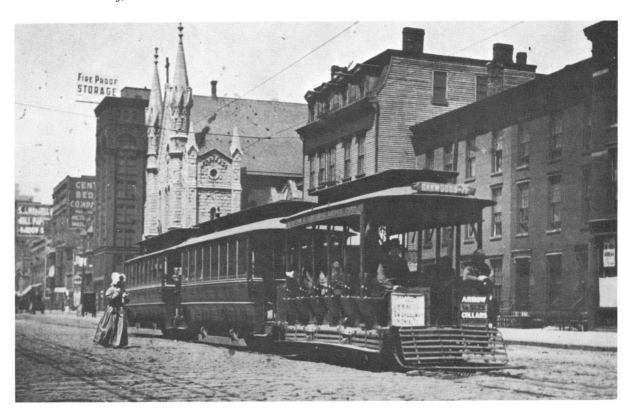

NORTH CHICAGO STREET RAILROAD

Low & Grim top grip   *Gauge: 4'-8½"*

After the unsatisfactory experience of the Philadelphia Traction Company's cable system, it is difficult to believe that anyone would have attempted a second installation of the Low & Grim top grip with the rest of the Philadelphia technology, but the Widener-Elkins interests, in collaboration with Charles T. Yerkes, did exactly that after acquiring the North Chicago Street Railroad in 1886. The company was the dominant operator of horsecars on the north side of the city, but it had been inhibited from laying cable by the Chicago City Railway's exclusive rights to trust patents in Chicago. As in Philadelphia, the top-grip technology offered freedom from the trust, and the prospect of cheap installation. Unfortunately, the consequences of widespread dissatisfaction and general public outcry were also the same as in Philadelphia.

Once again, the installation was entrusted to A. D. Whitton, the Widener-Elkins syndicate's house engineer. The initial system was to run from a terminal loop in the business district immediately south of the Chicago River to the city limits at Diversey Avenue. The company made use of existing investment to cut costs in two respects: first, it put the main powerhouse in a large building at Clark and Elm, previously used as a swimming pool and skating rink; second, it arranged to enter the central area through a tunnel built under the river by the city in 1871. The tunnel obligated Whitton to use La Salle Street for the river crossing, but the system's two main lines ran north along Wells and Clark, one block to either side. A mixture of this circumstance and the long distance required to move from one rope to another with a top grip created continual problems between the north end of the tunnel and the points where cars took the main-line cables just north of Illinois Street. Originally, Whitton laid out a single cable from his loop powerhouse at La Salle and Illinois, running west on Illinois, then north on Wells for about 150 feet to a terminal sheave, where it reversed, ran back along the same route, through the tunnel, around the loop to Monroe Street, back through the tunnel, east on Illinois and north another 150 feet into Clark, where it again reversed itself to return to the powerhouse. On the opening day of service, March 26, 1888, it was discovered that only about one out of four cars could roll around either of the let-go curves at La Salle and Illinois unaided. As at the 7th-9th and Market intersections in Philadelphia, the company had to station a team of horses to haul the top-grip cars to their pick-up points. The team, frightened at the crowds on opening day, dashed into a cluster of spectators rolling several in the mud. The company discovered that the loop cable, which made 14 turns, and had grades of 7 per cent on the tunnel approaches, had a life expectancy of only about a month. As the rope stretched, it became increasingly difficult for a car to grip tightly enough for the grades. In 1889 Whitton modified the system to provide a separate cable for the short trips into Wells and Clark. Even so, outcry persisted. The junction at Clark and Wells was a bottleneck, and the downtown loop, even after its revision, failed frequently.

Typical of the complaints against the company were:

> "It is stated that break-downs and delays on the Yerkes Cable Road have become more frequent than ever, until whole North Side is virtually up in arms against what is known as the 'Philadelphia Syndicate.' According to the local press it is a complete failure owing to the cheapness of the system put in.

At left, North Chicago operations on Dearborn Street in 1894. *(Chicago Historical Society)*

At left, a North Chicago train runs
north on Dearborn Street in 1902.
The grip car is one of the Brownell
& Wight combination cars used on
the Clybourn Avenue line. *(Chicago
Historical Society)* An earlier set of
Brill combination cars, below, was
intended for service on the Clark
and Wells lines, but proved too
long for the loop at the north terminus. The cars were cut down to
small single-truck grips. *(Pennsylvania Historical Society)*

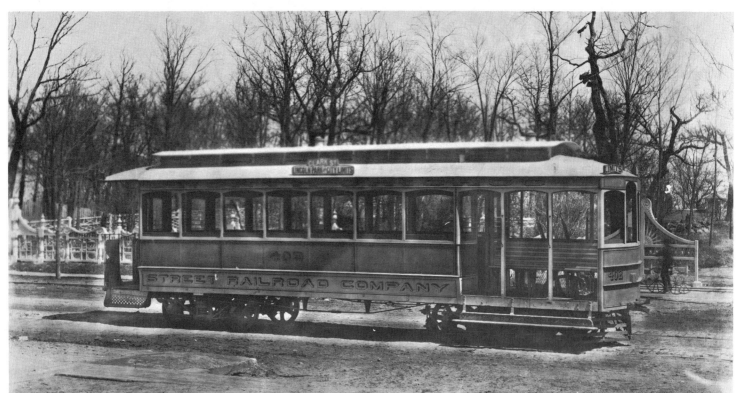

"Delays are frequent and many are wishing for a return to horse power."

The company was so sensitive to the complaints that it issued a pamphlet, *The North Chicago Street Railroad Company and Its Lines* in 1889 in its own defense. It argued that most of the problems centered about the terminal loop with its 320 curve pulleys, the breaking of any one of which caused the system to come to a halt. At peak hours, the cable handled about 65 cars, a load of 750 tons; each car required about 17 minutes to traverse the loop.

Withal, there is little doubt the North Chicago system was an improvement over pre-existing transportation. The Chicago River in the 19th century was a very major artery, with a continual parade of steamers and sailing vessels interfering with vehicular traffic across the bridges. The North Chicago cables provided the first mechanical traction across the water barrier which was not dependent on the bridges, and thus helped to regularize trips into the central area. The company, to receive its franchise, had agreed to move the Wells Street bridge to Dearborn and to build new bridges at Wells and Clark Streets. The water barrier had prevented any direct steam railroad access from the north side to what is now the Loop; northsiders had not enjoyed the direct service which several railroads operated straight south through the city. Lincoln Park, the north side beaches, the Ferris Wheel (which was re-erected near the Limits car house after the Fair of 1893), and the Relic House, a museum of the fire of 1871, all generated pleasure traffic for the company.

The company made two extensions. In February 1889 it opened a line from Clark and Centre (Armitage) to Lincoln and Wrightwood, and in May 1891 another from Wells and Division to Clybourn and Cooper. The former was operated from its own powerhouse at the terminus, but the latter was driven by a set of machinery in the Elm Street powerhouse originally intended for a North State Street line which was never undertaken. The Clybourn line was operated with Brownell & Wight combination cars, turned on a powered turntable — reportedly the only one east of Kansas City — in the car barn at the terminus. An earlier series of Brill combination cars had proved too long for the Limits loop and had been cut into short grips and trailers. The Limits and Lincoln trains were typically operated with these short grips and larger Stephenson grip cars, plus open and closed

trailers. The company reported a maximum of 157 grips, but as traffic declined following the introduction of electric cars on rival lines, several of the Stephenson grip cars were reduced to trailers. By 1902 regular operation required only 72 grips and 144 trailers. The company had 8.6 miles of double track — about half the mileage of the Chicago City Railway.

As the company's history progressed, outcry at the physical inefficiency of the cable system was replaced by widespread personal animosity to Yerkes, who became the archetypal venal traction tycoon of the late 19th century. Hostility to Yerkes was largely responsible for the franchise controversy of the early years of the 20th century. Yerkes had merged the North Chicago with the West Chicago Street Railroad into the Chicago Union Traction Company in 1899, and was looked upon as a monopolist. The settlement of 1905 entailed replacement of the north side cable lines along with the rest of the city's cable mileage. Union Traction, which had suffered vandalism at the end of its west side cable lines earlier in the year, announced that it would end cable operation on October 21, 1906, with a Clark Street-Limits train at 12:50 AM. Instead, the last cable cars were Lincoln and Clybourn grips about midnight. The first electric car ran on the announced schedule of the last cable car, and as anticipated, suffered some vandalism.

The company's tunnel remained intact until it was cut by the Dearborn Street subway. The north portal, in fact, was used for removal of earth from the tunneling, and the south portal closed. The north portal remains visible.

POWERHOUSES: La Salle and Illinois Streets. EQUIPMENT: Two 300 HP Corliss engines, one 26″ x 48″, one 28″ x 48″. Two Thomson-Houston generators operated arc lights in the tunnel and a third powered a system (apparently short-lived) of lights in the cars illuminated from a trolley wire with which short trolley poles on the roofs engaged and disengaged automatically at the portals. Powerhouse extant as Ireland's restaurant.

Clark and Elm Streets. EQUIPMENT: Four Corliss engines, two 36″ x 60″ and two 28″ x 60″.

Lincoln and Wrightwood Avenues. EQUIPMENT: Two 24″ x 48″ Corliss engines. Extant as Chicago Transit Authority facility.

The North Chicago was mainly operated with Stephenson grips of the 500 series on the main line and combination cars similar to No. 769 on the Clybourn branch. (*Smithsonian Institution; Chicago Historical Society; James J. Buckley*)

WEST CHICAGO STREET RAILROAD

Northern lines: Whitton   Gauge: 4'-8½"
double-jaw side grip

Southern lines: Vogel bottom grip

After the dismal experiences with top-grip technology in Philadelphia and on the north side of Chicago, the Widener-Elkins-Yerkes interests made no effort at a third installation based on the Low & Grim grip. When they turned to laying cable on their lines on the west side, A.D. Whitton designed a simple double-jaw side grip without carrying pulleys, and the company made an installation which was quite orthodox.

The original West Chicago system consisted of two lines, one straight west on Madison Street, the city's principal east-west commercial thoroughfare, and the other northwest on Milwaukee Avenue through the city's traditional German neighborhood. As in the case of the North Chicago, the Yerkes interests arranged to use an existing river crossing, a vehicular tunnel under Washington Street dating from 1869. The company invested about $200,000 in converting the tunnel to its purposes. Once again, the tunnel was poorly located relative to the lines the company was building, so that a second difficult approach was necessary. The tunnel powerhouse was placed at Washington and Jefferson at the junction of the two lines to issue the loop cable and the low-speed rope provided for the Madison Street trains to turn into Jefferson. Each of the two lines had a single centrally-located powerhouse. The Madison Street powerhouse had a low-speed cable within the powerhouse for switching movements of cars. The company originally intended a separate engine for the terminal loop at 40th and Madison, but decided upon an auxiliary. Much of the engineering for the line was done by Whitton's assistant, S. Potis, Jr.

The cable for the Milwaukee Avenue line was laid on June 7, 1890, and the Madison Street line was put in service on July 16, 1890. The company used Brownell & Wight combination cars on Milwaukee and grip-and-trailer combinations on Madison. The original physical plant was unsatisfactory in having a terminal loop which entailed six right angle turns, and brought the line only to La Salle Street, three blocks west of the principal retailing area, State Street. Yerkes had secured the right to run horsecars to State Street in 1890, but he could not reach an agreement with C. B. Holmes of the Chicago City Railway to bring his cables to State Street until 1892. In the fol-

lowing year he brought the loop east to State between Madison and Washington, crossing the North Chicago's terminal loop at four points. Since the extension to State Street was planned from the outset, the prospect of being inferior to another company at so many points may have given Whitton an additional incentive – if he needed one – not to use a top grip on the West Chicago. The company initially intended to retain the original loop for Milwaukee Avenue cars. In 1894 the SRJ reported that this arrangement was being implemented, though in later years only the State Street loop was used.

Yerkes planned a second pair of cable lines for the West Chicago to serve an area – even then a slum – along Halsted Street and Blue Island Avenue southwest of the central business district. For this installation, Potis, who was in charge of design, adopted yet another type of grip, the Vogel & Whelan bottom grip, with which the company had become impressed on the basis of the pilot installation in Butte. The Halsted and Blue Island lines required a separate downtown loop with its own tunnel, the only one of the three which had to be built specially for the cable car. The grade, as a result, was about 10 per cent, markedly steeper than the other tunnels. The company installed a ratchet system of emergency braking on the approaches. Yerkes encountered a series of legal actions in connection with the second loop which delayed completion until 1893. The powerhouse at 12th and Blue Island had proved a difficult engineering problem in that quicksand had required excavation 40 feet deep, and a foundation reportedly of a million bricks. The new lines were 6.0 miles, as compared with 9.2 for the original routes. With 15.2 miles of route, it was the second largest cable operation in the industry. The company had a maximum of 231 grips.

The West Chicago was a major carrier of 1850 cars of all types, according to its report for 1896. At that time it reported an operating ratio for its cable lines of 52.2, slightly less than the system as a whole. Its first electric line was built only in 1895, but thereafter it electrified the system, which covered the west side, quickly. The company, like the Chicago City Railway, had carried horsecars from connecting lines into the Loop on its cable trains. It made no attempt to handle electric cars behind the northern loop trains,

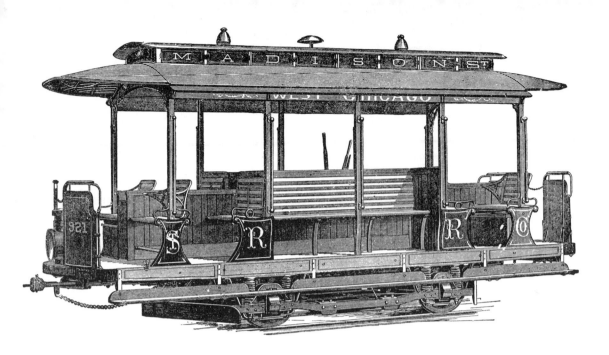

The West Chicago's Madison Street line was operated with light Brill grip cars, three examples of which are shown here, along with standard trailers. *(James J. Buckley; Chicago Historical Society)* The equipment of the Milwaukee Avenue line was apparently identical to the Clybourn Avenue combination cars of the North Chicago.

but it strung trolley wire in the southern tunnel for Van Buren Street electric cars to assist the grips up the grades as they were hauled around the loop by Halsted and Blue Island Avenue trains.

The incentive to get rid of the cable car was probably somewhat greater for this company than for the average operator, since its arrangement of a block of track on the left side of State Street with a pull curve at each end was about as bad a manifestation of cable technology as any in the industry. The cables survived through the merger of 1899 into the mass conversion of the Chicago system in 1906. Conversion began with Halsted Street in the first half of the year, followed by Blue Island Avenue in July. Madison and Milwaukee were converted simultaneously on August 19, 1906. At 12:45 AM, the crowd at Madison and Sheldon mobbed the penultimate grip, thinking it the last, overturned it, and stripped it of much of its hardware as souvenirs. The last train had police protection to bring it back to the 40th Avenue terminus about 2:30 AM.

Both tunnels were retained for electric service, though in later years the southern, presumably because of its steeper grades, was used only for training and other special movements.

POWERHOUSES: Washington and Jefferson Streets. EQUIPMENT: Two Corliss engines, 500 HP each; 100 HP Corliss added 1892. Extant as union hall.

Madison and Rockwell Streets: Two 36″ x 72″ Green engines, 1000 HP each, augmented in middle 1890s with 20″ x 40″ Fraser & Chalmers engine and 9″ x 12″ Russell high speed engine. Extant but unused. Formerly used car showroom and skating rink.

Milwaukee Avenue and Cleaver Street: Two 36″ x 72″ Corliss engines, 100 HP each.

Van Buren and Jefferson Streets: Two 38″ x 60″ Allis engines, 1500 HP each. Extant as Commonwealth Edison substation.

12th Street and Blue Island Avenue: Two 40″ x 72″ Allis engines, 1800 HP each. Foundation later occupied by Globe Theater, now razed.

Reference: George W. Hilton, *Cable Railways of Chicago* (Chicago: Electric Railway Historical Society, 1954). The information on North Chicago and West Chicago grips in this publication is erroneous.

TWELFTH STREET ELEVATION, NEW CABLE STATION—WEST CHICAGO
STREET RAILWAY.

Street Railway Journal Y.N.

The Halsted-Blue Island lines of the West Chicago Street Railroad were run from a powerhouse at 12th Street and Blue Island Avenue, which was integral with the building housing the company's general offices. On the opposite page, a Blue Island Avenue grip approaches Ashland Avenue in 1905. *(Chicago Historical Society)* At lower right is a cross-section of the Halsted-Blue Island lines' tunnel under the South Branch of the Chicago River.

Street Railway Journal N.Y.

BLUE ISLAND AVENUE ELEVATION, NEW CABLE POWER STATION—WEST CHICAGO STREET RAILWAY.

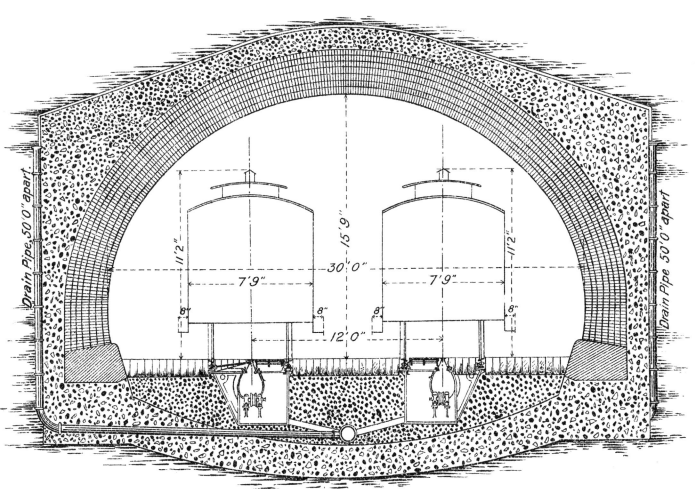

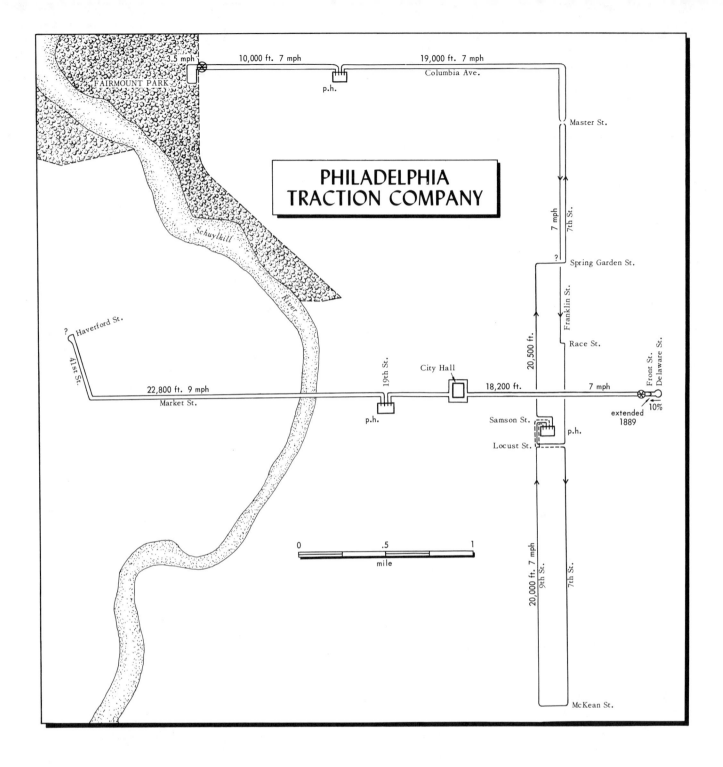

The Union Passenger Railway began cable service in Philadelphia with enclosed single-truck grip cars distinguished by round front ends. One of these cars, with a trailer, is illustrated on a ticket of the Philadelphia Traction Company from the collection of Harold E. Cox.

PHILADELPHIA

Population in 1890: 1,046,964

PHILADELPHIA TRACTION COMPANY

Low & Grim top grip   *Gauge: 5'-2½"*

The first, and in view of the size of the installation and population of the city, probably the worst example of an effort to build a system with non-trust patents was the Philadelphia installation of Peter A. B. Widener.

Philadelphia was a long-established, densely populated city which generated a large demand for public transportation. Widener had eagerly sought an alternative to the horsecar, and decided upon cable traction almost immediately upon its success on the Chicago City Railway in 1882. He was totally unwilling to deal wtih the patent trust, and arranged a complete non-trust technology based on the top grip of J. B. Low and A. K. Grim. As described in Chapter III, this grip was extremely hard on cable, had poor ability to pick up and eject the cable, and appears to have had no redeeming features. Most of the shortcomings of the system were the consequence either of use of this grip or of a cheap bolted conduit without yokes to prevent slot closure. The access plates were also so thin that the weight of traffic quickly forced them out of shape. In turn, the unsatisfactory experience with the system accounts for its small mileage relative to the size of the city.

The Union Passenger Railway, the predecessor of the Philadelphia Traction Company, opened the first portion of the system, about 1¼ miles along Columbia Avenue from the 23rd Street car house to Fairmount Park, on April 7, 1883. This short installation, about 3 miles from the center of the city, served little purpose, and was closed in about a month. In 1885, the Philadelphia Traction Company, which had succeeded the Union in the previous year for the express purpose of building a cable system, rebuilt this line with its orthodox conduit, replacing shallow cast iron tubes, and installed an auxiliary cable for the loop in Fairmount Park. The company also laid cable east from the powerhouse to 7th and Franklin Streets and south to Master Street, where it connected with a major horsecar line. The east cable was installed on January 10, 1885, and put in regular service on January 26. By March 18, the system had been halted by slot closure; the contraction was so severe that the track was put out of gauge enough to derail some horsecars.

Philadelphia Traction was also building a southward connection, and building an east-west line on Market Street. The latter was ready for test operation first, on May 16, 1885. Regular operation began from the Market Street powerhouse at 20th Street to the car house at 41st and Haverford on May 25, and the line east to Front Street followed on June 30. The company's other set of reduction gears was at 2nd Street to operate the Front Street loop. The system was so imperfect that operation had to be suspended twice in July, three times in August and once in November. At that time the SRJ reported the system represented an investment of $600,000 but that it would take $250,000 to correct the mistakes in it. The Columbia line was shut down on September 15, 1885, and not reopened until the southward connection was completed 13 months later.

A further problem was evident only when the cable from Sansom Street to Master Street was put in service on October 10, 1886. The crossings at 7th and 9th Streets at Market Street were the only crossings of top-grip lines ever attempted, and were as difficult as one might have anticipated. The intersections, like virtually all of the system, were flat, so that cars had no downhill momentum in any direction. Originally, the company had the 7th-9th cable above Market, but apparently before regular service on the new line was begun, put Market on top in an unsuccessful effort to dispense with horses to pull cars across. At 9th Street the carrying pulleys were so high as to foul the grips. In 1889 small auxiliaries of unspecified type were reported installed at both intersections to assist cars across, and around the curves to and from East Market Street. The north cable from Sansom Street also suffered from excessive curvature, especially the right-angle turns in and out of Race and Spring Garden Streets.

The final cable of the company ran south on 7th and 9th from the Sansom Street powerhouse to McKean Street. It was laid late in 1887 and put in service on January 10, 1888. This brought the system to its full length, the equivalent of just over 10 miles of double track, of which slightly over 6 were on the north-south line. Widener at the outset professed an

Surviving photographic coverage of the Philadelphia cable system is about equal to the company's operating history in quality. At left is the terminal loop at the foot of Market Street installed in 1889. Below is a view of the Market Street line east from the City Hall. *(Both, Harold E. Cox)*

intention of installing cable over his entire system of 180 miles but the existing lines were so unsatisfactory that he undertook nothing further. Passengers were reported in newspapers to be willing to walk a half mile to a parallel horsecar to avoid the cable lines. Both the New York *Times* and the Philadelphia *Times* criticized Widener for being close-mouthed about the unsuccessful system.

In 1889 the system was somewhat improved. The company began replacing the original tram rail on wooden stringers with 78-pound girder rail, and also strengthened the conduit. The eastern terminus of the Market Street line was brought east two short blocks from Front to Delaware Street, where it terminated at a loop of only 23¾ feet diameter (at the inside rail) in front of the Camden ferry terminal, reportedly on a short grade of about 10 per cent. Apparently the reduction gears for the Market Street loop were removed at this time. Similarly, the loop cable at Fairmount Park was removed before April 28, 1889, when the west Columbia cable was restored after a long period of idleness. Thereafter, the only major change in the line reported was elevation of the Columbia Street track over the Reading at 9th Street in 1892.

The company ran three cable routes: east-west on Market, north-south from McKean to the Park on Columbia, and a mixture of the two from the ferry terminal to the Park via the intersections at 7th and 9th and Market. Engineer A. D. Whitton originated his characteristic enclosed double-truck cars for this line, and the company also used single-truck equipment hauling horsecars as trailers. The company reported 161 cable cars in its annual report for 1893.

The company's car-building activities became an important enterprise; the company's shops built not only for itself, but for Widener-Elkins properties in Baltimore, Pittsburgh, and elsewhere.

The system, which might be expected to have been one of the first to be converted, lasted until 1895. The line south from Market Street was converted on April 27, and the rest of the north-south line on May 1. The west Market Street cable was stopped on June 19, and the east cable apparently after midnight on June 20. The cable slots were removed from Market in the following year. Some of the cable cars were rebuilt as electrics. At the time of the conversion, the *Scientific American* estimated the cable investment at $8 million.

Widener continued to be reluctant to discuss the cable experience in Philadelphia throughout his lifetime. He was reported in 1922 to have said that he would have been much better off to use the trust's

patents, even at the high fees the trust charged. The trust sued him, and in the settlement received a fee, apparently along with rights to the Low & Grim grip, which was listed among its holdings in 1893.

POWERHOUSES: Columbia Avenue, between 23rd and 24th Streets. EQUIPMENT: Two Porter Allen 100 HP engines, found unsatisfactory and replaced with two Wetherill Corliss engines, 24″ x 48″, 260 HP each, 1885.

Sansom Street, south side, between 8th and 9th Streets. EQUIPMENT: Two 350 HP Wetherill Corliss engines, 24″ x 48″. Replaced by 1891 with a 1000 HP Wetherill Corliss, 40″ x 48″. Powerhouse extant as substation for Market Street and Locust Street subways and 23, 47 and 50 car lines.

Market Street between 19th and 20th. EQUIPMENT: Two 350 HP Wetherill Corliss engines, 24″ x 48″.

References: Harold E. Cox, "The Cable Cars of Philadelphia," *Metropolitan Philadelphia Railway Association Newsletter*, VI, No. 3 (March, 1961), 3-4; *Scientific American*, LII (1885), 111, 117; SRJ, VI (1890), 327; "How the Cables Work," New York *Times*, July 30, 1886; L. M. Haupt, "Repairs to the Philadelphia Traction Company's Conduit," *Proceedings of the Engineers' Club of Philadelphia*, V (1885), 125-133; collection of John M. Strock.

A conductor loads a lady, complete with bustle, on a Market Street car in the 1890s. *(Harold E. Cox)*

Philadelphia Traction was notable for its own carbuilding. Above are a set of trucks and a separate set of trucks with a floor, built by Pullman for car bodies to be built in company shops. Note the broad gauge of the trucks. *(George Krambles)*

Below is one of Whitton's standard double-truck closed cars on Brill's transfer table. *(Pennsylvania Historical Society)*

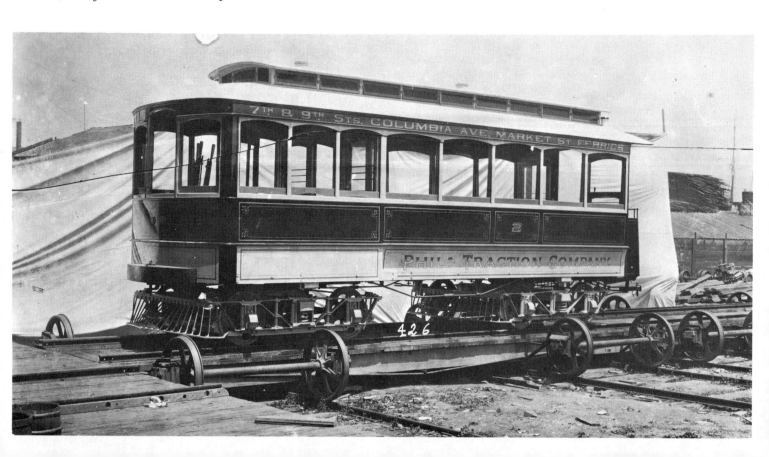

KANSAS CITY, MISSOURI

Population in 1890: 132,716

KANSAS CITY CABLE RAILWAY

Hovey double-jaw side grip;   *Gauge: 4'-8½"*
converted to Vogel bottom grip, 1889

Kansas City's terrain called for the cable car at least as much as San Francisco's; indeed, on seeing the city, one is surprised cable traction was not invented there. The city is located on continuously undulating upland, with a bluff called Quality Hill 116 feet high separating it from river flats called the West Bottoms below it. To the west, access to the secondary center of the metropolitan area, Kansas City, Kansas, required ascent of a smaller bluff. To the north of the business district of Kansas City, Missouri, the streets descend mainly at grades of 5 to 8 per cent to the North End, a produce market and wholesaling area. The descent to the West Bottoms was the more important of the two problems, since Union Depot sat at the bottom of the bluff, about opposite the west end of 9th Street. The existing communications to Union Depot were several simple wooden staircases and a roundabout horsecar line of the Metropolitan Street Railway via 5th Street and the North End — later to be the Metropolitan's Wyandotte cable line. In the middle-1880s Kansas City was experiencing a particularly strong land boom, and expanding rapidly. Thus, on all grounds, there was a considerable demand for cable traction. It was (as it remains) a city of low population density with a diffused pattern of employment which does not generate a heavy per capita demand for public transportation, however.

Cable traction in Kansas City is particularly identified with Robert Gillham, who designed no less than five lines in the area, beginning with the Kansas City Cable Railway. Gillham was born in New York in 1854, began practice of engineering in Hackensack, New Jersey in 1874, and removed to Kansas City in 1878. Almost immediately, he recognized the bluff as an engineering problem; his first thought was to build a funicular, but he was converted to endless-cable traction by the favorable experience in San Francisco. He applied for a franchise as early as 1881, but was rejected because of opposition of horsecar operators. He interested William J. Smith and George J. Keating,

implement dealers in the West Bottoms, in the project. Smith sold out his business to help finance the cable line. Keating was active only in the early years of the company; subsequently much of the equity in the company was held in Boston and Britain. Gillham on April 29, 1882 secured a franchise for a cable line from 8th and Woodland to Union Depot, using Grand Avenue for the transition from 8th to 9th Streets. Gillham designed the line to begin at an elevated terminal beside Union Depot, 28 feet above the ground, to proceed across the railroad tracks on a truss bridge, and then ascend the bluff on a trestle at an 18.535 per cent grade. The route continued across typical steeply undulating streets, with a major grade of 10.4 per cent for a block up to the right-angle turn into Grand Avenue. This produced an extremely difficult pull curve — one of the two notable "Dead Man's Curves" of the industry — which it was impossible to turn in partial release in either direction without running the most severe hazard of losing the grip on a major grade. Ordinary undulating terrain brought the line to Woodland Avenue, 1.9 miles from Union Depot.

ROBERT GILLHAM.

255

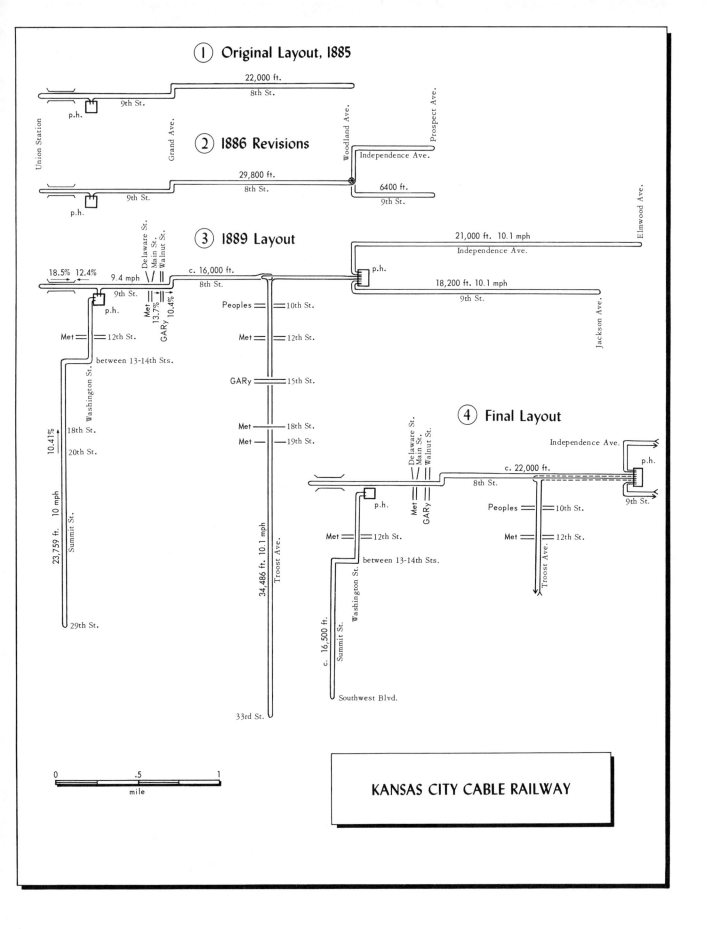

① Original Layout, 1885

② 1886 Revisions

③ 1889 Layout

④ Final Layout

KANSAS CITY CABLE RAILWAY

Gillham and Clift Wise designed the line with D. J. Miller's technology, then being installed on the Third Avenue Railway's lines in Harlem, New York, including the duplicate system of cables. As recounted in Chapter V, Gillham quickly came to dislike the duplicate system, and had it removed in July 1885. Initially, the line used a wheel-operated double-jaw side grip, variously reported to have been the Jonson grip with the lower jaws mobile and a grip similar to the later Earl Broadway grip with the upper jaws mobile. In any event, the grip proved unsafe on the descent to the Station. The line was scheduled to open in April, but because the track proved to be out of gauge by about an inch—an error which cost Smith about $100,000—and because the grip had to be replaced, opening was delayed until June 15, 1885. Gillham paid $17,000 to use the trust's Chicago City Railway grip of Asa Hovey. This arrangement created an anomalous situation of a line built with non-trust patents using a trust grip. When the Metropolitan Street Railway in 1887 bought exclusive use of trust patents in Kansas City, the KCCR was put in an ambiguous position. In any case, the Hovey grip, with its long jaws and high leverage, was well suited to the long pull up the bluff.

Since it provided a service the city had badly needed, the Kansas City Cable Railway proved itself one of the most notable successes in the industry. It regularly carried over 20,000 people per day, and on July 4, 1886, handled 37,500. Financially, it was the most successful company in Kansas City, returning about 30 per cent in its first year. Inevitably, it would be extended to the east and south, but Gillham, unfortunately, was not able to supervise the extensions. As Gillham stood in a pit watching the cable pass, a shopman dropped a grip on him, fracturing his skull, nearly killing him, and laying him up for about a year. The company replaced him with Clift Wise, who designed the extensions, and became a prominent cable engineer. Gillham was subsequently active in promoting rival lines.

The company first extended out Independence Avenue to Prospect Avenue on June 25, 1886, and then out 9th Street to the same avenue on November 24, 1886. Wise designed the new lines with an extension of the cable from the 9th and Washington powerhouse out Independence, but a separate cable as an auxiliary out 9th Street from 8th and Woodland. In a misguided effort at economy, Wise used a pair of drums on a single shaft, rather than reduction gears, fitted so that the mainline cable ran the 9th Street rope by the simple expedient of wrapping one around each drum. Wise put a tension device on the terminal

sheave at 9th and Prospect. This arrangement meant that, if anything stopped the auxiliary, it would create havoc with the rest of the physical plant. On August 31, 1887, a crew was sent to 9th and Prospect to tighten the tension device, but accidentally stopped the auxiliary cable. The mainline cable was stopped as a result, even though the engines were still driving it. The inevitable consequence was to bend the axle on the terminal sheave at Union Depot; service had to be suspended for several days.

Partly to get rid of this arrangement, but also in order to expand mileage, Wise began to redesign the system in 1887. In particular, the company had secured the franchise for Troost Avenue, a major north-south street about a mile east of the central business district; there would have been no practical way to run this line from the powerhouse at 9th and Washington. The company built a new powerhouse at 8th and Woodland, from which it ran a cable of 34,486 feet down 8th to Troost and then out Troost to 33rd Street. The mainline cable was cut back to 8th and Troost. Service began on Troost Avenue on November 18, 1887. Wise then devoted himself to revising the two lines east of Woodland. The Independence line was pushed east to Elmwood Avenue on July 12, 1889, and the east 9th Street line was extended to Jackson Avenue on December 8, 1889; each was given a separate cable from the Woodland Avenue powerhouse.

Simultaneously, the company was opening a line running straight south from the original powerhouse along Washington and Summit Streets to serve a residential area untapped by any of the city's other cable operators. The West Side Cable Railway had proposed to build into this area in 1888 with a route from 2nd and Wyandotte to 24th and Fairmount via Wyandotte, 17th, Belleview and 24th. The KCCR's line, opened on October 1, 1889, was the last in the city to be completed because of a large number of legal actions against the company. Gillham was reported to have returned to design it. Trains ran through from Washington along the main line and thence south on Troost Avenue. At this time, partly on the basis of observation of the Butte cable line, and partly because of the company's ambiguous relations with the trust, the management converted the entire system from the Hovey grip to the Vogel bottom grip, with which the company later reported itself highly pleased. As completed, the company had 10 miles of double track, and was considered one of the major operators in the industry.

Mainly because of problems at the intersection of 8th and Troost, the company undertook a further major revision in the physical plant in 1894. Cars had

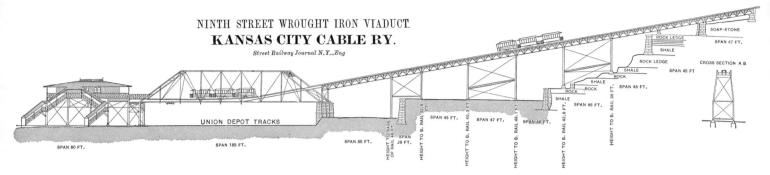

NINTH STREET WROUGHT IRON VIADUCT.
KANSAS CITY CABLE RY.
Street Railway Journal N.Y., Eng

UNION DEPOT TRACKS

SPAN 60 FT.   SPAN 185 FT.   SPAN 65 FT.   HEIGHT TO BASE OF RAIL 46 FT.   SPAN 29 FT.   HEIGHT TO B. RAIL 32.2 FT.   SPAN 45 FT.   HEIGHT TO B. RAIL 40.2 FT.   SPAN 47 FT.   HEIGHT TO B. RAIL 49.1 FT.   SPAN 46 FT.   HEIGHT TO B. RAIL 42.8 FT.   SHALE   ROCK   ROCK   SHALE   SPAN 46 FT.   HEIGHT TO B. RAIL 36 FT.   SHALE   ROCK   SPAN 46 FT.   SHALE   ROCK LEDGE   SHALE   SPAN 45 FT   ROCK LEDGE   SHALE   SPAN 47 FT.   SOAP-STONE   CROSS SECTION A B

difficulty moving between cables westbound, and cable life was reduced by the necessity of an exceptionally long rope bearing both mainline and Troost Avenue traffic. In the summer of 1894 the company took delivery of a large quadruple expansion engine which E. P. Allis & Company of Milwaukee had exhibited at the Columbian Exposition of the preceding year. This engine was more than adequate to handle the main line, Troost Avenue and the two branches to the east. Accordingly, the rope layout was modified to run the main line off a fourth set of winding machinery, intended for an unbuilt south Woodland branch. Speeds of the cables were reported increased from about 7 to 10 miles per hour.

The company had remained solvent in 1893 only through Smith's cashing in his life insurance and adding $100,000 to its cash. He was, naturally eager to merge it into another firm, and in April 1894 for a consideration of $852,000 arranged a merger with the Grand Avenue Railway, a better property physically, but one handicapped by lack of access to Union Depot. This merger was held illegal by the state supreme court in February 1895, but both companies came into the Metropolitan's expanding system later in the year. The cable car still served Kansas City well enough that the Metropolitan rebuilt the former KCCR main line in the summer of 1896, replacing the original stringers on wooden base with standard girder rail. On the other hand, the company in 1895 had decided on a long-term program of cable replacement.

Local worries concerning safety were highly concentrated on the former KCCR main line, both at the trestle on the west end, and at "Dead Man's Curve." The latter was a continual source of mild accidents; in 1897, for example, passenger H. W. Evans, returning from a dentist's office, was still so imperfectly in control of his faculties from anesthesia that he failed to take a firm grip at the curve, and was pitched into Grand Avenue. The trestle, though not so steep as its counterpart on 12th Street, was a chronic source of apprehension partly because the drop from Quality Hill was visually very abrupt, and partly because the

track dead-ended at the bottom. On the trial trip in 1885, passengers had been so fearful that they left at the top of the hill, and watched the train descend and return safely. On June 17, 1885, only two days after the line opened, a downbound car lost its grip on the incline, rolled down uncontrollably, crashed into the car waiting at the bottom, and injured 17 people, two severely. On the evening of February 8, 1888, the shank on a grip broke, sending a train down the viaduct into a waiting train, killing the gripman and seriously injuring two passengers. Subsequently, the accident experience was quite favorable. Trailers were equipped with a "dog" which could be lowered by the conductor to mesh with a rack on the upbound track or coiled cables on the downbound when the grip was lost. In the winter of 1890 this device was used 11 times.

In spite of the eagerness of the public to see the end of the 9th Street trestle, the entire KCCR cable plant survived into the 20th century because of the difficulty in arranging a replacement. As the century opened, the powerhouse at 9th and Washington burned on January 26, 1901. The Metropolitan was eager to convert the Washington-Summit line, which alone emanated from the burned powerhouse, but the 10.4 per cent grade on Summit between 18th and 20th was considered impossible for electric cars. As a consequence, the management converted the line south of Southwest Boulevard, routing the electric cars into the city over Southwest Boulevard and Main Street. The company strung trolley wire at 9th and Washington for an electric switcher to turn back the Troost Avenue trains which had formerly run through to Summit. Service was resumed from the powerhouse to Southwest Boulevard on July 22, 1901.

Otherwise the former KCCR system was intact when, on August 22, 1902, a downbound two-car train lost the grip on the trestle and plowed into a waiting train, killing gripman W. D. Taylor and injuring 17 passengers. Previously, only a single employee and no passengers had been killed in the viaduct's entire history. The Metropolitan's agreement with the city

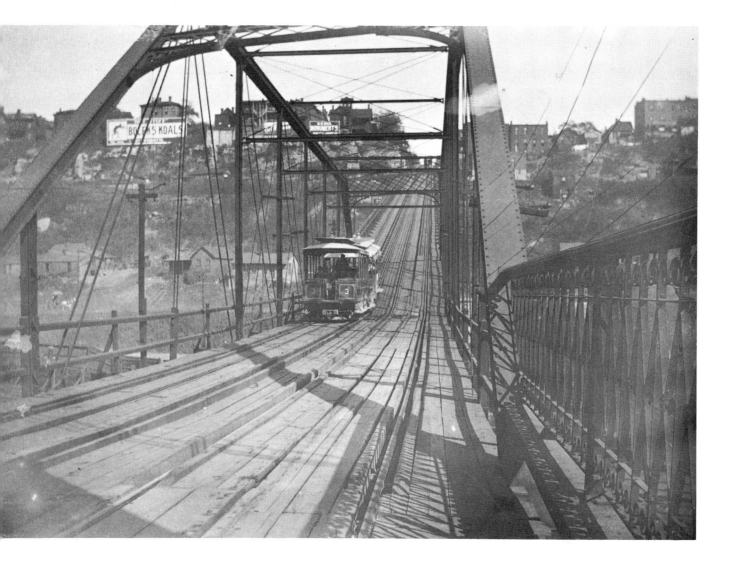

Most conspicuous part of the Kansas City Cable Railway was the viaduct ascending from Union Depot to the central business district to the east. Above is a photograph dating from 1895. *(Barney Neuberger)* Below is an earlier view. *(Earl Moore)*

These three photographs illustrate the Kansas City Cable Railway in the vicinity of "The Junction" at 9th and Main Streets. The Junction was in a valley with an ascent to the west shown above, and a steeper ascent to the east shown on the opposite page. This is a good example of a situation in which the superior road at a crossing, the Cable Railway, required a depression device to prevent its cable's fouling the inferior line's trains crossing in full release. *(Kansas City Public Library)*

entailed replacement of the trestle by December 1, 1903, in any case, but now public uproar was added to statutory obligation. The replacement was difficult because the alternative, the former Inter-State Rapid Transit line through the 8th Street tunnel, involved a grade of 8.8 per cent, such that for safety reasons the tunnel was restricted to a single car in each direction. Traffic on the 8th Street electric cars increased so greatly after the trestle accident that the company felt it necessary to reduce the tunnel's grade to 5 per cent to end the restriction. This project could not be completed until 1904, perpetuating the KCCR main line in the face of widespread dissatisfaction. The company in this period maintained a spare grip car at the trestle, which was attached to the rear of downbound trains as a safeguard against losing the grip.

Meanwhile, the Metropolitan was converting the rest of the system. Troost Avenue was converted on September 2, 1902, and east 9th Street on October 13, 1903. At length the modification of the 8th Street tunnel was completed so that the old KCCR main line along with the Independence extension could be converted on April 6, 1904. The only regret widely voiced was that the company had not typically collected fares from passengers who rode only up the trestle; such

hospitality would not be extended on the electric cars through the tunnel. The only remaining active KCCR cable trackage was the remnant of the Washington-Summit line from 9th Street to Southwest Boulevard. The Metropolitan at the time of abandonment of the incline announced it would not long continue the Summit cable. Upon completion of the Roanoke electric car line the Summit cable was abandoned on October 2, 1904. The portion of the line from 9th to 12th was restored in 1906 when the Metropolitan cut back its 12th Street line, and began operating its west loop from the 9th and Washington powerhouse. The 9th Street trestle itself was dismantled in 1905 with some nostalgia, but little genuine regret.

POWERHOUSES: 9th and Washington. EQUIPMENT: Two Wright engines, 24″ x 48″, probably of 250 HP, replaced with two 350 HP electric motors, 1897.

8th and Woodland: Two Wright engines, probably of 500 HP, replaced in 1894 with one Reynolds Corliss engine, 26″ + 40″ + 60″ + 70″ x 72″, E. P. Allis & Co., Milwaukee, reported as 3000 HP when exhibited at the World's Columbian Exposition, but as 1400 HP in service.

Above, two trailers of the Kansas City Cable Railway stand at Woodland Avenue. The closer trailer is of a type known on the line as a "Mother Hubbard." Below is the undistinguished car house of the Troost Avenue line. *(Kansas City Public Library)*

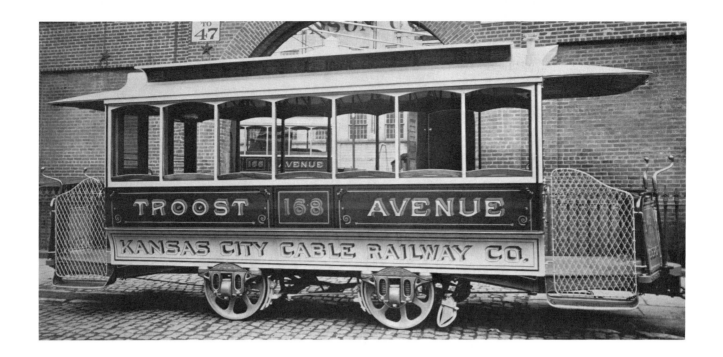

Troost Avenue has traditionally been Kansas City's most heavily-travelled transit route. Above is an early trailer for Troost Avenue at the Stephenson plant in New York. Below is another view of the Junction with an Independence Avenue train crossing. *(Smithsonian Instituiton; Kansas City Public Library)*

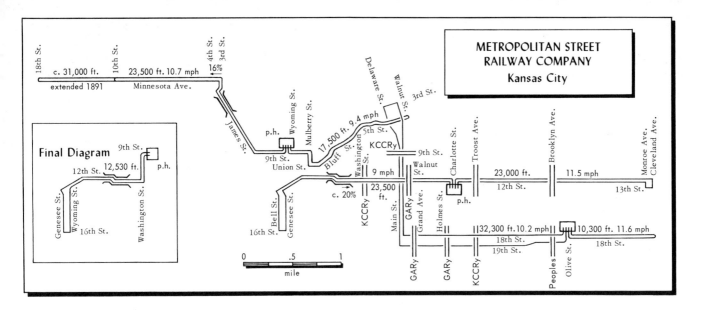

Below is the Junction from the Metropolitan Street Railway's approach down Main Street toward 9th. Northbound trains proceeded straight ahead on Main, and southbound trains such as this one came off Delaware Street at the left. (*Kansas City Public Library*)

Root single-jaw side grip   *Gauge: 4'-8½''*

The Metropolitan Street Railway, Kansas City's largest horsecar operator, was the system of Thomas Corrigan, prominent equally in urban transport and municipal politics. The company had four major lines into the central area, three of which were converted to cable. Corrigan in 1887 paid $50,000 for exclusive rights to trust patents, and had the system designed by the local engineers, William B. Knight and Daniel Bontecou.

Corrigan began his cable operations with the route running from 5th Street in the North End to Kansas City, Kansas, via Union Depot and the West Bottoms. It bore the name "the Wyandotte line," because it served the former town of Wyandotte, the principal component of Kansas City, Kansas, when the city was formed in 1886. This had traditionally been the principal horsecar line between the two cities. Although tortuous by cable standards, it had the advantage of traversing Minnesota Avenue, the main thoroughfare of Kansas City, Kansas. J. B. Stone reported that the line had 278 curve pulleys; he considered rope life of nine months, which the company reported, favorable under the circumstances. Like the company's other lines, this was run with two ropes from a single powerhouse. The east rope was put in service on May 12, 1887, and the west on October 27 of the same year. Initially, the route terminated at 10th Street in the Wyandotte area, about 4½ miles, but on May 30, 1891, it was extended 3778 feet to 18th Street, approximately the end of the inhabited territory. Cars ran on four-minute headway.

Simultaneously with the building of the Wyandotte line, the company was laying cable on 12th Street (of the Rag), one of the principal east-west thoroughfares of the city. This line was also to serve the West Bottoms, but the object was not so much to serve Union Depot, which the 8th and 9th Street lines of rival companies served more directly, as to reach the Kansas City Stock Yards on the east bank of the Kansas River. Since the main entrance to the Stock Yards was at 16th Street, the engineers arranged a loop on Bell and Genesee Streets to reach it. Knight was said to be fond of loops (though he had not used them on the Wyandotte line) and also provided one at the Cleveland Avenue terminus. The route was 4.25 miles long and almost entirely straight, but because of the terminal loops had 326 curve pulleys. The principal engineering problem in constructing the line was

the ascent of Quality Hill, which Knight and Bontecou dealt with by a trestle of about 1600 feet, flat from Mulberry Street to the base of the bluff, and then ascending very steeply at about 20 per cent. Completion of the trestle delayed the opening of the line, but it was ready for trial operation on April 7, 1888; revenue service began two days later. Until May 15 the company operated the 12th Street line with large Pullman combination cars, but they proved too heavy for the grade on the trestle, both in creating a safety hazard from weight too great for their brakes and in causing excessive wear on the rope. The company next planned to use them on the 18th-19th Street line, then under construction, but it stored them until 1897 when it rebuilt them as double-truck electric cars.

Construction of the 18-19th Street line was undertaken simultaneously with the completion of the 12th Street line. The route was to run from 9th and Main Streets — an intersection locally known as "The Junction" — south on Main through the central area, thence east on 19th to the powerhouse at Olive Street, and eastward to Cleveland Avenue on 18th. Westbound the line used 18th, which was too narrow for double track, all of the way west to Main. The terminus at the Junction presented a typical dilemma of cable technology: no solution was adequate. To turn the 33-foot combination cars then being considered for use, a turntable would have to be 30 feet in diameter. As usual in Kansas City, the track was on a grade such that mule-switching would be difficult. The company finally decided upon a balloon loop, which must have been of very restricted dimensions. The physical plant was intended for completion on November 1 but opened on October 23, 1888 — the only line in Kansas City (and one of the few anywhere) opened ahead of schedule. Its mileage was about 3.3.

The company suffered the unpopularity of dominant firms in the traction systems of many cities. The public and members of the City Council alike widely looked upon it as a monopoly, so that the hostility manifested itself in several franchise disputes. The company had been offered a cable franchise for its Broadway mule car line (which was 4'-1½'' gauge) only on condition it provide electric street lighting. The company refused and the line became the only one into the central area never converted to cable. More important was a long controversy concerning a terminal loop for the 18th-19th Street line in the

THE LACLEDE CAR CO. St. Louis, Mo.

Builders of Street Railway Cars of Every Description

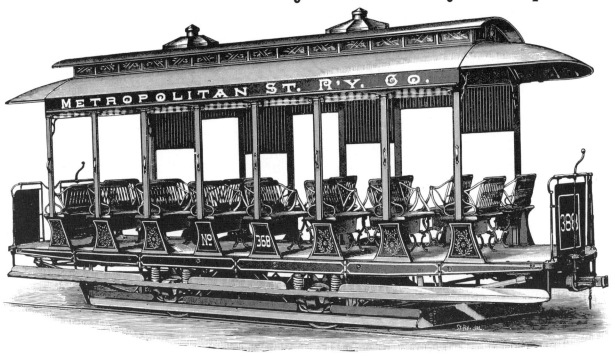

North End. The company disliked its balloon loop at 9th Street and was eager to provide a direct connection between the Wyandotte line on 5th Street and the rest of the cable system. Its preference was a terminal loop, involving almost exactly a mile of additional cable, down Main to 3rd Street, returning to the Junction on Delaware Street. The City Council and much of the press felt that the company's exclusive rights to use trust patents had inhibited development of cable traction in the city. Robert Gillham proposed that the loop be made joint among the various cable operators, with any company paying the Metropolitan a fee for use of the track. Gillham was eager to extend his People's Cable Railway, and was willing to build the loop, but did not have the franchise for Main Street between 9th and 10th.

In July 1888 the City Council voted the Metropolitan the loop franchise, attaching to it Gillham's proviso that other companies might use the trackage. Mayor Henry C. Kumpf vetoed the franchise on the ground that it did not require the Metropolitan to license the trust patents. Kumpf feared that the Metropolitan would use its patents to prevent completion of the Kansas City Cable Railway's Summit line, then under construction. Upon veto of the ordinance, the Metropolitan did go to court for an injunction against progress on the Summit line. Early in 1889 the Council passed an ordinance for the loop entailing a requirement that the Metropolitan license patents at a reasonable fee. The Mayor signed the franchise on February 5. The 5th Street dummy line from the North End to the East Bottoms was expected to be converted to cable as soon as it was given access to trust patents. The Metropolitan was undecided about accepting the franchise, and was widely expected to reject it once more, but almost immediately the company learned of Judge Wallace's decision in New York holding invalid the trust's patents on conduits. President C. F. Morse questioned the validity of any of his patents on the basis of this decision, and on February 15 accepted the franchise. Under its terms, the Metropolitan was obligated to accept transfers to the loop from any company, but not to let other companies use its tracks.

The press hailed the franchise as a victory against restriction, in general ignoring that the cable car had become uneconomic. Owing to the city's terrain and to an unfavorable experience with an electric line of John Henry in 1884, recognition of the obsolescence of cable traction came later to Kansas City than to any other; on April 11, 1887, the Kansas City *Journal* had discussed the alternative means of public transportation at great length without even mentioning the electric streetcar as a possibility for the city. The *Times* stated on February 16, 1889:

> Kansas City is today the great cable railway city of the world. With millions of dollars invested in these enterprises, she justly holds credit for being far ahead of the world in enterprises of this sort. Millions more of money would have been expended here had it not been for the monopoly of patents enjoyed by the National Cable Company, but now that their validity is no longer in doubt, capitalists will pour out their money like water in additional cable railways, and within a short space of years the horsecar, dummy line and electric motor will have given way to the cable system.

Few predictions, obviously, could have been less accurate. Only the Washington-Summit line of the KCCR was ever built under the compulsory licensing provision. A circuit court set the fee for licensing at $3000, but the Metropolitan refused the sum as inadequate. The city responded by revoking the Metropolitan's franchise for Highland Avenue, and requiring forfeiture of the franchise deposit of $10,000. Terms were arranged for the licensing and the Metropolitan received a franchise for an electric line on Vine Street, which had easier grades than Highland. The cable loop itself was built in the first half of 1889; the cable was laid by three grip cars and 38 mules on June 27.

The Metropolitan made only one further revision in its cable plant of 13.3 miles. In 1894 the Kansas City Stock Yards, with which the Metropolitan had some community of ownership, announced that it wished to expand one block to the east. The company in 1895 moved the terminal loop of the 12th Street line from Bell, which was obliterated, to Wyoming Street. Thereafter the system atrophied.

The Metropolitan began its lengthy and successful effort to absorb the city's entire street railway system with purchase in 1894 of the Inter-State elevated, which had already been electrified. In May, 1895, the Metropolitan acquired the Kansas City Cable Railway for $4,339,000 and the Grand Avenue Railway for $2,400,000, giving it control of the city's entire cable system with the exception of the People's Cable Railway, which it did not take over until 1899. The consolidated network was by far the largest of any single company, about 31.9 miles. In 1895 the Metropolitan had its system studied by consulting engineers from New York, who strongly recommended conversion of the entire cable mileage to electric lines. They estimated that the company could replace seven power-houses with one, avoid $100,000 per year in cable renewals, and cut damage to life and property nearly

Union Depot, object of much of the cable-laying in Kansas City, was the big Victorian structure shown above. The Metropolitan's track ran past the front of the building after a difficult descent via Bluff Street, below. *(Kansas City Public Library)* At the bottom of the opposite page is a woodcut of one of the heavy combination cars used briefly on the 12th Street line, reproduced from a Laclede advertisement. Other cars of this series were built by Pullman.

50 per cent. The Metropolitan decided upon a long-term program of conversion, partly for the intrinsic advantages, and partly to buttress its case for franchise renewal. Most of its franchises would expire early in the twentieth century, and the company, recognizing the chronic hostility of the municipal government, wanted to present as strong a case as possible. The city's cable network, which had represented a total investment of about $13.5 million, was in poor condition and obsolete; the Council was unlikely to award new franchises for its perpetuation. Partly because the cable system was so large, and partly because the city had an ordinance of 1888 requiring the consent of the owners of a majority of the footage along the right-of-way for conversion to electricity or steam locomotives, conversion was a prolonged process.

First of the Metropolitan's lines to go was the 5th Street-Wyandotte route, which was redundant upon the Kansas City Elevated. The line's east cable had some of the worst curvature in the industry, and the west cable traversed the James Street bridge, an all-metallic structure which expanded in the summer heat, giving the company the rare distinction of having slot closures from heat as well as from cold. Cable service was discontinued on November 1, 1898.

Of the Metropolitan's own original lines, the 18th-19th Street route was next to be converted on October 30, 1900. The company on June 2, 1903 was given a new franchise in an ordinance aptly known as the "Peace Agreement." The provisions explicitly required conversion of the remaining cable mileage. The 12th Street line presented the preeminent problem of a grade a streetcar could not traverse; the 20 per cent grade was roughly double what an adhesion vehicle could ascend or descend safely. The company dealt with the problem by converting the line from Washington to Cleveland Avenue on January 25, 1906, and revising the terminal in the West Bottoms, including

the trestle, to operate out of the former KCCR powerhouse at 9th and Washington. Cable trains regularly ran from 12th and Washington, where they were switched by a single-truck electric switcher, to the loop at the Stock Yards. Replacement of this trackage, though it motivated the populace less than getting rid of the 9th Street incline, was no less desirable on safety grounds. Here again, the safety experience had been better than one would reasonably expect. The worst accidents were concentrated in the twentieth century. On November 4, 1903, a grip broke, pitching a train down the incline, killing one passenger and injuring 72 others. On November 1, 1904, an eastbound train lost its grip and rolled back to the bottom without injuries, except to those who jumped. Thereafter, two trains were never permitted on the grade simultaneously in the same direction. In spite of this, on March 29, 1910, a westbound car derailed, and was struck by the following train.

The city drew up plans for building a viaduct for general traffic down into the West Bottoms mild enough for electric cars, and the company prepared to get rid of the last small remnant of its cable system. With David Barnhardt as gripman and F. H. Surbaugh as conductor, the last train left 12th and Washington at 1:00 AM on October 13, 1913, traversed the loop at the Stock Yards and returned to Washington Street 21 minutes later. The last small vestige of Kansas City's 37.8 mile cable network was extinguished.

POWERHOUSES: 9th and Wyoming Streets. EQUIPMENT: Two 30″ x 72″ Hamilton Corliss engines, 600 HP each.

Twelfth and Charlotte Streets. EQUIPMENT: Two 30″ x 72″ Hamilton Corliss engines, 600 HP each.

Eighteenth and Olive Streets. EQUIPMENT: Two 750 HP Hamilton Corliss engines.

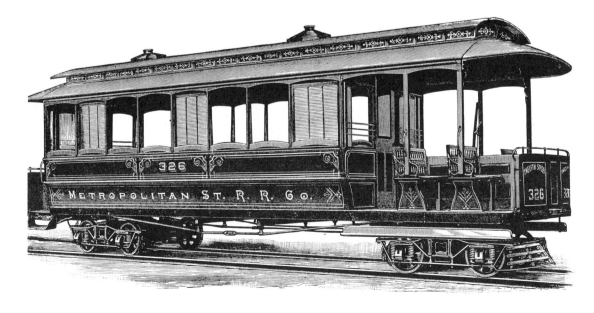

Above is a poor photograph of the bridge approaching Union Depot on the Metropolitan's line to Kansas City, Kansas. Below is the Metropolitan's trestle in the West Bottoms near the end of the cable era in Kansas City. The flat portion, on which the train is running, was about 40 feet over the railroad tracks below. The grade, reportedly of 20 per cent, is in the background. (*Kansas City Public Library*)

GRAND AVENUE RAILWAY

Single-jaw side grip   *Gauge: 4'-8½"*

The Westport & Kansas City Horse Railroad, a long-established operator led by Walton H. Holmes, together with his brothers, received a franchise in January 1886 for a line of cable or electric technology from central Kansas City to the old community of Westport. The Holmes brothers re-formed the company as the Grand Avenue Railway, and set out to build a route from the North End through the central area on Walnut Street to 13th, and thence to Westport via Grand Avenue and Main Street. Later in the year the Holmes brothers received a franchise for 15th Street (Truman Road). The decision to use cable technology was made in the spring of 1886, and the line was built during 1887. The downtown and 15th Street cables went into service on September 18, 1887, and the Grand Avenue or Westport cable on December 15.

In spite of the haste with which the physical plant was built, it was considered the best in Kansas City. William B. Knight and Daniel Bontecou, who had designed the Metropolitan, drew on their experience to produce a plant which was in many respects ideal. They put their powerhouse at 15th and Grand so that the three cables radiated straight out from it. The 15th Street cable had no curvature, and the Westport cable only a series of long pull curves on a moderate grade from Howard Avenue (24th Street) to 27th Street. The downtown cable, however, was beset with right-angle curves in and out of 13th Street as the line went from Grand Avenue to Walnut Street, following a route necessary to avoid franchise rights of other companies. The company's principal operating problem was an asymmetrical loop around 3rd, Grand, 1st and Walnut in the North Bottoms. J. B. Stone reported that the loop, which contained 66 curve pulleys, caused intolerable cable wear. Stone felt generally that the Kansas City engineers had overestimated the flexibility of cables, and built too much curvature into their systems. He considered operating conditions there so difficult that he expected Kansas City to consume more cable than the rest of the United States combined. As if in agreement with him, the Grand Avenue Railway moved quickly to get rid of the loop — rather the reverse of the behavior of the Metropolitan in the same period. In 1888, it was replaced with a small balloon loop to the left at 3rd and Walnut. If Knight and Bontecou executed the plans Stone attributed to them, the cable turned on a 12-foot terminal sheave, and the cars traversed

the loop on momentum. Stone estimated the change would reduce wear on the north cable in a ratio of 22:13.

Once this problem was out of the way, the physical plant was considered an economical one to operate. The company, alone among Kansas City operators, used combination cars exclusively, similar to the equipment of the North Chicago Street Railroad. It was reported in 1891 to own 80. Cars were reported to operate for only about 13¢ per car mile, as versus 15-16¢ per train mile for other companies. The company reached an agreement with the Metropolitan for use of trust patents. The grip was originally described as a Root, but was later reported to have been modified with longer jaws and removal of the carrying pulleys.

The company's fourth and last line was a route down Holmes Street, built by the subsidiary Holmes Street Railway after the city's most notable franchise controversy. Thomas Corrigan, Robert Gillham, and Col. James Lillis, with associates, promoted the Citizens' Cable Railway in hopes of building a line from Main and Missouri in the North End east on Missouri, south on Cherry and McCoy Streets (one block west of Holmes) to Springfield Avenue (31st Street), and thence back to its origin via Holmes and Missouri. In November 1887 the City Council voted the Citizens' a franchise; the Grand Avenue Railway received only 5 of 16 votes. Mayor Kumpf, however, vetoed the Citizens' franchise on the ground that the proposed route would entail rope drops at 10 points, whereas the Grand Avenue's proposed line south from 15th Street would cross only the Metropolitan at 18th and 19th Streets. Kumpf's veto was sustained by a margin of one vote, and the Grand Avenue Railway was given the franchise for its subsidiary. The line was a very simple one, with a single cable on a perfectly straight route from a powerhouse at the south terminus. It was, however, exceptionally hilly, requiring four depression pulleys. The 1.7 mile line cost $350,000. The company had visions of issuing a second cable south from Springfield as the city developed, but the cable era ended before plans were formulated. The Holmes Street Railway began operation on July 1, 1889.

No further additions were made to the Grand Avenue system. One of the most obvious cable routes in the area was out 15th Street down into the Blue River Valley and up again into downtown Indepen-

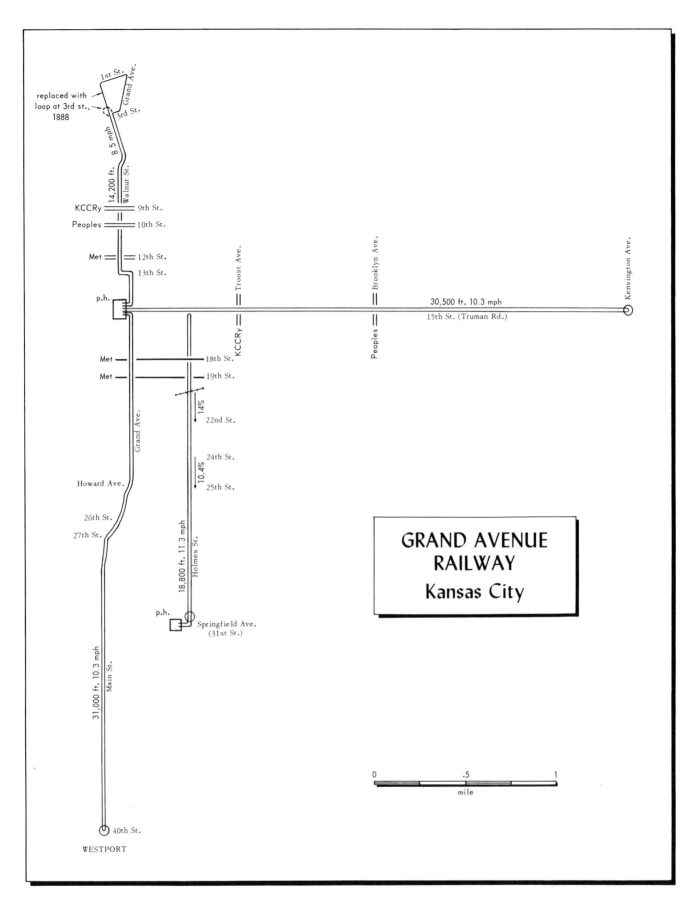

1st St.

Grand Ave.

replaced with
loop at 3rd st.,
1888

3rd St.

8.5 mph

14,200 ft.

Walnut St.

KCCRy — 9th St.

Peoples — 10th St.

Met — 12th St.

13th St.

Troost Ave.

Brooklyn Ave.

Kensington Ave.

p.h.

30,500 ft. 10.3 mph

15th St. (Truman Rd.)

Met — 18th St.

KCCRy

Peoples

Met — 19th St.

14%

22nd St.

Grand Ave.

24th St.

10.4%

25th St.

Howard Ave.

26th St.

18,800 ft. 11.3 mph

Holmes St.

27th St.

p.h.

Springfield Ave.
(31st St.)

**GRAND AVENUE
RAILWAY
Kansas City**

31,000 ft. 10.3 mph

Main St.

0   .5   1
mile

40th St.

WESTPORT

The Grand Avenue Railway originally terminated in the loop, shown above, in bluffs, since removed, in the North End area of the city. Below, a photographer with a warped sense of values was obviously trying to shoot one of the Fire Department's ladder wagons making a hard left turn off Walnut Street, but in the process he secured the clearest known photograph of a Grand Avenue Railway car — or, at least, part of it. (*Kansas City Public Library*)

At left, a Grand Avenue car takes the cable after the rope drop for the Kansas City Cable Railway at 9th and Walnut. Below is a group of gripmen, conductors and shop personnel at the Holmes Street powerhouse. *(Kansas City Public Library)* On the opposite page, open and closed versions of the Grand Avenue Railway's combination cars share a Brownell & Wight advertisement with single-truckers of the Pacific Railway and the Missouri Railroad.

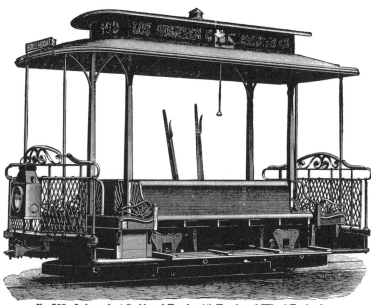
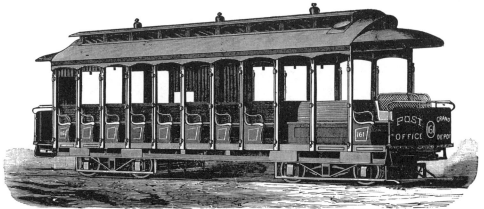
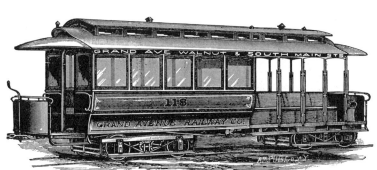

275

dence. The Centropolis Valley Cable Railroad in 1887 sought a franchise to build from the end of the 15th Street line to Independence, and in 1889 the Kansas City & Blue Valley Railway proposed the same project. Neither was built.

Lack of access to the West Bottoms spared the Grand Avenue the operating problems of its major rivals, but also divorced it from a major source of revenue at Union Depot. The worst reported accident of the company was a collision of a 15th Street car with a Santa Fe freight in October 1892, which killed four.

Kansas City required crossing guards for safety reasons where cable lines intersected. These guards became familiar figures in the city. Most were ephemeral figures historically, but the Grand Avenue's guard at 19th and Grand was Uncle Charley Fisher, known as "Santa Claus" because of his beard and corpulence. A lover of warmth and comfort in a job that offered little of either, Fisher rigged a semaphore arm to give his lantern signals from his curbside booth in harsh weather. The city's other notable crossing guard was Michael Tuite, known as "Old Wideawake" from his warning cry of "Wideawake—wideawake!" at the approach of cars at the Junction at 9th and Main. Tuite, an Irish immigrant, was reportedly a volunteer at the outset, but he was later retained by the Metropolitan.

As reported in connection with the Kansas City Cable Railway and the Metropolitan Street Railway,

the Holmes brothers first endeavored to merge with the former in 1894, and then sold out to the latter in 1895. The Metropolitan in which the Holmes brothers became officers, showed no great eagerness at converting the Grand Avenue system, which was in relatively good condition, and reasonably well patronized. The Westport line was converted on May 2, 1900, because of the Metropolitan's desire to modify the track on south Main Street to accommodate electric cars considerably larger than the cable equipment. Running time was cut about 10 minutes by the electric cars.

Conversion of the rest of the Grand Avenue system was required by the Metropolitan's "Peace Agreement" of 1903. The 15th Street, Holmes Street, and Walnut cables were all killed in the early hours of September 1, 1903; the last cars were scheduled to leave the north terminus at midnight the previous evening. The Walnut rope was relaid on the Washington-Summit line, but the rest were scrapped.

POWERHOUSES: 15th and Grand. EQUIPMENT: Two Allis engines, 450 HP each, and one 750 HP engine.

Holmes and Springfield. EQUIPMENT: One 250 HP engine.

Grand Avenue personnel. (*Kansas City Public Library*)

INTER-STATE CONSOLIDATED RAPID
TRANSIT RAILWAY

Gillham double-jaw side grip Gauge: 4'-8½"

This company operated two cable lines incidental to a steam dummy system running from Kansas City, Missouri to Kansas City, Kansas. The entire operation was integral with the Inter-State Investment Company, an effort at real estate development of Col. David W. Edgerton and associates. The rail operation consisted of 3.75 miles of surface steam dummy line in Kansas, a two-mile elevated structure across the West Bottoms to bring the trains to the Union Depot, a cable line of 0.8 mile to haul them into the central business district of Kansas City, and a separate cable installation, the Riverview line, of 1.6 miles in Kansas. The elevated was reportedly the first west of New York.

Both of the company's cable installations date from 1888, though the steam dummy mileage had been in service earlier. Edgerton had completed the steam line from the St. Louis Avenue station on the elevated at Union Depot across the West Bottoms and up into Kansas to Edgerton Place in 1886. Service began on October 10. Edgerton built an extension to Chelsea Park, an amusement area he had promoted, in 1887. To go from St. Louis Avenue into the central area, he faced the same problem of climbing the bluff that had faced the directors of the Kansas City Cable Railway and the Metropolitan, and he dealt with it in the same fashion, by resorting to cable traction. His intention, however, was to haul rapid transit cars from the dummy line behind grip cars, an operation which would have been impossible with the grades of 18 to 20 per cent which the other lines used. Consequently, the company found it necessary to tunnel the bluff to Washington Street to bring the line up to 8th Street, on which it was to terminate at Delaware. The tunnel, which cost about $150,000, was 810 feet of 8.8 per cent grade, 28 feet wide and 21 feet high, capable of accommodating double track.

Design of the cable line was entrusted to Robert Gillham, who began working on it early in 1887; tunneling the bluff began in April. Gillham used what was described as a heavier version of his usual grip with an elongated lever, mounted in a short grip car only seven feet long, designed without seats for passengers. The company is variously reported to have had eight or nine such cars, with which it planned service from Delaware Street to Union Depot on three-minute headway; steam trains ran on eight-minute headway to Wyandotte. The cable plant was completed in about a year, so that the cable could be laid on April 21, 1888. Gillham used a 1½ inch cable; the rest of the Kansas City lines used 1¼ inch ropes. Unlike the typical street railway, the company had steam locomotives available for laying the cable. A dummy engine was able to draw the cable up to Delaware Street, but once the cable had been threaded around the terminal sheave, the additional resistance was too much for the engine, and ten horses had to be added to bring it back to the tunnel mouth. Gravity enabled the engine to haul it down without further difficulty. Revenue service began on April 24.

Gillham was simultaneously designing a separate cable installation, the Riverview line, in Kansas. This was intended to be an ordinary street railway on Riverview Boulevard (Central Avenue), through a lightly populated, but rapidly developing area. It was a particularly simple installation of a single cable, with a long ascent from east to west no worse than 4 per cent. Construction of the Riverview line also began in April 1887, and the plant was ready for a trial run on May 21, 1888. The first run had to be made with one of the tunnel line's short grip cars and trailers borrowed from the People's Cable Railway, with which the company had a partial community of ownership. The Pullman grips and trailers intended for the Riverview line had not yet been delivered. The line's own equipment arrived about a week after the initiation of revenue service on May 22, 1888.

On October 4, 1888, the company announced that it intended to exchange equipment between the tunnel cable and the Riverview line. The weight of the rapid transit cars was proving too much for cable traction, and the Riverview line did not produce

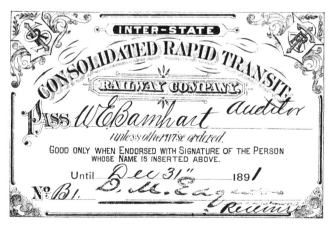

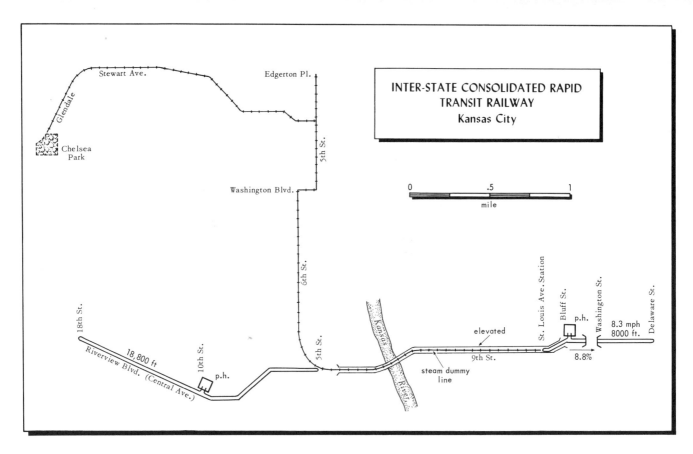

Washington Blvd.

Stewart Ave.

Edgerton Pl.

Glendale

Chelsea Park

5th St.

6th St.

18th St.

Riverview Blvd. (Central Ave.)
18,800 ft

10th St.

p.h.

5th St.

Kansas River

steam dummy line

9th St.

elevated

St. Louis Ave. Station

Bluff St.

p.h.

8.8%

Washington St.

8.3 mph 8000 ft.

Delaware St.

INTER-STATE CONSOLIDATED RAPID TRANSIT RAILWAY
Kansas City

0   .5   1
mile

enough traffic to occupy the equipment bought for it. The line was reported to have eight sets of equipment, but to operate with only two. The company equipped some rapid transit cars with stoves, and began hauling them on the Riverview line behind the former tunnel grip cars. The rapid transit trains were terminated at St. Louis Avenue, where passengers changed to the former Riverview grips and trailers to rise to 8th Street.

Although the Kansas City *Times* reported in November 1888 that the Riverview line was "producing quite a bit of traffic," the company rather quickly concluded that traffic had not warranted the project. As early as March 1889 the company was reported to be interested in abandoning it. In June the management applied to the Kansas City, Kansas city council for permission to convert to steam dummy, but no action was taken. In August a break in the cable caused the company to operate with steam dummies, demonstrating the practicability of steam traction on the line's modest grades. An ordinance for conversion was introduced on October 25, 1889, and passed on January 3, 1890. By March the SRJ reported the cable equipment up for sale.

Meanwhile, the Inter-State had gone bankrupt in October 1889, mainly from the debt incurred in building the tunnel, but Edgerton was appointed trustee. His receiver's inventory listed the investment in the tunnel cable installation as $533,610 and in the River-

view cable line as $255,981. In 1892 the company was reorganized as the Kansas City Elevated Railway, with Gillham as general manager. He had by this time faced the shortcomings of the cable traction with which he had become so thoroughly identified, and embarked upon a total electrification of the elevated system. Electric cars replaced cable in the summer of 1892, and the entire dummy system was electrified with street railway technology by March 1, 1893. In May, 1894, the Metropolitan bought out the Elevated, but continued it in separate operation under Gillham. Thus, the Inter-State became the first of the Kansas City lines to give up cable power, and the first independent company to come into the Metropolitan's expanding network. After the accident of 1902 on the 9th Street incline, passengers converted to the 8th Street electric cars in such numbers that the Metropolitan was forced to reduce the grade in the tunnel in 1903-04 to 5 per cent, thereby increasing its capacity. The change moved the upper portal two blocks east to Broadway. The tunnel remained a principal entry into downtown Kansas City for cars from Kansas City, Kansas, until the end of the streetcar era.

POWERHOUSE: West portal of tunnel at Bluff Street. Equipment unknown.

Riverview Avenue and 10th Street. Equipment unknown.

Only known photograph of Inter-State cable equipment is this small illustration of one of the non-passenger grip cars from *Mass Transportation* of January 1954.

The photograph above illustrates the methods by which the Inter-State Rapid Transit and two of its rivals dealt with the ascent of Quality Hill. In the foreground is the 9th Street trestle of the Kansas City Cable Railway. Immediately above is the Inter-State's elevated approach to its tunnel portal. The Inter-State's powerhouse is marked by a plume of escaping steam and a smoking chimney. To the left is the Metropolitan's line along Bluff Street to the North End area. *(Kansas City Public Library)*

Below is the tunnel portal in 1953, near the end of electric operation in Kansas City. The elevated had been substantially rebuilt in the interim. *(Charles J. Murphy)*

There are no known photographs of the Inter-State's cable operations, though these photographs illustrate the company's over-all operations. Above, one of the rapid transit trains is hauled across the West Bottoms by a steam dummy engine. *(Earl Moore)* Below is the Inter-State's station at Mulberry Street after electrification. The Metropolitan cable train in the foreground will turn left and run across the West Bottoms under the elevated structure. *(Kansas City Public Library)*

One of the Inter-State's trains waits at the Edgerton Place terminal, headed by a Baldwin dummy engine. *(Earl Moore)* The company converted from dummy to cable haulage at St. Louis Avenue station, the latter-day equivalent of which is shown in Charles J. Murphy's photograph from Quality Hill in 1953.

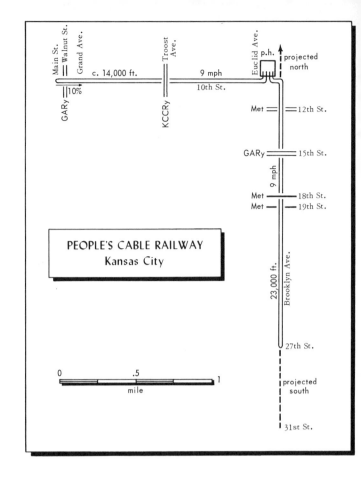

PEOPLE'S CABLE RAILWAY
Kansas City

The Pullman builder's photograph, below, is the only known picture of People's Cable Railway equipment. Pullman's order book indicates the equipment was delivered in tan and scarlet, but retrospective accounts report that cars were Pullman green toward the end of service. *(Barney Neuberger)* The company's principal engineering problem was the ascent of the 10th Street hill up from Main Street, shown above in a present-day view by Edward N. Middleton.

PEOPLE'S CABLE RAILWAY

Gillham double-jaw side-grip   Gauge: 4'-8½"

Least successful of the completed Kansas City companies was the People's Cable Railway, which operated a route of 3½ miles on 10th Street and Brooklyn Avenue. The line was projected in 1886 by J. Foster Rhodes of Chicago and a local real estate broker, Henry N. Smith, Jr., who conceived it integrally with a land development on Brooklyn Avenue. They received a franchise over the mayor's veto in February, 1887, and began to build the line. Their engineer was Robert Gillham, to whom the job was probably an easy one. The line began at 10th and Main, ran east up the steepest hill in the central business district and through typical undulating territory to 27th and Brooklyn, with a single right-angle turn of 55-foot radius at 10th and Brooklyn. The powerhouse was placed two blocks west of the intersection, giving the line an almost bare minimum of curvature.

Unfortunately, in other respects the line was not so well situated. The terminus at Main Street was east of Union Depot and the Broadway business area, and the decline of the land boom left the tributary area lightly populated. Because of the harsh winter of 1888, the company was able to do no construction until well into the year, and could not complete the 10th Street portion of the line until May 29, 1888. The Brooklyn Avenue segment had its trial trip on August 6. The company had projects for extension in both directions, though the plans were of somewhat different character. Originally Rhodes and Gillham, who became active in the management of the line, proposed to extend the 10th Street cable west under Main Street to Wyandotte Avenue and north to 8th Street for a connection with the Interstate Elevated, with which the line had some community of ownership. This course of action would have brought the cars to Union Depot, but at the cost of a very difficult reverse curve crossing Main Street. In 1889 Gillham changed his plans, and proposed to route the company's cars around the projected joint loop of the major companies on the Metropolitan's track on north Main Street of which he was the principal advocate. The company, however, became insolvent on July 1, 1889, and was unable to engage in any further construction. Indeed, it was reported in the SRJ to be willing to sell all its rolling stock and physical plant in order to liquidate completely.

The People's Cable Railway, owing to its financial troubles, also proved unable to build south. There the

incentive was not a desire to serve additional territory, but rather a franchise obligation to build to Springfield Avenue (31st Street), the south city limit. The company had no interest in doing so, since the end of the land boom had left the area almost unpopulated. The City Council was adamant on this point, and in 1892 declared the company's franchise bond of $10,000 forfeited on the ground of refusal to complete the line. In the previous year the bondholders, who were mainly in Chicago, tried to sell the property to the Kansas City Cable Railway, the president of which said he wouldn't take it free.

The company had also expressed an interest in building north along Brooklyn Avenue from the powerhouse, but nothing was done to advance the proposal.

Somewhat surprisingly, the People's survived the mass annihilation of American cable lines in the mid-1890s. The road had never covered its interest payments, but had run up a debt of nearly a million dollars, with annual deficits of $6000 to $12,000. On petition of the bondholders, the property was sold at a receiver's auction on March 14, 1896, and reorganized as the Brooklyn Avenue Railway. Service was cut from 5½-minute headway to 7-minute in 1897, to the dissatisfaction of the riders. In January, 1899, the Brooklyn Avenue Railway purchased the North East Electric Railway, and announced plans to convert the cable line to electricity. The two companies were consolidated into the Central Electric Railway, the bonds of which were guaranteed by the Metropolitan on May 1, 1899. Thus the 10th Street cable line came into the hands of the expanding Metropolitan system, which had little enthusiasm for perpetuating it. Cables were stopped on July 15, 1899 and Metropolitan electric cars began running on December 14, 1899. The line was formally incorporated into the Metropolitan in 1905. The former cable powerhouse was used for some years to house the flatbed motors equipped as floats for Kansas City's annual parade of the Priests of Pallas.

POWERHOUSE: 10th Street and Euclid Avenue.

EQUIPMENT: One 600 horsepower Hamilton Corliss engine.

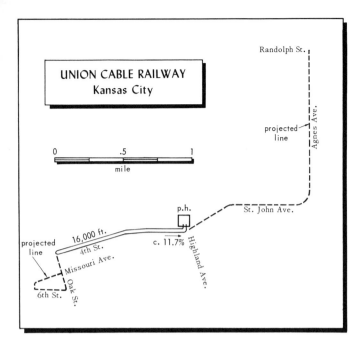

There are no known illustrations of the Union Cable Railway, but the photograph by Edward N. Middleton, below, shows the terrain which the line was intended to conquer. Fourth Street, greatly modified by a housing project, runs straight ahead from the photographer. The line climbed the hill in the distance; the powerhouse was at the left at the top of the hill.

Terry bottom grip   *Gauge: 4'-8½"*

Like the Rasmussen installation in Newark, the Union Cable Railway was a pilot project of a shallow-conduit system, designed to reduce the capital investment of cable traction. The effort was more successful, but barely so, and the experience can only be evaluated a failure.

The Terry grip was a bottom grip invented by S. H. Terry of Fulton, Missouri, intended for low-cost installation on horsecars. As mentioned in Chapter III, its action was based on a set of horizontal and vertical rollers at each end of a bobbin-shaped housing. When a wheel on the platform was tightened, the forward motion of the cable forced the rollers into the nose of the housing and pulled the car forward. The cable, which was orthodox, ran in a conduit 9¾" x 12", consisting of two pieces of cast iron bolted together. Pulley vaults, sunk 21 inches deep at 36-foot intervals, were designed to hold the cable eight inches below the slot. The powerhouse was also orthodox, though of lighter construction because the system was intended to require less energy than regular systems.

The Union Cable Railway was organized in 1887 by H. L. Coombs, Benjamin F. Coombs, M. G. Harmon and several other prominent North End commission merchants. Their purpose was to build a cable line of about 3¼ miles from the North End market area east along 4th Street, up the bluff to the region now largely occupied by North Terrace Park, and down again into the East Bottoms area, which was imperfectly served by existing transportation media. The route required a steep ascent eastbound, about 11.7 per cent, and would have required a descent of about the same magnitude to the east, if the route in that area had ever been defined. The line was intended to terminate on a loop in the market area, but nothing was built beyond a double-tracked line from 4th and Oak to the powerhouse at 4th and Highland. Cars were equipped with grips under the center of the body, with operating wheels on the two platforms, so that they were able to operate in either direction.

Had the system worked, the Union Cable Railway might have served as the entrance into Kansas City of a second line, the Blue Valley Cable Railway, which intended to build east into the valley of the Big Blue River and on to Independence. J. B. Stone on a visit to Kansas City wrote to his home office that he could find no evidence this project was being seri-ously pursued, and paid no attention to it. The company is known to have intended to use the Terry grip.

The Union Cable Railway worked closely with the Continental Cable & Grip Company of New York, which held the patent on the Terry grip. W. M. Broadwell, head of Continental, visited the property and had his engineer in attendance during construction in 1888 and 1889. The Union management had a great deal of difficulty financing the project, and had the line ready for operation, far behind schedule, only on December 20, 1889. Two cars operated, apparently in revenue service in an effort to secure the line's franchise deposit of $10,000. The Union had ordered ten cars from the St. Louis Car Company and expressed an intention of putting a third in service shortly. As it proved, the day of the operation on December 20, 1889 was the only one the company ever had.

At the time, newspaper accounts of the operation of December 20 were fairly favorable. A. W. Nesbit, who represented Continental at the opening, stated that the system's main problem was that the access plates and grip hatches were not made fast, so that passing grips knocked them loose. Revealing two respects in which orthodox technology was superior to the Terry system, Nesbit said that separate grip cars and trailers would be preferable to the line's mounting grips under car bodies, and also that standard concrete-and-iron would work out better than the line's bolted iron conduit. A reporter for the Kansas City *Times* wrote that the cars ran "smoothly and with good speed."

Retrospectively in 1900 an anonymous author in the SRR reported less favorably on the opening. He stated that the Terry system proved itself unworkable at once. The grip was incapable of making a smooth start; cars lurched about and knocked off hatches. The opening, this writer argued, was such an utter fiasco that the Union's numerous creditors immediately gave up on the project and brought several actions for recovery of debts.

In any case, the line's remaining history is entirely concerned with legal actions. Broadwell took over the line from its promoters, but it quickly went bankrupt. Efforts to put the line in operation went on as late as 1892, but in that year the cable was removed to prevent deterioration, and the city ordered the $10,000 bond forfeited for non-completion. Several operators

The Union Cable Railway's exit from the North End was 4th Street, the minor character of which is evident in Edward N. Middleton's photograph of 1970. Below are two advertisements from the Kansas City *Journal* demonstrating the ties between building the cable railways and real estate development in the area. *(Kansas City Public Library)*

showed interest in buying it, either in hopes of putting an electric line on 4th Street, or of scrapping the conduit. As late as 1897, Frank Dixon bought the line at a receiver's auction for $1260, less than its scrap value. Even then, Broadwell's attorney threatened further lawsuits. The property was eventually scrapped, and no electric line was ever built on its route. Investment in the stillborn cable facility was estimated at $300,000 of which about $50,000 was recovered by creditors.

POWERHOUSE: 4th Street and Highland Avenue.

EQUIPMENT: Built by Walker Manufacturing Company, Cleveland; details unknown.

Kansas City references: "Kansas City Cableography," SRG, III (1888), November supplement, 19; "Kansas City Cable Railway," *Kansas City Review of Science and Industry,* VIII (1885), 541-548; Kansas City *Times,* November 18, 1900; SRJ, IV (1888), 1; SRJ, VI (1890), 111-114; Bion J. Arnold, *Value of the Properties of the Metropolitan Street Railway of Kansas City* (1913), 3 vols.; Colin K. Lee, "Kansas City Cable Lines," unpublished MS in possession of its author, Webster Groves, Missouri; collection of Calvin B. Manon.

A NOTE ON RELATIVE ROPE POSITIONS IN KANSAS CITY

As the accompanying diagrams indicate, there were 22 crossings of cable lines in Kansas City. The problem of relative positions is of exceptional interest, partly because the city did not use seniority in allocation, and partly because the information on positions is incomplete.

The municipal government for safety reasons required the railway on the steeper grade to be given the superior position. The city is so hilly that only 18th-19th and Grand were essentially flat intersections, but at several the gradients in the two directions were not markedly different. Where two companies could not agree on positions, the City Engineer was empowered to decide on relative gradients, whereupon the City Council enacted an ordinance to specify relative positions. Ordinances determined positions at 9th and Main, 12th and Troost, 15th and Troost, 18th and Troost, 12th and Washington, and 18th and Brooklyn. Newspaper reports of accidents and especially of

a fortunate blizzard of February 12, 1894, which prevented cars from rolling over their rope drops normally, enable us to know the following: 9th and Walnut, 10th and Troost, 5th and Main, 5th and Delaware, 12th and Main, 12th and Walnut, 15th and Brooklyn and 18th and Holmes. Several other positions may be deduced from a statement in the SRJ that cars on the Metropolitan's 18th-19th Street line dropped rope ten times for cables of other lines. A similar statement that the Grand Avenue Railway had four rope drops is less helpful, for the author did not make clear whether he meant a number of specific points, or the number of drops required in a round trip. It is also not clear whether he included the subsidiary Holmes Street Railway. The problem is compounded by the poor documentation of the People's Cable Railway. This company, looked upon as a late-comer and interloper, was never described in detail in the trade journals and not much reported in newspapers.

In the course of research for a history of street railways in Kansas City, Terrence W. Cassidy found a manuscript log of changes in the system during conversion from cable to electricity. Entries in connection with removal of the People's cable in 1899 indicate that the Metropolitan immediately revised rope positions at 10th and Walnut and on Brooklyn Avenue at 12th, 18th and 19th. Presumably, ropes that had been inferior to the People's were raised to eliminate stationary depression devices. This appears to confirm the positions at 10th and Walnut and on Brooklyn at 12th and 19th, which had been based on inference. On the other hand, this discovery seems to raise the problem that the People's may have been made superior to the Metropolitan at 18th and Brooklyn at some unknown date, in spite of the ordinance mentioned above. Something other than relative rope position may have required the change at the intersection on removal of the People's cable, however. With that possible exception, all of the positions shown are consistent with surviving evidence and with the city's preference for the line on the steeper grade being superior.

A word on the speeds shown is in order. At the outset, the city restricted almost all lines to speed in the range of 7-8 miles per hour, but in 1888 became more liberal. The speeds shown are the latest reported, mainly dating from near the end of service, but other and usually lower speeds were widely reported.

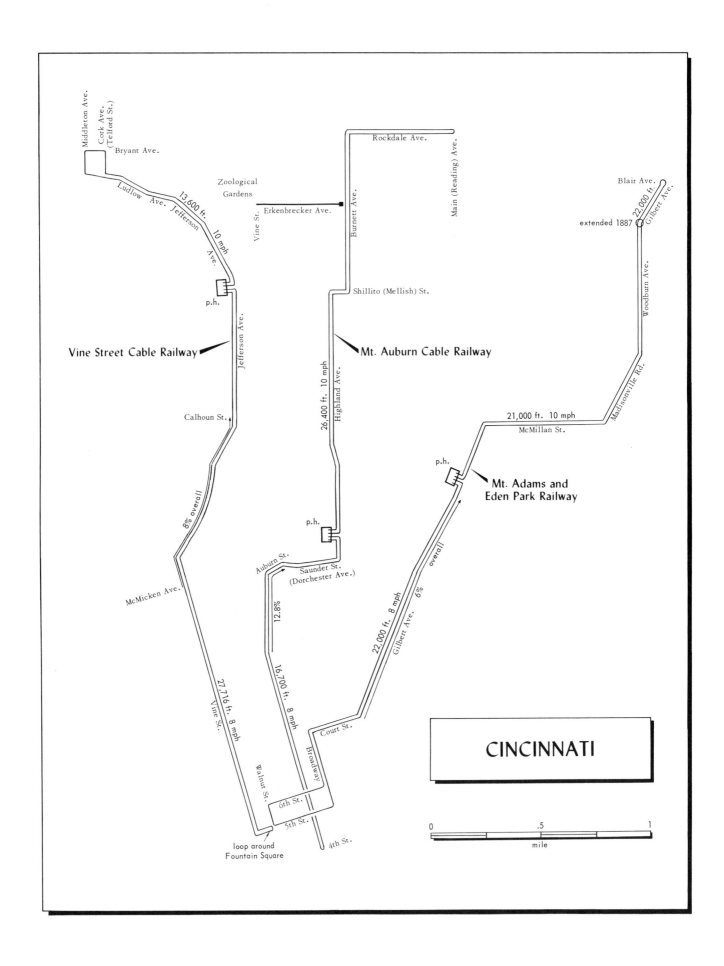

Middleton Ave.
Cork Ave. (Telford St.)
Bryant Ave.
Ludlow Ave. Jefferson Ave.
13,600 ft. 10 mph
Zoological Gardens
Vine St. Erkenbrecker Ave.
Rockdale Ave.
Burnett Ave.
Main (Reading) Ave.
Blair Ave.
22,000 ft.
Gilbert Ave.
extended 1887
Gilbert Ave.
p.h.
Shillito (Mellish) St.
Woodburn Ave.
Vine Street Cable Railway ▶
Jefferson Ave.
◀ **Mt. Auburn Cable Railway**
Calhoun St.
26,400 ft. 10 mph
Highland Ave.
Madisonville Rd.
21,000 ft. 10 mph
McMillan St.
8% overall
p.h.
Mt. Adams and Eden Park Railway
p.h.
McMicken Ave.
Auburn St.
Saunder St. (Dorchester Ave.)
12.8%
22,000 ft. 8 mph
Gilbert Ave.
6% overall
27,716 ft. 8 mph
Vine St.
16,700 ft. 8 mph
Walnut St.
Broadway
Court St.
6th St.
5th St.
4th St.
loop around Fountain Square

CINCINNATI		

0   .5   1
mile

CINCINNATI

Population in 1890: 296,908

MOUNT ADAMS & EDEN PARK RAILWAY

Lane single-jaw side grip   *Gauge: 5'-2½"*

Cincinnati, a pioneer city in its area, with a central business district at the base of hills ranging up from the Ohio River, was so obviously suited to cable traction that it received an installation as early as 1885. As in Pittsburgh, only a few major routes out of the central area were straight enough even for difficult cable systems, and thus the city had only three installations.

The Mount Adams & Eden Park Inclined Railway was founded in 1873 to establish a funicular for passengers from Lock Street east of the business district up Mount Adams to serve the Eden Park recreational area, and also to develop local real estate. The project was headed by James E. Mooney, a local tanner who, feeling that his other business interests prevented his directing the company, chose a young Pennsylvanian, George B. Kerper, to be president. The funicular opened in March 1876, and in the following year the company established a horsecar connection from Lock Street to Fountain Square at the center of the city via Fifth Street. In 1878 a separate horsecar line was established from the head of the funicular into Eden Park. In 1879 the company began work both to extend the upper horsecar line to the Avondale residential area, and to unite the two horsecar lines by converting the funicular to an open-platform capable of handling horsecars and road vehicles. The conversion operation was entrusted to Henry M. Lane, a recent graduate of MIT, and son of the head of Lane & Bodley, the city's largest machine shop. In April, 1880, the conversion was completed; the company went on to become the second largest street railway in the city, inferior only to John Kilgour's Cincinnati Consolidated Street Railroad.

Kilgour in 1880 merged his Consolidated with several other street railways to form the Cincinnati Street Railway. One of the components of the new system was a horsecar line on Gilbert Avenue parallel to the MA&EP horsecar line and funicular. When Kilgour in 1881 proposed to lay cable on Gilbert Avenue, Kerper felt his enterprise was menaced. After a rate

war and a long political struggle, the MA&EP bought the Gilbert Avenue line from the Street Railway for $270,000, of which $230,000 was to be paid in MA&EP stock. By this arrangement, Kilgour secured a minority interest in the company, enough for two directors, but not enough for control of it.

Kerper also planned to lay cable on Gilbert Avenue, but felt 5000 passengers per day was the minimum traffic to warrant the investment. The line, which served the city's most rapidly growing suburb, Walnut Hills, approached this figure by 1884. Lane, who was deputed to design the road, experimented with the Tom Johnson ladder cable system on May Street, but decided against it. Instead, Lane developed what he hoped would be a cut-rate version of standard technology, based on a grip similar to Hovey's Sutter Street side grip. He formed the Lane National Cable Construction Company, which became a prominent competitor to the trust. Both Kerper and Kilgour became partners in the company. Initially, the cable installation was limited to the steep portion of Gilbert Avenue from Court to Nassau Streets, a distance of barely over a mile. Horsecars were attached to a detachable grip at one end of the grade and detached at the other, all without stopping. Kerper missed the July 4 opening he had sought, and began cable service on July 8, 1885.

In April 1886 the company embarked upon extension of the cable installation to the entire car line, running from Walnut Street to a turntable at Woodburn and Gilbert Avenues along the route shown on the accompanying map. Lane built the line along McMillan Street, Madisonville Road and Woodburn Avenue, rather than directly along Gilbert Avenue, to avoid several long pull curves on difficult grades. Even so, the SRG reported that in curvature and other respects it was the most difficult cable road in existence when it opened on October 9, 1886. In the following year, the route was extended along Gilbert 2 blocks to Blair Avenue to a loop of only 30 feet radius, raising the mileage to about 3.8.

Above, a team drags the Mount Adams & Eden Park's first cable up the Gilbert Avenue grade. *(John H. White, Jr.)* Below, the first car operates on the line on July 8, 1885. At this time cable operation was limited to the ascent of the Gilbert Avenue hill; horses pulled the cars over the rest of the route. *(Smithsonian Institution)*

The company experienced some difficulty in keeping the cable on the driving drums, which in the interests of economy were on the shaft of the flywheel, but otherwise the line operated with not markedly worse than ordinary experience in accidents and breakdowns. The company's accident of October 2, 1887, recounted in Chapter IV, in which a loop of cable entrapped a grip so as to cause a collision at 5th and Sycamore, stemmed from the tortuous character of its approach to the business district, rather than from intrinsic limitations of Lane's cut-price technology.

J. B. Stone reported the line ran 285 trips per day, with a headway of 2½ minutes from 3:00 to 7:00 PM. He wrote that the outer cable lasted an average of 14 months and the inner nine months, in spite of greater curvature in the outer, merely because of the greater frequency of gripping and ungripping on the inner.

Kerper resigned the presidency of the company in 1890, leaving Kilgour free to incorporate it into his spreading Cincinnati Street Railway. The merger was not effected until August 1, 1896. The Eden Park horsecar line, including the funicular, had been electrified in 1890, as usual attracting much of the traffic from the cable line. Kilgour had become disillusioned with cables fairly early, but did not close the Gilbert Avenue line until February 1, 1898. Electric service was inaugurated the following day. The funicular, though earlier and more primitive, survived until April 16, 1948.

Lane had endeavored to design the line for $60,000 a mile of double track with $25,000 additional for machinery. Although he failed — investment was reported at $563,000 — it was a lightly built property. Lane used cast iron yokes anchored in concrete, but he substituted heavy creosoted planks for the walls of the conduit to save money. The company used single-truck open and closed cars from Pullman and Stephenson. When the line became fully cable-operated, the Lane grip was mounted under the car and controlled first by wheel and later by lever from the front platform; by 1890 the ejection spools were reported removed and the dies lengthened.

POWERHOUSE: Gilbert Avenue and Windsor Street.

EQUIPMENT: Two 28″ x 54″ Hamilton Corliss engines, 500 and 400 HP, respectively. Extant as Fenton-Wuerdeman-Thayer drycleaning plant.

References: John H. White, Jr. "The Mount Adams & Eden Park Inclined Railway, 'The Kerper Road'," *Bulletin of the Historical and Philosophical Society of Ohio*, XVII (1959), 243-276; SRG, I (1886), 284-290.

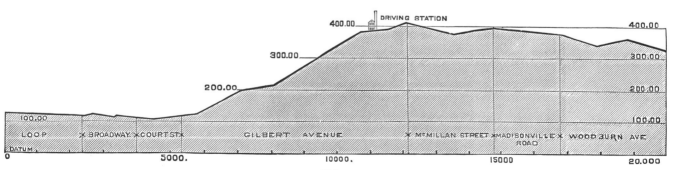

The Mount Adams & Eden Park was operated with substantial single-truck cars. Number 135 is shown here in a woodcut from the Stephenson catalog, and in a broadside in a typical Stephenson builder's photograph. (*Smithsonian Institution; Museum of the City of New York*) The timetable dates from 1886-87, when the line terminated at a turntable at Gilbert and Woodburn Avenues. (*Cincinnati Historical Society*)

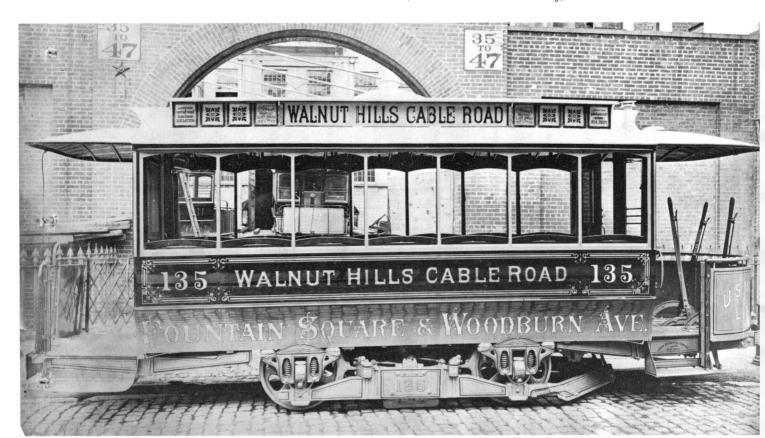

VINE STREET CABLE RAILWAY

Lane single-jaw side grip   *Gauge: 5'-2½"*

The Vine Street Cable Railway from beginning to end was a part of John Kilgour's Cincinnati Street Railway; although its cars were lettered with its own name, the line had no separate corporate identity.

Vine Street was Cincinnati's principal north-south thoroughfare, and also Kilgour's strongest franchise. Kilgour had shown interest in cable traction to the extent of undertaking a line without a franchise on Spring Grove Avenue in the northwest portion of the city in 1885, but a rival operator, the Cincinnati & Spring Grove Railway, brought a successful legal action to require Kilgour to secure authority from the Common Council. Kilgour cancelled his contracts for ironwork and abandoned the project. The population along Vine Street, apparently on the basis of the success of the Gilbert Avenue line, petitioned in August 1886 for a cable installation running to the Zoo. Kilgour did not build directly to the Zoo, but he did undertake a route of 4.05 miles along Vine, Jefferson and Ludlow from Fountain Square to a loop around a city block in the suburban area of Clifton. The route entailed an ascent of the Vine Street Hill of slightly under a mile of 8½ per cent grade, with frequent curvature.

Henry M. Lane was again engaged to design the line. It is somewhat surprising that he was able to deal with the Vine Street Hill ascent without a specially-designed grip of the sort used in Pittsburgh on long pull curves, but he used his usual side grip without any reported modifications. On the basis of a relative absence of complaint, Lane's Vine Street installation seems to have been more successful than his earlier effort on Gilbert Avenue. The powerhouse was at Corryville, above the principal grade, and about two-thirds of the distance to Clifton. J. B. Stone reported that the powerhouse was odd in having the north rope on the south winding machinery, and vice versa, presumably to minimize the distance a grip car had to roll between cables. Lane had the line ready for experimental operation on the lower cable on September 25, 1887. Revenue service began about a week later, and the upper cable was ready for operation on February 9, 1888. The completed line cost $627,000.

Stone reported that the company made 325 trips a day. The run from Fountain Square to Clifton was 25 minutes; alternate cars carried trailers. The company had one serious accident — as usual, intrinsic to the technology. On July 14, 1889, the gripman of a northbound car turned over the controls to his conductor for the trip to Clifton. On one of the several downgrades on the undulating track, the conductor lost his grip, and as was customary with side grips, he was unable to retake the rope. In tightening his handbrake, he pulled too hard on the lever, breaking the chain and causing it to wrap around an axle. The chain then lashed through the floor, terrifying passengers who were already frightened at the car's careening down the grade out of control. Several passengers jumped, of whom seven were injured and one, a woman, killed with a broken neck. Passengers who stayed in the car were safe, since it rolled to a halt just behind the leading car at the foot of the grade.

Initially Kilgour planned a second cable installation, a route up 8th Street to Price Hill, straight west of the central area. This was a particularly obvious cable route, combining a major gradient with service to substantial existing population. Both George B. Kerper and Henry Martin, the city's two other cable operators, expressed interest in building to Price Hill at various times; it is somewhat surprising that none of the three did so.

In 1890 Kilgour's general manager responded to an interrogation of the SRJ that the management had no intention to install any further cable mileage, but on the other hand, it had no present plans to convert the Vine Street mileage. On March 23, 1897, the board of directors of the Cincinnati Street Railway voted to convert all of its cable railways as soon as possible. It began with the Gilbert Avenue line, probably because of its greater curvature, and then turned to Vine Street, converting it on September 16, 1898.

POWERHOUSE: Vine and Jefferson Streets. EQUIPMENT: Two 450 HP Lane & Bodley engines.

References: SRJ, VI (1890), 16; collection of John H. White, Jr.

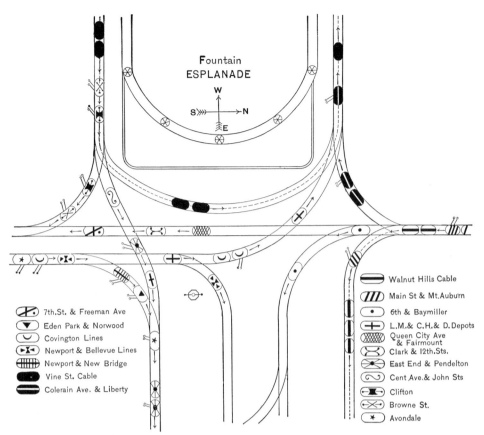

Fountain
ESPLANADE

W
S >>> N
E

7th.St. & Freeman Ave
Eden Park & Norwood
Covington Lines
Newport & Bellevue Lines
Newport & New Bridge
Vine St. Cable
Colerain Ave. & Liberty

Walnut Hills Cable
Main St & Mt.Auburn
6th & Baymiller
L.M.& C.H.& D.Depots
Queen City Ave & Fairmount
Clark & 12th.Sts.
East End & Pendelton
Cent.Ave.& John Sts
Clifton
Browne St.
Avondale

A SEEMING LABYRINTH—CORNER FIFTH AND WALNUT STREETS, CINCINNATI.

The Vine Street line looped around Fountain Square, the traditional center of Cincinnati, mixing with a large number of horse and electric cars plus the Mount Adams & Eden Park's Walnut Hills cable line at 5th and Walnut, above. The line had the usual mix of open and closed equipment, of which the open version is shown below at the Stephenson plant. (*Museum of the City of New York*)

The Vine Street colors of cream and gold lent themselves better to builders' photographs than to the mud of Vine Street itself. Above is a view in the central area, and below is the lay-over point on the outer terminal loop. Lane used a wheel to control his usual grip in this instance; the lever is a hand-brake. *(Both, Smithsonian Institution)*

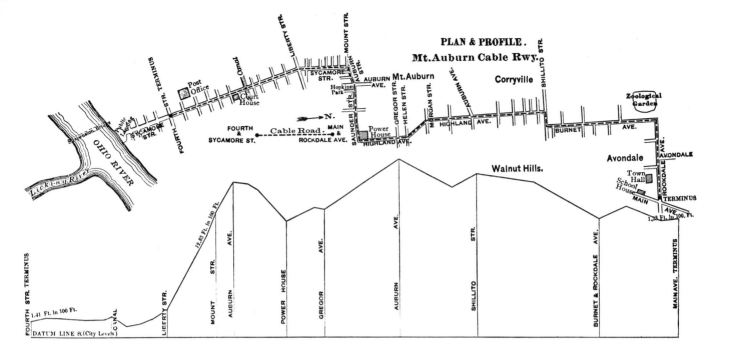

The Mount Auburn Cable Railway combined a steep ascent out of the central area with continuous undulation of the high-lying terrain. The map and profile above show the placing of the powerhouse relative to the grades. The odd mixture of stone and brick in the view of the powerhouse below is presumably the result of rebuilding after the fire of 1892. (*Smithsonian Institution*)

MOUNT AUBURN CABLE RAILWAY

Haddock bottom grip   *Gauge: 5'-2"*

Cincinnati's last cable line was an effort to provide direct service between the downtown area and Avondale surmounting the abrupt ascent of Mount Auburn and continual undulation of the terrain beyond. The promoter, Henry Martin, noted that the existing route was a mixture of a funicular on the hill and a horsecar below, each of which charged a 5 cent fare. He reasoned that a cable line for a single nickel would attract much of the traffic, and incidentally stimulate growth of the Avondale area, where he was a major real estate dealer.

Martin incorporated the company in June 1886, and secured a right to an exit from the central area via Sycamore Street. The route entailed a grade of nearly 13 per cent on Sycamore and Auburn Streets, including an exceedingly difficult pull curve at their intersection. The line descended Saunder (Dorchester) Street at grades of 5 to 8 per cent, to the powerhouse, and then passed through undulating streets through an area still lightly populated to Avondale. The property was built mainly in 1887; the line below the powerhouse was opened on March 13, 1888, and the remaining trackage on June 27.

The line was built by Worcester Haddock with non-trust patents, even more thoroughly a cut-rate enterprise than Lane's Gilbert Avenue installation. The worst of the line's several shortcomings was its iron conduit, naked of concrete; by 1891 the slot was reported to be varying between ½ inch and 2 inches in width. J. B. Stone in February 1889 wrote "This Road is just open, and construction is rather crude." The SRJ in 1891 reported that much of the conduit had been denuded by soil subsidence, and concluded, "There is very little to be said in favor of the mechanical construction of this line." The installation was about 4.5 miles, representing an investment of $640,000.

Initially, the company did well financially, grossing about $50 per day more than Martin had anticipated. He planned two extensions, one from Highland Avenue via Oak, Lane and Lincoln Streets to Woodburn Avenue in competition with the Mount Adams & Eden Park, and the other from Burnet Avenue to the Zoo via Erkenbrecker Avenue. The former was never built, but Martin built the latter in 1889 with a primitive arrangement of a large dummy car of about 100-passenger capacity, equipped with a steam engine and a winch which reeled in and played out a cable of about a quarter mile anchored at Burnet Avenue, laid on the street in a shallow conduit. When the city repaved the street about 1892, it removed the conduit and denied Martin, who had no franchise for this operation, the right to continue.

In March 1892 the company's powerhouse was destroyed by a fire, along with 24 cars. Even though the Cincinnati Street Railway had completed an electric line to Avondale in 1890 which had diverted a great many passengers, Martin set out to rebuild the powerhouse and reorder cars. He had the line back in service after 103 days, but traffic never fully recovered. As a consequence, the company went bankrupt in October 1893. John Kilgour showed immediate interest in buying the line, intending to abandon the grade on Sycamore Street, to electrify the upper trackage and to bring the cars into the business district over existing Street Railway track. The cable line was reportedly handling about 5000 passengers per day. The Street Railway did buy the line effective August 1, 1896, simultaneously with acquiring the Mount Adams & Eden Park, but surprisingly Kilgour made no immediate effort at conversion. Indeed, even though the Mount Auburn line had a physical plant far inferior either to the Gilbert Avenue route or the Street Railway's own installation on Vine Street, it outlasted the conversion of the city's two other cable lines in 1898 by four years. The line was converted to electricity at midnight, June 9, 1902; the last trip was operated by gripman Henry Bitters and conductor John Murphy, who had been in charge of the first trip in 1888.

POWERHOUSE: Saunder Street and Highland Avenue. EQUIPMENT: Two 24" x 60" Corliss engines, 350 HP each. Extant as storehouse for theatrical equipment.

References: SRG, III (1888), 22-23; SRJ, X (1894), 423; collection of John H. White, Jr.

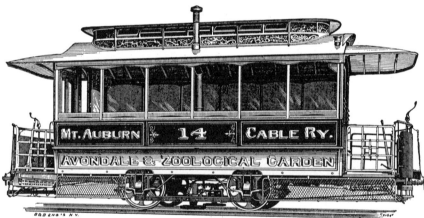

The original equipment of the Mount Auburn Cable Railway is exemplified by the photograph above *(John H. White, Jr.)* and by the engravings of grip 21 and trailer 14. Car 33 is one of the odd grip cars, truncated at the bulkheads, which the line bought after the fire of 1892. *(George Krambles)*

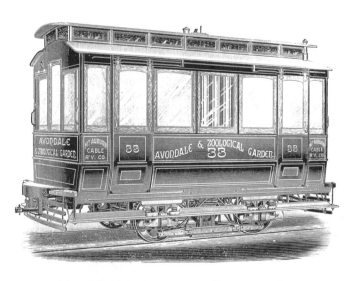

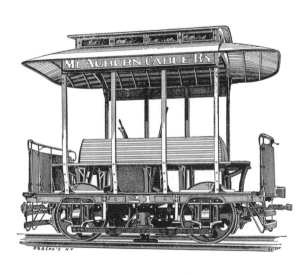

NEW YORK

Population in 1890: 1,515,301

THIRD AVENUE RAILROAD

Jonson double-jaw side grip   *Gauge: 4'-8½"*

New York in certain respects was ideal for cable traction. The city had the largest absolute population in the country, and the heaviest population density, but more important, its demand for transportation has always been so highly concentrated in north-south movements on Manhattan Island that the innate inflexibility of cable systems was least a handicap there. On the other hand, then as now, the city had the worst traffic congestion in the country, so that the imperfect control of the cable car presented a greater hazard of collision with horse drawn vehicles than elsewhere.

Except for lengthy disputes concerning patents and franchises, New York would probably have had an extensive cable network by the mid-1880s. The trust incorporated the New York Cable Railway which proposed a system of 72 miles, described in Chapter II, not finally rejected until 1890.

The trust, itself endeavoring to establish a cable system in New York, was particularly eager to put down non-trust-patent operations in the city. Since both companies which did, in fact, operate cable systems used non-trust technology, their history was integral with a great deal of litigation.

Somewhat surprisingly, New York's first cable line was built in Harlem, far from the city's greatest concentration of population, which at that time was below 14th Street. The line was projected by the Third Avenue Railway from the East River to the North River across 125th Street and Manhattan Street with a branch north on 10th (Amsterdam) Avenue to 186th Street. This was the only crosstown cable line ever built; no other city had enough population to justify a line that was not radial to the central business district. The 10th Avenue segment, which included the only important grade on the system, an ascent from the powerhouse to 137th Street with a maximum gradient of 7.5 per cent, was opened on August 31, 1885, for revenue service. Cars ran on 2 minute headway, 22 hours per day, reportedly from 125th Street and 8th Avenue. The 125th Street line went into service

December 1, 1886. Thereafter 17 cars were assigned to 125th Street and 10th Avenue jointly, with an additional 9 running on 125th Street alone.

The physical plant was the principal installation of the "American system" of D. J. Miller, entailing a duplicate cable and the Jonson grip, in which the lower jaws were mobile. This was an extremely capital-intensive system, involving over $250,000 per mile in the conduit and about a million per mile overall. Henry Root for the trust brought two infringement actions against the company, one for the use of orthodox yoke-and-concrete conduit, and the other for use of the Jonson grip. In 1889, Root lost the first but won the second. The company made a cash settlement with the trust and was free to continue its plans to lay cable on its main line on Third Avenue. After Miller's death at the age of 37 in 1889, the company engaged A. H. Lighthall in 1890 to design the main line with Miller's technology. In 1887 President Lewis Lyon had considered a Bentley-Knight conduit electrification to deal with the city's prohibition of overhead wires, and in the following year he visited Sprague's pioneer electric installation, but reported:

> I have just returned from a visit to Philadelphia and Richmond on this business to give one last look at electricity as a motive force. It may be the force of the future, but at present I am assured it is not practicable except on billiard table surfaces. If we applied it to Third Avenue we would have to have an extra motor to help the cars up the incline at Chatham Square, and that would involve trouble and loss of time.

Since the line ran straight down Third Avenue and the Bowery almost to the Post Office terminus at Park Row and Broadway, it was in one sense an easy project. There was little curvature, and no important grades except the mild ascent at Chatham Square. In several other respects, it was an extremely difficult undertaking. Notably, it was enormous, seven miles and 4468 feet, running from the old Post Office to the Harlem River; with the exception of the Cot-

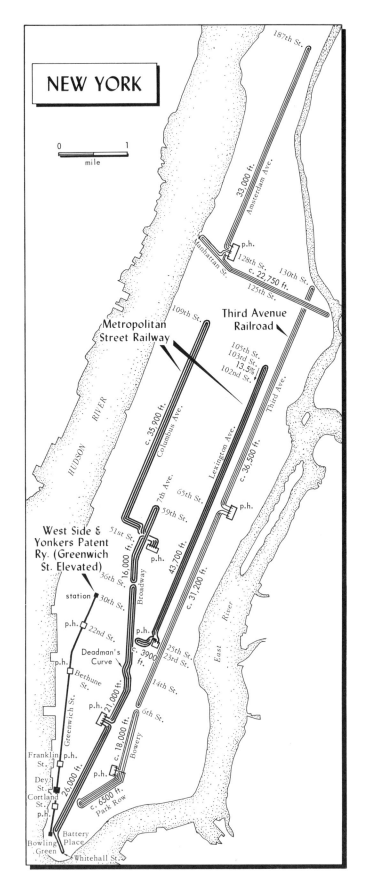

NEW YORK

0 ——— 1
mile

Metropolitan
Street Railway

Third Avenue
Railroad

West Side &
Yonkers Patent
Ry. (Greenwich
St. Elevated)

HUDSON RIVER

EAST RIVER

187th St.

Amsterdam Ave.

33,000 ft.

Manhattan St.

p.h.
128th St.
c. 22,750 ft.
130th St.
125th St.

109th St.

105th St.
103rd St.
13.5%
102nd St.

Columbus Ave.

Lexington Ave.

Third Ave.

c. 35,900 ft.

c. 36,500 ft.

7th Ave.

65th St.

59th St.

51st St.

p.h.

16,000 ft.

Broadway

36th St.

station
30th St.

p.h.
22nd St.

Deadman's
Curve

Bethune
St.

p.h.

21,000 ft.

Greenwich St.

p.h.

Franklin
St.
Dey
St.
Cortland
St.
p.h.

26,000 ft.

p.h.
25th St.
23rd St.
c. 3900
ft.

14th St.

6th St.

p.h.

18,000 ft.

Bowery

p.h.

c. 6500 ft.
Park Row

Battery
Place

Bowling
Green
Whitehall St.

43,700 ft.

c. 31,200 ft.

tage Grove Avenue line in Chicago, it was the longest
cable route in the country. With yokes at the normal
five-foot intervals, it entailed 4350 tons of ironwork
and 46,000 barrels of cement. The southern terminus
was a loop constricted to 41 feet radius by the spacial
limitations of the intersection before the Post Office.
Originally, the company planned to run the loop with
an auxiliary, but presumably on the basis of adverse
experience elsewhere, decided to issue three ropes
from the lower powerhouse southbound, two for the
duplicate system and one additional at very low speed
for the loop alone. Partly because of the narrow radius
of the loop, and partly for safety reasons, the company used large single truck cars, some of which
hauled trailers. The company again used the Jonson
grip, run off the front platform by lever or pilot wheel,
but equipped for automatic release of the cable at the
125th Street crossing and at other rope drops. The
grips operated with a pilot wheel had separate ejection levers at the gripman's right. Safety was a major
consideration, since all but the south end of the line
ran under the Third Avenue elevated, where visibility

was poor. The electric alarm system described in Chapter IV was adopted for such considerations.

In contrast to Baltimore and Washington, the Third Avenue cable installation was made at the desire of the company over the objections of the city. The company had to secure a writ of mandamus for authority to open the streets for the conduit. A mixture of the legal and technological obstacles prevented the company from undertaking construction until March 30, 1891. The line was opened north of 6th Street on December 4, 1893 and completed to the Post Office on February 11, 1894. Mail trailers operated through between the original uptown line and the main line, but passenger cars did not customarily do so. As anticipated, the line proved one of the most heavily-utilized transit facilities in the country. The company carried 36 million passengers in 1894 and reported a profit. Its investment at that time, almost entirely in 14 miles of cable facilities, was reported at $13.1 million.

Given the absence of heavy gradients and the omnipresence of accident hazards in New York, the cable car lasted only until electric conduit operation was demonstrably feasible. The company installed an experimental electrification on Amsterdam Avenue from 186th to 191st Streets in August, 1895, and was pleased with the experience. Between 1895 and 1898 the company acquired the 42nd Street crosstown and 10th Avenue lines, and an extensive network of horsecar lines in upper Manhattan, the Bronx and Westchester, all of which it intended to electrify quickly. As usual, consistency with the rest of an electrified system was added to the other incentives to get rid of cable traction. The company converted the cable lines in 1899, beginning with the 125th Street trackage on September 28.

POWERHOUSES: 128th Street and 10th Avenue. EQUIPMENT: Two 300 HP engines, augmented with 1500 HP engines, 1892.

Third Avenue and 66th Street. EQUIPMENT: Four Providence Corliss engines, 40″ x 72″, total of 7000 HP.

Bowery and Bayard Street. EQUIPMENT: Two Providence Corliss engines, total of 2500 HP.

References: Vincent F. Seyfried, *Third Avenue Railway System 1853-1953*, pp. 5, 9-17. Collection of Frank J. Goldsmith, Jr.

The crosstown line at 125th Street and 7th Avenue in 1895. *(Edward B. Watson)*

One of the first 125th Street crosstown cars rides the transfer table at the Brill plant in 1885. *(Vincent F. Seyfried)* The Third Avenue Railroad's closed cars cost $1485 to $1850, open cars from $1710 to $2180. Below is the 125th Street line from the 8th Avenue elevated station in 1893. *(Museum of the City of New York)*

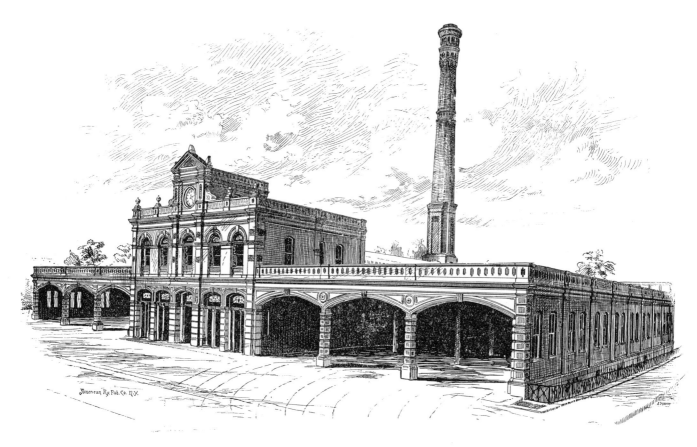

FRONT ELEVATION OF THE TENTH AVENUE CABLE RAILWAY BUILDING, NEW YORK CITY.

The Third Avenue Railroad served Harlem — at that time a middle-to-upper income area — with parlor cars at a 25¢ fare. Car E is an open version of the extra-fare equipment. *(Vincent F. Seyfried)*

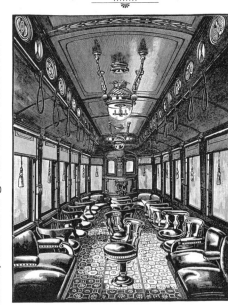
Car V was the winter version of Third Avenue Railroad's Harlem parlor car. A former horse-car converted to cable, the car made four round trips a day at the 25¢ fare. The interior appeared in an advertisement for the Pintsch gas system. Note the gas tank at floor level in the photograph. (*Edward B. Watson*)

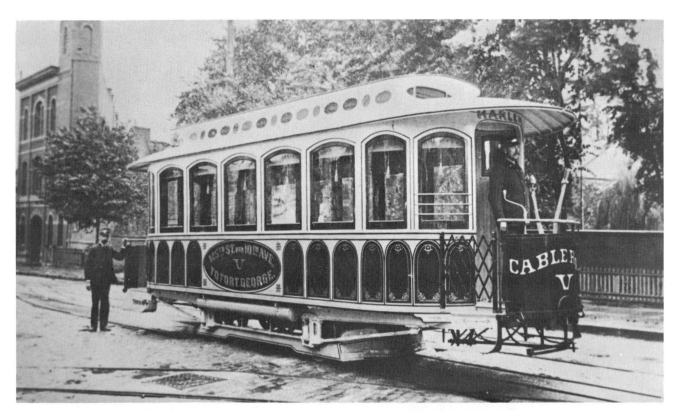

304

The company's main line was so thoroughly hidden by the Third Avenue elevated that few attempted to photograph operations. At Grand Street on the Bowery the elevated tracks parted, making possible these views of the line under construction in 1890 and in operation in 1896. In the upper view, yokes are being installed; the relocation of utilities so characteristic of New York is apparent. Ironwork for the main line cost about $66,000 per mile; complete Sprague installations with overhead trolley cost $20,000 to $30,000 per mile. *(New York Historical Society; Edward B. Watson)*

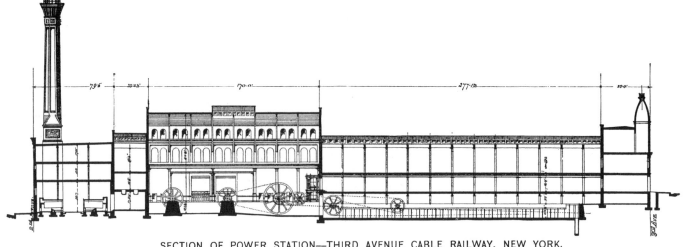

SECTION OF POWER STATION—THIRD AVENUE CABLE RAILWAY, NEW YORK.

The 65th Street powerhouse was the Victorian gem below. On the opposite page is the south terminus of the Third Avenue main line at Park Row and Broadway. The Metropolitan's Broadway cable line is at the left. The building is the New York Post Office, a distinguished example of the work of Alfred B. Mullet, architect of the old State, War and Navy Building in Washington. *(Museum of the City of New York)* Below is A. H. Lighthall's plan for the terminal loop.

COPYRIGHT 1896. BY J.S.JOHNSTON, N.Y.

POST OFFICE, N.Y.

(PARK ROW)

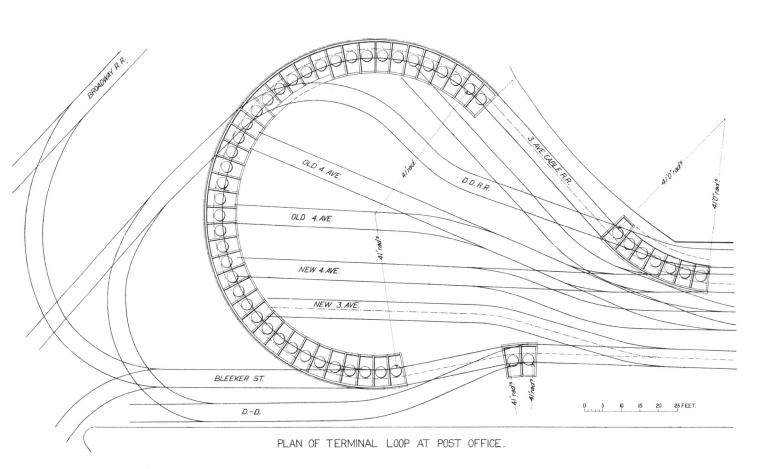

BROADWAY R.R.

OLD 4. AVE.

OLD 4. AVE.

NEW 4. AVE.

NEW 3. AVE.

BLEEKER ST.

D.-D.

3. AVE. CABLE R.R.

D.D.R.R.

4'.rad.

4'.rad's

4'.0'.rad's

4'.0'.rad's

4'.rad's

4'.rad's

0 5 10 15 20 25 FEET.

PLAN OF TERMINAL LOOP AT POST OFFICE.

Earl double-jaw side grip   Gauge: 4'-8½"

The long controversy concerning franchises which prevented cable traction on Third Avenue until 1893 also kept it off Broadway until the same year. The street, being long, mainly straight, and for most of its distance, relatively wide, was well suited to cable operation, and so important was it to New York that it promised to have the highest passenger volume, with the possible exception of State Street, Chicago, in the industry.

The Metropolitan Street Railway was formed in 1892 as a holding company for street railways, including the Broadway & Seventh Avenue Railroad, which had been building the Broadway cable line since securing the rights to Broadway from the Broadway Surface Railroad in 1889. The project, like the Third Avenue Railroad, was an enormous one, complicated by the extensive underground utilities already in place. The company also used the duplicate system, but with a grip operated in the usual fashion with the upper jaws mobile. Once again, this was an extremely expensive installation, with investment, including powerhouses, over a million dollars per mile. It was, in fact, described as the most capital-intensive cable installation of them all.

After lengthy delays, the Broadway line was ready for installation of cable and experimental operation early in 1893. Cable cars replaced horsecars as they became available between May 1 and July 1. Initially the line was served by 125 cable cars, increased to 150 during the first year, with a 40-second headway. The line carried about 100,000 people per day.

The company proceeded with two extensions of the system. Branching from the Broadway line at 7th Avenue and 53rd Street, a Columbus Avenue line was built to serve the west side. Opened on December 6, 1894, this route added another 100 cars to regular operation at 60-second headway. Finally, the company opened a long line up the east side on 23rd Street and Lexington Avenue on October 14, 1895. The route, which contained the longest cable ever attempted,

43,700 feet, also entailed the only major gradient on the entire system, a descent of Duffy's Hill between 102nd and 103rd Streets of 13.5 per cent. This was a very major route, hardly inferior to Broadway itself; service was provided at 20- to 30-second intervals for about 86,000 riders per day. Cars of all three lines shared Broadway, usually with alternate cars running all the way to the Battery, and alternate cars turning back at Bowling Green. South of the Houston Street powerhouse, cars ran at 20-second intervals, but between Houston Street and the junction at 23rd Street, cars ran every 15 seconds in rush hours.

The frequency of operation on Broadway created a major problem at 14th Street, where a long reverse curve had been necessary to bring the line around a corner of Union Square. This, the most notorious "Dead Man's Curve" in the industry, became a major source of accidents as cars threaded it in the usual fashion, at top speed. In 1895 the company invested $200,000 in an auxiliary to allow cars to turn the corner at reduced speed, but the arrangement had to be abandoned when it caused a queue of cars for the curve as far back at Canal Street. In 1897 the company fitted clips to the grips to hold the cable in the jaws on curves in partial release so as to allow lower speeds. Complaints against the hazards of "Dead Man's Curve" continued, however. The company also had chronic trouble at 53rd Street and 9th Avenue, where it had a short-radius pull curve with visibility obstructed by an elevated structure. Probably owing to the great frequency of gripping and ungripping, the incidence of loose strands was exceptionally high, and collisions with horse-drawn vehicles commensurate.

Initially, the company envisioned an extension of the Columbus Avenue line via 110th Street and Lenox Avenue, but apparently out of dissatisfaction with the existing cable installations, completed the line as an electric conduit operation. The development of the electric conduit in the middle of the decade inevitably foreshadowed the end of the cable car in New York. As in Washington, conversion was made difficult by the necessity of revising existing conduits while cable cars passed at short intervals — in this instance, only about 30 seconds. The company planned the conversion for the midsummer months, when traffic was least, but in fact converted in the spring of 1901. The Columbus Avenue cable was reported removed on May 11, and both the Columbus and Lex-

---

On the opposite page is the junction of the Metropolitan's Broadway and Lexington Avenue lines at 23rd Street and Broadway. The curve into 23rd Street, being traversed by two Lexington Avenue grips in the background, was apparently arranged as a pull curve. (*Smithsonian Institution*)

ington cables were reported gone by June 19. The last Broadway car left the Battery at 8:27 PM May 25, 1901, ending street cable operations in New York.

POWERHOUSES: Seventh Avenue and 50th Street. EQUIPMENT: Two Dickson engines, 36″ x 60″, 1000 HP each.

Broadway and Houston Streets. EQUIPMENT: Four Dickson Corliss engines, 38″ x 60″, 1200 HP each. The entire Broadway line was reported shifted to this powerhouse upon opening of the Columbus Avenue line. Extant as Cable Building.

25th Street, east of Lexington Avenue. EQUIPMENT: One Reynolds Corliss cross-compound 30½″ + 48″ x 48″, 1800 HP; one Allis Corliss 30″ x 60″. Extant as Consolidated Edison substation.

References: SRJ, X (1894), 106-111; collection of Frank J. Goldsmith.

The company's headquarters, at right, were designed by no less than McKim, Mead & White. *(GWH)* Below is an overhead view of the intersection of 23rd and Broadway. *(New York Historical Society)*

Above is one of the numerous illustrations of building the Broadway line in the vicinity of Union Square. (*Smithsonian Institution*) Below is the Metropolitan's sinister pull curve at the south end of Union Square, "Dead Man's Curve" at 14th Street and Broadway. (*Museum of the City of New York*)

A working model of a Broadway car from the Museum of the City of New York illustrates the Metropolitan's cable equipment. Most of the Metropolitan's mileage remained horse-operated until electrification. Here a Metropolitan horsecar waits to load in front of the Pennsylvania Railroad's North River ferry terminal. *(Smithsonian Institution)* The overhead view of 1898 on the opposite page demonstrates the close headway of the Broadway cable line. *(Museum of the City of New York)*

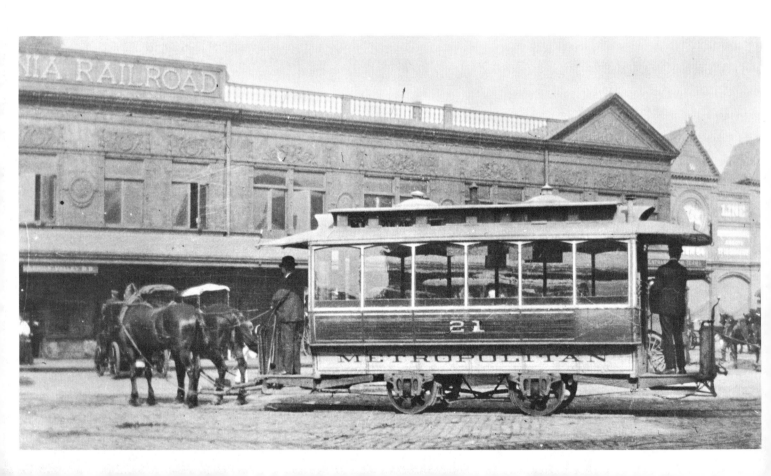

COPYRIGHT 1898

NEW YORK & BROOKLYN BRIDGE
RAILWAY

Paine roller grip; changed to   *Gauge: 4'-8½"*
bottom grip similar to Hallidie, 1885

John Roebling, who had experience with producing cable for funiculars, envisioned a cable-hauled rail operation of some sort on his Brooklyn Bridge from the outset. His son, Washington Roebling, who brought the vast project to completion, advocated cable traction to keep the weight of steam locomotives off the bridge. The Union Ferry Company was handling about 112,000 people a day, indicating a considerable demand for passenger crossings.

Design of the railway of slightly over a mile was entrusted to Col. William H. Paine, who joined the bridge project in 1869. Both Paine and the trust continually argued that Paine's design was entirely original, and was not based on Hallidie's San Francisco innovations. Notably, the cable was not in a conduit, but held three inches above the rails. In particular, Paine made the only use for a prolonged period of pure roller grip, in which four small sheaves below the center of the car held the cable; the sheaves were stopped to move the car, and allowed to revolve when the car stopped or reduced speed. Because the Paine grip was unable to start a car from a standing stop, the line first used a cable switching car on an auxiliary at the New York end, and later 0-4-0 switchers at each terminus.

The Brooklyn Bridge itself was opened on May 24, 1883. The railway had a test run on August 8, 1883, and was put in commercial service on September 24. Almost immediately it proved a success such that most of its history was a series of efforts to adapt the inflexible cable plant to rapidly increasing traffic. Paine had planned for single-car operation, but within a month two-car trains were instituted. The monthly passenger count rose from 477,700 in October 1883 to 2,593,104 in April 1888. In 1884, the line carried 9,234,690 passengers, but the completion of the Brooklyn elevated to the Fulton Ferry, adjacent to the Brooklyn terminus, more than doubled patronage. The line handled 19,964,000 passengers in 1885, and three-car trains were instituted in September. Trains ran around the clock, though between 1:00 AM and 5:00 AM the steam switchers handled trains across. By

1888 the trains handled 30,945,605 passengers, and the trustees of the Bridge found it necessary to expand the Brooklyn station platforms, replace some machinery in the powerhouse on the Brooklyn end, and install side-entrance equipment of the British sort to speed loading. Four-car trains were instituted simultaneously. In 1889 the New York terminal was expanded and cars equipped with a vacuum brake.

In 1885 the line gave up Paine's roller grip, which was proving inadequate for the growing volume of traffic, and adopted a bottom grip run off the front platform, very similar to Hallidie's original Clay Street grip. Indeed, it was so similar that the trust sued the Bridge's trustees for infringement and collected $4500 damages.

The railway's remarkable growth in traffic continued into the 1890s. Storage facilities were built for cars at the Brooklyn end in 1892, and both terminals were expanded again in 1893. In the same year a duplicate set of winding machinery was installed for a second cable, intended for a set of gauntleted tracks to permit closer headways and more intensive utilization of platforms. In 1894 500 volt trolley wire was strung over the railway for car-lighting.

By the mid-1890s the line was still operated with cable rapid-transit cars, switched between arrival and departure platforms and assisted out of the stations by small steam locomotives, ten 0-4-0 and two 2-4-2 tank engines. Even though the grades on the Bridge were only 3.77 per cent, the trustees continued to feel that cable traction was necessary to deal with them. On November 30, 1896, the railway put in service 20 heavy Pullman motor cars, equipped for electric switching around the terminals. Even though their introduction required laying of third rail along the entire railway, the trustees continued to require cable operation between stations. The change did bring about the end of use of steam locomotives on January 23, 1897, however.

The entry of Brooklyn into New York City on January 1, 1898, caused the Bridge to pass from its own trustees into the hands of the municipal Department of Bridges. The Brooklyn Elevated assumed control of the Bridge railway, and effected a physical connection at Tillary Street, Brooklyn. On Novem-

---

The *Scientific American*, at left, illustrated the Brooklyn Bridge operation in the late 1880s. (*Smithsonian Institution*)

ber 1, 1898, the Elevated initiated through service to the Manhattan terminus, using the electric Bridge motors to haul steam elevated trains from Tillary Street through the Brooklyn station on the Bridge, and to the pick-up point for cable operation. They ran across the Bridge by cable and switched electrically at the west end. In rush hours only Bridge equipment was used. After 8:45 PM, all trains crossed electrically. On July 16, 1899, through service was discontinued except for summer trains from Manhattan to Brighton Beach. The Bridge local trains ran by cable in the two rush periods, and electrically at other times. On October 1, 1901, through service was resumed, with Bridge trains handling the evening rush hour only.

The opening of the IRT East River tunnels on January 8, 1908, caused the Bridge local trains to be withdrawn on January 27, 1908, and cable operation to be stopped permanently — a decade or so after it ceased to be necessary or even useful. Rapid transit across the Bridge continued until 1944.

POWERHOUSE: Beneath tracks at Brooklyn end of Bridge. EQUIPMENT: Two 26″ x 48″ engines.

References: Charles L. Small, "The Railway of the New York & Brooklyn Bridge," *Bulletin of the Railway & Locomotive Historical Society,* no. 97 (1957), 7-20; Gabriel Leverich, "The Cable Railway on the New York & Brooklyn Bridge," *Transactions of the American Society of Civil Engineers,* XVIII (1888), 67-102.

Four of the big Pullman motor cars of 1896 are shown below. This equipment switched electrically at terminals, but crossed the bridge on a cable gripped from the wheel at the opposite side of the front platform from the controller. (*Edward B. Watson*) The right-of-way on the bridge was the simple construction shown at upper right. Note that the cable rode above the level of the rails. At lower right is an early view, dating from the days of steam switching at the termini, showing trains near the pick-up point for the cable. (*Rensselaer Polytechnic Institute — Smithsonian Institution*)

These two photographs illustrate the pick-up arrangements for the cable at opposite ends of the bridge. Above, in 1894 trains took the rope at the Manhattan end at this series of elevated carrying pulleys. The similar arrangement at the Brooklyn end is shown below in 1903 after third rail had been laid the length of the bridge, and a duplicate cable had been laid. (*Edward B. Watson*)

On this page are two views of the New York terminus, the upper in the days of electric switching and the lower when steam locomotives pushed trains to the pick-up point to take the cable. (*Edward B. Watson: Rensselaer Polytechnic Institute — Smithsonian Institution*)

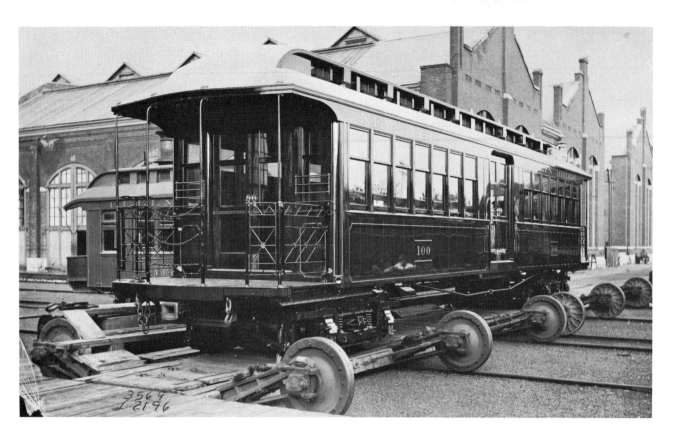

One of the heavy rapid transit cars built for the New York & Brooklyn Bridge Railway in 1896 is photographed on the transfer table at the Pullman plant. *(George Krambles)* At the top of the opposite page a train of this equipment loads at the Manhattan terminus. *(Rensselaer Polytechnic Institute — Smithsonian Institution)*

One of the New York & Brooklyn Bridge rapid transit cars ended her career as Mason City & Clear Lake Railroad work motor 19 in Iowa cornfields far from the urban reaches of home. (*LaMar M. Kelley — George Krambles*)

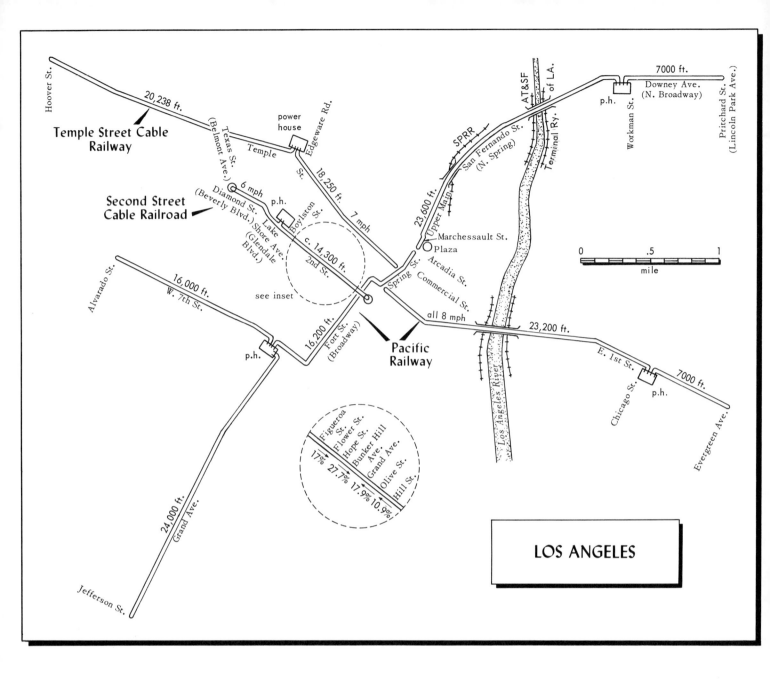

Hoover St.

Temple Street Cable
Railway

20,238 ft.

Texas St.
(Belmont Ave.)

power
house

Edgeware Rd.

Temple

18,250 ft.

7 mph

6 mph

Diamond St.
(Beverly Blvd.)

p.h.

Boylston St.

Second Street
Cable Railroad

Lake
Shore Ave.
(Glendale
Blvd.)

c. 14,300 ft.

2nd St.

see inset

Alvarado St.

16,000 ft.

W. 7th St.

p.h.

16,200 ft.

Fort St.
(Broadway)

24,000 ft.

Grand Ave.

Jefferson St.

SPRR

San Fernando St.
(N. Spring)

23,600 ft.

Upper Main

Marchessault St.
Plaza

Spring St.

Arcadia St.

Commercial St.

all 8 mph

AT&SF

Terminal Ry.

of L.A.

Los Angeles River

Workman St.

p.h.

7000 ft.

Downey Ave.
(N. Broadway)

Pritchard St.
(Lincoln Park Ave.)

0   .5   1
mile

23,200 ft.

E. 1st St.

Chicago St.

p.h.

7000 ft.

Evergreen Ave.

Pacific
Railway

Figueroa St.
Flower St.
Hope St.
Bunker Hill Ave.
Grand Ave.
Olive St.
Hill St.

17%   27.7%   17.9%   10.9%

LOS ANGELES

The Second Street powerhouse in the mid-1880s. *(UCLA Libraries)*

LOS ANGELES

Population in 1890: 50,395

SECOND STREET CABLE RAILROAD

Single-jaw side grip   *Gauge: 3'-6"*

Los Angeles was, as usual in its history, growing rapidly in the 1880s. It had been a small town of 11,183 in 1880, and was virtually quintupling in population in the course of the decade. Development of the western suburbs — which are now, of course, considered part of the immediate central area — was hampered by the natural barrier of Bunker Hill and the undulating territory immediately to the west. As in other cities, cable traction presented itself as an obvious solution.

The Second Street Cable Railroad was promoted by Jesse Yarnell and his associates in 1885, though after 1887 James McLoughlin was president. The line was integral with real estate promotion on Bunker Hill and immediately to the west. Construction began at Second and Spring Streets in March 1885, and was pushed west directly over Bunker Hill, thence west on Second Street to Lake Shore Avenue (Glendale Boulevard), and Diamond Street (Beverly Boulevard) to the top of another hill at Texas Street (Belmont Avenue). The line was put in service on October 8, 1885.

Though only 6,900 feet long, the Second Street line was notable in various respects. It was the first single-track cable line, essentially an adaptation of the trust's California Street technology to single-track operation. The engineer, J. M. Thompson, designed the property with turnouts placed so that the downbound car could drop the cable and pick it up again when returning to the main track. Since he used a single-jaw side grip (probably a Root, though one source says it was similar to Hovey's Sutter Street grip), he had to use turntables at each end. The single-track arrangement was considered so unsatisfactory that in 1887 the company announced an intention of double-tracking, but it was never able to do so.

Second, however inconspicuous the line was, it contained the heaviest grade of any American cable operation, 27.7 per cent, on the eastbound ascent of Bunker Hill from Hope Street to Bunker Hill Avenue. This was, as mentioned in Chapter II, steeper than any other American cable grade by more than 6.5 per cent, and within 1 per cent of the steepest in the world.

Third, the Second Street line was the first cable railway, apart from the off-the-street operation in Binghamton and the experimental line in Brooklyn, to be abandoned. Like many another, the line was built in anticipation of population which failed to appear in its lifetime. As the accompanying photographs indicate, the actual population was light throughout its history. The company had only six grips and an equal number of trailers. An affiliated steam dummy line running a mile and a half to the west also suffered from sparse on-line population.

The company, somewhat surprisingly in a city usually considered arid, was troubled by inundation during severe rains, the last of which brought the line to an early end. The conduit on the east escarpment of Bunker Hill acted as a storm drain, flooding the horizontal conduit east of Hill Street. In the winter of 1887 this problem caused the company to install an informal drain from the conduit into the excavation for the Bryson Building at Second and Spring, flooding out the excavation, but allowing the cable cars to resume service. In 1888 the line was closed from February 27 to March 11 when the terrain was so muddy that a replacement cable could not be trucked from the railroad freight station to the powerhouse.

On October 13, 1889, the line shut down when the cable deteriorated too much for further operation. The management reported that the line had been unprofitable for some time, and that it was unable to finance renewal of the cable. The suspension was intended to be temporary, but on December 24, 1889, Los Angeles had possibly the heaviest rainstorm of its history. In addition to the usual damage to the conduit on the hill, the storm caused Echo Park Lake to overflow, flooding the area immediately west of Bunker Hill. The cable line in the valley west of Figueroa Street was washed out, ending any real prospect of resumption.

A test of the machinery in the powerhouse in April, 1890 led to speculation that the line would be rebuilt. In May, it was announced that the company would be sold at auction to satisfy a judgment of $10,000 secured by Elizabeth Hollenbeck in an effort to recover her husband's investment; she argued that the company had violated its charter by failing to operate daily for a five-year period. The company passed into the hands of H. C. Witmer, who expressed his intention of restoring it as a double-track cable operation, including an extension along Fourth Street to the Southern Pacific station. In October 1890 it was announced that the line would be rebuilt as soon as materials arrived, but in December the conduit was removed in preparation for installation of an electric line on the flatter western portion.

POWERHOUSE EQUIPMENT: One Corliss engine, 14″ x 30″, built by Savage & Son, San Francisco; machinery by Union Iron Works, San Francisco.

The Second Street Cable Railroad's ascent of Bunker Hill from the west involved a cut which was, by the standards of a street railway, very extensive. The ascent from the east, below, was more orthodox. (*UCLA Libraries; Security Pacific Bank*)

TEMPLE STREET CABLE RAILWAY

Wood & Fowler double-jaw side grip   *Gauge: 3'-6"*

The hilly area immediately northwest of downtown Los Angeles is served most directly by Temple Street, a thoroughfare without any major grades, but steeply undulating throughout. Efforts at a franchise for horsecars had been continual since 1881, but the street was exactly of the character most difficult for horse traction — rather a street from Kansas City set in Los Angeles.

The patent trust in San Francisco had correctly spotted Temple Street as an ideal route for a cable line, and endeavored to interest local capitalists in the project beginning in 1883. A group interested in real estate development in the area led by Walter S. Maxwell and Prudent Beaudry began active promotion of the line in 1884, and secured enough funds to begin construction on December 28, 1885. The line was under construction until May 8, 1886, and was said to have been completed in only 62 working days. Apparently because of financial differences between the directors and the contractor, the property was not turned over to the company until July 13, 1886; operation began the following morning.

Like the Second Street line of the previous year, the Temple Street Cable Railway was a single-track operation, though it was of superior design. The track, only 8,725 feet long, had three intermediate and two terminal turnouts, and the cars were designed for double-ended operation. To avoid using turntables, Secretary F. W. Wood and Superintendent J. Fowler designed a wheel-operated double-jaw side grip which bore their names. The line was initially reported to have eight grip cars, built by the company under the supervision of G. W. Douglas of San Francisco, and a like number of trailers built by John Stephenson of New York.

The company, no less than the Second Street operators, found single-track operation unsatisfactory, but the Temple Street route was so much stronger in traffic (being to a greater extent a service for existing population) that the company was able to double-track the line in August 1888. Somewhat surprisingly, the directors reverted to single track for an extension of just under two miles from the powerhouse at Edgeware Road to Hoover Street, the western city limit, opened on April 30, 1889. With the additional trackage, investment was reported at $300,000. The extension brought the line into a rural area which attracted a large number of week-end travelers. Two more grips with trailers were added. The opening of the Boyle Heights line of the Pacific Railway in August of the same year offered an alternative cable route to the country, and reduced the Temple Street line's traffic so greatly that it never again paid a dividend.

Withal, the Temple Street line was successful, as cable operations went, long outlasting Los Angeles' two other companies. Together with the connecting Cahuenga Valley Railroad, a local dummy line, the Temple Street Cable Railway was part of a direct route from Los Angeles to the separate community of Hollywood. The cars operated on 10-minute headway. The corporation failed to meet its obligations in 1897 and was put in receivership. J. A. Graves, representing the bondholders, bought the line under foreclosure in January 1901. The company handled 1,305,596 passengers in 1900, in spite of the rivalry of electric lines, which were spreading rapidly about the area. There was considerable local pressure for conversion by this late date, based mainly on dissatisfaction with frequent breakdowns. Graves sold the line to Henry E. Huntington, who converted it to electric operation on October 22, 1902, as part of his Los Angeles Interurban Railway. It became part of the Los Angeles Railway in 1910 and continued as an electric streetcar line until 1946. The powerhouse was used as a car barn, but was later razed; builders of the Hollywood Freeway unearthed the foundation in 1949 and were forced to remove it.

POWERHOUSE EQUIPMENT: One Corliss engine, 16" x 36", 85 HP.

The Temple Street Cable Railway operated with orthodox grip-and-trailer trains, such as that shown immediately to the left. The steam dummy train, with a coach crudely concocted of old horsecars, was the company's connection for Hollywood. At the bottom, a high school is moved up and over the Temple Street track; a moving building was high among the things an inflexible cable line couldn't avoid.

On this page are the east end of the Temple Street line in the central business district and the powerhouse in what were then the western suburbs. *(Title Insurance & Trust Company; Security Pacific Bank; UCLA Libraries)*

Above are trains of the Pacific Railway on opening day of the Downey Avenue line, photographed on the bridge over the Los Angeles River. The same line's trestle over the Southern Pacific's freight yards was the imposing structure below — a fine demonstration of the lengths to which cable engineers went to avoid crossing railroad tracks. (*Security Pacific Bank*)

Eppelsheimer bottom grip   *Gauge: 3'-6"*

Unlike the two earlier Los Angeles cable lines, which were intended to serve limited areas for real-estate development, what became the Pacific Railway was projected as a comprehensive system of 60 miles, serving all of the populated area of the city, and even extending to Pasadena and Santa Monica. As usual in such projects, only a small part of the intended system was ever built, but the promoters did achieve a network of about 10½ miles which covered all of the city except the southeastern portion and the hilly area served by the two earlier installations.

The company was incorporated on July 8, 1887, as the Los Angeles Cable Railway by I. W. Hellman and J. F. Crank, the city's leading horsecar operators. On the basis of the unsatisfactory experience of the Daft installation on Pico Boulevard in 1887, they rejected electric traction, even though the system they envisioned was mainly flat and nowhere more than mildly undulating. Hellman and Crank leased their three existing horse railways to the cable company, announced their grandiose plans, and proceeded in 1888 with construction of the first segments, a line on West Seventh Street through East First Street to Boyle Heights, and another from South Grand Avenue through to the Eastlake district via Downey Avenue. The two lines shared a route through the central business district on Fort Street (Broadway).

Like many other cable promoters, Hellman and Crank found construction far more expensive than they had anticipated, and in order to bring the project to completion, sold a three-fourths interest in the company on October 31, 1888, to C. B. Holmes of the Chicago City Railway. Holmes organized the Pacific Railway Company, which assumed the property, then nearing completion, on September 9, 1889. The main powerhouse at Grand and Seventh was ready for occupancy as the line's general office on June 1, 1889, and on June 8 was put in service operating the Fort Street cable which both lines were to use jointly. The First Street powerhouse was activated on August 3 when the cable from Spring to Chicago on First Street went into service; the extension to Evergreen Avenue followed on September 28. In the interim, the Grand Avenue cable was started on September 14. The entire line north to the Eastlake area opened on November 2, and finally the West Seventh Street line, which had the only significant undulation on the system, was

put in service on December 7. Investment in the completed system was $1,715,000.

The designer, Augustine W. Wright of Chicago, used trust patents to reproduce the technology of the Powell Street line in both gauge and grip; the large number of rope drops in the central area undoubtedly made the bottom grip attractive. Wright, however, used separate grip cars and trailers, bought respectively from Brownell & Wight and Laclede in St. Louis. The system was considered an excellent one, among the best designed in the country. Wright's handling of the long pull curves at the Plaza was considered particularly adept. Wright considered it the most difficult cable system he had ever attempted.

The system's principal novelty was three long viaducts used to take the cable trains over the railroads which the lines north and east had to cross. The largest was a 1535-foot structure over the Southern Pacific on the north line, designed by Samuel G. Artingstall of Chicago. At the SP's insistence, the viaduct was put on a single line of columns, making it the only structure in the country, except for short stretches of the New York elevated, to have two tracks on single pillars. Entry was denied horsedrawn vehicles by the simple expedient of providing an 18 per cent approach. In part because of the ascents and descents from the three viaducts, the system contained 48 depression pulleys and 60 crown pulleys. Trains operated typically on 5-minute headway.

Upon assuming control of the company, C. B. Holmes replaced most of the management personnel. As general manager he installed a British tramway official, James Clifton Robinson, who upon his return to England in 1891 went on to fame and to knighthood as one of the leading figures in the tramway industry. Robinson in his short tenure in Los Angeles was among the most eloquent advocates of cable traction in the industry, and one of the leading enthusiasts for bottom grips. His chief engineer was Frank Van Vleck, later to be designer of the San Diego Cable Railway.

The downpour of December 24, 1889, which wiped out the Second Street Cable Railroad, also damaged the Pacific Railway, though not irreparably. The runoff from the streets filled not only the conduits with sand and debris, but also inundated the tension runs in the powerhouses. Robinson, possibly to avoid a

Pacific Railway equipment was predominately open because of Los Angeles' mild climate. Both views here are of Downey-Grand Avenue trains. *(Security Pacific Bank; Title Insurance & Trust Company)*

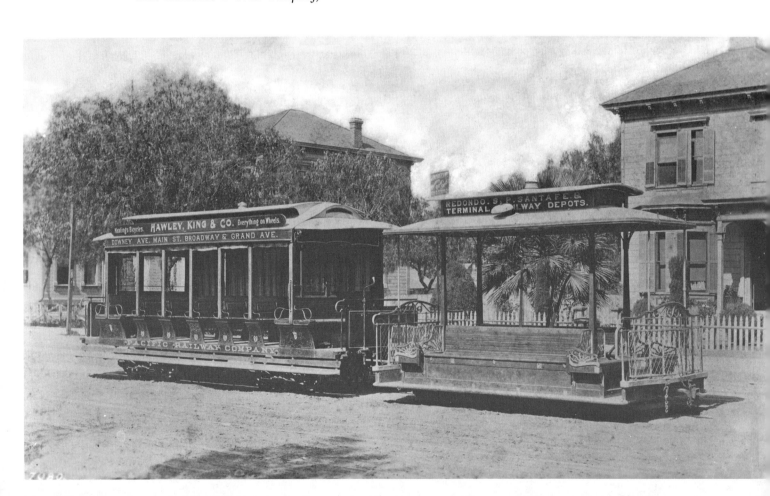

demonstration that the cable traction of which he was such a devotee was more liable to obstruction from natural disasters than either of its rivals, bet a cigar that he could have the Pacific system back in operation by 1:00 PM Christmas Day. Although sand and dirt were throughout the system, he ordered the engines started at 1:00, thereby winning his cigar, but grinding abrasive material into cables, pulleys and winding machinery alike. This foolhardy act, which is consistent with reports of Robinson's flamboyant behavior, involved the company in heavy costs for repairs to the system, and led to Robinson's being fired, or at least asked to resign. He was also prosecuted for diverting flood water from the main powerhouse to basements of adjacent buildings, though he was acquitted of the charge. Robinson went to San Francisco, where he became an independent consultant in planning of electric lines.

Partly because of damage from the premature resumption following the flood, but more basically because of competition from electric cars of the Los Angeles Consolidated Electric Railway, the Pacific Railway went into bankruptcy on January 21, 1891, with Crank appointed as receiver. Later in the year, the state supreme court ruled that the Consolidated Electric Railway had the right to use the cable company's trackage under a state law of 1890 granting street railways use of one another's track at a fee for a maximum distance of five blocks. For this privilege, the Consolidated had to pay only $15,000. Especially if the Consolidated could string wire over its track in the central area, the cable line was hopeless. Operating under a statutory speed limit of 8 miles per hour, it was less than ordinarily able to compete with electric cars, at best. Accordingly, on June 13, 1893, when the Pacific Railway was sold, the Consolidated was the only bidder, with a successful offer of $1,344,320. The Pacific Railway had represented an investment of about $2.5 million, including horse-car lines of about the same mileage as the cable system. The Consolidated absorbed the Pacific Railway on October 13, 1893.

The Consolidated was in turn succeeded by the Los Angeles Railway on March 23, 1895, organized by the bondholders out of dissatisfaction with the Consolidated's management. As general manager, the new corporation hired F. W. Wood of the Temple Street Cable Railway, who had a local reputation for making a success out of an unpromising enterprise on Temple Street. Wood immediately announced an intention to consolidate the operation of the entire system in a powerhouse at Central Avenue and Wilde Street; this implied immediate conversion of the remaining horse and cable lines.

Wood ordered fifty additional electric cars, and in October 1895 began stringing electric wires indiscriminately over the remaining horse and cable trackage. The conversion began abruptly on February 1, 1896 with the West Seventh Street and Fort Street cables, which were deteriorated beyond further use. The Grand Avenue cable was stopped on February 12, thus ending operation out of the main powerhouse. The Boyle Heights line was ended on March 13, and the Downey Avenue line on March 18, ending the big cable system's history in less than six years. Conversion of the horse trackage was completed in the same year.

Electric cars ran on the old cable trackage without immediate change, though the shallow-flangeway tram rail was replaced with T-rail over the course of the next six years. Initially, the electric cars ran over the long cable viaducts, for which the approaches had to be modified to reduce gradients, but they were later rerouted via city streets. None of the powerhouses survived; the site of the main powerhouse at Seventh and Grand is occupied, somewhat ironically, by Robinson's department store.

POWERHOUSES: Initially each of the three powerhouses contained one compound Fraser & Chalmers engine, 26″ + 42″ x 48″ of 700 horsepower. Since the system was expected to be expanded greatly, the Seventh and Grand powerhouse was designed for a second engine of the same type, but it was never installed. The two outlying powerhouses were grossly overpowered with their original equipment. The Downey Avenue powerhouse was also intended for two engines, but even the one installed was too large, and had been replaced by a 150 horsepower Wheelock by 1893. The Boyle Heights station was re-equipped with a 115 horsepower Wheelock.

References: Ira L. Swett, "Los Angeles Railway," *Interurbans,* Special No. 11 (1951); SRJ, VI (1890), 97-102; SRJ, IX (1893), 525-528; Edwin L. Lewis, "Historical Data concerning Street Railway Transportation in Los Angeles," typescript in Huntington Library, San Marino, California (1932).

Pacific Railway's lines on West 7th Street and South Grand Avenue diverged at the company's main powerhouse at lower left. Above is a woodcut of one of the company's characteristic open trailers, suitably misspelled, from an advertisement of the Calumet Car Company of Chicago. The other views show trains at the terminal and in operation. *(Security Pacific Bank; Title Insurance & Trust Company)*

BINGHAMTON

Population in 1890: 35,005

WASHINGTON STREET & STATE ASYLUM RAILROAD

Fairchild twin cable system   Gauge: 4′-0″ (?)

This small cable line of only ¾ mile is of interest as the experimental installation of the Fairchild twin cable system, described in Chapter III. It was ideal for this purpose, if only because of the simplicity of the problem to be solved. The Washington Street & State Asylum Railroad, as the title indicates, connected downtown Binghamton with the state mental hospital on the eastern outskirts of the city. The company sought some method of climbing the hill, variously reported at 10 per cent and 12 per cent, into the hospital grounds. The cable line could be laid entirely on private right-of-way with the cable exposed in the manner of funiculars, without a conduit. The system, which provided no method of dropping the cable, necessarily entailed loops at both ends. The company reported owning two cars that travelled at 12 miles per hour, which seems to imply that the cable ran at 6 miles per hour; the technology permitted the car to move at double the speed of the cable.

The cable line was opened on November 6, 1885, but its subsequent history is obscure. The record is almost entirely preserved in C. B. Fairchild's *Street Railways,* but although Fairchild, the promoter, could hardly have been more familiar with it, he was extremely vague about details. He reported that it operated for about two years, probably until some time in 1888. It was then replaced by what Fairchild called "the gravity system," presumably a funicular.

No other company is known to have shown serious interest in the Fairchild system, although it was apparently workable in service. The installation's most lasting accomplishment was bringing Fairchild into the street railway industry. His advocacy of the twin cable system had been his baptism in street railways. He became editor of the SRJ and the most distinguished trade journalist in his field.

POWERHOUSE: On Asylum grounds. EQUIPMENT: One engine of 40 HP, details unknown.

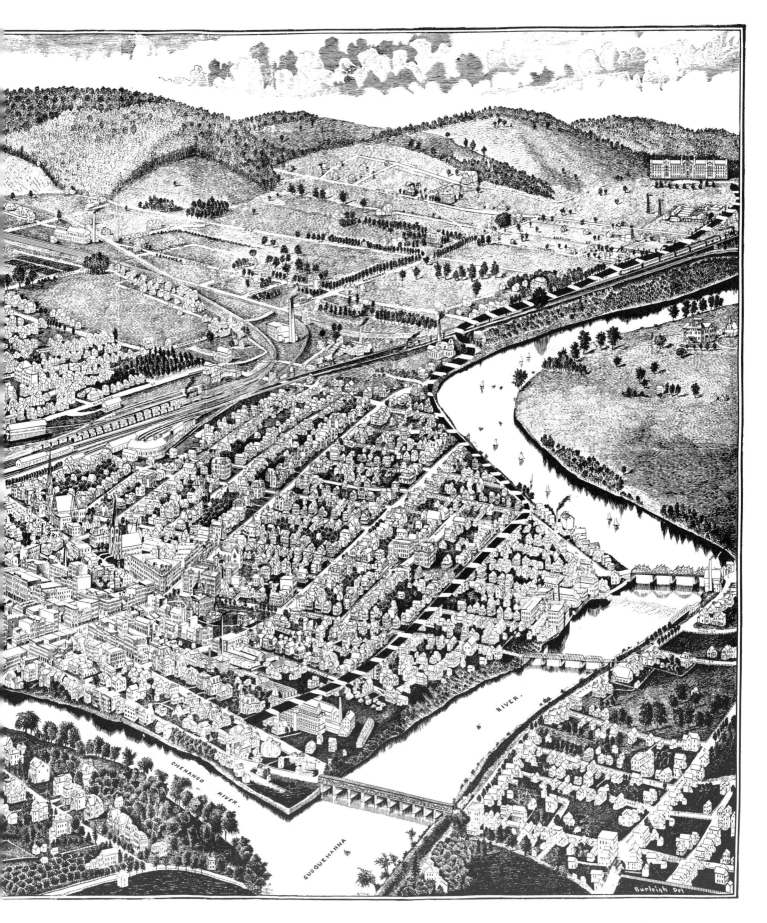

There are no known photographs of the Fairchild twin cable system in operation. This map of Binghamton in 1882 antedates the cable installation by three years, but the route of the Washington Street & State Asylum Railroad has been superimposed as a dotted line. The cable line ran on the last three-quarters of a mile of the route, climbing the hill to the mental hospital at the extreme upper right of the map. (*Broome County Historical Society*)

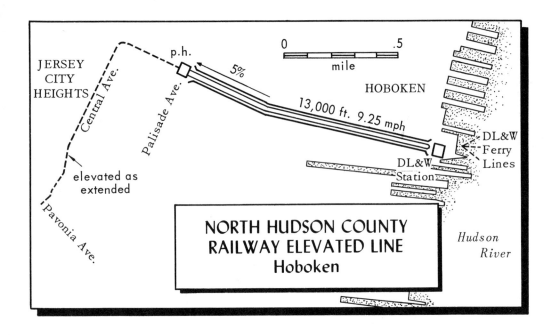

NORTH HUDSON COUNTY
RAILWAY ELEVATED LINE
Hoboken

The only known photograph of cable operation on the Hoboken Elevated is the illustration, below, from the book *Art Work of Jersey City*. The view apparently dates from immediately before electrification, since the trolley supports are already in place. *(Jersey City Public Library — Edward T. Francis)*

HOBOKEN

Population in 1890: 43,648

NORTH HUDSON COUNTY RAILWAY

Endres bottom grip   Gauge: 4'-8½"

Hoboken is a city characterized by a business district on flatland at its ferry terminal, with an abrupt rise to residential areas of Jersey City behind it. The combination of heavy traffic concentration at the ferry terminal and the elevation to the dormitory areas was an obvious one for cable traction. Actually, the company had established a funicular for horsecars as early as 1874, but this operation had the usual inflexibility of funiculars in adjusting to imbalances in traffic between the two directions. Consequently, the company late in 1882 resolved upon building an elevated rapid transit line from the terminal of the Hoboken Ferry to Jersey City Heights at Palisade Avenue, a distance of about a mile and an eighth. Approximately 3,500 feet of the structure from the Hoboken terminal were flat at an elevation about 15 feet off the ground, but the line then rose on spectacular trestlework at a grade just over 5 per cent to Palisade Avenue, gaining slightly over 100 feet. The structure was completed in 1885 and the line opened for traffic on January 25, 1886.

Mechanically, the line was unique in several respects. It used open-platformed elevated cars of the standard rapid-transit type of the time, equipped with the Endres bottom grip, illustrated in Chapter III, a ponderous but simple grip which closed on the cable laterally, more like side grips than bottom grips of the Eppelsheimer type. Cars carried a grip on each truck, wheel-operated off the front platform. Each truck was equipped with a pair of cable-lifters, which grasped the cable as if with pincers to lift it to the jaws. Cars could take rope at any point except at either of the two curves, though in practice they did not make intermediate stops between the two termini. The company used a 1¼" cable, the thickest in the industry, and made a practice of giving it a very light coating of cold tar. The line's engineer, J. J. Endres, felt that tar increased the diameter of the cable on the first wrap around the winding machinery, causing slack on subsequent windings, and also that a dry rope facilitated quick starts from the two sta-

tions. J. B. Stone on visiting the property argued that the relative nudity of the cable combined with the angularity of the edges of the cable-lifters to fracture the strands in the cable. The company found its cable deteriorated in a fashion different from any other company. Instead of generating long loose strands, the cable shed short pieces, usually from ¼" to 1", which congregated at the terminal sheave of the lower terminus. The management worried that this situation, which they were unable to explain, might cause a break in the cable, but Stone believed the rope capable of hauling loads three to four times what it carried. He recommended heavier coatings of hot tar, and rounding the edges of the cable-lifting mechanism to ease what he thought was a cutting action on the outer strands.

As cable lines went, this one was a success. The cable ran 20 hours a day, handling loads of about 10,000 daily passengers, with peak days of about 15,000. Owing in part to the absence of street-running or cross-traffic, the safety record was exceptionally good. The road had 14 cable cars, reportedly built by Pullman, plus two Baldwin 0-4-0T dummy engines for use when the cable system was out of action. Cable cars customarily ran singly.

In view of the relative absence of the usual complaints about cable traction, it is somewhat surprising the Hoboken line was so short-lived. The company in the early 1890s decided to extend the elevated from Palisade Avenue to the Hudson County Court House at Newark Avenue, Jersey City. Originally, the company planned to use cable traction on the extension, even though it was relatively flat. Newspaper accounts indicate that cable was laid over the extension in March, 1891, but President S. B. Dod apparently had second thoughts about extending the cable system. The company first announced it would use steam locomotives on the new line of an additional mile and an eighth, but by 1892 had decided to operate both the extension and the original line by electric traction. The extension was opened as an electric line on June

337

6, 1892, and for six months passengers transferred between cable and electric cars at Palisade Avenue station. In December, 1892, the cable operation was ended, and the new Brill electric cars ran through from the ferry terminal to Newark Avenue. The locomotives and Pullman cable cars went to the Palisade Railroad line of the North Hudson County Railway, where the cars are reported to have been rebuilt as electrics in 1895. The elevated line, which had a grade easily within the capacity of ordinarily-equipped electric cars, served as access to the ferries for Public Service of New Jersey streetcars until 1949.

POWERHOUSE: Beneath the tracks at the Palisade Avenue terminus. EQUIPMENT: Two 500 HP Corliss engines, 30″ x 60″, Watts-Campbell Co., Newark, N.J.

References: Edward T. Francis and George W. Walrath, "The North Hudson County Railway," *The Marker,* V, No. 2 (Sept., 1946), 1-12; SRG, I (1886), 63; *Scientific American,* LIV (1886), 111 ff.

The Hoboken elevated replaced the funicular, below, which had hauled horsecars up the bluff since 1874. *(Smithsonian Institution)*

The powerhouse of the Hoboken elevated was set in the ground floor of the station at Palisade Avenue, shown above in the electric car era about 1912. The elevated structure served to bring Public Service streetcars to the Hoboken Ferry until after World War II. Below are cars of Public Service's Oakland and Jackson lines on the trestle's upper reaches in 1911. *(Both, Edward T. Francis)*

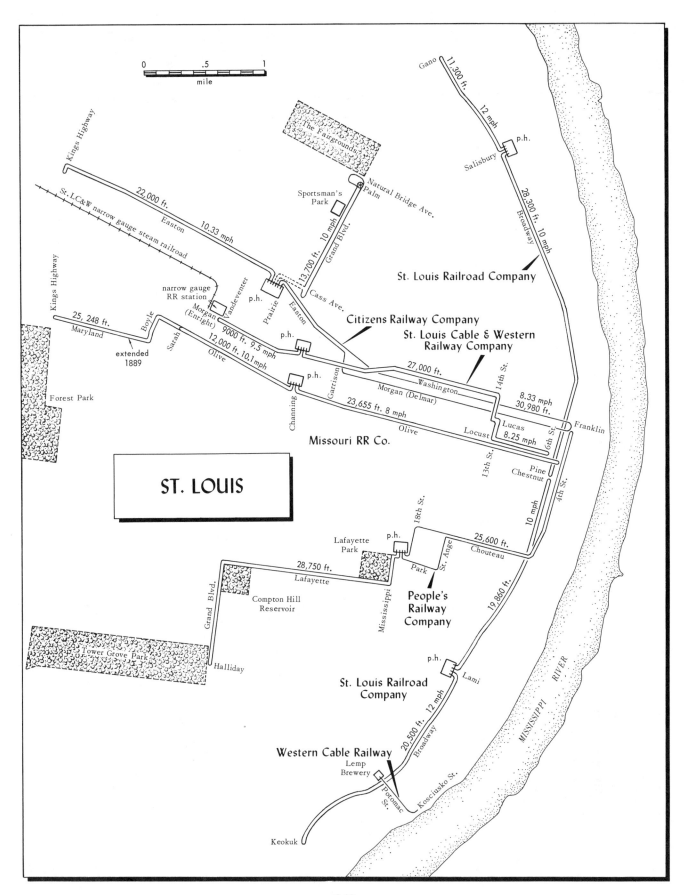

ST. LOUIS

340

ST. LOUIS

Population in 1890: 451,770

ST. LOUIS CABLE & WESTERN RAILWAY

Snelson & Judge double-jaw side   *Gauge: 4'-10"*
grip; converted to Root single-jaw side grip, 1888

The strange name of this company was in fact quite descriptive of its operations. The property was a narrow gauge steam railroad to the western suburbs, combined with a cable entry into the central business district. The narrow gauge had been organized in 1875 as the West End Narrow Gauge Railroad and completed from a station northwest of Grand and Olive in St. Louis to Florissant in 1878. Indianapolis interests, operating under the name of St. Louis Creve Coeur & St. Charles Railway, bought the line in 1883, and in 1884 reorganized it as the St. Louis Cable & Western in the intention of building a cable connection from the station to the central area. This was a somewhat more difficult project than it appears, since all the direct routes were preempted by existing horse-car lines. Consequently, St. Louis' first cable line had by far the most tortuous and difficult access to downtown. In particular, it was necessary to build four right-angle curves in making the transition from Wash (Cole) to Locust Street via 13th and 14th Streets. In all, the company had seven right-angle curves of short radii, and six more gentle curves. By far the worst was a reverse curve at Franklin and Grand Avenue. The line was 3.2 miles over-all; the company moved the terminus of the narrow gauge west to Enright and Vandeventer when it began cable operation in 1886. Trial runs began on April 1, 1886, and regular operation on April 15.

There are no known photographs of the St. Louis Cable & Western in operation, though the line was considered an important one in the industry. It used orthodox open grip cars with trailers — as all the later St. Louis cable lines were to do. The line was extremely difficult to operate, partly because the curvature was excessive, and partly because the original grip, which weighed 344 pounds, was too light for heavy duty. The company's worst problem stemmed from its effort to operate with a single cable of some 34,600 feet, in spite of the curvature. About 185 horsepower was required to move the cable unloaded, even though the terrain — as for all the St. Louis lines — was only moderately undulating and gently sloping upward from the Mississippi. The cable had a relatively short life, stretched heavily, and occasionally unwound. The problem was compounded by a higher than ordinary incidence of slot closures.

In October 1887 the company's cable equipment was concentrated at the east end to move the crowd dispersing from the annual Parade of the Veiled Prophet. The strain on the cable caused a 12-inch shaft to break in the powerhouse, and the cable to kink and unstrand in various places. Restoring the rope to workable condition shut the line down for nearly two weeks. In the fall of 1888 the company modified the intersection of Franklin and Grand to ease the reverse curve which was the worst single feature of the physical plant. This proved inadequate and the company undertook to modify the line by replacing the powerhouse with a new one, adjacent to the old, equipped to issue two cables. The new arrangement was put in service on June 28, 1889. The life of the company's cables more than tripled.

The Cable & Western initially attracted a great many passengers from the horsecar lines on parallel streets, but the success was self-defeating. To compete with the Cable & Western, the Citizens' Railway in 1887 and the Missouri Railroad in 1888 laid cable on nearby streets. Both had the advantage of more direct routes and more substantial physical plants. The Cable & Western, which also suffered from a heavy bonded debt, went bankrupt in 1889, and along with the narrow gauge was reorganized as the St. Louis & Suburban Railway in 1890. Since two lines in the city had already been electrified successfully, the new company, which was controlled by St. Louis interests, decided to convert the narrow gauge and the cable line to a single electric line at the St. Louis gauge of 4'-10". This course of action avoided a further reconstruction of the cable railway, which could hardly have been avoided, allowed trackage to be pushed farther into the western suburbs, and permitted operation with a consistent system for the entire mileage. The steam line was converted first, whereupon the cable operation was discontinued on October 27, 1891. The conduit was removed in favor of heavier track, and engines from the virtually new powerhouse were shifted to an electric generation station at DeHodiamont.

POWERHOUSE: Original equipment: Unknown. 1889 equipment: Two 30" x 72" Hamilton-Corliss engines.

Illustrations of the St. Louis Cable & Western are limited to the poor catalog illustration of a trailer, shown above, and some engravings of powerhouse equipment. *(National Museum of Transport)* As the Hodiamont car line, the former Cable & Western was St. Louis' longest-surviving electric streetcar operation.

A Citizens Railway grip is photographed at the Stephenson plant in New York. *(Smithsonian Institution)*

CITIZENS' RAILWAY

Eppelsheimer bottom grip;   Gauge: 4'-10"
converted to Volk bottom grip, 1889

The Citizens' Railway was a horsecar operator dating from 1859, at the inception of street railway service in St. Louis. After a long history of successful operation, the company suffered a drastic loss of traffic when the new St. Louis Cable & Western was built in 1886. Within a year the officers resolved on laying cable and began reconstructing the system on May 18, 1887. The job was given to Wright, Meysenberg & Co., which became St. Louis' specialist in cable installation. Partly because the company would be inferior to the Cable & Western at four points and would have several additional rope drops in the vicinity of the powerhouse, the officers arranged to use the trust's Eppelsheimer bottom grip. The company specified high standards of construction, and produced a physical plant much superior to the Cable & Western.

Construction began with the trackage from the powerhouse at Easton and Prairie Avenues to Fourth Street downtown via Franklin and Morgan Streets. This portion was ready for service on November 23, 1887. Unfortunately, the engineers had made inadequate provision for the city's difficult winters, so that in January the line was continually beset by slot closures, clogged conduits, and unstranding produced by a mixture of the cold weather and the increased resistance of the cars. By January 22, at the worst of the famous winter of 1888, further operation proved impossible, and the company restored horsecars. After some abortive efforts to resume service, the company gave up cable service until spring. After alterations to the slot and other revisions, the cable was put back in service on April 17. By May, the line was carrying 12 to 16 cable trains regularly, in place of 30 horsecars, and averaged $257 per day additional revenue.

In spite of the company's difficulties in the winter of 1888, it pushed on with laying cable on two of its four routes beyond the powerhouse. One, opened on May 23, 1888, ran west on St. Charles Rock Road (Easton Avenue) to King's Highway. The second, opened on May 26, ran down Grand Avenue past Sportsman's Park, the city's baseball park, to the Fairgrounds. This line had less regular traffic than the Easton route, but had the advantage of a great deal of off-hours traffic to the two attractions along it. Normal practice was to run two cars to King's Highway and the third to the Fairgrounds. The trip to King's Highway required 35 minutes, and to the Fairgrounds 25. The company regularly ran 35 trains. The horsecar lines were cut back to their intersections with the cable lines, but cable trains did not handle horsecars as trailers.

After the difficulties of the initial winter, the line is reported to have had no exceptional problems in operation. It did have chronic difficulty at its rope drop for the Cable & Western at 14th and Franklin. Cars had so many failures to let go properly there, that the company assigned a specialist to handle the grip across the intersection for the regular gripmen.

C. B. Holmes of the Chicago City Railway acquired control of the Citizens' Railway in 1888 through his holding company, the National Railway Company. Even though Holmes was an extreme enthusiast for cable traction, his control of the line was indirectly responsible for the end of cable operation. Holmes also secured control of the Cass Avenue & Fair Grounds Railway, which was electrified in 1892. The managers, recognizing the economies of scale of electrical systems, decided to electrify the Grand Avenue branch of Citizens' Railway jointly with the Cass Avenue & Fair Grounds. The Grand Avenue line was converted to electricity in mid-1893, and all 57 grips and 125 trailers were diverted to the main line. Plans for complete conversion were already in hand, however, and wire was shortly strung over the remaining cable track. After several days of mixed cable and electric operation, the cable was killed on December 26, 1894.

POWERHOUSE EQUIPMENT: Two 500 HP Corliss engines, built by Smith, Beggs & Rankin, St. Louis.

All photographs of St. Louis cable lines in action show grip-and-trailer equipment, but this large combination car lettered for the Citizens' Railway was photographed at the Pullman plant awaiting shipment. *(George Krambles)* The Missouri Railroad trailer is from a Brill catalog.

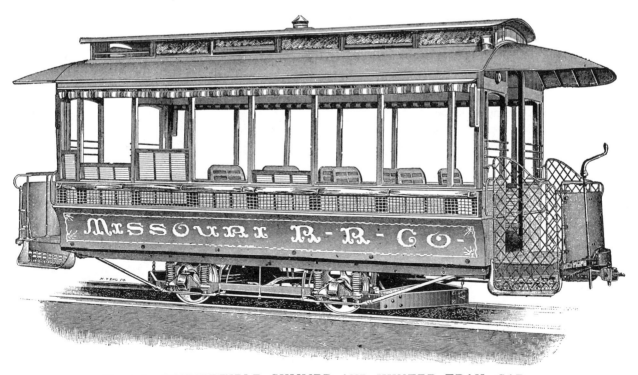

No. 432.—CONVERTIBLE SUMMER AND WINTER TRAIL CAR.

Extreme length, twenty-four feet six inches.
Length of body, seventeen feet six inches.
Width, seven feet seven inches.

Approximate weight { body, 4,300 lbs.
                     running gear, 1,400 lbs.
Seating capacity, twenty-eight persons.

Root single-jaw side grip;   *Gauge: 4'-10"*
converted to Jonson double-jaw (?)
side grip, 1896

Olive Street, occupied by the horsecar line of the Missouri Railroad, was the most promising street in St. Louis for cable traction, and one of the most attractive for the purpose in the country. A long, straight thoroughfare, Olive Street was the principal route straight west from the central area. A cable line promised to be economical to operate and relatively free of accident; the traffic on the existing horsecar line was probably the heaviest in the city, easily enough to justify investment in a cable system. The company's principal rivals, the St. Louis Cable & Western and the Citizens' Railway, had already laid cable.

Accordingly, in 1887 the Missouri Railroad undertook a cable plant, contracting for the installation with Wright, Meysenberg & Co., who were completing the Citizens' Railway. Construction began on August 19, 1887, and ran through the hard winter of 1888. The line was to run out Olive from Fourth Street to Sarah Street, with the powerhouse set at the only curve on the route, a mild turn at Channing Street. The cable was laid from the powerhouse downtown on March 17, 1888, and placed in revenue service on March 31. The outer cable was laid on April 11 and put in service on April 15.

As had been anticipated, the line was an instantaneous success. The directors almost immediately resolved to push the cable track west to King's Highway at Forest Park via Boyle and Maryland Streets. As the only cable route to Forest Park, the line could count on heavy week-end traffic. The extension was opened on June 1, 1889, bringing total mileage to 4.53.

The company operated with standard open grip cars from Brill and the local carbuilder, Brownell & Wight; in 1894 it was reported to have 40 grip cars and 200 trailers. Traffic was heavy enough to warrant carrying two trailers regularly and often three in peak periods. The Missouri Railroad is an ideal example of a line with such dense traffic as to appear to verify the mistaken impression of the early 1890s that cable operation was more economical than electric on heavily-travelled lines. Remarkably, this idea, which was generally dead elsewhere by 1893, persisted in the minds of the company's officers until 1896, when

they re-equipped the cable line completely with new enclosed grip cars, operated from a pilot wheel on the front platform. Both the grip cars and trailers were longer than the previous equipment, so that two-car trains became standard. At the same time the company converted to the Third Avenue Railroad's Jonson grip in hopes of providing smoother starts, easier alike on the passengers, the gripman and the cable. This re-equipment is all the more inexplicable in that the company had been operating two electric lines successfully for a full five years. The company was, of course, to regret the move.

In April 1897 the Missouri Railroad came under control of the Lindell Railway, one of the city's most important street railways — one which had moved directly from horse to electric traction. The two companies had a community of management, but legal actions prevented outright merger until a general consolidation of the city's major traction properties into the United Railways was effected by the investment bankers, Brown Brothers, in October 1899. United Railways was, in turn, leased to the newly organized St. Louis Transit Company for operation. As usual, the operator of a city-wide system had little enthusiasm for incompatible cable mileage, and moved immediately toward conversion. The Olive Street line was in markedly better physical condition than either of the other cable lines which St. Louis Transit inherited, and consequently was the last to be converted. The cable was stopped permanently on March 14, 1901, and electric cars began service the following morning.

Modifications of the curb line to ease the curves in and out of Boyle Street in what is now the Gaslight Square area, along with similar modifications on 13th Street by the St. Louis Cable & Western, are among the few visible reminders of the cable era in St. Louis. The company's powerhouse is also the only one still in existence.

POWERHOUSE EQUIPMENT: Two 30" x 60" Corliss engines. Cylinders reported enlarged at the time of the 1896 re-equipment. Extant, greatly altered, as the Drake Hotel.

On the opposite page and below are the original light grips and trailers of the Missouri Railroad. At right are the heavy grips and trailers with which the company re-equipped itself in 1896. Note the pilot wheel with which the grip was controlled on car 82. (*National Museum of Transport*)

The People's Railway traversed downtown St. Louis on 4th Street, above. The two lower views illustrate the aftermath of the cyclone of May 27, 1896. (*National Museum of Transport*)

PEOPLE'S RAILWAY

Root single-jaw side grip   *Gauge: 4'-10"*

The People's Railway, which had also been operating successfully as a horsecar line since 1859, served a densely populated area southwest of the central business district, together with Lafayette Park and the Compton Hill Reservoir. The company had ample traffic to justify laying cable, but the route, mainly on Lafayette and Chouteau Streets, had enough curvature to make it a difficult cable plant. The line was extended down Grand Avenue from Lafayette to Tower Grove Park when cable was adopted. Since the company entered the central area on Fourth Street, where the Citizens' Railway and Missouri Railroad terminated, it could avoid rope drops for any of the senior companies. Somewhat surprisingly, none of the St. Louis companies attempted to descend to the wholesaling area on the river flats below Fourth Street; much of the Kansas City mileage had been built for exactly such a purpose.

The directors' decision to adopt cable traction was a late one, made in 1889, probably motivated partly by the city's hostility to overhead electrical wires in the central area, but largely by the success of the three earlier lines. Construction was once again entrusted to Wright, Meysenberg & Co., who completed the plant and had it ready for trial operation on April 7, 1890. Regular service began on April 10. Traffic was initially up to expectations, so that the typical train was a grip and two trailers. All of the equipment came from Stephenson. In addition to its own trailers, trains of the company hauled horsecars

of the affiliated Fourth Street & Arsenal Railway from Fourth and Chouteau to the downtown terminus. The line was unusual in operating by cable around the clock, rather than providing horsecars in the night hours. Owl cars did not cover the Grand Avenue trackage, however. The powerhouse operated continuously from April 1890 until May 27, 1896, when a cyclone which caused havoc in the city removed the roof, but did not seriously damage the machinery. Remarkably, the line was restored to service the following day, even though the valve events had to be controlled manually at the powerhouse.

This company is one of the few established street railways which went bankrupt as a consequence of converting to cable. The cable plant had entailed a debt of $800,000, but the extension of electric lines into the area by the Lindell Railway and the Union Depot Railroad in the early 1890s caused an attrition of patronage. The company went bankrupt in March 1897 and was sold for $500,000 on February 9, 1899 to August Gehner, who on April 1 sold his equity for $725,000 to the interests forming the St. Louis Transit network. The line became part of the general consolidation of October 1, 1899. The physical plant was probably the most deteriorated of the three which survived to the merger, but it outlasted the Broadway line, and was converted only on February 14, 1901.

POWERHOUSE EQUIPMENT: Two 30" x 60" Hamilton-Corliss engines.

Broadway was decked out for an exhibition, above, in 1892. Below, a St. Louis Railroad train stops at Broadway and Chestnut in 1891. Note the city's characteristic proliferation of small gas fixtures for street lighting. *(National Museum of Transport)*

ST. LOUIS RAILROAD
Eppelsheimer bottom grip   *Gauge: 4'-10"*

St. Louis' longest, last, and in many respects most interesting cable line was the St. Louis Railroad. Whereas the rest of the installations were efforts to connect the central area with the residential areas to the west, the St. Louis Railroad was the city's one north-south line, running parallel to the river on Broadway at the top of the grade up from the river flats below. This was a major artery, serving a large number of commercial installations, in addition to the local population.

This company adopted cable traction because of the city's refusal to allow it overhead wires in the central area. The management had experimented with Sidney H. Short's Series System with a double overhead along the south end of its route. The officers had been satisfied with the experience, and were eager to install the system on the entire line, but failing to secure permission, opted for cable traction out of lack of alternatives. Wright, Meysenberg began work on the project on April 15, 1890. Only a few days earlier, the city council relented and granted the Union Depot Railroad permission to enter downtown with an orthodox overhead, but the St. Louis Railroad was already committed to the cable installation.

The system consisted of four consecutive cables run out of two powerhouses. The northernmost rope was ready for operation on December 23, 1890, and the other three on January 19, 1891. The linear arrangement of ropes required three rope drops, but the company was also junior to every other line in the city, and running crosstown, it had to cross all of them except the Cable & Western. Finally, although senior, it was necessarily inferior to the Western Cable Railway, a freight line at the Lemp Brewery that used a finite-cable technology in which the car was unable to drop its rope. All of these impediments gave a gripman eight intermediate rope drops in each direction. The company sensibly adopted a bottom grip to minimize the difficulty. The line required a fleet of 80 grip cars and 240 trailers, half open and half closed.

Since 1888 the St. Louis Railroad had been controlled by C. B. Holmes' National Railway Company, along with the Citizens' Railway and four horsecar lines. Holmes was replaced by D. G. Hamilton as head of the holding company in 1891, thereby removing one of cable traction's greatest supporters. The four horsecar lines were converted to electric as the decade progressed. Free transfer was provided between the six companies; since the Broadway line was a crosstown connection, it was pivotal to the entire system. The network, which was popularly known as the Hamilton Syndicate, expanded throughout the 1890s. In particular, it built an electric line north from the cable terminus at Gano Street in 1894. In 1898 the Hamilton Syndicate was sold to C. H. Spencer, head of the Southern Electric Railroad, which connected for Carondelet with the south end of the cable line at Keokuk Street. When transfers were instituted at this point in 1899, the cable route became an unnecessary impediment to through electric service from the north suburbs to the south. As a consequence, it would undoubtedly have been converted shortly in any event.

Spencer, however, sold out the former Hamilton Syndicate and his Southern Electric to Brown Brothers on July 13, 1899. The Broadway line was among the large number of street railways incorporated into United Railways in the merger of October 1, 1899, and leased to the St. Louis Transit Company. Probably because of its electric connections, it was the first of the three cable lines to be converted. Because of a shortage of electric power, the conversion proved one of the most prolonged in the industry. Electric wires were erected by January 1900, but electric cars replaced only the horse-drawn owl cars. In the general strike of May 1900, cables were cut at several points, and rocks placed across the track. Remarkably, the cables were repaired and the company's odd mixture of day-and-evening cable service with electric owl cars was restored. On October 8, 1900, this arrangement ended, and electric cars assumed the duties around the clock.

POWERHOUSES: Each station had two 36" x 72" Wheelock engines, nominally capable of 600 HP each. The cylinders were reported too large, and the power supply wasteful and unsatisfactory.

✤   ✤   ✤

The Western Cable Railway, which the St. Louis Railroad crossed, was a finite-cable operation, and thus properly outside of the scope of this book, but it is of interest, both *per se* and in its relation to the St. Louis Railroad.

The line, though nominally a common carrier, was essentially a plant facility of Lemp's Western Brewery, one of the leading midwestern brewers of the

Above, operation on the outer reaches of the St. Louis Railroad. Below, the company's Lami Street powerhouse became an auditorium after the cable era. The photograph shows it when offered for sale in 1904. (*National Museum of Transport*)

1890s. The brewery was located on Broadway about 2000 feet from the tracks of the St. Louis Iron Mountain & Southern Railroad, with a rise of about 95 feet from the track. The ascent along Potomac Street was essentially continuous, with its steepest portion 7.2 per cent. The connection required 35 to 42 horse-drawn wagons, and was considered both expensive and unsatisfactory. Lemp directed Col. Henry Flad to design a cable connection to replace the wagons.

Flad's arrangement was based on a hoisting engine (two cylinders 14″ x 15″) which hauled in and payed out a cable of about 2000 feet for moving freight cars down Potomac Street to Barracks Street, where it turned left into the Iron Mountain house tracks on a curve of 166 feet radius. In normal operation, an Iron Mountain switcher placed two loaded or three empty boxcars in front of a control car fixed to the end of the cable. An operator on this car controlled the operation through electric wires imbedded in the core of the cable, with which he signalled the operator of the hoisting engine. At the brewery the company operated a light switcher to spot the cars. Downbound, the train descended by gravity. In either direction the cable ran at 5 feet per second.

The operation had a safety device based on a rack projecting downward in the conduit. To stop in an emergency, the operator pulled a pin, which drove a pair of saw teeth upward into the rack. A cylinder of mixed water and glycerin was attached to the teeth by a chain to act as a shock absorber. This arrangement could stop a loaded train in four feet nine inches. Rupture of the cable broke the electrical circuit in the core, and actuated this device automatically.

The Lemp cable had a hand-operated depression pulley at Broadway to depress it for the St. Louis Railroad grip cars passing in full release. The Western Cable Railway was opened in June, 1891, but in a crossing of a finite-cable and an endless-cable line, the finite-cable line must be given superior position. Lemp's line handled about 40 cars per day in winter and 60 to 80 in summer, but there is no record of accidents at the crossing. The installation cost only $58,340, but it was considered successful. It operated throughout the history of the Broadway cable, and was not discontinued until February 12, 1921, after the brewery had been closed by Prohibition. A short portion of the slot may still be seen in Potomac Street.

References: Berl Katz, *St. Louis Cable Railways* (Chicago: Electric Railway Historical Society, 1965); Edward Flad, "An Inclined Cable Railway for Transferring Freight Cars between the Upper and Lower Yards of the Western Cable Railway Co., St. Louis, Mo.," *Journal of the Association of Engineering Societies*, XI (1892), 74-84.

The grip car of Flad's Western Cable Railway was this strange device. Grip car it was; it had no means of ungripping the finite cable. *(Stanford University Library)*

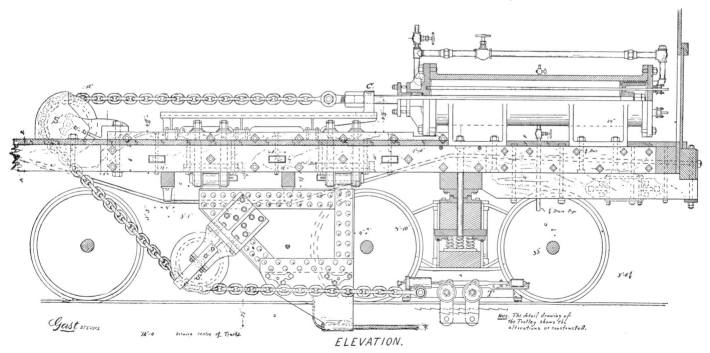

ELEVATION.

The Oakland Cable Railway connected downtown Oakland with an important secondary center in Emeryville. The station of the California & Nevada Railroad, a suburban narrow gauge, was at the outer terminus, and the California Jockey Club, a major race track, was close by. Above is one of the company's narrow-gauge combination cars, and below is the line at Broadway and San Pablo, the principal intersection of Oakland. (*Louis L. Stein*)

OAKLAND

Population in 1890: 48,682

OAKLAND CABLE RAILWAY

Root single-jaw side grip   *Gauge: 3'-6"*

James G. Fair promoted the Oakland Cable Railway, which he operated as an adjunct of his South Pacific Coast Railway, a narrow gauge between Oakland, San Jose and Santa Cruz. Fair initially considered using the Tom Johnson ladder-cable system, but decided on a narrow-gauge version of Market Street technology of San Francisco, built with trust patents.

The line was built from a turntable at Seventh Street up Broadway to the main intersection of Oakland at 14th Street, and thence out San Pablo Avenue to Park Street in Emeryville, a distance of about 2.4 miles. The Pacific Rolling Mills Company laid the line as contractor during 1886, completing it in time for opening on November 19, 1886. The route was almost entirely flat, and apart from some steam railroad crossings at the outer end, was one of the most simple engineering projects of any of the cable installations.

Fair sold the Oakland Cable Railway to the Southern Pacific on July 1, 1887, incidentally to leasing his narrow gauge to the railroad. The SP in 1889 extended the route from Seventh to Water Street to serve the Oakland Creek ferry terminal, thereby providing direct access to the San Francisco boats at the expense of some additional railroad crossings. The downtown turntable was moved about four-tenths of a mile in the process.

In the early 1880s the company was absorbed into the Oakland Railroad, the electric cars of which used the trackage on Broadway en route to Telegraph Avenue. Since the line had no gradients to justify cable traction, it is remarkable that it lasted much beyond 1893; it was not converted to electric traction until May 21, 1899, however.

POWERHOUSE EQUIPMENT: Two 150 horsepower Corliss engines, built by Risdon Iron Works.

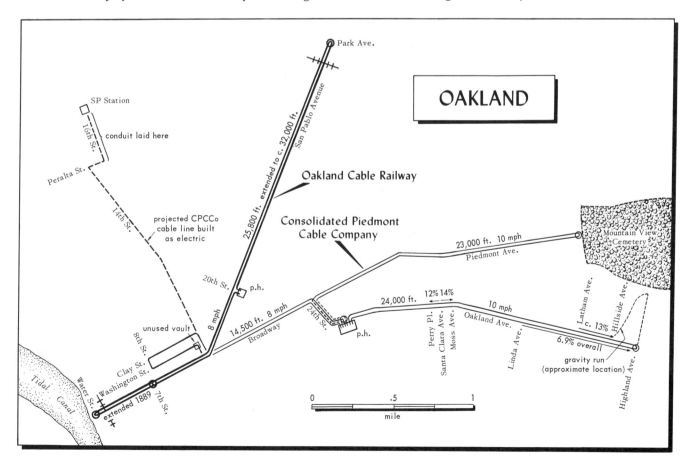

355

Below, car 1 rides the double-track turntable at Park Street in an early view. Above, crewmen pose for a collective portrait at the barn on San Pablo Avenue. *(Both, Louis L. Stein)*

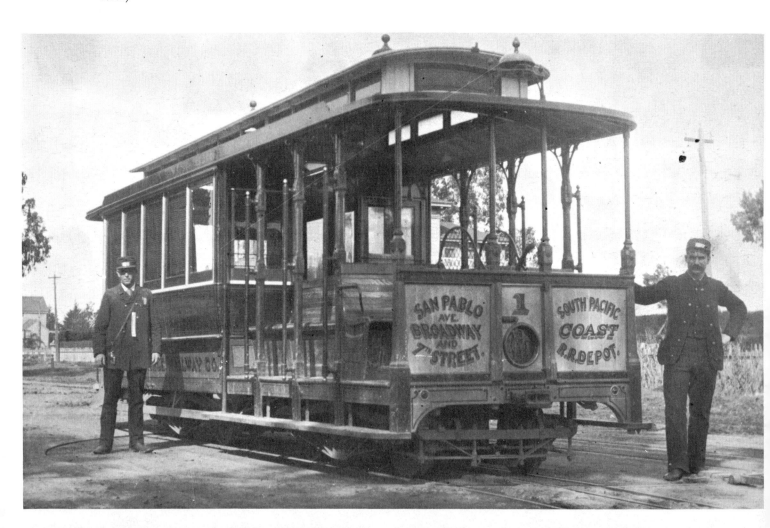

CONSOLIDATED PIEDMONT CABLE
COMPANY

McClelle bottom grip   *Gauge: 3'-6"*

Oakland's later, larger, and more complicated cable system, the Consolidated Piedmont Cable Company, was a joint venture of Walter Blair and Mark Requa, both large landholders in the Piedmont area behind Oakland, and Montgomery Howe and E. A. Herron, who had a background in local horsecar operation. As one might expect, the projected system was designed both for development of the high-lying Piedmont area and for serving the general transportation needs of the existing population.

The terrain was among the most difficult ever presented to a cable engineer. The line had to run from a flat business district up to an elevation of 341 feet at Piedmont, a distance of about 4 miles, with an intermediate summit of 125 feet and a descent to 71 feet before the final major grade up into the hills. Further, the Oakland Cable Railway had pre-empted Broadway, the main street of Oakland from the ferry terminal to 14th Street. A route was laid out beginning with a terminal loop in the retailing area along Clay, Eighth, Washington and 14th Streets, crossing the Oakland Cable Railway at the principal intersection of downtown Oakland, and running out to Piedmont on Oakland Avenue by the route shown on the accompanying map. The terrain has been greatly altered as the area has become populated; the gradient approaching Vernal (Highland) Avenue is currently about 13 per cent, but was reported as 14½ per cent as the line was completed.

The terminal arrangements at Vernal Avenue were unique. The cable terminated at a double-track turntable at Oakland and Vernal; most weekday cars were turned there and sent straight back down Oakland Avenue. As an alternative, the company provided a gravity run of about a mile from the turntable north along Vernal to Blair Park, a promotion of the management, and thence through open fields to a point around the present intersection of Oakland and Hillside. The views of San Francisco Bay along the gravity run were spectacular. At the turntable cars were prepared for the gravity run by hoisting their grips out of the conduit at an automatic grip trap with a block and tackle arrangement on the side of the car body. Grips were then lowered on return to Oakland Avenue.

The line was also unique in technology. The physical plant was built to the non-trust patents of John Isaacs, one of the promoters. Isaacs' principal novelty

was an all-concrete conduit, without yokes, laid at a rate of 300 to 400 feet per day from a horsedrawn steel mold. Isaacs estimated the saving at $15,000 to $20,000 per mile, relative to standard systems, even though the conduit was 24 inches deep. The line was arranged so that every curve except one was a let-go curve. All of the carrying pulleys were equipped with roller bearings. The powerhouse was a well-built structure near Lake Merritt which used lake water for steam generation, and in turn sold hot water to a swimming pool next door.

The line was surveyed in 1889 and completed in the following year. The hill cable was put in service on August 1, 1890, and the downtown cable about a month later. The company, intending to build its second line on 14th and 16th Streets to serve the Southern Pacific's Oakland station, provided a vault under the downtown cable at 14th and Washington, and in 1891 built a short stretch of conduit on 16th Street between Peralta Street and the station. Had the project been completed, the line would have required a cable of about 17,000 feet, run off reduction gears in the vault. Especially since the plan entailed an acute angle into Peralta Street and a right angle curve out of it, there is a very real question whether a cable of this length could have been run off reduction gears. We will never know, because the decision of the Oakland Consolidated Street Railway to electrify its Howe Street line to St. Mary's Cemetery caused Montgomery Howe to shift his efforts to laying cable on his Piedmont Avenue horsecar line, a block from Howe Street, and the direct access to the large Mountain View Cemetery. The company opened this, its second and last cable line, on August 3, 1892, two months before the Howe Street electric line. The new line was a long gradual ascent of Broadway and Piedmont Avenue of about 1.8 miles to the cemetery entrance.

By 1892 building a flat line such as the proposed 14th Street line with cable technology would have been obviously uneconomic, and Howe decided to build it as a narrow-gauge electric line, utilizing the cable track already built on 16th Street. The electric line was opened on November 2, 1892.

The heavy expenditures on the 1892 extensions, combined with the worsening depression, drove the company bankrupt on November 1, 1893. The company was sold under foreclosure on March 19, 1895, to a bondholders' committee for $62,000, barely 10 per cent of the investment, and reorganized as the Piedmont & Mountain View Railway. Efforts at conversion began almost immediately. The existing cars were electrified by applying two Thomson-Houston 15-horsepower motors to the rear truck. On June 10, the Piedmont Avenue line was converted, but the hill on Oakland Avenue was initially beyond the capacity of the small motors when the cars were heavily loaded. In the second half of 1896, the typical operation was electric on weekdays, when the cars carried few people to the lightly populated area, but cable on Sundays when they were heavily utilized. This arrangement ended in December, 1896, when the operation became all-electric.

POWERHOUSE: Oakland Avenue and 24th Street. Two tandem compound Corliss engines, 18″ + 32″ x 42″, 350 horsepower, built by San Francisco Tool Company. Extant as Shepard Cadillac Agency.

References: Erle C. Hanson, "Early Day Trolleys of the East Bay," *Western Railroader*, Nos. 232-233 (1959); SRJ, VI (1890), 583-585; SRJ, IX (1893), 457-458.

In the upper view on the opposite page, one of Consolidated Piedmont's open combination cars crosses the intersection of 14th and Washington in downtown Oakland. In the background, one of the company's electric cars approaches the unused vault at the intersection intended for reduction gears for the 14th Street line. Below is an open car at Blair Park on the long gravity run of the Oakland Avenue line. *(Both, Roy D. Graves)*

The photographs on this page show removal of the cable line on Washington Street. Above, a gang works on the vault at 14th and Washington. Below, workmen remove conduit for reprocessing in the machine at left. The coils of rope in the foreground are mats to be placed over the conduit while blasting. *(Louis L. Stein)*

The 14th-16th Street line of Consolidated Piedmont, planned as a cable line, was built as an electric operation, run with the miniature California-type cars shown above. Below is the company's powerhouse in the transitional period when only the Oakland Avenue line remained a cable operation. *(Both, Louis L. Stein)*

BROOKLYN

Population in 1890: 806,343

BROOKLYN CABLE COMPANY

Johnson ladder-cable non-grip system   Gauge: 4'-8½"

Brooklyn was a city so identified with the electric streetcar that its baseball team became known as the Trolley Dodgers. The city never shared New York's aversion to overhead electric wires, and the combination of streetcars for local trips with rapid transit for journeys into Manhattan suited the dormitory character of the area very well. Owing to the relatively secondary role of downtown Brooklyn, and the water barrier to Manhattan, cable traction was not so attractive as it would have been in another city of Brooklyn's size.

Brooklyn had two operating cable lines, plus the New York & Brooklyn Bridge Railway. The earlier of the two street cable lines was the Brooklyn Cable Company, which achieved a short-lived operation on about a quarter of a projected route from the Fulton Ferry to a set of cemeteries in central Brooklyn. The route, had it been completed, would have connected the major ferry terminal and downtown Brooklyn with a densely populated area in the Bushwick district. The line was to be the pilot installation of the ladder-cable technology of Milton A. Wheaton, customarily known as the Tom L. Johnson system. Johnson arranged, under the name of the Brooklyn Cable Company, to install the system on track of the Atlantic Avenue Railroad, which was to receive 14 per cent of gross receipts. The arrangement was a typical one for an experimental technology.

The Johnson system, as described in Chapter III, was based on a pair of steel cables of ¾" diameter, connected at 6-inch intervals by steel crossbars which meshed with a large cogwheel on the car. No cars are known to have been bought for the line, and it is presumed the cogwheels were mounted on existing horsecars. The line was absolutely straight, thereby avoiding what must have been one of the system's most difficult aspects.

The company was enfranchised by the Brooklyn Common Council in enactments of July 7 and October 4, 1886. A powerhouse was built at Grand and Park Avenues, which was intended to issue ladder cables west to the Fulton Ferry and east to Broadway along Park. Presumably a second powerhouse would have been required for the line from Broadway to the cemetery. Actually, the segment from the Grand Avenue powerhouse along Park to Broadway was the only portion of the line ever built. This was opened on March 6, 1887. Cars operated off the cable for the distance of about a mile and a half, and were hauled west by horse with the cogwheels removed. Many of the passengers came from an elevated station at Park and Washington, three blocks west of the powerhouse.

The line was a failure from almost any point of view. The route as built was unpromising, serving a secondary commercial street between the parallel horsecar lines of the Brooklyn City Railroad on Myrtle and Flushing Avenues. As mentioned in Chapter III, the technology was demonstrably unworkable.

Insofar as the line had any prospects, they depended on extension to the cemeteries. When the state supreme court denied the company the right to lay track on Central Avenue, it became hopeless. Operation was discontinued on July 15, 1887, and the line returned to horse traction of the Atlantic Avenue Railroad. The company's properties, consisting mainly of the powerhouse, were sold at a foreclosure sale late in 1889 to satisfy a judgment of $9,750. There are no known photographs of the operation.

The failure of this system, like that of the Rasmussen and Terry systems, helped kill the cable car by demonstrating the impracticability of the shallow-conduit systems designed for cheap conversion of horsecar lines. William Richardson, president of the Atlantic Avenue Railroad, had watched the Park Avenue installation avidly, and announced plans for either a similar installation or one of the D. J. Miller system on his connecting line on Vanderbilt Avenue and Prospect Park West. The failure dissuaded him, and so contributed to Brooklyn's early recourse to the electric car.

POWERHOUSE: On west side of Grand Avenue just north of Park Avenue. EQUIPMENT: One 250 HP engine, details unknown. Poole & Hunt machinery.

Two of the open cars of the Brooklyn Heights Railroad pass on upper Montague Street near the Borough Hall end of the cable line in 1905 in the postcard view above. The area has retained its Victorian flavor to the present exceptionally well. Below is car 5 at the lower terminus in 1899. The equipment was built with enclosed platforms and railroad roofs, but shortly modified into this configuration. Platforms were again enclosed before electrification. *(Edward B. Watson)*

Wheel-operated Gillham   *Gauge: 4'-8½"*
double-jaw side grip

The shortest, but one of the most successful American cable lines was this installation of a mere 2774 feet in Brooklyn. The line was designed to connect the Borough Hall area, Brooklyn's central business district, with the Wall Street Ferry at the foot of a long grade of about 9½ per cent down Montague Street. The promoters considered a Bentley-Knight electric installation, but decided on cable in consideration of the gradient. Robert Gillham was retained to design the physical plant. The line was ready for trial operation on July 15, 1891, and opened for passengers on July 20; it was operated by the construction company until February 1, 1892.

The line was double-tracked and substantially built. It was operated out of a powerhouse about 2000 feet off the line on State Street. The company lost a legal action to lay track to the powerhouse, and ran the cable through a blind conduit under State and Hicks Street. Downbound cars dropped rope at Hicks Street and picked up the outbound cable off an elevating sheave. Cars took rope with gypsy chains at both termini. Gillham modified his standard grip for operation off a wheel on the front platform. At the outset the company used a locked-wire cable for which it bought steel welding equipment to splice, but shortly converted to a standard hemp-centered model.

The company had eight enclosed cable cars and seven open ones. Cars were stored at the bottom of the grade to the north of the line, and with their grips removed, taken to the Brooklyn City Railroad depot at Third Avenue and 58th Street for servicing. Cars had a combined wheel- and track-brake operating off a single lever. They were reported to have air brakes at least experimentally in 1895. The operating history was apparently favorable. A car lost its grip early in 1892 and rolled down to the ferry, injuring two of its 15 passengers, and open car 20 was destroyed in a wreck in 1905.

This tiny cable operation, somewhat surprisingly, was the inception of one of the city's largest transit undertakings, the Brooklyn Rapid Transit Company. In 1893 the Brooklyn Heights Railroad leased the Brooklyn City Railroad, the largest street railway in Brooklyn, and in 1896 formed the Brooklyn Rapid Transit, including much of the city's streetcar and elevated network.

Since the cable line served exclusively to climb a grade, and was heavily patronized, it was one of the longest-lived in America — by far the longest surviving in the East. Brooklyn Rapid Transit dropped service on the line Sundays and holidays in 1898, but did not convert it to electricity until September 25, 1909. The fourteen surviving cars were electrified and retained in service. The line lost its principal purpose when the Wall Street Ferry was abandoned in 1912, but it was retained until May 18, 1924, when it was itself abandoned. The closed cars were then scrapped, as the open cars had been in 1917. The powerhouse after the end of cable operation was converted to a printing plant for Brooklyn Rapid Transit transfers.

POWERHOUSE: State Street at Willow Place. Extant as garage. EQUIPMENT: One 250 HP tandem compound, C. & G. Cooper & Co., Mount Vernon, Ohio. Walker machinery.

References: SRJ, VII (1891), 395; collection of Edward B. Watson.

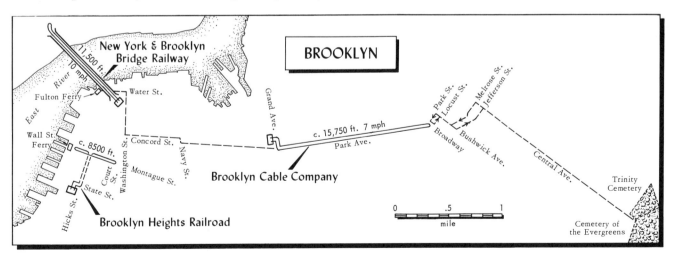

The Brooklyn Heights line made its physical connection with the rest of Brooklyn Rapid Transit's streetcar lines at the switch, above, into Court Street. Note that BRT appended a small C to the numbers of the cable cars, as shown on car 15 at the right. Borough Hall is festooned for Memorial Day, 1903.

The cable powerhouse was the unimposing structure below. The machinery was in the basement, feeding cable out into a blind conduit to the left of the photograph.

The view of 1914, above, shows the Montague Street grade after electrification of the cable line. The car, which seems to have motivated the photographer less than the grade, is number 2, one of the former cable cars. At lower left is the plush-upholstered, stove-heated interior of car 7 in 1905. At lower right is open car 15 in 1911, two years after electrification. *(All, Edward B. Watson)*

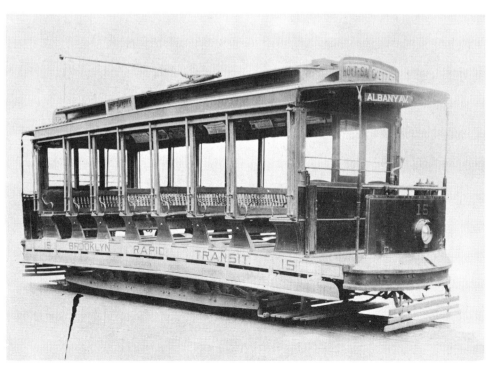

The Cable Tramway of Omaha was among the least photographed cable lines. Above is a standard Stephenson builder's photograph of grip number 3. *(Museum of the City of New York)* Below is a train awaiting departure from the south terminus at Union Station. *(Bostwick-Frohardt Collection, KMTV, Omaha)*

OMAHA

Population in 1890: 140,452

CABLE TRAMWAY COMPANY OF OMAHA

Side grip (see text)   *Gauge: 4'-8½"*

The Cable Tramway Company of Omaha was intended both to develop the undulating residential areas characteristic of the Missouri Valley cities and to break the dominant position of the Omaha Horse Railway in the city. The Cable Tramway was projected by Samuel R. Johnson of Omaha with several associates, and franchised by the City Council on October 7, 1884. Financial difficulties prevented construction until 1886.

The line was intended to connect the Union Station at 10th and Jones Streets with the central business district and finally with residential areas to the north and west. The promoters' original intention was to build north on 10th to Farnam Street, the city's main thoroughfare, thence west to 20th, and north into the residential area. The Horse Railway managed to prevent the Cable Tramway's use of Farnam through an injunction. The Tramway revised its plans to provide for two east-west routes, one on Dodge and the other on Harney Street. Both were ascending westbound, Dodge the more steeply. This arrangement left the company looping around the central business district rather than passing directly through it, a circumstance which was to prove one of the line's several handicaps. Finally, the plans were amplified to include an extension from the junction at 20th and Dodge straight west to 26th Street, apparently to provide an entrance into the city for a projected line called the Metropolitan Cable Railway (of which W. H. Paine was engineer), intended to develop real estate along Underwood Avenue between 48th and 69th Streets. The Tramway shared parts of both 10th and 20th Streets with the Horse Railway and was forced to pay the older company $8000 per year damages for diversion of traffic.

The cable system as built was an exceedingly odd one. As the accompanying map indicates, the entire network was run with two cables, one for the 10th-Harney-20th-Dodge line, and the other for the portion of the 10th-Dodge-20th line above Harney. The purpose of this arrangement seems mainly to have been providing pull curves in all upbound directions at 20th and Dodge, which is near but not precisely

at the summit of a major hill, but especially since the powerhouse was at 20th and Harney, rather than at the intersection, the consequence was to build an enormously greater degree of curvature into the system than was necessary. Had the powerhouse been at 20th and Dodge and the line run with four cables, the

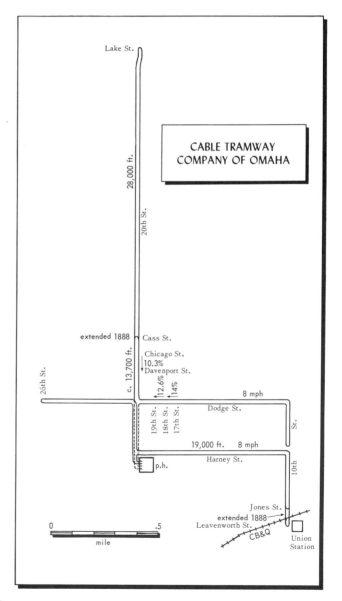

367

curvature would have been much less than half of what was in fact built into it. C. B. Fairchild on visiting the line in 1892 observed that noise from the conduits was more noticeable than in other cable railways owing to the excessive friction in the system, and also that cable wear was exceptionally great. Cables lasted only about 90 days. The designer was Robert Gillham of Kansas City, who was hardly unfamiliar with problems of this character.

The SRJ reported very specifically that the line used "the original Hovey California grip with spools and wheels," which is to say the Sutter Street single-jaw side grip. If so, this is Gillham's only known deviation from his usual double-jaw side grip. J. B. Stone, who visited the property in 1888 and 1890, reported, "The grips that they use are similar to the Chicago grip with rollers at each end," which is consistent either with the Sutter Street or Gillham's own grip. Newspaper accounts fail to describe the grip.

The system was hurried to completion toward the end of 1887, and opened on December 29. The original terminus of the northern line was Cass Street, though an extension northward was intended from the outset; on June 28, 1888 the line was extended to Lake Street. In the same year a minor extension of about a block was made on 10th Street from Jones to a point south of Leavenworth to bring cars to the west door of Union Station. The completed system was 4.2 miles, representing an investment of about $600,000. Stone stated that at the time of his 1888 visit the company planned a third route south from the powerhouse along 20th Street to Poppleton Avenue and west to 34th Street, a distance of about 1½ miles, but the line was never built.

The Tramway was among the least successful cable lines. It failed in 1888 and was reorganized as the Omaha Cable Tramway Company on May 1, 1888 without change of ownership. At this time the Horse Railway intended to lay cable on its Farnam line from 10th Street to a powerhouse at 41st, using D. J. Miller's duplicate system. The Horse Railway also envisioned extension south to Hanscom Park and northwest into newly developing territory, but it first gave up the idea of the extensions and then the projected Farnam line in favor of electrification. Stone in 1890 wrote that the electric system in Omaha showed greater progress than anywhere else he had visited.

Omaha is characterized by exceptionally broad streets which were apparently responsible for a relatively favorable safety record of the cable system. The blind cable for the north line in the conduit on 20th between Harney and Dodge appears to have been close to the Harney cable, which the grips held. On January 6, 1888 a gripman on a northbound car accidentally took the blind cable and did not discover his mistake until it descended into the vaultwork to head east on Dodge, dragging his grip downward with it. The impact sent him sprawling across the grip car, and in the words of a reporter for the *World-Herald*, taught him "that a cable may be a little more dangerous than the after section of a mule."

As might be expected, the Cable Tramway was among the most short-lived cable lines. On January 1, 1889, the company was merged with the Horse Railway and a suburban line, the Omaha Motor Company, into the Omaha Street Railway, which controlled all of the street railway lines in the city. Like several other operators, the new company was more eager to convert its horse mileage than its cable lines, but circumstances made it desirable to convert the Harney line relatively early. On July 1, 1890, coincidentally with the opening of the Farnam Street electric line, the company announced it would shortly convert the Harney Street cable line because it intended to build a viaduct on 10th Street over the tracks at Union Station which would obliterate the south end of the cable line. The conversion apparently took place July 7, 1890.

The conversion of the Harney line left the Dodge line terminating rather pointlessly at 10th and Harney in a wholesaling and warehousing area of no particular distinction. Somewhat surprisingly, no moves were made to convert the line until 1894. The City Council granted permission for the conversion in October, but the company announced that it would not convert until the present cable was worn out. The attractions of conversion were so great that most companies disregarded the condition of the current cable. The Omaha Street Railway erected wire over the cable line in the fall of 1894, and prepared to convert around the end of the year. On January 1, 1895 the line was reported still operating, but conversion was expected within a week. The line was converted during January 1895, and the electric cars were reported to have passed their first major test by operating up the Dodge Street hill perfectly in a heavy snow of January 24.

POWERHOUSE: Southeast corner of 20th and Harney. Extant as J. V. Thorndike Co. garage.
EQUIPMENT: One Wright engine of 400 HP.

References: SRJ, VI (1890), 114-116; Dennis Thavenet, "A History of Omaha Public Transportation," unpublished M.A. thesis, University of Omaha library, 1960.

ST. PAUL

Population in 1890: 133,156

ST. PAUL CITY RAILWAY

Hovey double-jaw side grip   *Gauge: 4'-8½"*

St. Paul, an old-established meat-packing and railroad city, is set along the Mississippi with its central business district on flat land at the center of an amphitheater formed by the hills to the west, north and east. The St. Paul City Railway built two unconnected and in certain respects dissimilar cable lines to climb the hills to the west and east. However appropriate the terrain, the climate was the most severe in which cable traction was ever attempted. The company recognized the problems of ice accumulation in the conduit it would face, and also the extreme expansion and contraction of the yokes in prospect, but it was under pressure from the city council to adopt cable technology.

The earlier of the two lines was designed to climb a grade of 16 per cent on Selby Hill directly west of the business district, and then to run along Selby Avenue across relatively flat land through a residential area. It presented engineering problems both in requiring a 16 per cent grade with a curve in it, and in pursuing a course through the central area along 3rd and 4th Streets with curvature at three intersections. The line served a street of wholesaling firms and central offices, ending at the Northern Pacific general office building at Broadway. Since the line was built to face the widest range of temperature of any of the cable installations, the slot was necessarily the widest in the industry, enough so that the SPCA complained of the toe and heel calks of horseshoes being caught in it periodically. Even so, the line was troubled by slot closure and snow accumulation as it was being readied for service. There were local fears that the line would be able to operate summers only.

The company hired Clift Wise of Kansas City to design the installation and supervise its construction.

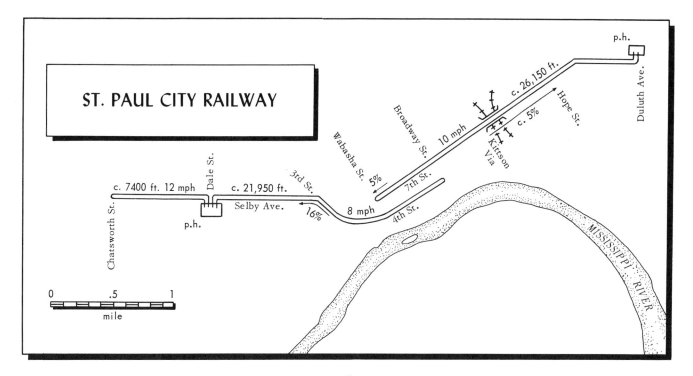

CLIFT WISE.

He used straightforward Chicago City Railway-Kansas City Cable Railway technology. The line was built in 1887 and opened on January 21, 1888, after several days' delay from a blizzard. Almost immediately, on January 27, 1888, a gripman on an eastbound train lost the grip descending the Selby Hill, causing a derailment which killed one passenger and injured several others. The accident destroyed one of the company's twelve original grips, involved it in lawsuits over the course of several years, and provided one of the main examples for bottom-grip enthusiasts, who argued that the disaster followed directly from the absolute inability of a side grip to recover the cable once it had been dropped unintentionally.

The Selby line at its opening was reported to run to St. Albans Street, a block beyond the powerhouse at Dale Street. Mileage reported for it in 1888 and 1889 of 2.3 is consistent with this. In August 1890 it was reported in the SRJ to be about to be extended; the extension brought it to a point between Milton and Chatsworth Streets, an additional 0.6 miles.* A further projected extension to Fairview Avenue was built as an electric line in 1891.

In the interim, the company opened its east line, a route of about 2.7 miles from 7th and Wabasha in the retailing area to 7th and Duluth at the top of a long grade of about 5 per cent up the hill to the east. Much of the route was on a viaduct over extensive railroad yards east of the central area. Operation

---

*This chronology is not certain. The company's book of operating orders directed the Chatsworth extension to be opened on January 21, 1888.

began on June 14, 1889. By 1892 it was reported that electric cars were operating in the snow more effectively than the cable cars.

Since the west line contained a grade beyond the capacity of adhesion vehicles and the east line did not, the east line was converted early in the mass replacement of cable lines in the mid-1890s, but the west line survived until some form of mechanical assistance for electric cars could be worked out. The 7th Street route was converted on September 1, 1893, but the Selby line survived until June 3, 1898, when a counterbalance was arranged out of the former Selby cable cars and the conduit on Selby Hill to assist electric cars on the 16 per cent grade. This arrangement, which was almost identical to the second counterbalance in Providence, served until October 10, 1906, when a tunnel was drilled to provide an ascent streetcars could make with ordinary adhesion. Some cable yokes were uncovered when the streetcar tracks were removed in this area in 1954.

The former Selby grip cars, equipped with electric motors for use on the counterbalance, became shop switchers for the Twin City Rapid Transit Company, and somewhat surprisingly, proved to be the last rail vehicles the company operated upon its conversion to buses in the 1950s.

POWERHOUSES: Selby Avenue and Dale Street. EQUIPMENT: Two Allis-Corliss engines of 600 HP each. Became ice plant, and was recently razed.

Seventh Street and Duluth Avenue: EQUIPMENT: One Allis-Corliss engine of 600 HP.

References: Ira Swett *et alia, Electric Railways of Minneapolis and St. Paul,* Interurbans, Special No. 14 (1953); collections of Byron D. Olsen and Russell L. Olson.

A bearded conductor, above, tightens the brakes on the trailer of a train descending the 16 per cent grade on Selby Hill. The beard was undoubtedly a help in dealing with St. Paul's grim winters. Immediately above the grade, the Selby Avenue line passed the Victorian mansion of N. W. Kittson, below. The site is now occupied by St. Paul's magnificent Catholic cathedral. *(Both, Minnesota Historical Society)*

The St. Paul City Railway was unusual in using a railroad roof on some of its cable equipment. *(Above, W. S. Craig)*

Below is the only known photograph of the 7th Street line in St. Paul. As the picture indicates, the line traversed the central business district on a long, flat street, but terminated on the one block at which a grade was present for gravity switching. *(Minnesota Historical Society)*

NEWARK

Population in 1890: 181,830

ESSEX PASSENGER RAILWAY – NEWARK & IRVINGTON STREET RAILWAY

Rasmussen non-grip system   *Gauge: 5'-2¼"*

The Rasmussen installation in Newark is of exceptional interest, since its failure, occurring in the same year as Sprague's successful electrification in Richmond, convinced many street railway operators that there was no hope in shallow-conduit, low-capital cable technology, and so reinforced their incentives to turn to electric streetcars. The installation had been eagerly awaited in the industry, but the failure was so complete that no one could hold hope for the system thereafter.

The technology, described in Chapter III, was based on a sprocket wheel on the car which meshed with iron collars on the cable. To move, the operator tightened a band brake, which he loosened to allow the sprocket wheel to revolve when he stopped for a passenger. The cable carried its own trucks, which ran on rails in the conduit.

It should be stated at the outset that the descriptions in the press of the system and of the modifications in it are not consistent, partly because several changes were made in an effort to make it function effectively, and partly because Rasmussen's representatives systematically minimized the failure to the point of misrepresenting what was happening in an effort to continue confidence.

After the experimental installation in Chicago in 1886, F. E. Hinckley, president of the United States Cable Railway Company, arranged an installation, intended to be permanent, of slightly over two miles on Market Street and Springfield Avenue, Newark, New Jersey. It was a major route, covering one of Newark's two most important streets in the downtown area, and terminating at the Pennsylvania Station. The track on Market was owned by the Essex Passenger Railway and that on Springfield by the Newark & Irvington Street Railway. The installation was made at the expense of Hinckley and his associates; the street railways were to have the option to buy it within two months of initiation of regular operation. The line gained 185 feet in altitude, but had

no serious grades; the system was probably not well suited to severe gradients.

The conduit was laid in the second half of 1887, and on November 1 was near enough to completion that opening was announced for January 1, 1888. It was then discovered that the collars were imperfectly anchored in babbitt, and tended to move along the cable. Intended to hold a 5-ton load, they proved capable of only 2½ tons. By December 13, 1887, the technology had been modified to drop the sprocket wheel, which had apparently proved itself impossible quickly, in favor of a retractable sprung arm of four prongs which engaged the two-wheel trucks on which the cable rode on rails in the conduit. January 1 came and went without operation, but by February 14, 1888, general manager H. W. McNeill could announce that only winter weather was preventing the opening. On March 6, 1888, McNeill and 20 other officials of the company and of the street railways managed a trial trip from the powerhouse at Bedford Street to the upper end of the line at 4 miles per hour – half the speed for which the system had been planned. The lower cable had reportedly not yet been laid. By September it was reported that the Market Street rope was installed and operating irregularly, but that the complicated cable would not turn the terminal sheave at the Pennsylvania Station properly. Trucks occasionally entered the conduit at a right angle, set up a great deal of friction and ignited oil in the journals. The iron trucks also proved a problem in breaking on contact with the rivets and bolts at the line's minor curve at Market and Mulberry Streets. The original trucks seem to have been too brittle for the attachment of cars by the grip arms – for which, of course, they had not been designed. At this time ten horsecars were reported fitted for cable operation. Only car No. 1 is known to have been fitted; it was raised six inches and given lowered steps.

In the winter of 1888-89, one final effort was made to revise the line. By this time the local press and

NEWARK & IRVINGTON STREET RAILWAY -
ESSEX PASSENGER RAILWAY
Newark

trade journals were losing interest in the property, and thus the final changes are poorly documented. The changes involved imbedding bronze balls in the cable, riveted around the hemp core and surrounded by the strands of the cable. The account in the SRJ indicates that the trucks were superimposed directly on the cable over the balls. Control of the enterprise was said to have passed into the hands of an operator named Heckert of Yonkers, New York. In this final arrangement, the cars were equipped with a link belt between two 18-inch wheels, from which projections descended to engage the trucks on the cable. This represented a reversion to an early idea of Rasmussen's, since the description of his system in the M&SP in 1885 is of a technology of this character. While the upper cable was converted to the new arrangement in the winter months, the lower cable froze in place on Market Street.

The promoters remained superficially confident. In early February 1889 Superintendent William Hopkins said of the system, "It's just as sure to be a success as the sun is to shine." He reported (probably inaccurately) that construction of a Rasmussen system of 20 miles had begun in Milwaukee, that the promoters of the Newark experiment had bought control of the street railway in Memphis for a Rasmussen installation, and that negotiations were in progress in Duluth. Rarely has optimism been so ill-founded, for early in March the employees put extensive claims for back wages in the hands of a counsel. Since, as far as is known, the line had never been able to provide revenue service, this action brought efforts to perfect it to an end. By November 1889 the cables had been removed and the conduit was being taken away as quickly as possible.

The failure, which was reportedly of about $250,000, prevented the spread of the system to Milwaukee and the other cities in which it was being considered. Rasmussen himself was reported to have gone insane in frustration at the outcome. In Newark the experience was almost forgotten, so that discovery of the vaultwork for the terminal sheave on Springfield Avenue in 1896 caused a query in the SRR how such a thing could be found in a city that had not experienced cable traction.

POWERHOUSE: Springfield Avenue and Bedford Street. EQUIPMENT: One engine, built by Iowa Iron Works, Dubuque, variously reported at 180 and 250 HP.

References: "The Coming Power to Move Street Cars," (Chicago: Rasmussen Cable Co., 1887); collection of Edward T. Francis.

The powerhouse of the Rasmussen installation in Newark was this unpretentious structure at Springfield and Bedford. Subsequently, the building became a substation for Public Service. (*Edward T. Francis*)

GRAND RAPIDS

Population in 1890: 60,278

VALLEY CITY STREET & CABLE RAILWAY

Phenix double-jaw side grip   *Gauge: 4'-8½"*

Grand Rapids, Michigan, was the only medium-sized city between the Missouri River and Pittsburgh to have a cable installation. The city is located in the valley of the Grand River, with a long continuous ascent from the central business district to residential areas to the east. Moreover, the city was growing rapidly, and suffered from what was considered a monopolistic horsecar operator, the Street Railway Company of Grand Rapids. The Common Council of Grand Rapids in 1884 ordered the Street Railway to build a cable line on Lyon, Union and Bridge Streets, covering the main ascents east from the business district. The company refused, and continued to show no interest in cable traction throughout the cable era.

In 1887 H. P. Breed of Minneapolis, A. J. Bowne of Grand Rapids and several associates founded the Valley City Street & Cable Railway to build the proposed line. The design was entrusted to William Phenix, who had developed a non-trust set of patents on the basis of his experience on the Chicago City Railway, the Mount Adams & Eden Park, and the St. Louis Cable & Western. The company paid the trust royalties in 1889, however. Phenix essentially proposed to adapt Chicago City Railway technology to single-track operation to economize on capital. A mixture of the management's desire for single track, the city's preference for the route, and the necessity of avoiding existing lines of the Street Railway caused Phenix to build one of the most complicated plants ever attempted, and one of the least successful.

The Valley City, like many cable operators, envisioned a mixed horse and cable system, which would be progressively converted from horse to cable as funds became available. Eventually, it hoped to cover the city, but its immediate target was a loop line on Lyon, Grand, Bridge, and Canal Streets, with an extension to the Fulton Street Cemetery via Union and Fulton Streets, and a north-south line on Ottawa plus various secondary streets. This pair of routes would cover most of the populated area of the city east of the river.

In keeping with the company's plan of progressive development of the system, it first built a single line on Lyon Street from a powerhouse between Union and Grand to a terminal sheave at Canal Street. The

WM. PHENIX.

cable was laid on April 13, 1888, and service began on the 18th. By the time of the opening, the company had secured franchises for the loop line and for the northward extension along Ottawa. The north Ottawa line was particularly attractive, since it promised to terminate close to the passenger station of the Detroit, Grand Haven & Milwaukee, which was about a mile north of the central business district. This route was opened March 7, 1889, by the unsatisfactory expedient of extending the Lyon cable to the north via Canal and Bridge Streets, including five right angle curves. This was intended as an interim arrangement while the company built the loop line, but it proved the most long-lasting of the company's remarkable variety of rope diagrams.

375

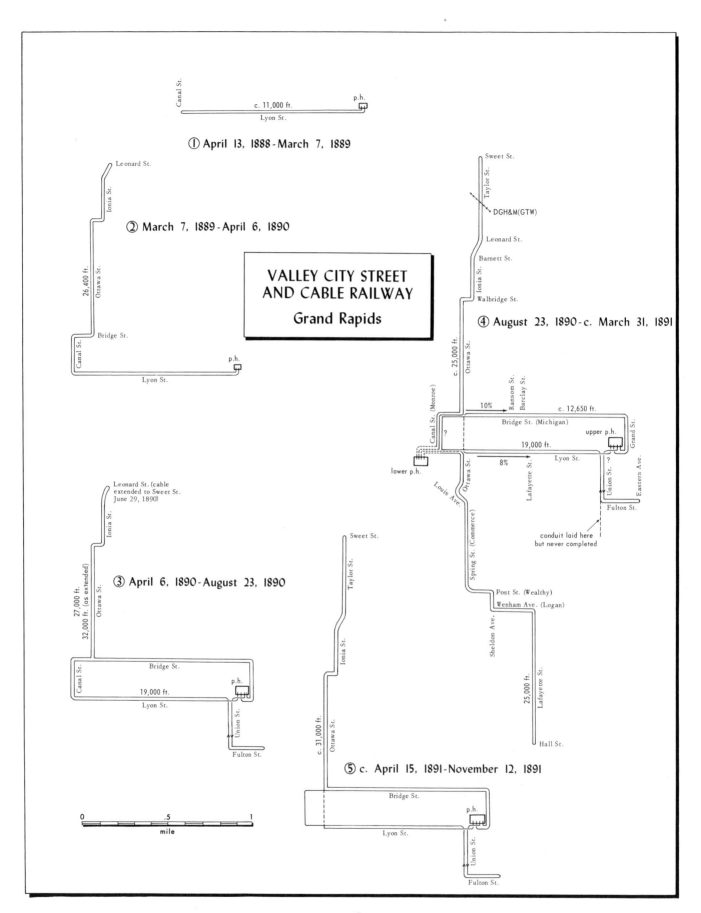

Canal St.

c. 11,000 ft.   p.h.

Lyon St.

① April 13, 1888 - March 7, 1889

Leonard St.

Ionia St.

② March 7, 1889 - April 6, 1890

26,400 ft.

Ottawa St.

Bridge St.

Canal St.

Lyon St.

p.h.

Sweet St.

Taylor St.

DGH&M(GTW)

Leonard St.

Barnett St.

Ionia St.

Walbridge St.

VALLEY CITY STREET
AND CABLE RAILWAY

Grand Rapids

④ August 23, 1890 - c. March 31, 1891

c. 25,000 ft.

Ottawa St.

Canal St. (Monroe)

Ransom St.
Barclay St.

10%

c. 12,650 ft.

Bridge St. (Michigan)

upper p.h.

Grand St.

?

19,000 ft.

lower p.h.

Lyon St.

Louis Ave.

Ottawa St.

8%

Lafayette St.

Union St.

?

Eastern Ave.

Spring St. (Commerce)

Fulton St.

conduit laid here
but never completed

Leonard St. (cable
extended to Sweet St.
June 29, 1890)

Ionia St.

③ April 6, 1890 - August 23, 1890

27,000 ft. (as extended)

32,000 ft.

Ottawa St.

Sweet St.

Taylor St.

Ionia St.

Post St. (Wealthy)

Wenham Ave. (Logan)

Sheldon Ave.

Canal St.

Bridge St.

19,000 ft.

Lyon St.

p.h.

Union St.

Fulton St.

25,000 ft.

Lafayette St.

Hall St.

⑤ c. April 15, 1891 - November 12, 1891

c. 31,000 ft.

Ottawa St.

0   .5   1

mile

Bridge St.

Lyon St.

p.h.

Union St.

Fulton St.

The loop line was opened on April 6, 1890, after laborious preparation. Although mainly single track, the loop was intended for operation in both directions. One cable ran from the powerhouse west a half block, thence south on Union Street to serve the Union-Fulton extension, and back to Lyon for a clockwise run around the loop. The counterclockwise loop cable was initially routed up the northern line. Especially after the extension north from Leonard to Sweet Street on June 29, 1890, this cable, now 32,000 feet, was grossly too long for its degree of curvature. The company as a permanent arrangement wanted the north line and a projected south line operated from a second powerhouse at the foot of Lyon Street. It received permission for this change from the Common Council on April 22, 1890, and quickly built a powerhouse similar to the original at Lyon and Campau Streets. The south line and the lower powerhouse were completed during the summer of 1890, so that between August 23 and September 4 the system could be converted to what was expected to be its final organization.

The Valley City's cable system, full blown, consisted of a clockwise and a counterclockwise loop line, both of which ran over the Union-Fulton extension, and a single north-south line which shared the loop line's trackage on Canal and adjacent portions of Lyon and Bridge. Mileage was 6.9. The cable layout in the vicinity of Canal Street was among the most involved ever built. Southbound cars on the north-south line and counterclockwise loop cars held the southbound rope of the north line inbound to the lower powerhouse; the counterclockwise loop cable ran blind through Ottawa Street from Bridge to Lyon. Northbound cars off the south line shifted from the south cable to the clockwise loop cable at Ottawa and Lyon, but apparently shifted to the outbound north cable at the vault on Canal Street so as to pull the curve from Bridge into Ottawa. They apparently held their cable in their left jaws, while the clockwise loop cars held their cables in the right jaws. To allow all this Phenix designed double track for the stretch used jointly by the two lines, for short distances above and below the loop on Ottawa, and on the loop line itself as far up the hill as Barclay Street.

The south line was the company's weakest operation, and the immediate cause of the demise of the cable system. Essentially it was an effort to parallel the Street Railway's Division Street horsecar line, but the necessity of finding unoccupied streets involved the company in a devious route of limited traffic potential and utterly unworkable curvature. In particular, the line had four right-angle curves in crossing

from Spring to Lafayette Streets, and a slot too narrow for the local winters — probably the worst, save only St. Paul, of any of the cable systems — so that excessive friction caused the rope to sever frequently. Grand Rapids was the only system in which outright severance rather than loose strands was the principal problem with the cable itself. The first cable on the south line served 134 days at an average cost of $56.30 per day, some five times what the line was grossing. Early in 1891 the first cable was replaced leaving the company's weakest line with its only new cable.

Simultaneously, the north cable wore out. The company substituted horses on February 27, 1891, with no intention of restoring cable service, which both the management and much of the public had come to dislike intensely. The Common Council was of the opposite opinion, and quickly ordered the company to restore service on pain of loss of its operating rights and denial of further franchises. The Valley City management was in a vulnerable position, since it was awaiting a franchise to merge with the Street Railway, which was extending electric lines throughout the city. The company had no choice but to reopen the north line, but it was eager to avoid buying a new cable and thus throwing $6000 of still good money after about a million of extremely bad.

President Bowne on March 30, 1891, secured acquiescence of the Council to a plan whereby the cable should be removed from the south line, relaid on the north, and spliced to the counterclockwise loop cable in a transitional period while the lower powerhouse was changed to electric. The south line which had only recently been reopened after a flood, was abandoned immediately — not electrified. By April 15 the north line was rigged once again to operate out of the upper powerhouse, though this time it returned via the blind conduit on Ottawa Street. This arrangement necessarily ended the counterclockwise loop trains, which had no means of traversing Canal Street: the north line trains terminated at Ottawa and Bridge.

The final rope layout entailed the fourth arrangement — all different — of the intersection of Bridge and Ottawa. Given the inflexibility of cable vaultwork, the ability of the Valley City's engineers to rearrange the movement of cables through that intersection is remarkable. From the last revision of the system in April to the end, the company cut its cable speeds from the former 9.75 miles per hour to about 7.5 to reduce friction on the cable and thus to avoid the prospect of another replacement. The low speed of operation provided one last source of complaint, over and above the public outcry over accidents and suspensions of service which was particularly conspicuous in Grand Rapids.

The company, which merged with the Street Railway as the Consolidated Street Railway Company on July 1, 1891, continued its efforts to convert the cable system, and on October 9 ran its first electric cars on the loop line. The grades were difficult enough to present real problems for the early electrics, but the transitional difficulties were resolved in about a month, and on November 12, 1891, laborers began removing the cable from the conduit.

POWERHOUSES: Upper, Lyon between Grand and Union. EQUIPMENT: One 160 HP engine, details unknown, replaced by two 24″ x 48″ Wheelock engines, 350 HP each. Walker machinery.

Lower, Lyon and Campau Streets. EQUIPMENT: Two 24″ x 48″ Wheelock engines, 350 HP each.

References: George W. Hilton, "The Cable Car in Grand Rapids," *American Railroad Journal*, II (1967-68), 16-30.

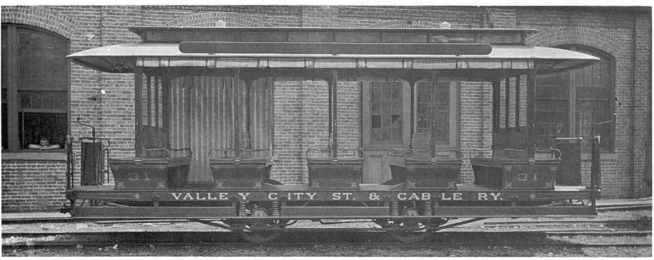

The only known photograph of cable cars in Grand Rapids is the view immediately
above, thought to date from the opening of the Valley City's north Ottawa Street line.
Below is the upper Lyon Street powerhouse. The horsecar on the opposite page ran
on the west side of the Grand River, an area in which the company never managed to
lay cable. *(All, Grand Rapids Public Library)* Open trailer 31 is shown on completion
at Pullman. *(George Krambles)*

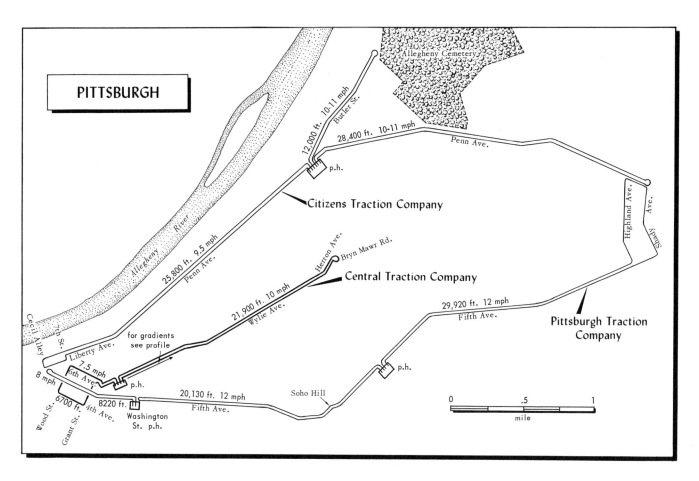

PITTSBURGH

Allegheny Cemetery

12,000 ft. 10-11 mph — Butler St.

28,400 ft. 10-11 mph — Penn Ave.

p.h.

Citizens Traction Company

Highland Ave.

Shady Ave.

Allegheny River

25,800 ft. 9.5 mph — Penn Ave.

Herron Ave.

Bryn Mawr Rd.

Central Traction Company

21,900 ft. 10 mph — Wylie Ave.

29,920 ft. 12 mph — Fifth Ave.

Pittsburgh Traction Company

Cecil Alley

7th St.

Liberty Ave.

for gradients see profile

7.5 mph

6th Ave.

p.h.

8 mph

Wood St.

6700 ft. — 4th Ave.

Grant St.

8220 ft.

Washington St. p.h.

20,130 ft. 12 mph — Fifth Ave.

Soho Hill

p.h.

0 — .5 — 1
mile

A single-truck grip of the "butterfly" type, in which passengers sat back-to-back, facing outward for the full length of the car, lettered for the Pittsburgh Traction Company, stands on Brill's transfer table. (*Historical Society of Pennsylvania*)

380

PITTSBURGH

Population in 1890: 238,617

PITTSBURGH TRACTION COMPANY

Whitton top grip   *Gauge: 5'-2½"*

Pittsburgh, one of the hilliest cities in the world, was a less suitable place for cable traction than one would expect. The streets are so tortuous that only a few were straight enough even for what would be by the standards of any other city a cable line with an enormous degree of curvature. Further, ascent of the bluffs up from the rivers was so steep as to be beyond even the cable car; accordingly, Pittsburgh was principally characterized by funiculars, and escaped with only three cable lines.

Two of the city's three lines connected the central business district with East Liberty, the secondary business district, and the third bisected the intermediate area with a shorter line. This limited network rather effectively covered virtually all of the city that could have been served by cable traction, given the technology's limitations.

The first of the three lines to be built was the Pittsburgh Traction Company's route from the central area to East Liberty via Fifth Avenue. By Pittsburgh standards, this was a relatively easy route, about 5.4 miles of gently rising line along moderately straight and wide streets. Fifth Avenue skirted the city's central ridge to the south, and served the Oakland area, site of Pittsburgh's present impressive cultural center, even then a major secondary focal point for traffic. The principal engineering problem was dealing with Soho Hill, a long double reverse curve of about a half mile on a 4 per cent grade approaching Oakland. The worst curve was of only 250-foot radius, but it was flanked by curves of 350-foot radius on either side. The Widener-Elkins syndicate, which owned the company, deputed its usual cable engineer, A. D. Whitton, to design an arrangement whereby cars could traverse Soho Hill at less than full speed and also stop for passengers; the reverse curve was simply too long for the normal practice of traversing the curve at top speed at full grip. Whitton designed an extremely large and heavy top grip, weighing 400 pounds, capable of trailing the cable in partial release on a curve. He fitted Soho Hill with 290 consecutive curve pul-

leys. The grip required an especially deep and expensive conduit, but somewhat surprisingly, the effort was quite successful, so that cars traversed the long curve in partial release and even stopped for passengers regularly over the course of the line's history.

Whitton's other major problem was arranging a terminus in the central business district. The company had rights only to Fifth Avenue, but Whitton wanted to use his usual double-truck enclosed car, which was single-ended. Consequently, he was forced to terminate at a loop of only 27-foot radius at Fifth and Liberty in what is hardly more than a broad intersection. J. B. Stone, who reported it was only 25-foot radius, said it had over 50 curve pulleys, and was the sharpest he had seen. This arrangement was able to handle Whitton's 28-foot double-truck cars, but subsequently the company bought single-truck open equipment of the "butterfly" type, probably for facility in traversing the loop.

The outer portion of the line was completed in September, 1888, and the inner portions were ready for service on October 9, 1888. In contrast to Whitton's installations in Philadelphia and Chicago, this one worked quite well, and was reasonably successful by the standards of the industry. It carried over eight million passengers in 1893, and stayed in the black in spite of the worsening business conditions of the early 1890s. The line had reduced travel time between East Liberty and the central area from about an hour and 45 minutes to 30 minutes. The installation was very expensive, an investment of about $1.4 million.

As elsewhere, the cable line lost much of its attraction when paralleled by an electric line, in this instance the Forbes Avenue line, a block to the south, of the Duquesne Traction Company of the Magee-Flinn syndicate, Pittsburgh's other major traction operator. The Widener-Elkins and Magee-Flinn interests arranged a pooling of revenue in 1891, and in 1895 agreed to merge the city's most important railways into the Consolidated Traction Company. Both the

Pittsburgh Traction Company's cable line and the parallel Forbes Avenue electric line thus became part of the same combine. As usual in such circumstances, there was little place for a cable operation in a comprehensive electric system, and preparations for conversion began immediately. The last Fifth Avenue cable car left the downtown loop at 11:45 PM on Sunday, August 23, 1896, and presumably tied up at the Oakland barn after midnight on the following day.

The line was closed for two months while a force of 1400 men removed the yokes by crane; even in death cable traction was a massive operation. Electric service was inaugurated on October 17, 1896, and the crew immediately went to work on conversion of the Penn Avenue line of the former Citizens Traction Company.

POWERHOUSES: Washington Street. EQUIPMENT: Two 20″ x 48″ Wetherill-Corliss engines, 175 HP each.

Oakland powerhouse: Two 28″ x 60″ Wetherill-Corliss engines, 500 HP each.

References: SRJ, VI (1890), 257; VII (1891), convention supplement, 12-15.

382

At right, Pittsburgh Traction grips traverse Fifth Avenue. *(E. Harper Charlton)* Below are the line's two principal operating problems, the loop at Liberty Street and the ascent of Soho Hill. *(Pittway Corp.)*

Above, cars of the Citizens Traction Company lay over on their loop in downtown Pittsburgh. *(Russ Cashdollar)* Car 201 appears on a cracked glass plate negative on downtown trackage. *(Pittway Corp.)*

CITIZENS TRACTION COMPANY

Whitton top grip   *Gauge: 5'-2½"*

Pittsburgh's second cable line, the Citizens Traction Company, had precisely the same termini as its first installation, even to the same intersections in the central area and in East Liberty. For most of the intermediate distance the two lines were over a mile apart. The Citizens line served Penn Avenue, for about half its length on relatively flat land along the Allegheny River, and for the remainder up a grade of 5 per cent for about 0.8 miles to undulating land, before a long descent to East Liberty. For the last two blocks the line shared Penn Avenue with the terminal loop of the Pittsburgh Traction Company, giving the street one eastbound track between two westbound. A branch of the Citizens Traction Company ran out Butler Street for just under a mile to the Allegheny Cemetery. The entire system was about 5.9 miles.

The company was formed July 6, 1887 by John G. Holmes and associates to lease the city's pioneer operation of 1859, the Citizens Passenger Railway, and a lesser horsecar line, the Transverse Passenger Railway. The management immediately set out to convert the system to cable, using Whitton's technology — even though this was not at the outset a Widener-Elkins property. The system was a simple and well designed one, with a single powerhouse at the intersection of the main line and the Butler Street branch. There Whitton encountered the inevitable problem of dealing with the excessive distance a top-grip car required to roll between ropes. Inbound cars dropped the cable several hundred feet short of the intersection and took advantage of the long downgrade to roll to the pick-up point. Initially upbound cars were hauled across by horses, but the expense and low speed of this operation caused the company to resort to runs on momentum, which somewhat surprisingly proved effective; only three or four cars a day typically failed to make the crossing. In one respect the line was the reverse of the Pittsburgh Traction Company: it terminated in a loop on city streets at the downtown end, and on a balloon loop at East Liberty. Both companies provided pits for the inspection of the grip on every trip, the Citizens at Cecil Alley on the downtown loop and at the termini of its two lines. The company was more than ordinarily conscious of safety; it placed a set of signal boxes along the line to protect itself against involvements in loose strands. The conductor was able to trip a gong and actuate an indicator at the power-

house to show which cable was involved. The system was intended to stop a car in 300 feet at any point on the line. Partly because of the safety features, and partly because of the deep conduit required by the Whitton grip, the property was very capital-intensive, reportedly representing an investment of $1.6 million, though this figure may include some non-cable facilities.

The line was completed on December 23, 1888; the main line opened for revenue service on January 1, 1889, and the Butler branch followed on January 10. Horsecars served Pittsburgh so poorly that anything which replaced them had an immense advantage. The company experienced a 55 per cent increase in traffic almost immediately, and by 1890-91 was hauling 12.5 million passengers per year, about double the figure of 1887-88. Operation was generally accounted successful, but the company was characterized, like most top-grip lines, by short cable life, in this instance compounded by short radii on terminal loops. Ropes lasted less than seven months, so that the company was forced to charge off $100 per day for cable expense.

The company began electric operation with a line on Frankstown Avenue in April, 1893, but in 1895 carried nearly 14 million passengers on its cable cars and only 2.8 million on electrics. The cable line offered service as frequently as once a minute in rush hours, and was one of the most heavily utilized transit routes in the United States. The company would doubtless have converted the cable line in the mid-1890s in any case, but when it was absorbed into the Consolidated Traction Company in 1895, the terms of the lease provided for conversion to electricity by November 1, 1897. The company had no inclination to push the terminal date, and began work on the replacement as soon as the Fifth Avenue cable line had been removed. The portion from the powerhouse to East Liberty was discontinued following a trip by car 227 from the central area at 12:18 AM on November 9, 1896. In this instance, electric cars replaced cable cars immediately, but operated on a single track while cranes removed conduit from the other. The company announced at the time that the remainder of the main line and the Butler branch would continue in cable operation until spring. Cable cars were still running when a major fire destroyed several buildings in the vicinity of Cecil Alley on May 1, 1897; several days later cable operation was resumed after rubble had been cleared away. The line survived until June 14, 1897, when it was converted.

POWERHOUSE: Penn Avenue and Butler Street.
EQUIPMENT: Three 28″ x 60″ Wetherill-Corliss engines, 500 HP each. Wetherill machinery. Natural-gas burning boilers.

References: SRJ, VI (1890), 256-257; VII (1891), convention supplement, 10.

Like most street railways of the time, Citizens Traction used different liveries for its two lines. Here in two builder's photographs car 128 is shown emerging from the Pullman plant in the yellow and white of the Butler Avenue branch and car 204 in the dark red of the Penn Avenue line. This practice, which added color and variety to our streets, had the incidental advantage of identifying cars simply for illiterates and non-English speaking persons, who were still numerous in our cities. The greater flexibility of the electric car in assignments between lines and the decline of illiteracy resulted in homogeneous color schemes in most American cities by the early 20th century. *(George Krambles)*

CENTRAL TRACTION COMPANY

Root single-jaw side grip   *Gauge: 5'-2½"*

Pittsburgh's third cable line was more typical of the industry, both in technology and in terrain, than either of its earlier and more conspicuous counterparts. The line replaced an existing horsecar route on Wylie Avenue along the ridge of the hills at the center of the peninsula between the Allegheny and Monongehela Rivers on which the central portion of the city is situated. The company had been considered relatively weak. The route was reasonably straight, but with a very steep grade out of the central business district and continual undulation on the ridge. (See the profile illustrated.) Accordingly, the line was an almost ideal example of a cable installation serving the purpose for which the technology was best suited.

George I. Whitney reorganized his Central Passenger Railway as the Central Traction Company on December 21, 1888, and immediately set out to build the cable line. Design was entrusted to George Rice, who had supervised construction of the two earlier installations in the city. Presumably because the line would be inferior to the Pittsburgh Traction Company at two points on its terminal loop, he forewent the top grip of the earlier roads, and used the trust's Root grip. Most of Rice's problems were concentrated in the terminal loop, which contained a curve at Webster and High Streets of only 30-foot radius, another of 40-foot, six of 45-foot and one of 50-foot. Naturally, he preferred to run this as a separate cable at low speed, but this course required him to put his powerhouse at the bottom of the grade out of the central area. This grade, now obliterated by the Civic Auditorium, was 2000 feet long, apparently varying from 9.5 to 12.75 per cent, but reportedly 11.1 per cent over-all. As usual, placing the powerhouse at the bottom of a grade maximized the strain on the terminal sheave at the terminus, Herron Avenue and Bryn Mawr Road, so that the original had to be replaced with a more substantial one. The Herron Avenue gravity loop ran through a car house, which contained a pit for inspection of the grip — a precaution particularly characteristic of Pittsburgh. The route was the equivalent of 2.9 miles of double track, and including about 2 miles of unconverted horsecar line represented a reported investment of $1.2 million — a figure which seems excessive.

The cable road was built mainly in 1889 and opened on February 24, 1890. The tributary popula-

tion was light, relative to the city's two other lines, but the company was uniformly profitable. The physical plant, which contained stationary depression pulleys at the two crossings of Fifth Avenue and an unspecified but large number of movable depression pulleys elsewhere, was very hard on rope, but otherwise the operation seems to have been fairly successful. In 1892 traffic warranted addition of trailers. The company in the same year built an extension of a mile on Centre Avenue in the form of a Westinghouse electric system; in a man-bites-dog accident, an electric car became unmanageable near the east terminus and struck a cable car in November, 1894, injuring four passengers. The Westinghouse Air Brake Company in 1890 equipped a car experimentally with a straight air brake, actuated off a front axle. The experiment lasted about a year, and was accounted generally successful.

In the extensive merger of 1895, the Consolidated Traction Company leased the Central Traction Company for 950 years, effective April 2, 1896. The Widener-Elkins interests lost little time in getting rid of the cable operation. With almost no advance notice,

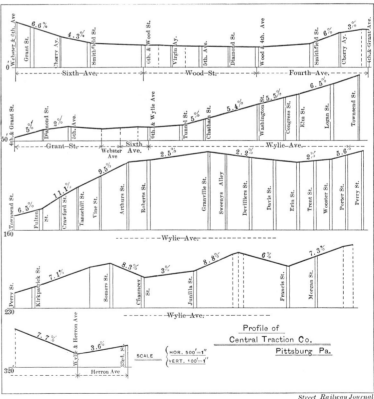

Profile of
Central Traction Co.
Pittsburg Pa.

SCALE { HOR. 500'=1"
        VERT. 100'=1"

Street Railway Journal

the Wylie cable was killed shortly after midnight on August 30, 1896, and immediately replaced by an electric line.

POWERHOUSE: Wylie Avenue and Tunnel Street.
EQUIPMENT: Two 28″ x 60″ Wetherill Corliss engines, 500 HP each.

References: SRJ, VI (1890), 257-258; VII (1891), convention supplement, 16; collections of Peter Weiglin and Ken Douglas.

The Central Traction Company used a particularly handsome livery of yellow, cream and gold. Here one of the company's 16 grips from Pullman appears in one of that builder's characteristic blind-side views. The interior view at right shows two brake levers in the operator's compartment on the front platform, plus a slot for placing of the grip. Street railways customarily installed grips themselves on taking delivery of cars. *(George Krambles)*

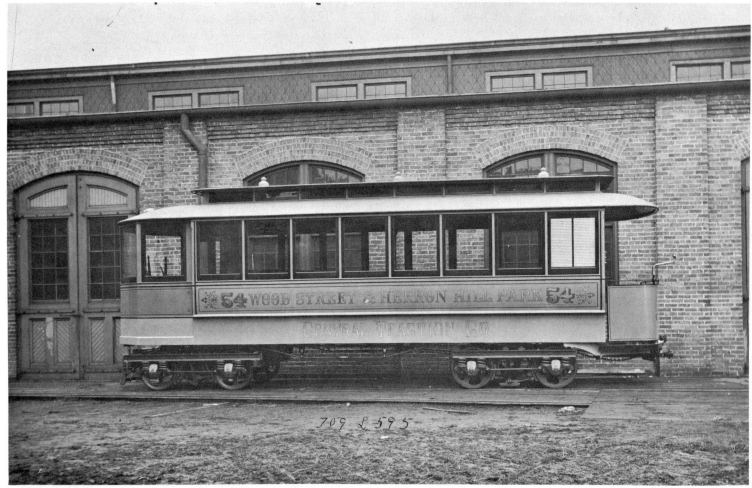

SEATTLE

Population in 1890: 42,837

SEATTLE CITY RAILWAY

Single-jaw side grip   *Gauge: 3'-0"*

Not even San Francisco and Kansas City had more obvious geographical characteristics for cable traction than Seattle. The city lies on a ridge running north and south along an isthmus between Puget Sound and Lake Washington. The central business district is along Puget Sound at the foot of a steep ascent of the ridge to the east. As in many of the cities growing rapidly in the 1880s, the high-lying land was inaccessible with horse-drawn vehicles.

Seattle's first — and always its most famous — cable installation was the Yesler Way line, running 2.5 miles straight east from the Pioneer Square area to Lake Washington. It was promoted by J. M. Thompson, George A. Moore, A. S. Moore, J. B. Metcalfe, Josiah O. Low, Junius Rochester and John Leary, doing business as the Seattle Construction Company. Thompson designed and supervised construction of the line in collaboration with the Pacific Cable Construction Company in 1888; it was reportedly Pacific Cable's first installation north of San Francisco. The project was integral with real estate development along the route; the tributary territory was said to have only 13 houses in 1888, and passengers who put their heads out of windows in the first cars were reported to be in danger of bumping tree trunks along the way. The line opened with an excursion and banquet on September 27, 1888, and began revenue service two days later.

The Yesler Way line was characterized in its history by an exceptional number of changes in route. Initially, the route was a single-track loop running eastbound on Yesler and westbound on Jackson Street, three blocks to the south. Both streets involved descending to Lake Washington from the high-lying land on long and high trestles, approximately 18 per cent on Yesler, and 15.62 per cent on the ascent of Jackson. The line was operated from a powerhouse on a small bluff above the Lake, approximately at Power Avenue. Fairchild considered the placing of the powerhouse short of the Lake incomprehensible, since the arrangement required coal and supplies to be brought up from Lake Washington by a cable haulage device.

Originally, the route ran south from Yesler to Jackson parallel to Lake Washington, and then ascended the Jackson trestle. Although less steep than its counterpart on Yesler, the Jackson trestle was flimsier and, in popular opinion, more hazardous. This view was verified when on August 17, 1890, an upbound car lost its grip, ran away, and derailed when the trestle swayed. The accident caused the line to be modified to run lefthanded up the Yesler trestle, and to cross to Jackson on Rainier Avenue, approximately at the present 31st Avenue. The western terminus was Occidental Avenue and Yesler, where Thompson had placed a turntable to avoid a pull curve at a major intersection. Especially since grip and trailer had to be turned separately, the turntable was a serious bottleneck in the system.

The line was successful in attracting population to the hills, but had a checkered financial history. Because of its poor initial financial showing, the Seattle Construction Company, a typical subsidiary organized to build the property, operated the line until the fall of 1889. The property was then sold to Fred E. Sander, one of the original promoters, who in 1890 organized the Lake Washington Cable Railroad to operate the line. Sander built a boathouse, pavilion and other facilities known collectively as Leschi Park at the Lake Washington terminus for promotional purposes, and then sold the line on August 23, 1890, to L. S. J. Hunt, who incorporated it as the Seattle City Railway. The tributary area was reported to have 3000 houses by 1891, but the company went bankrupt in 1893. In spite of continual efforts to refinance the line in the 1890s, it was reorganized as the Seattle Railway only after a foreclosure sale on September 21, 1901. The new company was controlled by the Seattle Electric Company, and the line for the rest of its history was integral with the city's streetcar system.

Meanwhile the line had been substantially rebuilt and relocated in 1899 and 1900. The physical plant had been a poor one, probably the cheapest ever attempted with trust patents. Thompson had placed his yokes 8 feet apart, with fir planking between the rails; there is no mention of concrete. The conduit was a

389

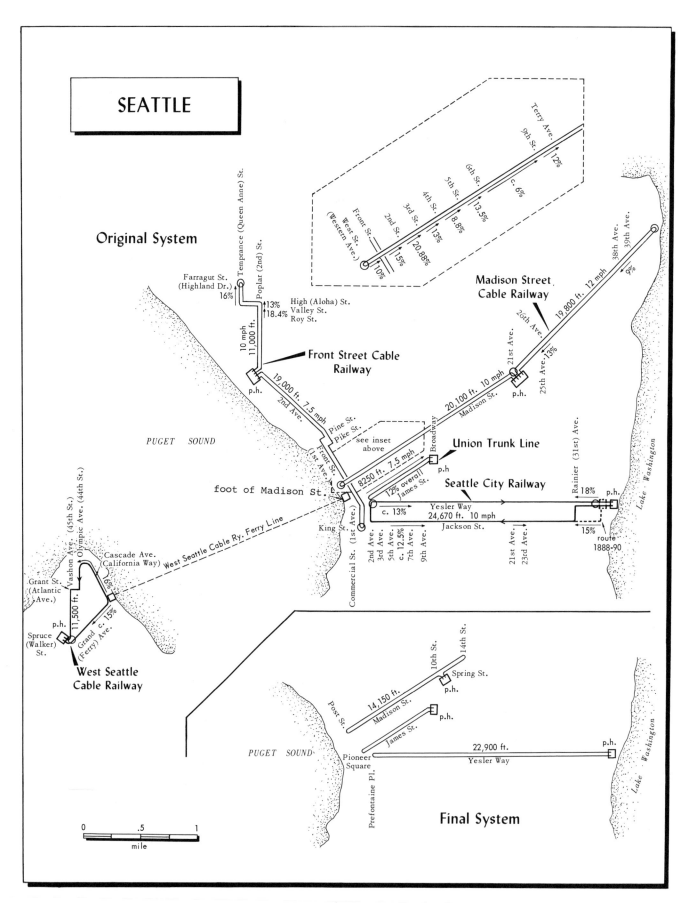

SEATTLE

Original System

Temprance (Queen Anne) St.
Poplar (2nd) St.
Farragut St. (Highland Dr.)
16%
13%
18.4%
High (Aloha) St.
Valley St.
Roy St.

10 mph
11,000 ft.

Front St. (Western Ave.)
10%
15%
20.88%
13%
8.8%
13.5%
c. 6%
12%
2nd St.
3rd St.
4th St.
5th St.
6th St.
9th St.
Terry Ave.

see inset above

Front Street Cable Railway

p.h.
19,000 ft. 7.5 mph
2nd Ave.
Pine St.
Pike St.
Front St.
1st Ave.

Madison Street Cable Railway
19,800 ft. 12 mph
9%
38th Ave.
39th Ave.
26th Ave.
25th Ave. 13%
21st Ave.
p.h.
20,100 ft. 10 mph
Madison St.

PUGET SOUND

foot of Madison St.

8250 ft. 7.5 mph
Broadway
Union Trunk Line
p.h
12% overall
James St.

Seattle City Railway
Rainier (31st) Ave.
18%
p.h.
15%
route 1888-90
Lake Washington

c. 13%
Yesler Way
24,670 ft. 10 mph
Jackson St.
2nd Ave.
3rd Ave.
5th Ave.
c. 12.5%
7th Ave.
9th Ave.
21st Ave.
23rd Ave.

King St. (1st Ave.)
Commercial St. (1st Ave.)

West Seattle Cable Ry. Ferry Line

Olympic Ave. (44th St.)
Vashon Ave. (45th St.)
Cascade Ave. (California Way)
6%
Grant St. (Atlantic Ave.)
11,500 ft.
Grand c. 15%
(Ferry) Ave.
p.h.
Spruce (Walker) St.

West Seattle Cable Railway

0 .5 1
mile

Final System

14,150 ft.
10th St.
14th St.
Spring St.
p.h.
Post St.
Madison St.
p.h.
James St.
22,900 ft.
p.h.
Pioneer Square
Prefontaine Pl.
Yesler Way

PUGET SOUND
Lake Washington

390

sheet iron construction with no system of drains. The line was variously reported to have cost only $220,000 and $300,000 to complete. Ever since 1889 it had been proposed to double-track Yesler and to operate as a separate line. The work was undertaken in 1899 and completed in June 1900. Jackson was reconstructed as an electric line and cable cars ran in both directions with righthand operation on Yesler. A major project in the reconstruction was a new powerhouse on the shore of Lake Washington at the foot of the Yesler grade.

Since the line had grades far beyond the capacity of adhesion vehicles, it easily survived the mass annihilation of cable systems elsewhere. In 1912 the powerhouse was converted to electricity. On June 14, 1920, the line was cut back slightly from Occidental to Prefontaine Place at the Pioneer Square end. Briefly, May 16 to June 23, 1932, the line was operated by one-man crews. Because of the line's heavy grades, cables were replaced frequently, and often relaid on the city's other cable lines.

Because of the line's spectacular scenery and antique character, it had considerable local fame — far more than any of the city's other cable operations — but it failed to achieve the national fame of its counterparts in San Francisco. Accordingly, it was discontinued on August 10, 1940, as part of the general replacement of rail transit in Seattle, with relatively little opposition. Had it survived the war, it would undoubtedly have become a major tourist attraction.

POWERHOUSE EQUIPMENT: Originally, one 120 HP Corliss, replaced c. 1890 by one Allis Corliss engine, 250 HP and one Hamilton Corliss engine, 200 HP. Steam power replaced with one 500 HP, 2200 volt, 3-phase General Electric induction motor, 1912.

One of the Yesler Way line's trains stands at the Lake Washington end in the early period of the line's history when the operation was still in the hands of the construction company which had built the property. (LeRoy O. King, Jr.)

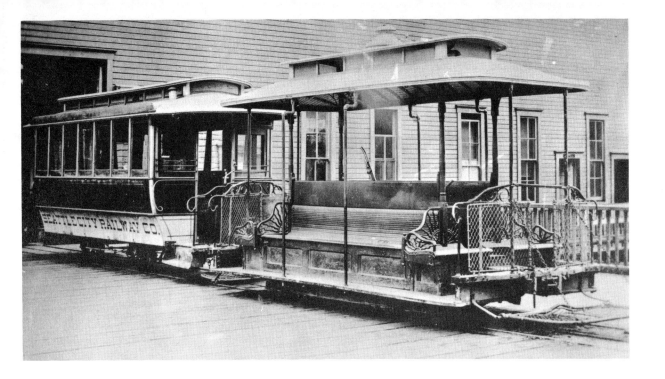

A Yesler Way train in the era of the Seattle City Railway stands before the line's second powerhouse at Lake Washington. *(LeRoy O. King, Jr.)*

The Jackson Street trestle by which the Yesler Way line ascended from Lake Washington was widely looked upon as a hazard. The structure's evil reputation was verified in 1890 when a strong wind swayed the trestle enough to cause a car to derail and lose its grip. The accident resulted in the trestle's being abandoned in favor of an ascent on Yesler Way itself. *(Seattle Historical Society)*

Part of the Yesler Way line's Leschi Park development was steamer service on Lake Washington. The company acquired the first steamboat on the lake, *Edith E.*, and in 1889 ordered the larger sidewheeler *Kirkland*. The steamers ran to Juanita, Kirkland and Houghton from a pier near the powerhouse. *(Seattle Historical Society)*

Above, a car ascends from the Yesler Way powerhouse shortly after the rebuilding of the line at the end of the nineteenth century. *(Seattle Historical Society)* The rebuilding entailed re-equipping the line with California type double-ended cars, one of which is shown, below, crossing Second Avenue early in the twentieth century. *(George Krambles)*

Car 3 of the Yesler Way line crosses Second Avenue, probably around 1903. A similar car of the James Street line crosses in the background. *(Washington State Historical Society)* This equipment was enclosed in 1913-14 in an effort to eliminate accidents to passengers riding on the open steps. Car 2 in the enclosed configuration is shown loading at the west end of the line on the last day of service, August 10, 1940. *(Seattle Historical Society)*

FRONT STREET CABLE RAILWAY

Single-jaw side grip   *Gauge: 4'-8½"*

Alone among Seattle's cable lines, the Front Street Cable Railway was intended not to climb the escarpment behind the central business district, but rather to run along the base of the escarpment along what was then the city's major commercial street, and finally to climb Queen Anne Hill to the north. The company was a promotion of A. B. Stewart, A. P. Mitten, Maurice McMicken, Jacob Furth and associates, all of whom were engaged in civic affairs and in real estate development in Seattle. Active in the project were J. M. Thompson of Pacific Cable and Col. J. C. Haines, who had been among the promoters of the Yesler Way line. Haines was adamantly opposed to electricity as dangerous and impractical. He expected rain to short-circuit the wires, believed the current would cause arcing, and even expected electricity to magnetize the passengers' watches. Haines contended with Frank H. Osgood, an electric railway advocate, for a franchise on Front Street, and won.

The line was built in three segments, of which the first and most important ran from the powerhouse at 2nd Avenue and Depot Street (Denny Way) down 2nd Avenue and Front Street (1st Avenue) to Yesler Way at Pioneer Square. At Pike Street the company's construction gang engaged in a battle with the track-laying crew of the Seattle Electric Railway & Power Company. Service began on March 13, 1889. In 1890 the line was extended southward four blocks from Yesler to King Street to serve the major railroad stations. The third and last segment was the ascent of Queen Anne Hill via Poplar (2nd), High (Aloha) and Temperance (Queen Anne) Streets, authorized in 1890 and completed on March 1, 1891. The northward extension was separately incorporated as the North Seattle Cable Railway, but operated integrally with the Front Street trackage. The mileage on Front Street was built of old T-rail and angle iron, but the northern extension was built with an entirely wooden conduit, a cheap and impermanent construction that would have had to be replaced under the franchise within ten years. Total mileage was about 2.7.

Early in 1893 the promoters sold a majority interest in the line to D. T. Denny and associates, who proposed to incorporate it into their Seattle Consolidated Street Railway. This project was not consummated and the company remained in the hands of Stewart and his associates until it went bankrupt. The property was sold under foreclosure in 1898 to Frank Jones of Portsmouth, New Hampshire, representing the bondholders, who reorganized it as the First Avenue Railway. Owing to the line's cheaply-built physical plant and its weak financial performance in the 1890s, the condition by 1898 was extremely poor. It had been paralleled by an electric line of Osgood's on 2nd Avenue since 1889. The company was so unpopular for its low standard of service that the city government twice threatened it, on February 14, 1898, and January 3, 1899, with forfeiture of the franchise for dereliction of its obligations. Jones' new corporation forestalled the action against it by claiming it was not in active control of the property until January 13, 1899. The city council, however, refused Jones a franchise for conversion to electricity, which in effect forced him to sell out to the Seattle Electric Company in 1900. Seattle Electric formally absorbed the property on September 8, but the line was converted to electricity four days earlier, on September 4, 1900. In order to assist electric cars up Queen Anne Hill, Seattle Electric installed a counterbalance on Queen Anne Avenue between Mercer and Galer Streets.

POWERHOUSE EQUIPMENT: Two compound non-condensing engines, 18" + 42" x 48", 150 HP each.

A visit of President Harrison to Seattle brought forth this crowd, and incidentally halted the Front Street Cable Railway's operations briefly. The equipment is a pair of grip-and-trailer trains flanking an ex-Omnibus combination car. *(University of Washington Library)*

The Front Street Cable Railway had a major curve at Pioneer Square, below. C. B. Fairchild commented that the company's practice of carrying advertising banners on the sides and roofs of cars, visible on the approaching combination car, might have been a source of revenue, but was in poor taste. *(University of Washington Library)* Above is the Front Street powerhouse. *(Seattle Historical Society)*

MADISON STREET CABLE RAILWAY

Single-jaw side grip   *Gauge: 3'-6"*

Madison Street, Seattle's principal thoroughfare from the central business district to the northeast, was an exceptionally promising cable route. The street had extreme gradients leaving the central area, continual undulation on the high-lying land, and then a long descent to Lake Washington without the necessity of a trestle such as the Yesler Way line had entailed. The Queen City Cable Company endeavored to build on Madison Street in the late 1880s, but even after ordering ironwork in Kansas City, was unable to begin building.

The Madison Street Cable Railway was formed in 1889 by H. G. Struve, A. B. Stewart and their associates in the Front Street Cable Railway, who were once again interested in real estate development on the outer reaches of the line. In this instance, the eastern mileage was almost uninhabited, but potentially very desirable residential land. They also envisioned Madison Park, a resort development on Lake Washington parallel to Leschi Park on the Yesler Way line.

The line in certain respects was an ideal cable installation. Madison Street had only a single curve at the powerhouse, so that neither rope had any curvature. The worst gradients were concentrated on the west end, where 20.88 per cent between Second and Third Avenues was the third steepest grade in the industry. The physical plant was designed with trust technology by J. M. Thompson, who was simultaneously engaged in supervising construction of the Portland Cable Railway; his assistant, Andrew Jackson, was in charge of the installation on Madison Street. The line was first built from the powerhouse between 22nd and 23rd Avenues to a turntable at West Street (Western Avenue). Trial runs were made on March 28, 1890, and revenue service began a few days later, probably on April 1. Construction on the line east began immediately. It was ready for experimental operation on June 21, 1891, bringing the line's total mileage to 3.6. Investment was reported at $550,000.

The Madison Street line was a success from the outset; in July 1891 it carried 175,520 passengers. At first traffic was highly concentrated on Sundays, but population quickly developed along the route. Originally the company owned 16 Stockton combination cars, of which 11 were regularly operated. Gripmen were allowed to install glass windshields at their own expenditure of $10. Crews were not required to turn cars manually at the ends of the line; the turntables were power-operated by gears and a clutch off the cable.

The company had a subsidiary, the South Seattle Cable Railway, which intended a cable line to the south from the central business district, but in fact built a steam dummy operation, converted within a year to an electric line.

In 1898 the Madison Street Cable Railway operated 417,032 car miles and handled 1,784,439 passengers, about double the traffic of the Front Street line. The line avoided receivership in the 1890s, principally because it had been built largely out of cash of the promoters, and was incorporated into the Seattle Electric Company on September 8, 1900. Since the line east of the powerhouse had no grades beyond the capacity of electric streetcars, cable operation from 21st Avenue to Madison Park was discontinued on October 5, 1910. Since the only portion which could be justified at that late date was the ascent from the waterfront, the line was further cut back to Broadway on August 31, 1911, and operated from a new powerhouse a block east of Broadway. Somewhat surprisingly, the line was restored as far east as 14th Avenue on May 25, 1913. In this truncated form, it served a purpose similar to the Union Trunk Line's James Street cable route, connecting crosstown electric lines with the central area. As part of the modification of the plant, the cars were rebuilt as double-enders, the turntable discontinued and the line cut back about a block at the west end.

The cut-back of 1910 ended the line's handling of freight. Previously, owing to the undeveloped character of the eastern area, the company had hauled freight in trailers behind its standard combination cars; this traffic had been partly responsible for the line's favorable financial experience during the depressed 1890s.

The residual Madison Street cable line of 1.2 miles served a useful function in the city's transportation system, and survived until the end of rail transit in the city. The conversion was effected with a federal loan of $10,200,000, with which the entire streetcar system was replaced by buses. The last Madison Street car was scheduled for April 13, 1940, though the last car reached the barn after midnight. The original equipment, greatly rebuilt, survived to the end of operation.

POWERHOUSE: 22nd-23rd Avenues and Madison. EQUIPMENT: Two 24" x 48" Hamilton Corliss engines, 250 HP each. Replaced by electric motors after merger of 1900.
Broadway and 10th Avenue. Electric equipment.

At left is an early view of the Madison Street line's heroic ascent out of downtown Seattle. *(Seattle Museum of History and Industry)* Below is the company's original powerhouse at 21st and Madison. *(Seattle Historical Society)*

A particularly handsome car of the Madison Street line was number 52, a former Front Street Cable Railway combination car, rebuilt by the Front Street shops from a cable trailer. (*Washington State Historical Society*)

Though the Yesler Way line received most of the publicity, the Madison Street line served by far the largest population of any of the Seattle cable operations. The line served the Perry, a pioneer high-rise apartment building. Car 42 is one of the company's convertible combination cars operating with its sides enclosed. (*Washington State Historical Society*)

The ridiculous combination above is not an effort to satisfy a large number of enthusiasts simultaneously, but rather the Madison Street Cable Railway's celebration of the arrival of the Great Northern Railway's main line from St. Paul in 1893. *(University of Washington Library)*

At the end the Madison Street line was operated with its original equipment, rebuilt into the general enclosed double-ended configuration of the other surviving Seattle cable lines. *(Barney Neuberger)*

On the opposite page is the West Seattle Cable Railway's fine Queen Anne powerhouse with a characteristically empty car. *(Seattle Museum of History and Industry)*

WEST SEATTLE CABLE RAILWAY

Single-jaw side grip (?)   *Gauge: 3'-6"*

This unique operation was a project for real estate development at the tip of the West Seattle Peninsula, about 2.2 miles across Elliott Bay from central Seattle. The proprietor, the West Seattle Land & Improvement Company, was organized by Col. Thomas Ewing, H. G. Struve, head of the Madison Street Cable Railway, several other Seattle financiers, and Homer King and George W. Grayson of San Francisco. The project began with establishment of a ferry line from the foot of Madison Street to the peninsula in November, 1888. Ewing in 1890 went to San Francisco to arrange with J. M. Thompson of Pacific Cable to design the line. Remarkably, the physical plant was a very substantial one, far more so than any of the lines in downtown Seattle itself. Thompson designed a standard conduit with iron yokes and concrete, including corrugated concrete pavement; the proprietors claimed it was the best built cable installation on the west coast. The line was built quickly in the summer of 1890, beginning on June 1 and opened on September 6 with a ceremony for 100 guests.

The route was a loop running from the ferry slip approximately at the foot of the present Atlantic Street up a grade of 16 per cent around the bluff at Duwamish Head and thence south along the route indicated by the accompanying map to a powerhouse in the vicinity of the present intersection of 46th Avenue and College Street. The route returned to the ferry slip via the diagonal Ferry Avenue. It was expected that the line would be extended south as the area was populated, but no further trackage was attempted. The completed route was slightly over 2 miles of single track. Investment was reported at only $75,000, a figure which seems inadequate.

The company bought four Stockton combination cars of the Powell Street type, and initially offered service at 15-minute intervals. The promoters sold $300,000 worth of lots in the first year, but the worsening depression prevented any appreciable further development. By 1893 a single car was reported operating hourly in connection with the ferry, with the cable stopped between trips. More frequent service was offered in the summer season. The cable line was never profitable *per se;* in 1896 it lost $10,000. President H. S. King of the company tired of the losses and ordered the cable operation stopped on August 31, 1897. Residents were reported to feel they could live without the cable line, but not the ferry. King kept the boat, the *City of Seattle,* in service, but raised the ferry rate from 10¢ to 20¢. The ferry line survived until 1923. The slip is still distinguishable, and the route of the cable line is particularly well preserved, even to modifications of the curb line at the curves into and out of Grant (Atlantic) Street.

POWERHOUSE EQUIPMENT: One Wheelock engine, variously reported as 100, 200 and 300 HP.

The West Seattle Cable Railway's ferryboat, the double-ended sidewheeler *City of Seattle*, had the strange design feature of two pilot houses unified around the stack amidships. The little craft spent most of her career on the Martinez-Benicia ferry on San Francisco Bay. Her engine was removed in 1948, but she is still in existence as a residence north of Sausalito. *(Seattle Historical Society)*

Below, a West Seattle Cable Railway car stands near the bottom of the long descent to the ferry terminal.

UNION TRUNK LINE

Single-jaw side grip   *Gauge: 3'-6"*

Like its counterpart in Tacoma, the James Street line of the Union Trunk line was designed to provide access for a set of electric lines to the central business district over a street too steep for adhesion operation. The Union Trunk Line operated 6.75 miles of narrow gauge electric line on four routes, mainly on streets without serious gradient problems. The cable line served to climb James Street from Pioneer Square to the common powerhouse of the cable and electric lines at James and Broadway, a distance of .75 mile. The route, which is shown in its entirety in Chapter V, was an over-all grade of about 12 per cent, at its worst 18.65 per cent between Second and Third Avenues. The company's original intention was to haul its electric cars behind short, 14-foot grip cars on the cable line, but it found this impractical, and ran the grip cars singly, requiring passengers to change at the powerhouse.

The Union Trunk Line was formed in 1890 in the expectation of running a mixed cable and electric system by merger of three companies, two of which were building on projecting electric lines and the third the cable operation. The cable line was being built by the James Street Construction Company, but is thought to have been intended to operate under the name of the James Street Trunk Line. The promotors envisioned a north-south cable line on Broadway and various routes to the east, but the new management was interested in cable only for the James Street grade. The cable line was built in 1890 and 1891, and opened on March 19, 1891. The company was reported in 1896 to own eight cable cars, although regular operation called for only four. The cable trip required only six minutes.

Fred E. Sander, who had been involved in the Yesler Way line, was vice-president of the company, but otherwise it was controlled by interests apart from the loose association of real estate and transit promoters who had brought forth all of the city's other cable lines. The company was less successful than the Madison Street Cable Railway, but markedly more successful than any of the city's other cable lines. It was, apart from the Madison Street line, the only cable company to survive until the merger of 1900 without bankruptcy. The company promoted Madrona Park on Lake Washington, which it served with electric cars. The standard of service was considered below the other electric lines, so that the company was also threatened with franchise forfeiture in 1898 and 1899.

The Union Trunk Line passed into the hands of Seattle Electric on January 19, 1900. Seattle Electric converted the powerhouse to electricity, re-equipped the cable line with double-truck cars, some from Hammond and some made in company shops, and standard-gauged the electric trackage. The municipal government acquired the street railway system from Stone & Webster in 1919, but continued to operate the James Street line along with the other cable operations. It considered converting all the remaining cable lines throughout the 1930s, but did not do so until the mass conversion of 1940. The James Street line was the first of the three to go; service was abruptly terminated at midnight February 17, 1940, when the cable wore out. The line was simply abandoned; nothing replaced it. Alternative routes were available with easier gradients than James Street.

POWERHOUSE EQUIPMENT: Two 300 HP Lane & Bodley engines, also used to run the dynamos for the company's electric system. Replaced with electrical equipment after merger of 1900.

References: SRR, I (1891), 371-376; SRJ, IX (1893), 310-316; Leslie F. Blanchard, "A History of the Seattle Street Railway System, 1884-1919," *Puget Sound Railroader,* IV, No. 1 (January 1960), 17-27, and *The Street Railway Era in Seattle* (Forty Fort, Pennsylvania: Harold E. Cox, 1968); Unpublished MS, "Seattle's Cable Railways," (WPA, 1941), in Seattle Municipal Reference Library. Collection of Lawton Gowey.

One of the Union Trunk Line's grip cars is shown above at the company's joint cable-electric powerhouse with two of the electric cars which the cable line was intended to haul into the central business district. When the electric cars proved too heavy for the cable line, the grip cars ran singly, as below. On the opposite page is the James Street line operated with California type cars early in the century. Note that the light cable equipment could not take oxidation off the rails as well as the electrics with which they shared the dual gauge track in the foreground. *(Seattle Historical Society; Lawton Gowey; Washington State Historical Society)*

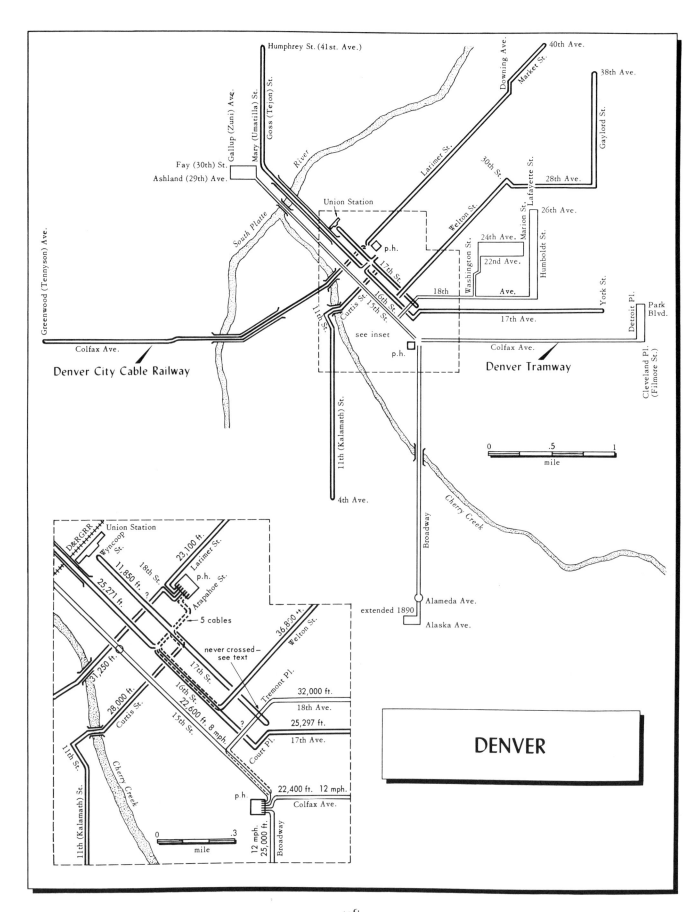

Humphrey St. (41st. Ave.)

40th Ave.
38th Ave.

Downing Ave.
Market St.
Gaylord St.
28th Ave.

Larimer St.
30th St.
Lafayette St.
26th Ave.

Fay (30th) St.
Ashland (29th) Ave.

Goss (Tejon) St.
Mary (Umatilla) St.
Gallup (Zuni) Ave.

River
South Platte

Welton St.
Washington St.
Marion St.
Humboldt St.
24th Ave.
22nd Ave.
Ave.

Union Station

p.h.

17th St.

16th St.
15th St.
Curtis St.
11th St.

18th
York St.
Detroit Pl.
Park Blvd.

17th Ave.

see inset

Greenwood (Tennyson) Ave.

p.h.

Colfax Ave.
Colfax Ave.

Denver City Cable Railway
Denver Tramway

Cleveland Pl. (Filmore St.)

11th (Kalamath) St.

4th Ave.

Cherry Creek

Broadway

0 .5 1
mile

extended 1890
Alameda Ave.
Alaska Ave.

D&RGRR

Union Station

Wyncoop St.

18th St.

23,100 ft.

Larimer St.

p.h.

Arapahoe St.

11,850 ft.

25,271 ft.

5 cables

36,850 ft.

Welton St.

never crossed — see text

31,250 ft.

17th St.

16th St.

15th St.

Tremont Pl.

32,000 ft.

18th Ave.

25,297 ft.

17th Ave.

28,000 ft.

Curtis St.

22,600 ft. 8 mph.

Court Pl.

11th (Kalamath) St.

Cherry Creek

p.h.

22,400 ft. 12 mph.

Colfax Ave.

12 mph.
25,000 ft.

Broadway

0 .3
mile

DENVER

DENVER

Population in 1890: 106,713

DENVER TRAMWAY

Lane single-jaw side grip   *Gauge: 3'-6"*

Denver had no problem of major gradients, but its great silver boom of the 1880s coincided with the short period in which cable traction was economic, and as a consequence it received one of the most comprehensive systems of any city.

Denver was one of several cities which turned to the cable car after unsuccessful experimentation with pre-Sprague electrics. Several property owners on 15th Street in the central area, led by John Evans, formed the Denver Electric & Cable Company in 1885 to install a conduit electric line of a technology invented by Professor Sidney H. Short of the University of Denver. The company changed its name to the Denver Tramway in 1886 and gave up the Short system in the following year with the intention of running horsecars. Since its charter provided only for electric or cable traction, a local court held the use of horses *ultra vires,* and virtually drove the company to a cable system.

The Tramway's management hired Henry M. Lane of Cincinnati to make an installation of his non-trust technology on a system of three lines radiating from a powerhouse at Colfax and Broadway. This was widely cited as an ideal cable installation, since the lines ran straight down 15th Street, Colfax Avenue and Broadway without any curvature at all, apart from the central intersection and the terminal loops. The company managed to secure as much as 20 months' life out of the cables. Both the 15th Street and Broadway lines had widely-spaced tracks, flanking an existing horsecar line of the Denver City Railway. This arrangement allowed Lane to install a turntable on 15th east of Larimer between the tracks for the turning of Broadway cars; Colfax cars ran through to the loop west of the South Platte River. The Tramway's cable system opened on December 22, 1888.

If the three original lines of the Tramway were well suited to cable technology, the fourth was precisely the reverse, the most unworkable line ever attempted. The powerhouse had been built with four sets of driving machinery, of which the fourth was intended for a route northeast to Downing Street, running out Stout and returning on California. Apparently because the rival Denver City Cable Railway was building cable lines out 17th Avenue and Welton Street, the Tramway revised its plans, and used the fourth set of machinery for a route on 18th Avenue. Owing to the curvature necessary to take the cable from the powerhouse to 18th Avenue, the line would have been difficult at best, but the company sought to saturate the territory between 17th Avenue and Welton, as it might have done in the horsecar era, with two loops, one on Lafayette and Humboldt Streets, and the other on Washington and Marion Streets. This cable had by far the heaviest degree of curvature ever attempted in a single rope, and as might have been anticipated, proved thoroughly unworkable. J. B. Stone reported that the Washington Street loop operated only from November 3 to December 11, 1889, when it had to be removed partly because of the excessive curvature in the cable, and partly because cars turning from 18th into Washington tended to derail or to have difficulty in taking the rope. The track was removed, and the cable reduced by about 8450 feet. The company's only other extension was one of two blocks from Broadway and Alameda to a new loop at Alaska Avenue in 1890. The Tramway's cable system had a total mileage of 9.3 and an investment of about $2 million.

The company began a fifth line, hurriedly building four blocks of conduit from 15th to 19th Streets on Lawrence Street in December 1889 in the intention of having a route straight out Lawrence to its intersection with 35th and Downing Streets. The cable was to run from its own powerhouse at the outer terminus. Possibly because of dissatisfaction with the 18th Avenue line, completed the previous month, the company did not pursue the project, and instead removed the conduit.

Since the Tramway had never been eager to operate cable traction, it is not surprising that the system was among the first to go. Even after excision of the Washington Street loop, the 18th Avenue line was unsatisfactory, partly in its heavy curvature,

409

partly in being too close to the 17th Avenue line of the Denver City Cable Railway. The rival company was building its 17th Street line through the central business district in 1891, and was eager to avoid a rope drop at Tremont Place. The Tramway was willing to give up the cable line so as to avoid the crossing if the City Cable Railway, which held franchise rights to all streets not occupied by the Tramway's existing lines, would allow it to place an electric line in replacement on 19th rather than 18th Avenue. This compromise was quickly worked out, and the 18th Avenue cable was killed on November 28, 1891.

The City Council had granted the Tramway blanket authority to convert its cable lines to electricity in an ordinance of April 9, 1891. The Tramway waited only for the improvements in the streetcar in 1893; simultaneously, the city was exerting pressure on the company to relocate the 15th Street and Broadway lines to the center of the street. The Broadway route was converted on May 1, 1893, and both Colfax

and 15th Street on July 6. President Rodney Curtis stated that the conversion was tentative, and that cable service might be restored, but he added that Denver's aridity was ideal for electric operation. He said that the conversion reflected no shortcoming of cable traction, but merely indicated the company's desire for a consistent electric technology on all its lines. It is impossible to say whether this represented an honest opinion, or merely a desire not to spoil the market for his cable equipment. The company offered its cable equipment for sale in the journals, but is not known to have found any takers.

The Tramway, doubtless relieved to be free of cable traction, would find itself in cable operation again in 1899, when it assumed the larger, more complicated, but less satisfactory network of the Denver City Cable Railway.

POWERHOUSE EQUIPMENT: Two Wetherill engines, 32″ x 66″, 750 HP, and 28″ x 60″, 500 HP.

The Denver Tramway operated with a unique type of single-truck car, distinguished by a low-mounted side-facing seat at each side of the gripman. Open and closed versions are shown here in the white livery of the Colfax line and the maroon of the Broadway line. At lower left is the terminal of the Broadway line at Alaska Avenue. Directly below is the company's powerhouse. *(Denver Public Library; State Historical Society of Colorado)*

The most unpopular feature of an exceedingly unpopular cable system was the Denver City Cable Railway's let-go curve at 16th and Welton, above. Outbound cars had to take the curve at high speed to roll to the pick-up on Welton, out of the photograph to the right. *(Denver Public Library)* Below is one of the company's trains passing the Jefferson Block early in the 1890s. *(Edward B. Watson)*

DENVER CITY CABLE RAILWAY

Gillham double-jaw side grip   *Gauge: 3'-6"*

Denver's second and larger cable system is notable for being the most extensive ever run out of a single powerhouse, and also for being the only example of a company forced by the municipal government to operate with cable technology long after cable traction had ceased to be economic.

On May 19, 1888, the Denver City Railway, the area's leading horsecar operator, reorganized itself as the Denver City Cable Railway, and in distinction to the Tramway, contracted for $30,000 for exclusive rights to trust patents for the Denver area. Henry Root promptly came to Denver to threaten the Tramway with an infringement suit, but apparently failed to proceed with it. The Cable Railway entrusted design of the property to Robert Gillham, who produced a narrow-gauge version of his Kansas City technology. He centered the operation in a powerhouse at 18th and Lawrence which was expected to issue 13 ropes for a system covering the entire city. The company had free choice of streets other than those already occupied by the Tramway under its franchise, but it achieved only a system of seven cables, which did, however, radiate into all four quadrants of the city. Both companies built their lines to serve existing population, rather than speculatively to develop real estate, and thus had considerable traffic potential. As a consequence, traffic held up in the depressed 1890s better than in most cities.

The company began operation with its diagonal line across the city on Larimer Street on October 16, 1889. About November 1 this was followed with a diagonal line across the city in the opposite direction on Goss Street, 16th Street and 17th Avenue, plus a branch out Welton Street. The Welton line was notable for a cable of 36,850 feet, the longest attempted until that time. With the exception of the two Larimer Street ropes, all the cables issued from the central powerhouse through a blind conduit down Arapahoe Street. This conduit was also used for the company's two later lines, a second route through the central area via 17th Street, opened on December 22, 1891, and the so-called West Denver line, which left the business district on Curtis Street to run south on 11th (Kalamath) Street. The opening of the West Denver line on June 6, 1892, brought the powerhouse to an output of about 30 miles of cable. The entire system operated at 10 miles per hour. With 15 miles of line, the company had the third largest system in the country.

Even though the Cable Railway attempted no additional lines after 1892, the management appears initially to have been satisfied with cable traction. As the Tramway was converting its system in 1893, the Cable Railway spent $15,000 on new gearing for the powerhouse. Such satisfaction as the management had was short-lived. A mixture of electrification of its rival and the depression of the early 1890s drove the company bankrupt. A receiver was appointed on November 10, 1895, and the company was reorganized as the Denver City Railroad in August 1896. The excision of "Cable" from the title presumably indicates the management's intention to join the industry in conversion.

Unfortunately, the company's effort to make a conversion which was almost universally desired resulted in a lengthy political struggle which perpetuated the cable car in Denver almost to the end of the century. The city in 1897 endeavored to force the company under its franchise obligations to repave the centers of the streets it occupied in the central area, but the company, which had barely been able to meet operating expenses since 1893, could not comply. The city directed the Barber Asphalt Company to do the paving, and then endeavored to collect the bill of $29,117 from the cable company. When the management refused to pay on the ground it could have had the job done for $18,000, the city brought a legal action which drove the company into receivership once again on October 3, 1898. Interests connected with the Tramway bought it in December, and on March 3, 1899, merged it into its rival in an effort to take advantage of the Tramway's blanket authority to convert its cable lines of 1891. The City Railroad had secured council approval of its own conversion statute over the mayor's veto in 1898, but the Board of Supervisors had exercised its power to reject it.

The Tramway moved to convert the former Cable Railway immediately, but was told by the Denver Board of Public Works that its authority of 1891 did not extend to the newly-acquired system. Since the cable system was now part of a large and reasonably prosperous electric network, the city recognized that it was able to secure a large fee for the conversion, greatly in excess of the $29,117 it had been trying to recover from the Cable Railway. Supervisor Benton Cannon estimated the benefit to the company of the conversion at $480,000, of which he felt the city could confiscate a large portion. The Tramway was endeavoring to tie the conversion in with issuance of an indefinite franchise, thereby alienating the *Rocky Mountain News* and Denver *Post*. The Denver *Times* argued strongly for the conversion, stressing the safety hazards at 17th and Curtis and 16th and Welton, both long let-go curves which cable trains traversed at high speeds to roll to the pick-up points. The cable system was deteriorating rapidly, since the company was unwilling to make any further investments in it. In May 1899 the Tramway was enjoined against stringing electric wires over the tracks without permission.

In March 1900 the Tramway and the city reached an agreement whereby the company would pay $102,000 as a fee for the conversion, $30,000 immediately and the remainder within a year. Supervisor Cannon argued that in light of the expected savings, the city should have extracted a higher fee, but the other municipal officials concerned with the matter approved, and the agreement went into effect. Although the Board of Aldermen approved the agreement only on March 21, the first electric car ran experimentally on the West Denver line on March 25, and the cable was killed on March 28. The Welton line was converted on the 29th, 17th Avenue on the 30th, and finally Larimer at 1:00 AM on April 1, 1900. The unmatched speed of the conversion is a good indication of the urgency a cable operator felt at

getting rid of the system when forced to operate it for seven years after it had any pretensions of being economic.

POWERHOUSE EQUIPMENT: Two 750 HP engines, 36″ x 60″, William Wright, Newburgh, N. Y. Extant as restaurant.

References: George W. Hilton, "Denver's Cable Railways," *The Colorado Magazine*, XLIV (1967), 35-52. SRJ, IX (1893), 135-147.

* * *

Note: Denver had a large number of projected cable lines, all of which were completed as electric lines or simply abandoned before work was undertaken. The reported lines were:

DENVER & WEST SIDE CABLE RAILWAY. A promotion of H. A. W. Tabor in 1888, this company was variously reported as projecting lines west from the business district to Sloan's Lake, with a branch to Sheridan Heights, and from central Denver to Highlands and Barnum.

NORTH DENVER CABLE COMPANY. George W. Bowman in 1887 secured a franchise to build from Denver to Barnum and Fort Sheridan. Bowman was also reported to be promoting the DENVER & BOULEVARD CABLE RAILWAY.

THE SOUTH DENVER CABLE RAILWAY was projected in 1889 to run from the end of the Broadway cable to Rosedale and South Denver.

The Denver City Cable Railway is the best depicted cable system, partly because of its long involuntary survival, partly because the great photographer William H. Jackson was active in Denver. Jackson, unlike his counterparts in Kansas City who typically produced photographs of cable track naked of cars, habitually waited for a cable train to add interest to his foregrounds. On these pages are trains of the company passing the Union Pacific shops and approaching the intersection of 16th and Larimer in downtown Denver. On the following pages is a superlative example of Jackson's style, a broadside of Larimer Street in the early 1890s. *(All, State Historical Society of Colorado)*

DRUGGISTS.

WHOLESALE DRUGGIST

LUMBER

FLITCH'S GARDEN
COOPER LAKE
MANHATTAN BEACH.

SLOAN'S LAKE   SLOAN'S LAKE

LARIMER STREET LOOKING NORTH FROM 15TH   DENVER

Since the Denver City Cable Railway's 16th Street viaduct, unlike the company's similar structure on the Sloan's Lake line, carried street traffic, the municipal government contributed to the company's investment in the long overpass. (*State Historical Society of Colorado*) Below is one of the company's trains at 16th and Lawrence. (*Edward B. Watson*) On the opposite page is a train on 17th Street at the rope drop for the blind conduit on Arapahoe Street. (*State Historical Society of Colorado*)

Above is the Butte City Street Railroad's powerhouse at Centerville. The cable line's odd design of three-rail operation with frequent passing sidings is evident in the view of the south terminus, below. The combination of a paved conduit and a street deep in mud was only too common among cable lines, even in cities without the frontier character of Butte. This situation was responsible for the heavy fall of dirt into cable conduits. (*C. Owen Smithers & Son*)

BUTTE

Population in 1890: 10,723

BUTTE CITY STREET RAILROAD

Vogel & Whalen bottom grip　　　　　*Gauge: 3′-6″ (?)*

Though by far the smallest city to be served by cable cars, Butte had geographical characteristics which made cable traction attractive. The city lies on the south escarpment of a mountain, so that the streets ascend from south to north at successively increasing gradients. In the late 1880s, like many other mining cities, Butte was undergoing a major boom, and in particular was expanding to the north. The city approximately tripled in population in the 1880s. The typical pattern was to live in Butte and to work in mines on the escarpment to the north. The most important of the suburban communities was Walkerville, site of three major mines or mills.

The Butte City Street Railroad Company was organized in 1887 by Willard Bennett of Butte and financed in Boston. For about six months the company operated as a horsecar line, but then converted its operations to steam dummy. Although this form of transportation, of which the company eventually had 8 miles, was well suited to Butte's frontier character, the grade up to the mine suburb of Walkerville was too steep for locomotives. Accordingly, the company planned a cable line from Main and Galena Streets in downtown Butte to B and South Streets in Walkerville, about a mile and a half north and 490 feet elevated above Butte. The line went for five blocks up Main Street on grades of 5 per cent and 7 per cent, and then ran up through the intermediate town of Centerville to Walkerville over lengthy trestlework. The grade varied, but reportedly reached a maximum of 13.2 per cent above the powerhouse.

The operation was unusual in several respects. Notably, it was the pilot installation of the bottom grip of Charles Vogel and Frank Whalen, the most promising of the grips designed to minimize the depth of the conduit. Second, it was the only line to be built as a three-rail operation with center-bearing rail throughout. This odd arrangement was the result of a compromise between the company, which wanted an orthodox double-tracked system, and the city, which wanted only a single track on Main Street. The Vogel grip was incapable of single-track operation.

At several points sidings were provided where downbound cars, taking advantage of the Vogel grip's ability to drop the cable and pick it up at any point,

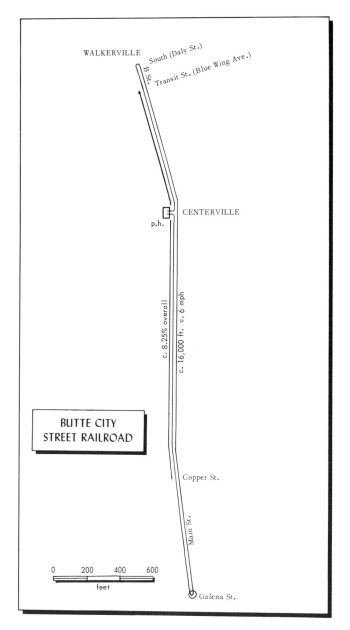

421

released and rolled around northbound trains. The company in later years felt it had enjoyed negligible capital saving, not worth the inconvenience of the arrangement. Strangely, the line had a turntable at the bottom, but double cross-overs at the top.

The line was built mainly in 1888, and ready for the laying of cable on February 25, 1889. A trial trip was made on March 14, but the gripman ruined the only grip on the property by failing to release before hitting the dead man just short of the Walkerville terminal sheave. There was some difficulty getting the early grips to function properly, but Vogel, who was having them manufactured in Cleveland, sent some to Butte which allowed the line to open for revenue service on April 12, 1889. It had to be shut down on April 19 for shortening of the cable 40 feet, but otherwise operated successfully in a purely technological sense. Cars carried wheel, track and slot brakes.

In March 1891 the company was merged into the Butte Consolidated Street Railway Company. In that year the cable line carried 596,744 passengers on 25,261 trips. At the end of the year the line had its only serious accident. About midnight on Christmas, a trailer was left outside the powerhouse while grip cars were changed. The brakes on the trailer were set, but someone maliciously released them and the car, containing eight passengers, rolled down the grade into Butte. At the mild curve into Main Street, the car derailed at high speed, killing William Cunningham, and injuring all but one of the other passengers. Lawsuits from this accident bedeviled the company throughout 1892, and combined with the growing depression to reduce the enterprise to low ebb by 1893. In April 1893 the company lost a suit for patent infringement for use of the Vogel grip, brought by the San Francisco trust. By December 6, the company was unable to meet its payroll. Manager J. R. Wharton told reporters that the company's electric lines, to which the steam dummy operations had been converted, covered expenses, but the cable line lost $15 per day. He petitioned the city council to close the cable operation until May 1894 without forfeiting the line's charter, but was apparently refused. Wharton continued to be eager to get rid of the cable line, but expressed willingness to run it through the Christmas season. He reported it paid its way in December, 1893, but indicated he would shut it down at the end of January 1894 if no way could be found to make it profitable. In the middle of January — not the most comfortable time for the change — he discontinued running trailers after the open grip cars as an economy measure. Although the line was expected to be shut down momentarily, it survived until the Butte Consolidated Street Railway went bankrupt in August, 1897.

Wharton, as receiver for the company, almost immediately moved to do what he had intended in 1893, close the cable line without losing his franchise to serve Walkerville. He petitioned the council on September 18 to end cable service and to institute an electric line over a longer and more gentle route in the following spring. On this occasion he was accepted, and on September 19, 1897, he brought the cable line to an end. On the following day crews began to remove the cable and to tear up the track. Since the line was located largely on trestlework which was destroyed, visual evidence of it was almost entirely eradicated and nothing remains in Butte to memorialize it.

POWERHOUSE: Centerville. EQUIPMENT: One 125 HP engine, E. P. Allis & Co.

Reference: SRJ, IX (1893), 246.

SIOUX CITY

Population in 1890: 37,806

SIOUX CITY CABLE RAILWAY

Phenix double-jaw side grip   *Gauge: 4'-8½"*

The Sioux City Cable Railway was among the best examples of a line built as a real estate promotion in the land boom of the late 1880s which became an utter failure during the depression of the 1890s. Sioux City, in common with other Missouri Valley cities, had a low-lying, flat central area, with undulating highlands above it which were potentially valuable residential areas. The project of developing high-lying land north of the central business district with a cable line was conceived by two prominent local figures, Daniel T. Hedges and John Peirce. They incorporated the cable line May 5, 1887, and secured a franchise to build north on Jackson Street, a major thoroughfare with a grade of 790 feet ranging between 7.29 per cent and 10.91 per cent leaving the business district. Construction was delayed by the prospect of the city's easing the grade, but the project was never undertaken. Track-laying began September 17, 1888.

Peirce in mid-1888, after first intending to use the Rasmussen system, made a tour of the cable cities to the east in an effort to determine a technology for his line. He was most impressed by William Phenix's installation in Grand Rapids. As early as the summer of 1888, only the original Lyon Street line in Grand Rapids was in service, and the problems which manifested themselves in the full system were not apparent. Peirce was impressed mainly by the capital savings of a single-track system. Phenix looked upon the commission as a very favorable one, and in fact moved to Sioux City to become superintendent of the cable line. Peirce's plan was to lay a grid of cable lines about the city, run from a centrally located powerhouse at 29th and Jones Streets. Only the original Jackson Street line was ever built, but newspapers variously reported a projected system of 12, 15, 24, 25, 38, and 50 miles, including an extension to the suburb of Leeds. The figures above 25 miles are improbable, but Peirce intended to lay cables along the major north-south streets, connected to the powerhouse by conduits along 29th Street. Such a course would have involved him in conflict with the Sioux City Street Railway, a horsecar system headed by J. F. Peavey.

The disparity between the actual line and the company's plans was also responsible for the enormous size of the powerhouse. The building was about 175 feet square, located at 29th and Hawthorne (Jones) Streets, one block east of the Jackson Street line. It was reported to be one of the largest cable powerhouses in the country and served also as the car shop and barn of the company. Owing to its large excess generating capacity, the company sold steam for heating of local buildings, and also generated electricity for the northern residential area. The company provided electric street lighting on Jackson without compensation.

The original line of the company was built from the powerhouse straight south on Jackson Street from 29th Street to 3rd Street, a block south of 4th Street, the city's financial business thoroughfare. Phenix' conduit was only 18" x 18"; the cable rode on carrying pulleys abreast three inches apart. Rail-laying and paving were reported completed in November, 1888. The company's original intention was to run horsecars over the line for the first winter and to initiate cable operation in the spring. On reconsideration, the company decided the Jackson Street hill was too steep for horses in icy weather and made no effort to operate until the powerhouse was completed. Construction began in December, the foundation was reported complete in February, and the engines ready by May. The cable was laid on May 28 and 29 by 10 horses, with 8 additional for the grade, and revenue service was inaugurated on June 1, 1889. An estimated 16,000 people rode the line in its first week, largely because of its novelty. The original cable was 22,271 feet, operated at 8 miles per hour.

Initially, the Sioux City Cable Railway received eight grip cars and sixteen trailers from Laclede, the St. Louis car builder. Later the roster expanded to 14 grips and 20 trailers, including five double-decked cars from James A. Trimble of New York. The grip cars were more substantial than on Phenix's Grand Rapids system, reportedly about the same size as on the St. Paul Selby cable line. The company regularly

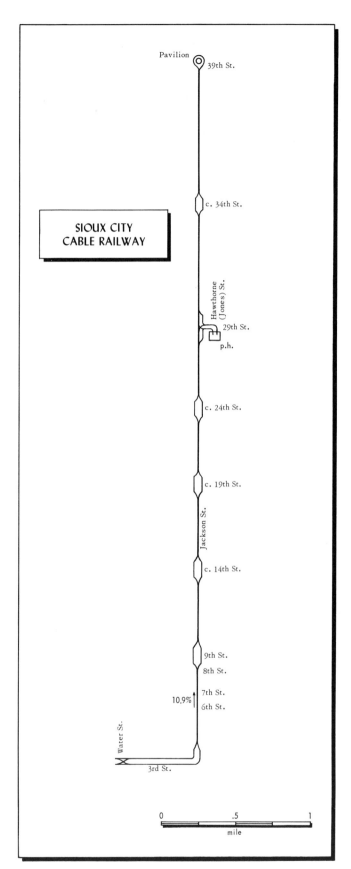

ran 6 trains with only about 30 per cent of the powerhouse's potential output.

Upon completion of the original line, the company undertook a northern extension on Jackson from 29th to 39th, where it planned a pavilion and an outdoor recreation area. Work on this line occupied almost a year, but the line was reported ready for laying of cable in April 1890. The line terminated in a balloon loop variously reported as 600 feet and 700 feet in circumference, at the center of which the company's pavilion was built during 1890. The octagonal structure, which contained a large mural of the Battle of Gettysburg, served as a theater, dance hall, and general recreational facility. Since the area served by the extension was very lightly populated, the pavilion was depended upon as a principal generator of traffic. The north line operated at 11 miles per hour with a separate cable of about 9,500 feet.

The original terminal at 3rd and Jackson was reasonably central to the Sioux City business district, which was at that time somewhat to the east.* In 1891 the Illinois Central and Great Northern announced their intention of building a Union Station on the south side of 3rd at Douglas Street. The Cable Railway responded by undertaking an extension from 3rd and Jackson five blocks west to Water Street, running successively past the Station, through the city's red light district and into a wholesaling and warehousing region. The Union Station did not open until August 15, 1893, but most of the city's railroad stations were in the area. Work on the cable line's extension was undertaken in February, the cable was laid May 27, 1892, and the line was opened for traffic almost immediately thereafter. The extension brought the length of the south cable to about 27,900 feet and reduced its life expectancy through increasing curvature. The original cable which opened service in June 1889 served until December 1, 1890, but thereafter the company had a more normal and less favorable experience. The Third Street extension also involved the company in a complicated and apparently unique terminal arrangement. At 3rd and Water the line ended in a double cross-over at which the grip cars engaged in "Dutch switching" of trailers by means of a rope. That is, a grip car headed west towed the trailer off

---

*Two newspaper accounts state that the original terminal was at 3rd and Jones, one short block to the east of Jackson. This may indicate the line turned the corner east at 3rd and Jackson. All other accounts indicate operation on Jackson only, including transit directory listings. The famous Sioux City elevated, which terminated at 3rd and Jones, was not opened until 1891.

424

FIG. 1.—POWER STATION—SIOUX CITY CABLE RAILWAY CO.

a rope before taking the turnout to the eastbound line. The conductor cast off the rope and coasted to the end of the westbound line. The grip car then towed the trailer east over the other turnout by attaching the rope to the other end of the car. The train was then made up on the eastbound track for the trip north.

By the time of the extension to 3rd and Water the Sioux City Cable Railway had already begun to decline. Initially it had been quite profitable, grossing around $95 a day as versus expenses of $50 in its first five months. In November 1888, while the cable line was abuilding, J. F. Peavey announced his intention to electrify the entire Sioux City Street Railway with Sprague technology. He undertook this in 1889 and finished the job on April 6, 1890. In particular, the Street Railway had an electric line on Pierce Street, two blocks west of Jackson, which offered 10-minute headway. The cable line, which had run trains on 4½-minute headway in 1889, was down to 15-minute headway by January 1894. Meanwhile, the company had been weakened by two accidents. On May 22, 1892, cable-oiler Ole P. Holmes fell on the lower rope on the tension run and was drawn under the tension sheave, killing him instantly. On April 2, 1893, a grip car killed a child named Earl Hungerford on 3rd Street, involving the company in $2500 damages. A storm in the spring of 1893 inundated the conduit and denuded both cables. The company refused to pay its license fees on the ground the city had done it $7,000 to $8,000 damage through using its conduit as a storm sewer.

Symptomatic of the Cable Railway's declining fortunes was the City Council's behavior with respect to its large network of projected lines. Peirce had intended on completion of the Jackson line to build north from 39th Street about a quarter mile and thence east to Leeds. His next and more important project was a second north-south line on Court Street, four blocks east of Jackson. On March 5, 1891, the Council revoked the Cable Railway's franchise for Court Street and awarded one for an electric line to Peavey's Street Railway. Peirce was in England endeavoring to sell bonds without success, and could make no show of financial responsibility to retain his franchise. His other franchises for unbuilt lines were allowed to expire on May 5, 1892. Phenix, apparently recognizing that the large system he had been brought to superintend would not be built, gave up the general managership in 1890 and left town. His successor, W. H. Mack, resigned effective January 1, 1892 and was replaced by Peirce's son-in-law, C. H. C. Moller.

The Sioux City Cable Railway went bankrupt in 1893 as a result of a lien of $5,859 filed by Broderick & Bascom for a replacement cable. By August 1893 Moller, who was appointed receiver, was paying his men in receiver's certificates. Also in 1893, D. T. Hedges died, leaving an estate containing 1720½ shares of the company's stock and $150,000 worth of its bonds, on which he had borrowed $75,000 from Kennedy, Tod & Company of New York. Hedges' executor arranged for Peirce to acquire all the securities in return for assuming the debt of $75,000. This settlement placed Peirce in full control of the bankrupt corporation. The cable line represented an investment of about $440,000, but by March 1894 it had run up deficits aggregating about $200,000 in its short history. Peirce was reported to be keeping it running only as a matter of faith with householders who had bought property along the line in Peirce's addition, out of which he and Hedges had made about a million dollars during the land boom.

Late in March 1894 Peirce went to Chicago to contract for Westinghouse equipment for electrification. The cost of conversion was reported to be only $20,000, a trivial sum compared either with the cable line's investment or its current deficits. The company planned to use its existing cars, equipped so that open or closed car bodies could be placed on detachable electric trucks. The first poles were placed along the line in April. Meanwhile, the cable line was allowed to deteriorate. One of the winding drums had broken and was bolted together in a makeshift fashion pending the conversion, scheduled for May 16. Shortly before midnight May 15, 1894, the drum broke violently, sending ironwork about the powerhouse as if it had exploded. Moller made no attempt to have the winding machinery, which was badly damaged, repaired for the few additional hours expected of it, and so the history of the Sioux City cable car line closed somewhat early in a wholly fitting debacle. Electric cars began running on May 16, as scheduled.

Robert E. Tod of Kennedy, Tod & Company, the line's principal creditor, who was endeavoring to bring together all of the Sioux City traction lines into a single property, began negotiating for its purchase. Even as an electric line, the company remained unprofitable because of the light population on the northern trackage. In November 1895 the Federal Court approved sale of the Sioux City Cable Railway to Tod at a modest $15,142.44 for incorporation into his Central Traction Company. This in turn was merged into the Sioux City Traction Company in 1899 in a consolidation of all the city's street railways. Because of the Jackson Street hill, the worst in the city, the Traction Company was unenthusiastic about the former cable line, and in 1901 abruptly over a weekend removed the trackage between 5th and 29th Streets. Of the two principal structures of the cable line, the pavilion passed eventually into the hands of the Sioux City Country Club, and the powerhouse served as a storage facility and heating plant. Neither is in existence, though part of the vaultwork at the powerhouse is conspicuous in a small park which occupies the property, and more surprisingly, big blocks of cinders from the fire boxes survive in a children's play area.

POWERHOUSE EQUIPMENT: Two Williams automatic cut-off engines, 250 HP each.

References: SRJ, IX (1893), 159; Peter Kocan, "A History of Street Railway Transportation of Sioux City," unpublished MS in Sioux City Public Library (1943).

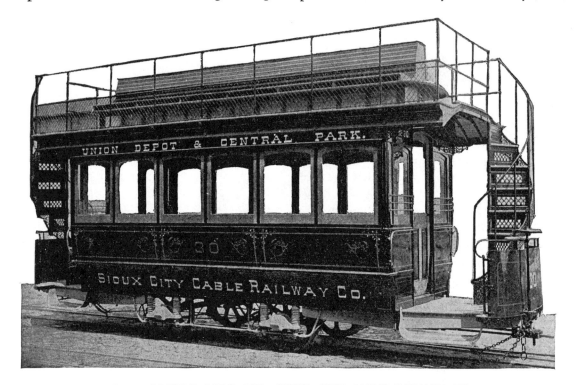

FIG. 2.—DOUBLE DECK CAR—SIOUX CITY CABLE RAILWAY CO.

SPOKANE

Population in 1890: 19,922

SPOKANE CABLE RAILWAY

Double-jaw side grip (?)   *Gauge: 3'-0"*

Spokane, settled in the hills along the Spokane River, had the geographical characteristics to evoke cable traction, but the line proved a rather extreme example of one built for real estate development in a city of too limited population to support the enterprise once the land boom of the 1880s ended.

The Spokane Cable Railway was promoted in 1888 by C. H. Moore, Frank R. Moore, Alfred S. Moore, J. D. Sherwood and their associates for real estate development on both the north and south sides of the city. They arranged for the north line to be built with trust patents by J. M. Thompson of the Pacific Cable Construction Company, who produced essentially a single-track version of his recent Yesler Way line in Seattle. The three-mile road was intended to run north from the central district across a newly-constructed wooden bridge, across the area immediately north of the river on Boone Street, and finally diagonally through Natatorium Park and over a second long wooden bridge to Twickenham, a subdivision of the Moore interests on a site later occupied by Fort George Wright. The line mainly served a plateau, and had no grade over 7½ per cent. Curvature was moderate, but the line was built with two easily-avoidable crossings of a railroad at Monroe and Boone.

The installation was unique in being powered by water. A small power station was built on the north side of the Spokane River beneath the Monroe Street Bridge in which water-powered turbines activated the cables through gears. About 30,000 horsepower was available, although the cable required only about 150. In part the power requirement was so low because the company used a ⅞-inch cable, the smallest diameter in the industry.

The line north of the river was opened on September 21, 1889. The portion from the river to the Northern Pacific station opened in October. Regular operation required four grips and trailers. There is no direct evidence of the grip style which Thompson adopted, but the absence of turntables and the ability of cars to reverse directions short of the terminus are consistent only with a double-jaw side grip.

Before the opening, Thompson left the company, and was replaced by Howard C. Holmes, who had designed the Ferries & Cliff House Railway in San Francisco. Holmes talked the management into making the projected 1.3 mile south line double-tracked. He ordered double-ended California cars of the sort Thompson had used on his Alder Street shuttle in Portland, but apparently continued to use the side grip of the north line. When Holmes' cars arrived, they proved of the wrong gauge (probably the Portland 3'-6" rather than 3'-0"), and while they were modified, service on the south line was begun on October 31, 1890 with north-end equipment. Even though the equipment was interchangeable, the two lines were not physically connected across the Northern Pacific tracks; passengers were expected to make a walking connection. The completed system cost about $250,000.

While the south line was abuilding, the company's Monroe Street bridge over the Spokane River burned completely on July 23, 1890. The bridge had been settling at the south end, and had been widely considered dangerous previously. The fire also damaged the power plant, but it was restored enough to re-open the line north of the river about October, 1890. On February 23, 1891, the company received authority to convert the north line to electricity and shortly did so.

The south line was initially powered from the hydro plant north of the river, but apparently shortly after the end of the north line, the Washington Water Power Company, which had acquired this and all other street railways in the city, opened a larger hydro station on the south bank of the river, out of which it operated both the cable line and the electric lines which were spreading about the city. The line south had almost everything working against it. Terminating south of the Northern Pacific tracks, it did not literally enter the central business district. It had severe grades, including two blocks over 16 per cent between 5th and 7th Streets. It had been built to serve a real estate development known as the

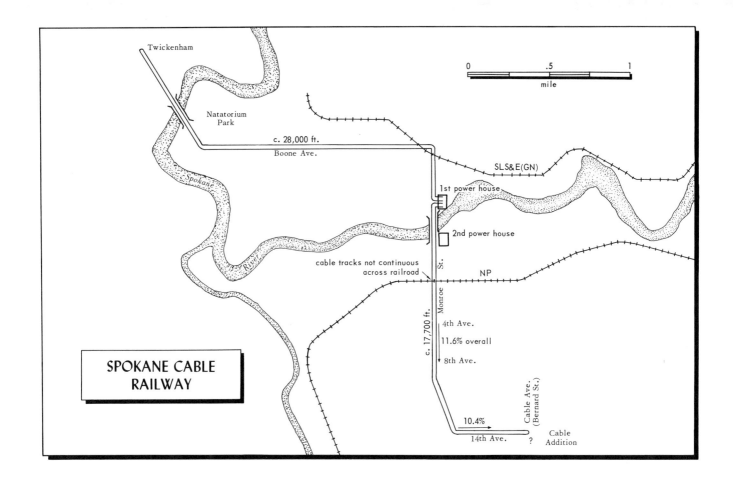

SPOKANE CABLE RAILWAY

Twickenham

Natatorium Park

c. 28,000 ft.
Boone Ave.

Spokane River

SLS&E(GN)

1st power house

2nd power house

cable tracks not continuous across railroad

NP

Monroe St.

c. 17,700 ft.

4th Ave.

11.6% overall

8th Ave.

Cable Ave. (Bernard St.)

10.4%

14th Ave.   ?   Cable Addition

0   .5   1
mile

The two lines of the Spokane Cable Railway were operated with dissimilar equipment. Below is one of the north line's grip cars, a Stockton catalog model, probably shown on Boone Avenue. (*Eastern Washington State Historical Society*)

Cable Addition which had barely developed at all, owing to the deteriorating business conditions of the early 1890s. The north line had served the Northwest League baseball park at Natatorium Park, but the south line had only its meagre residential population. The Spokane *Review* in 1894 described the cable line as something "whose existence is almost unknown except to the few persons who climb the Monroe Street hill in the rattletrap car that operates from Second Avenue to a point out in the woods beyond." The area was so undeveloped that it is difficult to identify the terminus; present-day sources place it variously at 14th and Bernard, McClellan or Division Streets, of which Bernard appears to accord most closely with maps of the company. The line operated infrequently with two of the California cars, carrying few passengers. In May 1894 the company sought a subsidy of $400 per month from local residents, but failed to secure it. This brought the operation to an end, on or about July 22, 1894. It was one of the few cable lines simply abandoned, rather than replaced with electric cars. The line, though one of the most obscure during its life, is memorialized in the destination "Cable Addition," on one of the city's bus lines.

POWERHOUSES: Hydro-power turbine installations. Second station extant, but unused.

Reference: SRJ, IX (1893), 253-254.

The Spokane Cable Railway's south line was equipped with California type cars, also standard models of the Stockton Combine Harvester & Agricultural Works. The car below was sketched by Peter Copeland of the Smithsonian Institution from a halftone in the Spokane *Spokesman-Review* of 1936.

Flimsy bridges were a notable characteristic of the north line of the Spokane Cable Railway. The span above was the line's exit from downtown Spokane. The structure, which was widely expected to collapse, surprised the local population by burning instead. The company's other bridge, below, connected Natatorium Park with Twickenham — considerably more successfully. (*Eastern Washington State Historical Society*)

PROVIDENCE

Population in 1890: 132,146

PROVIDENCE CABLE TRAMWAY

Wheel-operated double-jaw side grip   *Gauge: 4'-8½"*

Providence presented the only combination of population density and natural barriers sufficient to require cable traction in New England, and accordingly had the only cable line in the entire region. In addition, Providence was one of several cities in which cable traction was looked upon as relief from a monopolistic horsecar operator.

Since 1865 Providence had been served by the Union Railroad, which through the 1880s had made no effort to convert away from animal power. As a result, the company was forced to serve the East Side, which included Brown University and the city's highest-income residential area, by means of an exceedingly indirect horsecar line, circumventing the west escarpment of College Hill. The situation was a source of continual dissatisfaction to local residents, who saw in cable traction an obvious possibility of direct access from the East Side to Market Square at the foot of College Hill and to the central business district to the west. The Union Railroad had previously rejected an elevator and a vehicular tunnel as prohibitively expensive. Walter Richmond, an East Side resident, endeavored to interest the company in a cable line, but failed. The Union management explicitly argued that no solution was practicable.

Richmond began his own efforts at promoting a cable line by incorporating the Providence Cable Tramway Company on April 25, 1884. In the mid-1880s he made an extensive trip through the midwest during which he claimed to have inspected every cable car line from Pittsburgh to Omaha. He was most impressed with H. M. Lane's installations in Cincinnati, and contracted with Lane to design his line. Apparently fearful of a legal action for using Lane's non-trust technology, Richmond arranged to license National Cable Railway Company patents in 1889.

The Providence Cable Tramway had more difficulty in securing its franchise than any other line in the industry. The Union Railroad opposed Richmond at every stage, but on December 2, 1887, he secured the right to ascend College Hill on College Street,

turn hard left into Prospect Street at the main gate of Brown University, and then run across College Hill north of the Brown campus along Angell and Waterman Streets to Red Bridge at the Seekonk River. Daniel F. Longstreet, General Manager of the Union, argued strongly that cable traction was inappropriate for the narrow, curving streets of New England, and that even under the best of circumstances, the days of the cable car were numbered. He also suggested that action on the franchise be deferred until the success of the Rasmussen line in Newark could be ascertained.

Richmond's franchise represented only a partial victory, since the westernmost extremity of the line was at Market Square, some distance east of the central business district. He sought the right to run his trailers over more than three miles of the Union's trackage on Westminster and High Streets through the central area to Broadway and High in Olneyville on the opposite side of the city. Richmond did not consider his project viable without this right, but Longstreet interpreted his efforts as trying to compensate for the expected losses of cable operation with a share of the profits from the Union's strongest line. Most of the 32 council hearings on the Cable Tramway's affairs concerned this point. In 1889 the Tramway received the permission it sought, but by way of compromise the council required that the Tramway's trailers be operated by Union drivers and horses while on Union track. It also granted the Union rights to use short distances of Tramway track on Angell and Waterman Streets. Richmond was so elated at his victory that his grip cars carried "Olneyville" in addition to "Red Bridge" on their clerestories.

The layout of the line presented Lane with some extremely difficult engineering problems. Since the line had a loop return at Red Bridge and turnouts at Market Square, he was unable to use his characteristic single-jaw side grip. Instead, he adopted a wheel-operated double-jaw side grip essentially identical to the Wood & Fowler grip of the Temple Street line in Los Angeles. Lane's worst problems were all con-

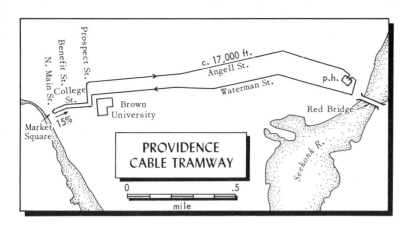

PROVIDENCE
CABLE TRAMWAY

0   .5
mile

A train of the Providence Cable Tramway ascends College Street approaching the line's difficult pull curve at the front gate of Brown University. Note the company's characteristic lefthand operation. *(Brown University Library)*

centrated in the westernmost two blocks of the line. The route began at the foot of a grade of 15 per cent from Market Square to Benefit Street, a major thoroughfare, and continued up an additional block of diminishing but still difficult gradient on a narrow street to the entrance to Brown, where the track turned a pull curve of only 40-foot radius into Prospect Street. This curve, which had a good claim to being the most difficult on any cable line, was so restrictive that Lane had to adopt grip cars only 12 feet long, though capable of seating 18 passengers. Beyond Prospect Street the line was undulating almost to the end. Beginning halfway along South Angell Street, the line ran sharply down at about 8 per cent to the Red Bridge. Unfortunately for the company, Richmond was unable to secure land for a powerhouse at Market Square, as he originally intended, and so was forced to put his powerhouse on the descending portion of South Angell Street. Since the grade was too heavy for upbound cars to roll past the powerhouse, Lane had to use Angell Street for the eastbound track, necessarily involving the line in left-hand operation on College and Prospect Streets and, no doubt, compounding the hazards of the pull curve at their intersection. The westbound track on Waterman Street entailed no particular problems; the grade up from Red Bridge to Cooke Street was mild, and the rest of the trackage merely undulating. The line's only other feature of note was Lane's treatment of the Benefit Street intersection. To simplify the ascent of the College Street grade, he deepened his conduit from the normal 21 inches to 54 to allow the cable to have a deep catenary at Benefit Street, thereby avoiding a pair of movable depression pulleys at the east side of the intersection. J. B. Stone, upon visiting Providence, noted that the route had 135 curve pulleys with an average angle of 5 per cent. He considered the Tramway simple but well built for a light-traffic operation; it had only 3.43 miles of track and represented an investment of about $250,000.

The Tramway's history was short, uneventful, but on the whole successful. Lane supervised construction during 1889, and had the route ready for laying of the cable by December 9, 1889. The trial trip was made two days later, but the turnouts at Market Square were not yet completed. Municipal officials were taken on a trip on Christmas Day, and free trips were offered half-hourly during the rest of December. Revenue service began on January 1, 1890. The line initially operated at 6½ miles per hour, but cable speed was increased to 9 miles per hour after about a year. At the outset the company had a great deal of diffi-

culty with the cable owing to inexperience of the gripmen. The first cable lasted six months, during which it had three or four outright severings, and a total of 17 splices. Lane shortly installed depression pulleys just short of the terminal sheave in an effort to regularize strain on his tension carriage. Probably because of the pull curve at College and Prospect, the company continued to have frequent ruptures in the cable throughout its existence.

Contrary to Longstreet's expectations, the Cable Tramway proved uniformly profitable. The company was solidly in the black from 1890 to 1894. In its best year, 1893, it carried 3,044,212 people. The management established a picnic area near the powerhouse to stimulate pleasure trips. The line carried 19,000 people on its first Fourth of July. The Union Railroad was impressed enough with the early successes that it bought a majority control of the Tramway on October 23, 1890. The Union's intention was to absorb the cable line and to dissolve the Tramway corporation, but being unable to buy the last two shares of stock, could not do so. As a result, the Union leased the property for 50 years beginning January 1, 1895. Meanwhile, the Union had electrified its own system completely between January 20, 1892, and April 24, 1894, and had incidentally come to the usual conclusion about the relative merits of cable and electric traction. Conversion, owing to the College Hill grade, promised to be exceptionally difficult.

Beginning in April 1894 Tramway grip cars had hauled electric cars up the hill, reportedly the former trailers, each equipped with a single electric motor. The Union management decided on the same solution adopted in St. Paul: a counterbalance using the former cable conduit. The cable line was closed permanently at midnight on January 26, 1895. Until February 15 passengers had to walk or take horsedrawn vehicles up the hill while the counterbalance was installed. The delay was required mainly for installation of second motors in the former trailers; the grip cars had been able to haul only single-motored equipment up the hill, but the counterbalance required two-motored cars. The counterbalance was an extremely simple one, designed by J. P. F. Kuhlmann of Seattle, who had built similar systems on Rainier Avenue in Seattle and Front Street in Portland. The system required two weights of six and one-half tons each, running on rails in the conduits. Electric cars latched onto the weights and assisted one another up and down the hill with their motors. The system could move cars only in a 1:1 ratio, which was inappropriate during rush hours. Consequently, the arrangement was modified by Milton H. Bronsdon of the company to operate with former grip cars, motorized and enclosed, designed to couple to the latches on the hill, but to switch freely at Market Square. Normally, the ex-grip cars pushed up two electric cars, but they could ascend or descend alone to give the system a degree of flexibility. The arrangement survived until a tunnel, still in use by buses, was opened for electric cars between Market Square and Thayer Street in 1914.

The Providence Cable Tramway survived as a corporate entity within the Union as late as 1934. The powerhouse was particularly long-lived, serving successively as a plant of the American Emery Wheel Works and the Arden Jewelry Manufacturing Company until recently destroyed in revision of approaches to the new Red Bridge.

POWERHOUSE: 169 South Angell Street. EQUIPMENT: Two Harris Corliss engines, 150 and 180 horsepower.

References: Albert W. Claflin, "The Providence Cable Tramway," *Rhode Island History,* IV (1945), 41-53; V (1946), 11-28. SRJ, VI (1890), 117; VII (1891), 227.

The photograph of Market Square below is a good capsule view of the operations of the Providence Cable Tramway. A two-horse team draws one of the company's trailers to a waiting grip car which will shortly haul it up College Hill on the right. The trailer is lettered "Olneyville," the community at the opposite side of the city which the company had laboriously secured the right to serve through trackage rights on the Union Railroad. *(Rhode Island Historical Society)*

The cable cars went back into service in Milton H. Bronsdon's modification of the counterbalance which replaced the Providence Cable Tramway. The two views on this page show them pushing an electric car up College Street and switching in Market Street at the bottom of the grade. *(Richard L. Wonson; Rhode Island Historical Society)*

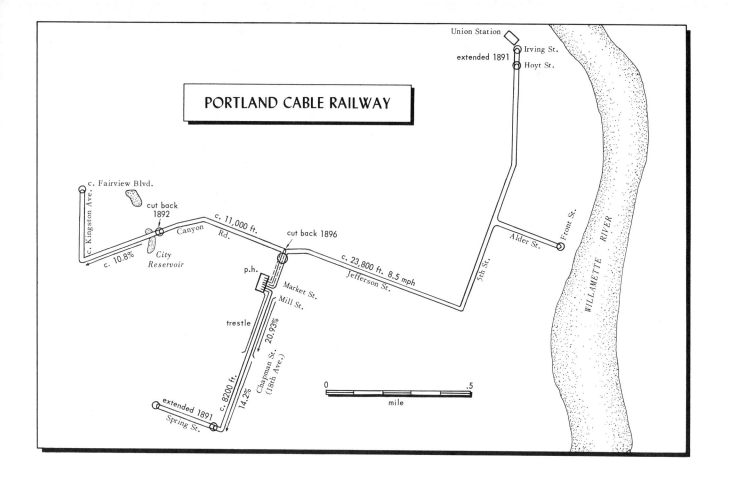

PORTLAND CABLE RAILWAY

Union Station
extended 1891
Irving St.
Hoyt St.

c. Fairview Blvd.
c. Kingston Ave.
cut back 1892
c. 11,000 ft.
Canyon Rd.
cut back 1896
c. 23,800 ft. 8.5 mph
Jefferson St.
5th St.
Alder St.
Front St.
c. 10.8%
City Reservoir
p.h.
Market St.
Mill St.
trestle
20.93%
Chapman St. (18th Ave.)
14.2%
c. 8200 ft.
extended 1891
Spring St.

0 .5
mile

WILLAMETTE RIVER

Car 17, the Portland Cable Railway's only double-ender, was permanently assigned to the company's Alder Street shuttle line. The handsome car is loaded on a flatcar for shipment from the Stockton Combine Harvester & Agricultural Works in California. (*Roy D. Graves*)

PORTLAND, OREGON

Population in 1890: 46,385

PORTLAND CABLE RAILWAY

McLellan bottom grip   *Gauge: 3'-6"*

One of the cable lines most clearly called forth by geographical problems was the Portland Cable Railway, designed to develop the extremely high-lying land of Portland Heights. Both in scenery and engineering, this was one of the most spectacular cable lines, but unfortunately, its financial success was by no means commensurate.

The Portland Cable Railway was promoted by Jefferson T. McCaffrey of Philadelphia and his associates, who were also involved with real estate development in the tributary area. Work began on October 1, 1887, in the expectation of having the line finished by March 1888, but financial problems prevented completion until Washington's Birthday, 1890. The road was built with Powell Street technology by the Pacific Cable Construction Company under the direction of J. M. Thompson. Pacific Cable, which had built mainly in milder climate, grossly underestimated the severity of the winters; the company was so badly afflicted with slot closures that its own engineer, R. A. McLellan, had to design a grip, very similar to the Eppelsheimer Thompson had intended, but with a narrower shank to minimize entrapments. Even so, the line was one of the worst sufferers from slot contraction in the winter months.

Though a small installation of only 3.7 miles, the line was built in an exceptionally large number of segments. Originally, the route ran from a turntable at Front Avenue up Alder Street, through the retailing area on Fifth Street to Jefferson, and thence to the base of the range of hills immediately west of the central district. There it turned south on 18th Street for its ascent to Portland Heights, from 161 feet above sea level at Mill Street to 608 feet at the turntable at Spring Street. About 270 feet of the ascent was on a wooden trestle at 20.93 per cent, apparently the second worst grade on any American cable line. Since the blocks immediately above the trestle were nearly as bad, the placing of a turntable at the top of a series of grades on which it would have been impossible to control the car with brakes alone was dangerous. Perhaps fortunately, a car failed

to take the rope coming off the turntable on the second day of service and ran away on the grade without serious injury. As a consequence, the company relocated the turntable in June 1890 a few feet to the west, so that a car was pushed off onto flat land to take the rope. Cars thereafter proceeded around a short curve before descending the grade.

The company's first extension on Fifth Street from Alder to Hoyt Street, a block from Union Station, opened on August 9, 1890. Fifth Street, on which the company traversed the central business district, became an important retailing street by the middle 1890s, but was secondary to streets to the east during the cable line's existence. A mixture of this circumstance and the low population on Portland Heights chronically depressed the line's traffic; the company carried only 1,260,000 passengers in 1892.

The company made two short extensions in 1891. In September it pushed the Fifth Street line one block from Hoyt to Irving, bringing the tracks to Union Station. At that time, the turntable from Alder and Front was relocated at Fifth and Irving, and the Alder portion converted to a shuttle operation with a double-ended car. On November 3, the line on

J. M. THOMPSON.

437

Portland Heights was built about a quarter mile west to the end of Spring Street.

In an effort to develop some pleasure traffic, the company built a second route up the hills to a tract west of Washington Park in the area of the present Arlington Heights. The tract was named Melinda Heights in honor of the wife of Amos N. King, promoter of the addition, but it was customarily known as King's Heights — the name the cable cars carried on their destination signs. This extension, the last the company attempted, was opened on April 8, 1892. Partly because it was built through undeveloped territory, and partly because it proved short-lived, the exact location is uncertain, but it apparently terminated at a baseball diamond near the present intersection of Kingston and Fairview Boulevard. The line was single-tracked, and operated by upbound cars pulling the cable, but coasting back in full release. The city's decision to build its present reservoir in 1892-93 in what is now Washington Park caused the line to be cut back at the end of the 1892 summer season.

The company, which had been heavily in debt from the outset, inevitably went bankrupt and was reorganized in September, 1892, as the City Cable Company under F. I. Fuller of the Portland Construction Company and S. Prentiss Smith of the Pacific Coast Steel Company, the principal creditors. In 1894 the line was sold to the Portland Traction Company for $41,718.14, the exact amount of its indebtedness. The property represented an investment of about $500,000. Fuller, who had come to the line as receiver, was retained as general manager, and instructed merely to cover variable expenses — something the line typically had been unable to do.

On May 1, 1896, the company converted the cable system to electricity with the exception of the ascent from the powerhouse to Portland Heights, which was far beyond the ability of adhesion vehicles. The company had operated with 23 Stockton cars, 10 open, 12 single-end combination, and one double-ender for the Alder shuttle. Of these, six open cars and ten combination cars were electrified by placing electric motors on the rear trucks. The bodies were necessarily raised 8 inches in the process. It was still possible to carry grips on the front trucks of the electrified cable cars. At various times after 1896 the company ran cars from Union Station under electricity to the powerhouse, where they took grips and pulled up the ascent, and at other times it required passengers to change from electrics to cable cars at a newly-installed turntable at 18th and Jefferson. The former cable trackage remained 3'-6" to the end of electric operation.

The incentive to get rid of the remaining 0.8 mile of cable mileage was, naturally, very great, but there was no prospect of electrifying the line as it stood. Portland Traction in 1904 built the first portion of its famous Council Crest electric line to serve the area by an entirely different route, and so was able to end the remaining cable operation.

POWERHOUSE: 18th between Mill and Market Streets. EQUIPMENT: Two Hamilton Corliss engines, 300 HP each, built by Hoover, Owens & Rentschler Co., Hamilton, Ohio. After the conversion of 1896 the electrified portion of the line was run off Portland Traction's regular grid, not from this powerhouse. The steam engines were replaced with a 125 HP General Electric motor to run the Portland Heights cable.

References: SRJ, IX (1893), 302-304; collection of David L. Stearns.

Photographers, who apparently avoided the Portland Cable Railway's street operations, devoted their attention to the company's spectacular ascent of Portland Heights. Above, the vast wooden trestle is under construction. Below, two of the line's closed combination cars traverse the 20.93 per cent grade of the trestle. *(Oregon Historical Society)*

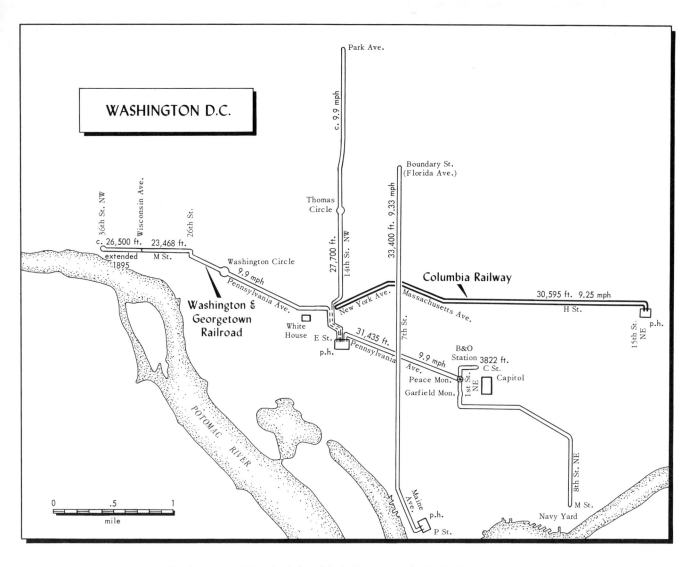

WASHINGTON D.C.

Park Ave.

c. 9.9 mph

Thomas Circle

Boundary St. (Florida Ave.)

33,400 9.33 mph

27,700 ft.

14th St. NW

c. 36th St. NW

Wisconsin Ave.

23,468 ft.

26th St.

M St.

extended 1895

26,500 ft.

Washington Circle

9.9 mph

Pennsylvania Ave.

Washington & Georgetown Railroad

White House

New York Ave.

Massachusetts Ave.

7th St.

Columbia Railway

30,595 ft. 9.25 mph

H St.

15th St. NE

p.h.

E St.

p.h.

31,435 ft.

Pennsylvania Ave.

9.9 mph

B&O Station

3822 ft.

C St.

Capitol

Peace Mon.

Garfield Mon.

1st St. NE

8th St. NE

M St.

Navy Yard

Maine Ave.

p.h.

P St.

POTOMAC RIVER

0   .5   1
mile

Benjamin Franklin doubtless felt little envy as he looked out upon what he didn't invent — cable traction — from the pedestal at the left at 10th Street and Pennsylvania Avenue, Washington. Note that the eastbound train carries a railway post office. (*Library of Congress*)

WASHINGTON

Population in 1890: 230,392

WASHINGTON & GEORGETOWN
RAILROAD

7th Street: Root single-jaw side grip   *Gauge: 4'-8½"*

Pennsylvania Avenue: Double-jaw side grip

Henry Hurt, president of the Washington & Georgetown Railroad, in 1887 stated, "Of all places, Washington is best adapted to a cable road." He slightly overstated his case, but there is no question that Washington's geographical properties were excellent for cable traction. The city was old-established, densely populated, and because of the heavy concentration of civil-service employment, highly centralized. Further, it was a planned city of broad, straight streets in a radial pattern, set on a long, gentle ascent from the Potomac River toward the Maryland hills.

Hurt announced his intention to apply to Congress for a charter for cable operation as early as 1886, but did not receive it until February 20, 1889. On the basis of a five-week tour of western street railways in 1887, he chose Daniel Bontecou of Kansas City to design the first line, a route of 3¼ miles from the 7th Street Wharves up 7th Street to Boundary Street (Florida Avenue). As in Kansas City, Bontecou used trust technology; construction was supervised by William B. Upton, who also designed portions of the engineering work. Edmund Saxton of Kansas City was contractor.

The 7th Street line was opened on April 12, 1890, and quickly proved one of the most successful cable lines. The street was the city's principal north-south shopping street, the residential area was thoroughly developed, and the baseball park was at the terminus. Service was provided by two- or three-car trains at 3½ minute intervals with 24 grips and 64 trailers; 16 trains were regularly required. Since the line was straight except for the curvature at the powerhouse and at the corner of 7th and Water Street (Maine Avenue), cables lasted about 18 months, and by the standards of cable operators, power consumption was quite modest.

A mixture of the success of the 7th Street line and Congressional pressure caused the company to undertake conversion of the remainder of its system to cable traction. Congress in 1889 required that street railways in the District of Columbia convert their remaining horsecar lines to some form of mechanical or electric power by 1892, but prohibited overhead electric wires (which were already in use by the Eckington & Soldiers Home Railway) in the area south of Boundary Street, effective in 1893. Since effective conduit electrification was not developed until 1895 (simultaneously in New York and Washington), the incentive to build cable lines in Washington was possibly greater than anywhere else during the period of rivalry between cable and electric cars from 1888 to 1893. The company would undoubtedly have used electricity for its further conversions if overhead wires had been allowed.

The second Washington & Georgetown cable system was a considerably more complicated engineering project. The company was blessed with the franchise for Pennsylvania Avenue, which it used for a pair of lines, one from the Navy Yard to M and 32nd Street (Wisconsin Avenue) in Georgetown, and the other from the old B&O station just north of the Capitol to 14th Street and Park Road. All of this it proposed to run out of a single powerhouse, one of the largest and best equipped in the industry, at 14th and Pennsylvania. Serving the B&O station required an auxiliary off the Navy Yard cable, and the rest of the system had considerable curvature. The 14th Street cable could easily have been run from the powerhouse straight north to Park Road, but instead it was run along the east side of the Treasury on 15th Street, and northeast on New York Avenue before reaching 14th. The horsecar line had been routed in this fashion to avoid a grade of about 5 per cent along the east side of the Willard Hotel on 14th Street between Pennsylvania and F Street. This grade was trivial by cable standards, but the Treasury corner at 15th and New York had developed into a major transfer point, such that the company was eager to continue to serve it with cable cars. Cars of both lines held the 14th Street cable outbound as far as 15th and F, where Georgetown cars dropped rope and picked up the

The 7th Street line of the Washington & Georgetown Railroad was among the country's most prosperous cable lines. One reason for the prosperity was the city's baseball park at the terminus, to which the swinging load below is destined. In the background is a battery car of the Eckington & Soldiers Home Railway. *(LeRoy O. King)*

442

Pennsylvania Avenue cable with a gypsy. Inbound, cars of both lines pulled the Georgetown rope to F Street and coasted to 14th Street in full release. The company also used hand-operated gypsies at termini and at the powerhouse, but it had three automatic gypsies activated by the passing grip, designed by Upton for taking the rope at the 7th Street crossing and at the vault for the auxiliary at the Peace Monument. Washington's broad boulevards gave gripmen excellent visibility, and thus contributed to a fairly favorable accident experience. The one qualification to Hurt's view of the perfection of the city's geography for cable traction was L'Enfant's traffic circles at intersections of the main boulevards, which required long pull curves of the sort most difficult for cable engineers.

The two Pennsylvania Avenue lines were opened on August 6, 1892. The only extension the company ever made was about 1500 feet from 32nd along M to the newly built central office at the Aqueduct (Key) Bridge, completed July 12, 1895. There the Georgetown line terminated in a loop which cars traversed by momentum and gravity through the ground floor of the building. Apparently in anticipation of this arrangement, since all other termini were turnouts, cars on the Pennsylvania Avenue lines were equipped with double-jaw side grips; they carried the rope in the right jaws on all lines. Each of the two lines provided service at 3-minute intervals, bringing a car down Pennsylvania Avenue every 90 seconds. Twenty-eight trains of 2 or 3 cars served the Georgetown line, and 22 the 14th Street line. The new lines brought the company's cable roster to 98 open grip cars, 24 from Laclede and 74 from Stephenson, plus 164 open trailers and 151 closed, built variously by Laclede, Stephenson, J. M. Jones, and the American Car Company. The two Pennsylvania Avenue lines aggregated 7.9 miles of line, and were among the most heavily patronized street railway routes of any type in the country. The company stayed in the black in the early 1890s. The cable system was 11.1 miles total, and because of the extensiveness of the main powerhouse, represented an investment of about $3.5 million.

On September 21, 1895, the Washington & Georgetown merged with the Rock Creek Railroad to form the Capital Traction Company. Given the relative success of the cable operation, the company showed less of the obsessive fervor to get rid of the cables

than the typical street railway. Doubtless the system would have been replaced with electric conduit lines by the turn of the century, but the conversion was abruptly precipitated by a fire which completely destroyed the 14th Street powerhouse on the night of September 29, 1897. Before the fire had been extinguished the company arranged to lease almost all of the available commercial horses in the city, and was able to provide service the following morning with the cable trailers used as horsecars on five-minute headway on the Georgetown line, and 4½-minute headway on 14th Street. Restoration of the powerhouse at that late date would have been grossly uneconomic, and the company began immediately to convert the cable conduit for electric operation. In spite of the continuing use of the track by the horse-drawn trailers, the 14th Street line was ready for electric conduit operation by March 12, 1898, and the Georgetown line by March 20.

The 7th Street line was, of course, unaffected by the powerhouse fire, but the company turned to its conversion immediately upon completing the Pennsylvania Avenue electrification. The two electric rails had to be put in the 7th Street conduit while the cable was operating, and while cable trains passed every few minutes. This difficult operation was completed late in May. In the early morning hours of May 25, 1898, the cable was cut at Boundary Street, and reeled in, with a grip car holding the severed end on each track. Electric operation began later that morning.

POWERHOUSES: Water and 4½ Streets, S. W. EQUIPMENT: Two compound Reynolds-Corliss engines, E. P. Allis & Co., 250 HP each. Walker machinery. 14th Street and Pennsylvania Avenue, N. W. EQUIPMENT: Two 36″ x 72″ Reynolds-Corliss engines, 750 HP each, E. P. Allis & Co. Site occupied by District Building.

References: G. F. Cunningham, "Cable Cars in the Nation's Capital," *The Turnout,* April 1953, pp. 45-54; John A. Boettjer, "Street Railways in the District of Columbia," unpublished M. A. thesis, George Washington University (1963); SRJ, VI (1890), 324; VIII (1892), 510-512; X (1894), 757-759; collections of LeRoy O. King, Sr. and Jr.

The Pennsylvania Avenue RPO service was operated with handsome Brill trailers. Cable RPOs also operated on Cottage Grove Avenue, Milwaukee Avenue and Madison Street in Chicago, on Third Avenue in New York, and Sacramento and Market Streets in San Francisco. (*LeRoy O. King;* Letter: *Robert A. Truax*)

444

Mrs. C. H. Davis' anonymous correspondent, author of the letter on the opposite page, could hardly have waited longer to use the Pennsylvania Avenue cable RPO, since the envelope is postmarked on the day of the fire which destroyed the line's powerhouse and brought cable operation to a quick end. The fire, which burned for three days, reduced the powerhouse to the Roman ruin shown below. (*LeRoy O. King; Library of Congress*)

The view of Pennsylvania Avenue at left illustrates the density of the Washington & Georgetown's traffic. Georgetown cars were green and cream, 14th Street yellow and cream.

Below is the overflow load at the time of the encampment of the Grand Army of the Republic in Washington in 1893. (*LeRoy O. King*)

Single-jaw side grip   *Gauge: 4'-8½"*

The Columbia Railway was an old-established and prosperous horsecar operator dating from 1871 whose property consisted of a single line from the Treasury corner to 15th and H Streets, N. E. This was the city's principal traffic artery straight east from the central business district, but in 1895 it was still horse-operated. The company had been particularly troubled by the dilemma of Washington operators after they had been ordered to convert from horses, but prohibited from using the only thoroughly satisfactory alternative, overhead electrification. The company was reportedly considering electrification as early as 1888, but seems to have been in a quandary after Congress' conflicting edicts of 1889. It experimented unsuccessfully with a compressed air motor in 1892, and the following year went so far as to draw up a contract for electrification with a conduit system already in use in Budapest. It then failed to sign the contract, and operated on extensions of its right to use horses. Finally, on August 6, 1894, the shareholders authorized installation of a cable system. By the time the system opened on March 9, 1895, it was by far the last to be completed in the country; the last previous company to start cable operation afresh had been the Baltimore City Passenger Railway in May, 1893.

The Columbia Railway entrusted design of its line to William B. Upton, who had been Bontecou's first assistant in designing the Washington & Georgetown system. Somewhat surprisingly, Upton took as his model the New York Broadway line, rather than any of Bontecou's installations. He used large single-truck cars of the Broadway sort (though two feet shorter), operated by a wheel-actuated grip off each platform. Unlike the Broadway installation, the line used a single-jaw side grip, however. The company did not use trailers.

The installation was one of the simplest ever attempted. The line was 2.8 miles long, with only 349 feet of curvature, distributed between three curves, all between 150 and 250 feet radius. Upton did not attempt the Broadway line's duplicate system. The line terminated at an ordinary crossover at the Treasury corner; the block between 14th and 15th on New York Avenue was the only one in the United States served by two parallel double-track cable lines. The company regularly handled over 3 million passengers a year, and was uniformly profitable. In 1898 it received a franchise for two extensions into the Ana-

WM. B. UPTON.

costia area, thereby increasing its attractiveness as a merger prospect.

In April 1899 the company's stock was purchased in its entirety by the Washington Traction & Electric Company, which was bringing together what became the major rival of Capital Traction. This company had previously acquired the Metropolitan Railway, which had introduced successful conduit electric operation to Washington on its 9th Street line on July 29, 1895. The new owner envisioned using the Columbia Railway's route as the entry into downtown Washington for electric cars radiating beyond 15th and H into the dormitory area beyond. Accordingly, it lost no time in converting the line to electricity. As on 7th Street, the conduit was revised for electric running while cable operation continued. The cable line was ready for conversion on July 23, 1899, slightly more than four years after its inception. As the Benning car line, it was one of the most heavily travelled electric lines in the city until its conversion to buses in 1949. It also served as the entry to the city for the Washington Baltimore & Annapolis interurban.

POWERHOUSE: 15th and H, N. E. EQUIPMENT: Two Corliss engines, 22" x 60", E. P. Allis & Company. Walker machinery.

References: Cunningham, *op. cit.;* SRJ, X (1894), 759-761; SRR, V (1895), 141-144.

The Columbia Railway's equipment was 40 Stephenson grip cars, equally divided between open and closed models. Painted in an impressive livery of royal blue and silver, these cars replaced 44 horsecars and 180 horses. (*Museum of the City of New York*)

The company's powerhouse survived into the early 1970s as a D.C. Transit garage.

SAN DIEGO

Population in 1890: 16,159

SAN DIEGO CABLE RAILWAY

Van Vleck bottom grip   *Gauge: 3'-6"*

The San Diego Cable Railway was an almost perfect example of a cable line built in the late 1880s to develop high-lying residential land which quickly failed in the depressed 1890s. In spite of its short life, it is one of the most interesting cable operations, mainly because its designer left the most detailed record of any of the single-track cable lines.

The company was promoted early in 1889 by Alderman John C. Fisher; David D. Dare and C. W. Collins of the California National Bank; real estate broker D. C. Reed; George Copeland, promoter of an unsuccessful electric line; and George B. Hensley, secretary of the Pacific Beach recreation area. Copeland held the franchise for Fourth Avenue through the Florence Heights area, but because of conflicting franchises of other companies it was necessary to enter the downtown area on Sixth Avenue. The line was an effort to connect the steam suburban railroad depots in the vicinity of L Street with the developing residential areas in Florence Heights, Hillcrest and University Heights. The company was incorporated on July 22, 1889, with a capitalization of $500,000.

Designing the line was entrusted to Frank Van Vleck of the Pacific Cable Railway in Los Angeles, who endeavored to modify the technology with which he was familiar to the requirements of the single-track line the promoters wanted in San Diego. Van Vleck adopted the orthodox 3'-6", and in one of the most clever accomplishments of any cable designer, adapted the Eppelsheimer bottom grip to the off-center operation of a single-track line. He dealt with the difficult problem of curvature on a single-track line by providing passing sidings at each pull curve, with double track for short distances on C Street and at a diagonal crossing of Walnut Street. Through the historical research of the late Richard V. Dodge, we know the entire track layout of the system, as shown on the accompanying map. Although Van Vleck defended building the system on the basis of its grades after Sprague had demonstrated to his satisfaction the superiority of the electric car on level terrain, the system's

gradients were in fact quite modest. The ruling grade was 8 per cent just south of Fir Street, and elsewhere several stretches had 6 per cent. The line ran from an elevation of 8 feet above water level at L Street to 360 feet at the northern terminus, a distance of 4.7 miles. Most of the gain in altitude was concentrated on Fourth Avenue, which was fairly continuously upward from C Street to University Avenue. The powerhouse at Spruce Street issued two cables, the "city cable" of 24,600 feet at 8 miles per hour, and the "suburban cable" at 27,000 feet at 10 miles per hour. Equipment was twelve Stockton combination cars of the Powell Street model, and two open cars of the same size. Investment in the line was reported at $300,000.

The system was under construction in the second half of 1889 and the first half of 1890. The car "El Escondido" made the first trip at 1:30 PM on June 7, 1890, between L Street and the powerhouse. Governor Robert W. Waterman and Mayor Douglas Gunn attended ceremonies at the powerhouse in honor of the opening. The company had received only one cable, but on receipt of a second opened the suburban portion of the line in the fourth week of July. On September 9 the company opened a private park and pavilion, later known as Mission Cliff Gardens, at the north or "Bluff" terminus. It also operated a sports area under the name of Recreation Park on University Avenue. It was hoped these promotional projects would compensate for the sparse population on the northern segment. The company initially planned some 6 miles of additional line, including a route east on C Street, but nothing further was undertaken.

Deteriorating business conditions, a succession of minor accidents of the sort usual on cable lines, failure of the tributary area to develop, and opening of a rival electric line on Fifth Avenue on September 21, 1892, all combined to ruin the company exceptionally quickly. The California National Bank of San Diego, which had financed the line in cooperation with Philadelphia capitalists, failed in November 1891. Of

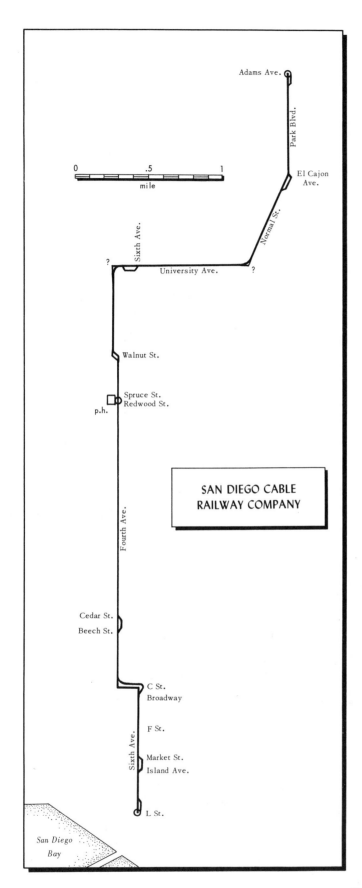

Adams Ave.

0 .5 1
mile

Park Blvd.

El Cajon
Ave.

Sixth Ave.

Normal St.

?   University Ave.   ?

Walnut St.

Spruce St.
Redwood St.
p.h.

SAN DIEGO CABLE
RAILWAY COMPANY

Fourth Ave.

Cedar St.
Beech St.

C St.
Broadway

F St.

Sixth Ave.

Market St.
Island Ave.

L St.

San Diego
Bay

the two officers of the bank active in the Cable Railway, Collins committed suicide, and Dare, who was on a European trip, elected not to return to America. A claim of $4000 of the Spreckels Brothers for coal caused the company to go into the hands of the courts under a succession of receivers. One of these, C. W. Pauly, reported in April that the company was losing about $1100 per month. To delinquency of the coal bill, taxes and wages was shortly added the prospect of the cables wearing out. In August Receiver Hensley secured permission of Judge Puterbaugh to replace the cables, and promptly ordered two new ones from Worcester. The suburban cable had to be shut down pending renewal. The first replacement cable arrived on October 4, but the company could not afford to move it to the powerhouse for installation. Efforts at a subsidy by residents along the line had failed, and Hensley could not sell receiver's certificates. On October 15, with the second renewal cable en route from Worcester, Attorney E. W. Britt, representing the principal bondholder, the California Title Insurance & Trust Company, appeared before Judge Puterbaugh to request an order shutting down the Cable Railway for lack of funds to continue. Judge Puterbaugh complied, and Receiver Hensley ended the operation on that evening, October 15, 1892.

Initially it was expected that the line would be returned to service, and as late as January 16, 1893, the cables were moved in the conduit to prevent rusting. The property remained intact, though subjected to vandalism, until 1896, when it was sold for $17,600 to George B. Kerper of Cincinnati, who converted it to electricity, installing motors in the old cable cars, under the name Citizens Traction Company. This enterprise failed, and the property passed into the hands of the San Diego Electric Railway, which converted the line from Fifth and University to the northern terminus to standard gauge as an extension of its Fifth Avenue line, and abandoned the rest. One of the electrified cable cars, greatly altered, has survived as a museum piece in the hands of the Railway Historical Society of San Diego.

POWERHOUSE: Two Wetherill Corliss engines, 18″ x 42″ and 22″ x 42″, 250 and 350 horsepower. Rope-driven machinery.

References: Richard V. Dodge, "San Diego's Grip Cars," *Dispatcher* (Railway Historical Society of San Diego, 1962); Frank Van Vleck, "Light Cable Road Construction," *Transactions of the American Society of Mechanical Engineers,* XII (1891), 56-84; SRJ, VII (1891), 337-340.

Given the San Diego Cable Railway's short life and small size, photographic coverage is remarkably good. Above, a car moves down Sixth Avenue near the south end of the line. The company's cars bore Spanish names. Below, the line's designer, Frank Van Vleck, leans at left on the front platform of Las Penasquitas – appropriately enough, "The Little Pains." *(Title Insurance & Trust Company)*

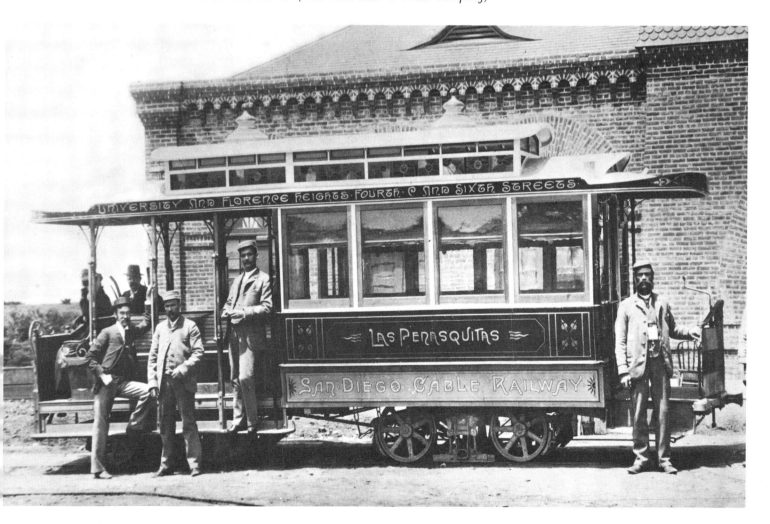

The San Diego Cable Railway's powerhouse was photographed before completion. Above, the turntable at the front is under construction, and below the winding machinery is awaiting stretching of the cable. *(Title Insurance & Trust Company)*

The company's labor force, plus a newsboy who worked the cars, turned out for the photograph at the powerhouse, above. This is the only known photograph of the line's open cars. Note the man, possibly Van Vleck, displaying the company's grip at the center.

Below is one of the combination cars, electrified with a minimum of alteration after acquisition of the bankrupt property by George B. Kerper. (*Title Insurance & Trust Company*)

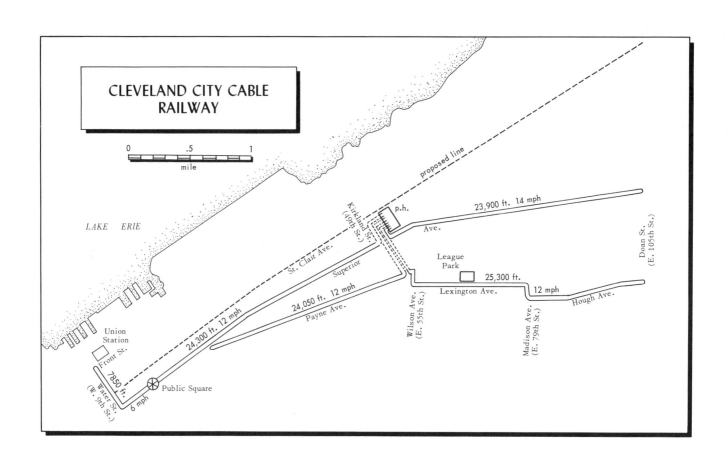

CLEVELAND CITY CABLE RAILWAY

0 .5 1
mile

LAKE ERIE

proposed line

23,900 ft. 14 mph

p.h.

Kirkland St. (49th St.)

St. Clair Ave.

Ave.

Doan St. (E. 105th St.)

Superior

League Park

25,300 ft.

24,050 ft. 12 mph

Payne Ave.

Lexington Ave.

12 mph

Hough Ave.

24,300 ft. 12 mph

Wilson Ave. (E. 55th St.)

Madison Ave. (E. 79th St.)

Union Station

Front St.

7850 ft.

Water St. (W. 9th St.)

6 mph

Public Square

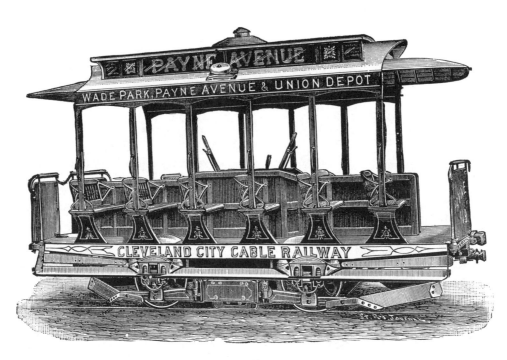

454

CLEVELAND

Population in 1890: 261,353

CLEVELAND CITY CABLE RAILWAY

Gillham double-jaw side grip   *Gauge: 4'-8½"*

Cleveland, like Kansas City, had a Union Station at the foot of a grade down from the central business district. The grade in this instance was under 6 per cent, and the city is free of Kansas City's universal undulation, but the solution of a cable railway was pursued in both cities. In Cleveland, cable traction was limited to the city's east side because Tom L. Johnson, the city's dominant traction magnate in other areas, somewhat surprisingly considered the city too low in size and population density to justify a cable installation.

The east side horsecar operator, Frank DeHaas Robison, was impressed with cable traction on the basis of the experience in Kansas City and Chicago. In 1889 he merged the St. Clair Street Railroad and the Superior Railroad to form the Cleveland City Cable Railway, and bought the rights for trust patents for the installation. Robison's intention was to run three lines in a radial pattern from Union Station out the major thoroughfares of the east side: Payne Avenue (and connecting streets), Superior Avenue, and St. Clair Avenue. Only the first two were built, but the powerhouse at Superior and Kirtland (49th) Street was designed to operate the entire system with six cables. Col. William H. Paine was construction engineer and Robert Gillham was consultant; the technology was similar to the Chicago City Railway and to Gillham's Kansas City installations.

The company's first and simpler line, Superior Avenue, was opened on December 17, 1890. The Payne Avenue line was reported in experimental operation at that time, and cable cars entirely replaced horsecars on the two routes over the course of about two weeks. The system totalled about 9.2 miles. As the map indicates, the outer cable of the Payne Avenue line had a considerable degree of curvature, such that it had to be operated at 2 miles per hour less than the outer Superior cable. The inner Superior cable operated an auxiliary at half speed to Union Station off a set of reduction gears, illustrated in Chapter V, at Public Square, which the cable line bisected. In the 1890s — one source indicates after about two years of service — the company removed the reduction gears and extended the inner Payne Avenue cable to Union Station, bringing it to about 36,750 feet. Removal of reduction gears was common, but why the company chose to extend the Payne rather than Superior cable is difficult to explain; this course of action entailed greater revision in the vaultwork at the intersection of the two lines, and resulted in a longer cable with greater curvature than an extended Superior cable would have had. Possibly the company was already considering early electrification of the stronger Superior line. To bolster traffic on the Payne Avenue line, Robison built Cable Park for amusement at the terminus, and in 1891 opened League Park on the line at Dunham and Lexington for the Cleveland Spiders of the National League, of which he was owner. In 1892 the company ran cars on each line at intervals of 2 to 3 minutes in rush hours and 7 minutes in base service, some of the most frequent service in the industry.

In June 1893 the company was merged with Senator Marcus A. Hanna's Woodland Avenue & West Side Street Railroad into the Cleveland City Railway, the corporate entity under which the cable lines served out the rest of their history. The new company announced it had no intention of converting the cable lines, but it strung trolley wire over some of the trackage in the central area. Robison in 1892 had decided against laying cable on the St. Clair Avenue route, and the City Railway completed it as an electric line in September 1893.

The cable lines operated throughout the 1890s as electric cars were spreading throughout the city. The City Railway converted Superior Avenue on July 1, 1900 and Payne Avenue on January 20, 1901. Robison's Cleveland Spiders, incidentally, in 1899 produced the worst season's record in major league history, 20 victories and 134 defeats. While this is hardly a major cause of the end of the cables, it is not too much to say that the team produced little traffic to help the Payne Avenue line survive.

POWERHOUSE EQUIPMENT: Two 1600 HP William Wright engines, 38" x 60". Oil-burning boilers. Walker machinery. Partly extant as Lennox Haldeman lathing and plastering shop.

References: Kenneth S. P. Morse, *A History of Cleveland Streetcars* (Baltimore, 1955), pp. 1-2; *Cleveland Leader*, December 18, 1890; SRJ, VII (1891), 277-281.

Unaccountably, the Cleveland City Cable Railway, though it bisected Public Square and operated for a full decade, generated hardly any photographic coverage. Here a train carrying trailer 131 turns from Water Street into Superior. The cable line shared the street with early electrics. *(Cleveland Public Library)*

BALTIMORE

Population in 1890: 434,439

BALTIMORE TRACTION COMPANY

Root single-jaw side grip   *Gauge: 5'-4½"*

Baltimore, an old, densely-populated city with continuous undulation of the terrain, had the most obvious geographical characteristics for cable traction of any eastern coastal city; the cost of operation of horsecars was reportedly the highest on the eastern seaboard. Remarkably, cable traction did not come to Baltimore until 1891, after every other city except Tacoma, and even then it came only because of pressure from the city government.

In the 1880s the heads of the city's major horsecar lines had expressed fairly uniform hostility to cable traction. In particular, in February 1889 president James S. Hagerty of the Citizens' Passenger Railway stated he doubted that cable cars would ever come to Baltimore because electric cars were so close to perfection. Some four months later this company merged with the People's Line to form the Baltimore Traction Company, which in turn came under control of the Widener-Elkins syndicate of Philadelphia. Widener, in spite of his adverse experience in Philadelphia and Chicago, was sympathetic enough to cable traction that he was willing to install it in Baltimore when the city government showed continuing hostility to overhead wires on safety grounds. A. D. Whitton, Widener's usual engineer, designed the system, but he mercifully spared the city another installation of the top-grip technology he had used in his first two attempts. Whitton adopted a Root grip, but used his characteristic large double-truck enclosed cars, built in the company shops in Philadelphia.

Baltimore Traction's purpose was to lay cable along existing horsecar lines to Druid Hill Park to the northwest and to Patterson Park to the east. The layout was a difficult one, especially since it involved three loops, one a large one through the central business district. The original route, via Druid Hill Avenue, was ready for service on May 23, 1891. It was the equivalent of about 4.6 miles of double track.

Since the line combined service to a substantial population with heavy week-end pleasure traffic to the two parks, it had a high absolute level of utilization. The company was at minimum satisfied with cable traction enough to convert a second route to

Druid Hill Park to cable. This alternate route of about 2½ miles via Fayette and Gilmor Streets, opened on August 30, 1892, was mainly notable for the odd arrangement the company made. for the powerhouse. Unwilling to duplicate the elaborate powerhouse it had put on Druid Hill Avenue, the company acquired the disused Epworth Methodist Church at Gilmor and Mosher Streets. The company removed as little of the interior as possible — leaving the balcony and chandelier in place — and installed two Corliss engines. With sly humor, the company officially named the installation "the Epworth powerhouse."

Cars for the Gilmor line ran only to the downtown loop, thereby creating a problem at Lombard and South Streets. Since the cable ran from the east powerhouse, cars had to let go on Lombard and pick up rope on South, but owing to a jog on Lombard the curve was too long to traverse on momentum. The company stationed a team of horses to assist cars around the corner — an expensive expedient which was an especial incentive to get rid of this line. The company served the Gilmor line not only with double truck cars of its usual sort, but also with open grips and trailers, painted Tuscan red with silver trim, of orthodox cable type. Trains of the two varieties alternated so as to serve smokers and non-smokers with different vehicles.

Unsurprisingly, the Gilmor Street line was one of the most short-lived in the industry. On October 17, 1894, when the line was only two years old, the company's directors voted to convert it to electricity, along with several lines the horsecars of which the cable cars hauled as trailers. Conversion of the Gilmor Street line was expected to save the company $20,000 per year. The route was ready for the conversion on March 3, 1895. President T. Edward Hambleton stated that his company had laid cable only because the council had refused to approve electricity, but that he had gone to "a higher power" for the right to electrify. Naturally, the company lost little time in preparing to convert the Druid Hill Avenue line. In the interim, the Gilmor cars were repainted in Druid Hill Avenue colors; thereafter, the open Gilmor cars ran

457

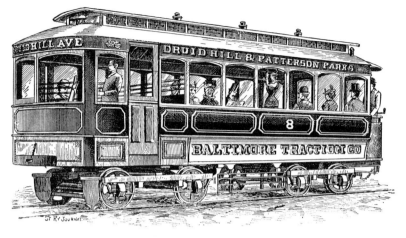

in the summer months, and the Whitton closed cars only in the off-season. They had but a single winter to serve, for the company converted the remaining line on October 4, 1896.

POWERHOUSES: Druid Hill Avenue and Retreat Street. EQUIPMENT: Two 500 HP Corliss engines. Extant as general manufacturing and storage building.

East Pratt Street and Central Avenue. EQUIPMENT: Two 500 HP Corliss engines. Extant as garage for municipal garbage trucks.

Epworth powerhouse equipment: Two Corliss engines, 36″ x 60″. Poole machinery. Extant as laundry and cleaning plant.

Baltimore Traction began service on Druid Hill Avenue with 20 of A. D. Whitton's double-truck cars of the type he had already used in Philadelphia and Pittsburgh. The cars were 32 feet long and seated 40 passengers. Ordinarily horsecars served as trailers. Livery was brownish yellow, white and gold. *(George F. Nixon)*

All of Baltimore Traction's powerhouses have survived. At the bottom of the opposite page are the Druid Hill Avenue plant, at left, and the East Pratt Street powerhouse. On this page is the Epworth powerhouse, its ecclesiastical character undimmed, in its present guise as a drycleaning plant. The cutaway drawing below shows how Baltimore Traction installed the usual cable equipment in the former church. *(Photographs, GWH)*

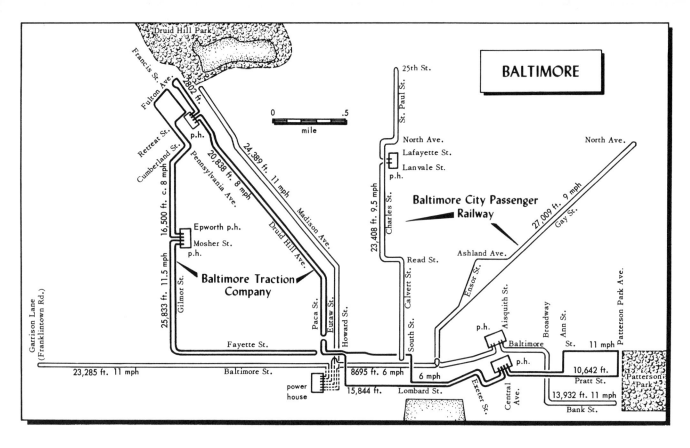

A train of Baltimore City Passenger Railway's Blue Line passes Calvert Station. (*Enoch Pratt Free Library*)

BALTIMORE CITY PASSENGER RAILWAY

Double-jaw side grip   *Gauge: 5'-4½"*

The opening of the Baltimore Traction Company's cable lines caused an immediate diversion of passengers away from the parallel horsecar lines of the Baltimore City Passenger Railway, which suffered a reduction in its dividends by half. The company, the largest in the city, had shown no enthusiasm for cable traction in the 1880s; President Oden Bowie, a former governor of Maryland, had stated in June 1889 that the company could not afford to run cable cars, and said he was looking into electric power. He felt that the necessity of a two-man crew on a grip car neutralized the savings over horsecars, since his company could feed eight horses for the salary of the second man. Retrospectively, E. Austin Jenkins, a director of the company said:

> We adopted cable power reluctantly, but were forced to do so owing to the popular clamor against electricity. To keep up with the progress of the times, it was necessary to displace the horsecars and electricity was looked upon with dread by the people. The popular prejudice was so strong against the use of electricity that the City Passenger Railway was forced to build cable lines.

On the other hand, when the company made its decision to lay cable, Bowie stated that he had studied the Sprague electrification in Boston (probably Sprague's least successful early installation) and concluded that his company could not make money with an operating ratio as high as the Sprague cars. He anticipated an operating ratio of 42 per cent with cable cars, as versus 60 to 95 per cent with Sprague electrics. Especially in light of the park tax, 9 per cent of gross receipts extracted from Baltimore street railways for maintenance of city parks, he felt the additional investment in a cable system was justified. Whether Bowie was honestly converted by comparing the Boston electrics with the Baltimore Traction Company's cable system, or was merely making a superficial show of enthusiasm for what was being forced on him is impossible to say. In any case, the City Passenger Railway in 1891 set out to convert to cable three most heavily-travelled lines, and had the system ready for service in 1893.

The company, which operated six lines, designated by color of the equipment, began cable operation on May 22, 1893 with the Blue Line, 2.2 miles, essentially a north-south route along Charles Street. South of Read Street it operated on Calvert, partly to avoid Mount Vernon Square and partly to serve the Pennsylvania Railroad's Calvert Station. Above North Avenue it ran on St. Paul Street to avoid the high-income residential portion of Charles, and incidentally to approach the baseball park near the terminus at 25th Street. The cable era coincided with the flourishing of the Baltimore Orioles in the National League.

On July 23, 1893, the company put in service the Red Line, a route along Baltimore and Gay Streets, with a minor diversion along Ashland and Ensor to avoid a narrow stretch of Gay. Between Gay and Eutaw Streets, the Red Line shared trackage with the White Line, opened as a cable operation on August 20, 1893. As the accompanying map indicates, the White Line closely paralleled the Baltimore Traction Company's main line from Druid Hill Park to Patterson Park. Since the Traction Company had already pre-empted Baltimore Street, the White Line approached Patterson Park via Broadway and Bank Street. Total mileage was about 10.7.

The City Passenger Railway's technology was orthodox, though there is no indication it used trust patents. The system was designed by its chief engineer, A. N. Connett, who designed a simple double-jaw side grip for it. His ingenuity was demonstrated principally in a variety of depression and elevation devices for dealing with the quick changes in gradient characteristic of the city.

A N. CONNETT.

Initially, the City Passenger Railway operated with open grip cars, 62 from Brill and 10 from Stephenson, hauling enclosed trailers in the usual fashion. About the end of 1896, the company began rebuilding the equipment, converting the closed trailers to grip cars, and the open grip cars to trailers. The former trailers were placed on substantial Peckham trucks and re-equipped with the Broadway, or Earl double-jaw side grip, wheel-operated off the front platform. Ostensibly, the purpose was to improve visibility for the grip-man and reduce accidents. In this it was successful enough that the company increased its cable speeds slightly after the change.

Actually, the change was probably the first step toward electrification. The Peckham trucks were heavy enough to carry electric motors, and the company, which had already electrified its outlying lines, had become enthusiastic about Westinghouse motors. The city remained adamant concerning overhead wires in densely populated areas, but the incentives to convert were so great that the company went to court to secure the right to electrify. Bowie was forced to fight the case through a lower court to the state court of appeals, where early in 1897 he received permission. Because of the necessity of installing electric motors in existing equipment, the conversion was a slow one, effected by replacing cable trains with electric as equipment became available. The first trolley car ran on the Blue Line on June 6, 1897, and

conversion was probably completed early the following year. The company then began work on the remainder of the cable system. Electric cars first ran on the White Line on June 28, 1898, and on the Red Line on August 30, 1898. Conversion of both was completed on March 23, 1899, shortly after the company had been absorbed into the United Railways.

Neither of the Baltimore companies made much effort to remove underground equipment. Cables were removed immediately, but carrying pullies, sheaves and other fittings of the conduit were typically left in the ground. The slots were visible well into the new century before the streets were resurfaced.

POWERHOUSES: Eutaw south of Baltimore. EQUIP-MENT: Two Reynolds-Corliss compound non-condensing engines, 24″ + 38″ x 60″.

Baltimore and Aisquith Streets. EQUIPMENT: Similar to above, 22″ + 36″ x 60″. Extant as ice cream factory of Hendler Creamery Co.

Charles Street between Lafayette and Lanvale. EQUIPMENT: Similar to above, 20″ + 30″ x 60″. Poole machinery. Extant as Charles Theater and Famous Ballroom.

References: George W. Hilton, "Cable Car Days in Baltimore," *Capital Traction Quarterly,* I, No. 4 (1965), 9 pages; SRJ, X (1894), 94-97, 160-61; collection of Mike Farrell.

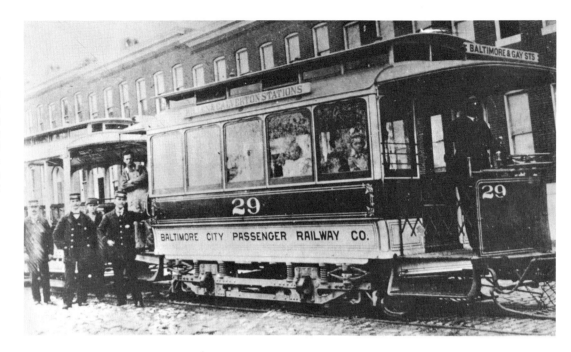

Baltimore City Passenger Railway began operation with orthodox grips such as the Red Line car on the opposite page. *(Museum of the City of New York)* About 1896 the company began rebuilding trailers into closed grip cars such as number 29 at right. *(Louis C. Mueller)*

The Blue Line's powerhouse and car barn double as the Charles Theater and the Famous Ballroom — possibly the most elevated status of any of the former powerhouses. (GWH)

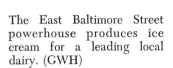

The East Baltimore Street powerhouse produces ice cream for a leading local dairy. (GWH)

The Tacoma cable line began operation with single-truck grip cars, as shown in the photograph at the left, which incidentally gives a good impression of the heroic grade the line was designed to climb. *(LeRoy O. King, Jr.)* The company next moved to handsome Pullman combination cars, such as number 35, photographed at the Pullman plant. *(George Krambles)* Finally, the line was re-equipped with steel cars of vaguely Stone-and-Webster design, as shown at the bottom of the page. *(Washington State Historical Society)*

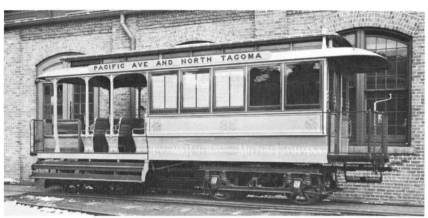

TACOMA

Population in 1890: 36,006

TACOMA RAILWAY & MOTOR COMPANY

Root single-jaw side grip   *Gauge: 3'-6"*

If one were to choose the single cable line which was most justified by geographic and economic considerations, the Tacoma installation would be the probable choice. The city's central business district lies virtually at water level at the foot of a steep grade up Court House Hill to a secondary business district and extensive residential areas. Although only about three-fourths of a mile long, this hill entails an over-all grade of about 10 per cent, with gradients on individual blocks ranging from 9 to more than 14 per cent. It was such an obvious place for cable traction that a Vogel line had been promoted unsuccessfully in 1888.

The Tacoma Railway & Motor Company was founded in 1890 to build a network of 46 miles of electric track comprehensively about the city. The company had no interest in cable traction generally, even for undulating portions of the system, but specified it in the corporate charter for the ascent of the hill out of the central area as a means of connecting the electric cars on the higher and lower levels. Indeed, in 1890 the company was reported to have asked to have the charter modified to use electric traction even on the hill, but to have been refused by the City Council. The charter had provided for a double-track line on 13th Street, but petitions from local property owners caused it to be built as a loop on A, 11th, K and 13th Streets. The route ascended 11th and descended 13th, thereby ascending the slightly milder of the two streets; the worst single block was 14.29 per cent between Tacoma and G Streets on 13th.

The installation was designed by W. B. Knight and constructed by Edmund Saxton, both of Kansas City, who had it ready for service on August 4, 1891. Investment was reported at $110,000. Five grip cars provided 4-minute headway on a round trip of only 12 minutes. The line was heavily utilized from the outset, and owing to its gradient, was protected against the general forces for annihilation of the cable cars in the 1890s. It was, in fact, the only American cable line to be modernized in equipment *pari passu* with electric lines, finally being equipped in 1917 with pay-as-you-enter steel cars of the sort common on electric systems. Examples of the three successive styles of cable equipment are shown in accompanying photographs.

As in Seattle, the cable line survived until the mass replacement of electric streetcars in the 1930s. The last cable car ran on April 8, 1938 at 1:10 AM.

POWERHOUSE: A and 13th Streets. The cable line was originally powered by a 30-year-old 200 horsepower Corliss engine, secondhand from a sawmill. This was reported replaced in 1913, probably by electric power. The powerhouse also generated for the company's electric lines throughout its history.

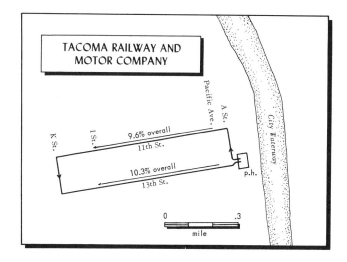

465

MAJOR PROJECTED LINES

The cable car ceased to be economic so abruptly that several projects died in the womb. These are of interest, both as local history and as indications of the calculations of cable promoters, hardly less than the completed lines. Since the street railways in most major cities, such as Buffalo and Indianapolis, for example, considered converting their major horsecar lines to cable, the decision on which projects to include is necessarily arbitrary. In general, I have included cable projects if a substantial amount of work was done on them, or if they were widely erroneously reported as completed, or if they were particularly important in the general history of cable traction.

Dallas

Population in 1890: 38,067

DALLAS CABLE RAILWAY

The Dallas Cable Railway came closer to completion than any of the other unexecuted projects — indeed, close enough that it is often listed among completed cable lines. The project was a promotion of Albert W. Childress, a broker and real estate dealer, in association with merchants along Elm Street in downtown Dallas. In 1890 Elm Street had no street railway of any sort, and was handicapped for retailing relative to Main Street, a block away, which had a long-established mule car line. Early in the year, the project was expected to be built as an electric line to provide entry for several suburban electric railways already under construction. Surprisingly, at a meeting of April 22, 1890, the Elm Street property owners voted in favor of a cable installation proposed by the Pacific Cable Construction Company. Dallas interests were to subscribe to a minimum of $184,000 in stock, and Pacific Cable was to provide the rest of the funds; the project was estimated at $600,000. The trust proposed to use Market Street technology, but a 3'-6" gauge.

The line was projected to run from Houston Street up Elm to Haskell Avenue, turn right and proceed to a turntable at Haskell and Lindsley, just short of the Texas & Pacific Railway tracks, and near the entrance to the Texas State Fair Grounds. The powerhouse, intended to be the duplicate mechanically of the Portland Cable Railway's plant, was to be on the north side of Haskell, just east of Elm. If Pacific Cable intended one cable for Haskell and one for Elm, as seems likely, the line would have been an almost ideal cable installation, with only a single pull curve on Elm at the T&P tracks, and no grade over 2 per cent. Large

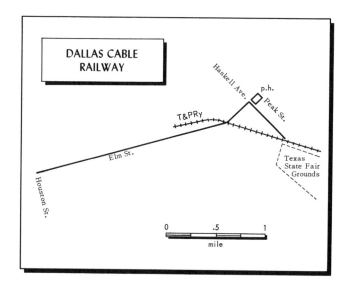

combination cars were to run at 10 miles per hour at 3-minute intervals. Thus, for all its expense, the Dallas Cable Railway would have been a high-capacity operation. Simultaneously, however, the Dallas Rapid Transit arranged an entry into the central area via Commerce Street, the third of the city's main streets, with an electric line costing only $100,000.

Concerted work on the cable line began on July 31, 1890, when the company put 75 men on Elm Street excavating for the conduit between Ervay and Akard. Although the company hoped to have the line ready on October 5 for the opening of the State Fair, construction lasted barely more than a week — just long enough to disrupt Elm Street badly. W. A. Dennis, local manager for Pacific Cable, stated that work was proceeding as fast as delivery of iron would allow, but the city believed the enterprise lacked funds for completion, particularly since Pacific Cable paid its franchise deposit of $17,500 with a check that bounced. On August 26 Dennis ordered out a gang to replace the pavement on Elm, and the project appeared dead. Mayor W. C. Connor recommended that the City Council revoke the company's franchise, but the Council merely allowed it to expire.

Childress, however, announced in November he intended to pursue the project without Pacific Cable. In December he received a new franchise, enabling him to undertake construction on February 15 and obligating him to complete the line by August 31, 1891. Childress reported that Dallas parties had subscribed $85,000 and stated that if the sum could be raised to $100,000 or $125,000, outside financiers would bear the rest of the cost. At the end of January he announced he had raised $100,000 and had arranged with unidentified New York capitalists to build the road. In March he told the press he had contracted for all the machinery, engines, rails and ironwork with the firm of C. E. Keller & Grigsby Bros. Work was resumed at Akard and Elm on May 4, and in spite of a strike (which the company lost), by June 3 Childress could report that 3000 feet of conduit were laid, and all of the iron was on the property. The foundation and first story of his powerhouse had also been completed. Apparently unable to secure land on Haskell, he had undertaken a powerhouse facing Elm near the corner of Elm and Peak, a block east of Haskell. By June 24, it was said to be two-thirds completed, and 12 grip cars with 12 trailers had been ordered. The order of separate grips and trailers indicates a change from the original plan, but what other changes in technology were intended is not clear.

On July 28, 1891, one of Pacific Cable's creditors, C. J. Pitman, secured a writ of garnishment against the Cable Railway for $2860. Work on the cable line ceased almost simultaneously, though Childress claimed that his affairs were being put in order for resumption of construction. On September 7 he obtained an extension of the completion date to July 31, 1892, but there is no evidence of further work. Remarkably, after almost a year of inactivity, Childress obtained an extension until March 1893 as the end of July 1892 approached. Alderman Conroy in the debate on the extension of time delivered a bitter denunciation of Childress and his associates, arguing that the company had not paid its laborers, had bilked local residents out of $25,000, and was merely trying to prevent any other operator's building on Elm Street.

Once again, there is no evidence of further construction. Main Street had been electrified in 1890, and the Elm Street project, in addition to its other

The proposed Haskell Avenue powerhouse was to cost $150,000. *(Texas State Library)*

difficulties, was becoming simply obsolete as electric lines spread about the city. Apart from the uncompleted powerhouse, the company's only real asset was the right to use Elm Street. Childress' best hope was to gain the right to convert the project from cable to electric, and this he did in an ordinance of January 24, 1893. His series of favorable actions from the Council in spite of the Cable Railway's dismal history was his only real success. Armed with the right to put an electric line on Elm, he quickly sold out to the Queen City Railway, which built the line in short order.

The question arises how much of the cable line was actually built. Childress claimed that about two-thirds of the conduit and two-thirds of the powerhouse were completed before building ceased in 1891. The SRJ in 1894 reported that material had been distributed over the whole line, but that only 1¼ miles of conduit, about a third of the project, ever went into the ground. The line was undoubtedly built in the central business district, and yokes were discovered years later on Elm west of the T&P crossing. The proposed powerhouse was completed as part of the carhouse complex of the Dallas Railway & Traction Company at Elm and Peak. A corner of it still survives.

Reference: George W. Hilton, "The Dallas Cable Railway," *Southwest Railroad Historical Society Newsletter,* V, No. 2 (December, 1966), 2-4.

The second projected powerhouse of the Dallas Cable Railway reached partial completion as the brick structure in the foreground. When the cable project was abandoned, the powerhouse was completed as a carbarn, shown above in 1917. The second powerhouse was apparently not built to the plan of the first. (*John J. Meyers*)

St. Joseph, Missouri

Population in 1890: 52,324

ST. JOSEPH CIRCLE RAILWAY

St. Joseph had some of the same geographical characteristics as Kansas City: a union station on river flats, a central business district up a grade from the flatlands, and high-lying residential areas being developed during the land boom of the late 1880s. The grade up from the station was mild compared with Kansas City, but the residential area was more steeply undulating.

St. Joseph had two major projects for cable lines, neither of which was completed. The earlier was the St. Joseph Circle Railway, more frequently known as the Circle Cable Railway. This was an effort to build from the Union Station at 6th and Mitchell Streets through the central business district directly north of the station, and thence east to the residential area along Jules and Francis Streets. Potentially, this was the more important of the two projected lines, if only because it would have served Francis Street, one of the city's two main business thoroughfares, but relatively little was done to bring the project to fruition.

The Circle Railway was projected by Col. James Lillis of Kansas City and others who had been connected with the Kansas City Cable Railway. They were also projectors of the Citizens' Cable Railway, unsuccessful applicant for the Holmes Street franchise in Kansas City. This group also had a community of financial interest with the Cable Tramway Company of Omaha. As in the related lines, Robert Gillham of Kansas City was to be engineer; presumably the company was to use Gillham's characteristic double-jaw side grip. The line was to run west from the Union Station at 6th and Mitchell two blocks to 4th Street, thence north to Angelique Street, where the line diverged, running north on 7th Street into the central business district and east on Francis Street through the residential area to 22nd Street. Returning, the line was to run west on Jules Street and straight south on 4th to Mitchell. The company secured a franchise for this route in April, 1887, but partly to reduce curvature and partly to avoid putting a double-track line on 4th Street beside the horsecar line of the existing Union Street Railway (which was overtly hostile to the cable line) the company sought and secured in May 1887 a revision of the franchise whereby the line was to run north from Mitchell, and cross to 7th on Messanie Street. The use of Messanie instead of Angelique would have obviated a short reverse curve at 6th and Messanie. The line as revised would have required only a single-jaw side grip. The company's franchise contained the favorable provision that the city should grade Jules and Francis Streets for the company's benefit. Both streets had grades of about 10 per cent east of 12th Street, which presumably were intended for reduction. The company was obligated to begin building within four months of the completion of grading.

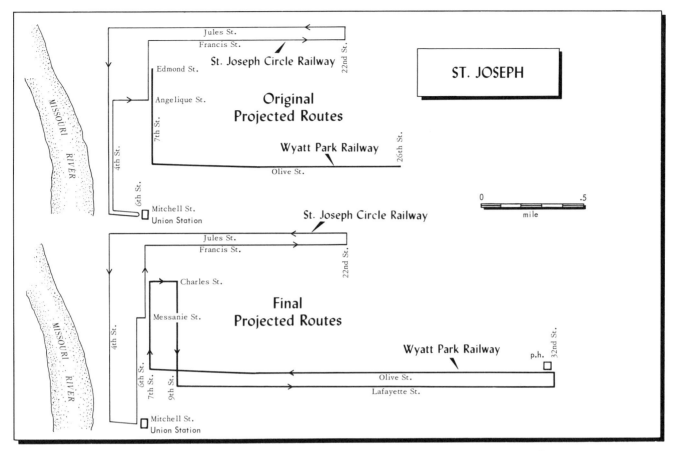

In September 1887 a carload of castings was shipped from Galesburg and Lillis was reported in town supervising distribution of iron yokes along the line. Beyond this, nothing was done, either by the city or the company in the next few months. There is no indication that a site for the powerhouse was ever chosen. In October a member of the city council suggested revoking the company's franchise for failure to undertake construction. Simon Sterne, a well-known New York financier who had interested himself in the project, said the line would be built as soon as the city graded the streets, but he admitted that only 5 per cent of the stock had been paid in. The company was unhappy that 6th Street was being paved with asphalt, increasing the difficulty of its projected excavation, and it claimed that both credit stringency and shortages of material were impeding its building of the portions of the route which required no grading.

As far as can be ascertained from newspaper accounts, the last flurry of effort on this project was some grading the city undertook at 20th and Jules in May 1888. A local group was reported interested in undertaking the project if Lillis and his associates withdrew, but the project lay idle until 1889, when the Wyatt Park Railway bought out the company to secure its franchise. The City Council on March 4, 1889 issued the Wyatt Park Railway a franchise for an electric line on Jules Street, thereby ending any prospect of the cable line's being built.

WYATT PARK RAILWAY

St. Joseph's second projected cable line was integral with Wyatt Park, a real estate promotion of A. L. Wyatt, John M. Huffman, W. J. Hobson, and other local businessmen. Located to the east of the central district beyond a major hill on Olive Street, Wyatt Park was an even more obvious area to be developed by cable traction than the region served by the Circle Railway.

The Wyatt Park Railway was incorporated in June 1887 and granted a franchise in July for a route from 7th and Edmond Streets, just below the central business district, south to Olive and east to 26th Street. Partly out of a desire to avoid putting a double-track line beside the Circle Railway's intended single track on 7th, and partly to avoid a grade of over 10 per cent eastbound on Olive Street, the Wyatt Park Railway in August secured a revision of the franchise to run south on 9th and east on Lafayette, looping back at Charles Street in the central area. The rope dia-

469

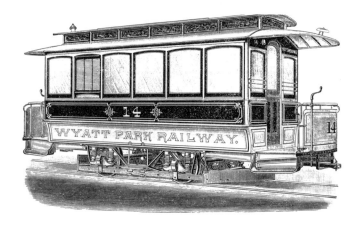

arranging for the line to be designed by D. J. Miller, whose New York installations were the most capital-intensive in the industry. Miller inspected the route, expressed satisfaction with it, and estimated the line would handle 6000 to 8000 passengers per day. He estimated the average cost of construction of cable lines at $200,000 to $250,000 per mile, but thought the Wyatt Park could be built for $150,000 per mile. There is no indication he intended to install his duplicate system, but presumably he intended to use his customary double-jaw side grip. As in the case of the Circle Railway, the revised diagram would have required only a single-jaw side grip. The promoters hoped to build the line for $450,000 of which $200,000 had been paid in. Financing was local, but they contracted with J. T. Lerned of Plainfield, N. J. to construct the property. Lerned arrived in November 1887 and stated he hoped to have the installation completed by March 1888. The time chosen coincided with the winter of 1888, one of the worst of the nineteenth century. The Wyatt Park was less fortunate than the Circle Railway in its franchise: it was required to do its own grading. The company planned some extensive grade reduction, including a

gram would have been a figure-8 with a crossing at 9th and Olive. It is perhaps pushing things a bit far to speculate on rope positions on unbuilt lines, but 9th would probably have been put above Olive to take advantage of a mild downgrade for westbound cars.

W. J. Hobson, who was in charge of construction for the promoters, estimated that the line could be built for $60,000 per mile, only two-thirds of what the Kansas City Cable Railway had cost. Unaccountably, he endeavored to implement this optimism by

Apparently in preparation for cable operation, the Wyatt Park Railway bought a set of trailers from the St. Louis Car Company (*above, George Krambles*) and a low-speed Corliss from the Sioux City Engine Works. The typical cable engine which ran at 55 to 80 RPM, could be used to run a dynamo, but a railway intending electric operation usually opted for an engine of 100 to 200 RPM.

14-foot cut on Lafayette. By the opening of 1888 some grading was said to have been done on Olive, but progress had come to a halt and rumors were rife that the project had been abandoned. By January 12 Lerned had returned to New Jersey.

Meanwhile, on September 6, 1887 the Union Street Railway opened a line of Sprague electric cars. This installation antedated even the Richmond Union Passenger Railway, and was argued locally to be the first wholly successful electric street railway in the country. As between the withdrawal of Lerned, the success of the rival electric line, and the pall on construction cast by the winter of 1888, the Wyatt Park Railway was widely thought to have been abandoned, but in March Hobson announced he had been to New York where he had arranged financing with a new syndicate. He also announced that the line would be built to the patents of A. H. Lighthall, which were essentially a non-trust version of Henry Root's designs for California Street in San Francisco. This was probably the closest the shady Lighthall ever came to having a line built to his own technology. Lighthall went to England where in late March he ordered 3500 yokes for the line. He returned to St. Joseph where he spent the spring in preparations for building, though no actual work beyond grading seems to have been done. The management apparently tired of Lighthall, and while he was in New York on company business in June, Hobson dismissed him, saying the firm would give him no further time to commence work on the line. Finally, on July 17, 1888, Hobson announced the Wyatt Park Railway would be built as an electric line with Sprague technology by D. W. Guernsey of St. Louis. As an electric line on 6th and Olive Streets, but by-passing the Olive Street Hill to the south, the Wyatt Park Railway was reported finished in September 1889. In 1891 it passed into the hands of the Union Street Railway and became a part of the city's early and complete Sprague electrification.

Boston

Population in 1890: 448,477

WEST END STREET RAILWAY

The West End Street Railway's proposed cable installation is the most famous of the projected lines, if only because President Henry M. Whitney's last-minute decision to use electricity was the beginning of the end for the cable car. This event has been widely recorded, but the exact character of the intended cable lines is of some interest *per se*.

In retrospect, Boston is a particularly obvious place not to have had cable cars. Its mixture of com-

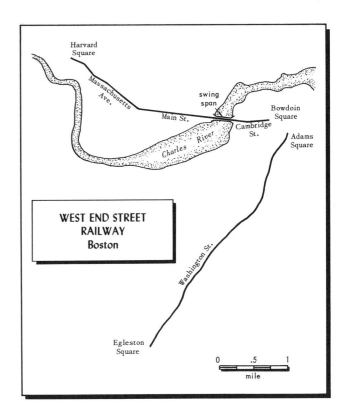

WEST END STREET RAILWAY
Boston

prehensive water barriers, tortuous downtown streets and an absence of major grades made cable traction unattractive, even though the city was large, densely populated, highly centralized and rapidly growing. In 1886 the Widener interests had proposed a Boston Cable Railway to run from the central business district to Brookline and Cambridge, apparently on a triangular route, using the unfortunate Philadelphia technology, but the project was never implemented.

The West End was the largest street railway in the country, an enterprise of 2000 cars and 8000 horses. Whitney was acutely aware of the necessity of replacing the horse, but he had a sensible skepticism of cable traction throughout the middle 1880s. His general manager, Daniel F. Longstreet, was reportedly in favor of cables (though this is inconsistent with his stated view of cable traction in Providence), but Whitney remained unconvinced until C. B. Holmes late in 1887 or early in 1888 went to Boston to speak persuasively in favor of the cable car. Whitney was won over, so that between February and April 1888 he announced extensive preparations for a pair of unconnected cable lines using Chicago City Railway technology. He brought Robert Gillham to Boston to work out engineering details, further indicating that a heavy double-jaw side grip was planned. Both lines were intended to pick up horsecars from converging lines to be brought in trains into the central area.

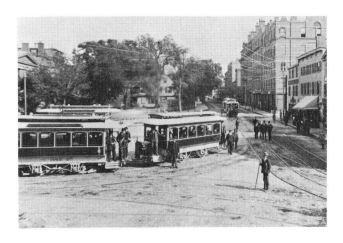

Had the West End's cable lines been built, trains would have approached Harvard Square by Massachusetts Avenue, shown here in the background of a view of the square in the 1890s. (*O. R. Cummings*)

Passenger density would probably have been among the heaviest in the country.

Whitney intended first to build from Bowdoin Square in Boston out Cambridge Street, the West Boston Bridge (now the Longfellow Bridge), Main Street and Massachusetts Avenue to Harvard Square, Cambridge. Target date for completion was December 1888. The second line was to run from Adams Square in Boston south along Washington Street to Eggleston Square in Roxbury. Both were and still are major transportation arteries of the city; they are, respectively, the routes of the present Harvard subway and the Forest Hills elevated. The Harvard line had been the route of the city's first horsecar line in 1856.

The two routes were feasible for cable traction, though by no means ideal. Both had a great deal of mild curvature at corners (the Roxbury line, in particular), and both were mildly undulating toward the outer ends. The Cambridge line would have had a short, sharp upgrade into Bowdoin Square for easy gravity switching. Whitney intended to run each line with a single cable from a powerhouse at the far end. He planned a powerhouse of two 30″ x 60″ engines (one to be a spare) at Harvard Square, to which it would have been a somewhat anomalous addition. A similar plant was planned for Roxbury, but no site was apparently decided upon. O. R. Cummings, who examined the company's minute books, found no evidence that land for either powerhouse was acquired. As an effort to adapt cable traction to Boston's difficult geographical characteristics, the system was very intelligently conceived.

In July 1888 the SRJ reported that the company had temporarily postponed the Harvard Square line in response to pressure from the Cambridge City Council to use an overhead electric system. In the August issue Whitney was reported in Richmond inspecting the Sprague electrification, and the Cambridge line was said to be set aside for the year, if not permanently. Cummings' investigation of the corporate records indicates Whitney had decided upon electrification as early as June, 1888. As far as is known, no actual construction of the cable lines had been undertaken when Whitney's famous decision was made.

Minneapolis

Population in 1890: 164,738

MINNEAPOLIS STREET RAILWAY

As in most other respects, Minneapolis is dissimilar to St. Paul in terrain. The city is mainly flat or gently undulating, with no marked difference in altitude between the central business district and the dormitory areas. It shares, of course, St. Paul's fierce climate, and thus the street railway had a double incentive to avoid cable traction. The Twin Cities' street railways had come under the common control of Thomas Lowry, President of the Soo Line, in 1886. A joint committee of the city councils of the two cities had inspected the street railways of Cleveland, Baltimore, Richmond, Boston, New York, and Philadelphia, and had concluded in favor of cable, relative to electric railways. Owing to St. Paul's physical characteristics, Lowry was willing to lay cable there, but he was reluctant to do so in Minneapolis. In 1889, with a conspicuous show of dissatisfaction, he agreed to the Minneapolis City Council's directive, and under-

Plans of the stillborn Minneapolis system progressed through design of the grip cars. (*Russell Olson*)

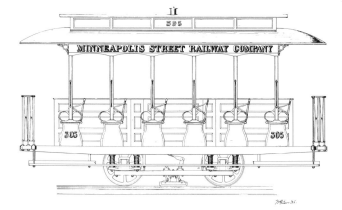

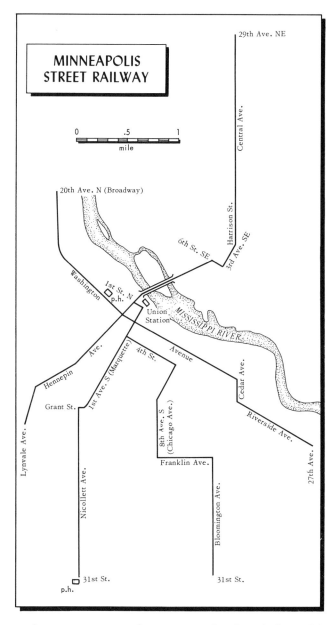

MINNEAPOLIS
STREET RAILWAY

0   .5   1
mile

29th Ave. NE

Central Ave.

20th Ave. N (Broadway)

Harrison St.

6th St. SE

3rd Ave. SE

Washington

1st St. N
p.h.

Union
Station

MISSISSIPPI RIVER

Hennepin Ave.

1st Ave. S (Marquette)

4th St.

Avenue

Cedar Ave.

Riverside Ave.

Grant St.

Lynvale Ave.

Nicollett Ave.

8th Ave. S
(Chicago Ave.)

Franklin Ave.

Bloomington Ave.

27th Ave.

31st St.
p.h.

31st St.

took construction. Plans were developed by Clift Wise, who presumably intended to use the same technology as in St. Paul.

The system would have been a large one, 14 miles at the outset and 21 miles by 1891. As the accompanying map indicates, it was to be radial from the central business district to all of the densely populated areas of the city. The system was to be centered in a powerhouse at 2nd Street and 3rd Avenue North, which was to issue two cables each (through conduits) for the Washington Avenue and Hennepin-Central Avenue lines. The Nicollet Avenue line was to be run from a separate powerhouse at its 31st Street terminus. A similar arrangement was presumably envisioned for the Bloomington Avenue line, which was

to be part of the second stage of construction. The central powerhouse was also to issue a low-speed cable for a downtown loop over which all cars would move counterclockwise past Union Station. Relative to cable lines elsewhere, it was a well-conceived system, which apart from climatic impediments, would probably have been fairly easy to operate.

In the second half of 1889 the company built the two powerhouses and did a small amount of excavation for construction along the Nicollet Avenue line at Grant Street. Nicollet was occupied by an existing motor line of the company, and would doubtless have been the route of heaviest traffic. The company bought about $400,000 worth of equipment for the powerhouses and conduits, which it stored in three locations.

Meanwhile, the Minneapolis Street Railway opened its first electric line on 4th Avenue on December 4, 1889, and was highly pleased with its operation in the winter weather, relative to the St. Paul cable lines. Lowry quickly moved to convert his franchise to electric. The Minneapolis *Tribune* was a strong advocate of an electric system for the city; on January 11, 1890, it wrote: "The fact is that except for hills, nobody regards cables as the ultimate solution of the local transit problem. The cable system is extremely expensive, and it is a cumbrous, awkward method of locomotion that is bound to be superseded." The City Council granted permission for the system to be built as electric on August 8, 1890, by a vote of 30-0, and Lowry quickly complied. The cable machinery was sold as scrap, though both powerhouses were completed as part of the electric system.

A cable powerhouse which never issued a rope, the intended central power station of the Minneapolis lines survives as the Colonial Warehouse. (*Byron D. Olsen*)

Milwaukee

Population in 1890: 204,468

MILWAUKEE CABLE RAILWAY

The flourishing city of Milwaukee was chosen for the second installation of the Rasmussen system, but the utter failure of the pilot installation in Newark prevented any serious effort to build the Milwaukee line.

The Milwaukee Cable Railway was organized in 1887 by John A. Hinsey, president of the city council, and several other local figures. Rasmussen's associate, H. W. McNeill, was vice-president of the company and its general manager. The firm's greatest asset was Hinsey's considerable political power, which manifested itself in a remarkable ability to secure franchises. He began with a simple and well-conceived pair of lines on State and 18th Streets, for which he received a franchise on December 19, 1887. At the time the central business district was almost entirely on the east side of the Milwaukee River, so that the company was involved in a crossing of navigable water of the sort that drove the Chicago lines to tunnels. Hinsey's franchise provided for drawing of cars by horse over the Wells Street bridge, but presumably the company would have required a separate powerhouse for the short trackage on Milwaukee and Oneida (Wells) Streets east of the river. The line, standard gauge and double track, was to be completed by December 1, 1888. The council had provided that any other cable system might be substituted if the Rasmussen system proved a failure, but Hinsey remained an enthusiast for the Rasmussen technology, which he hoped would enable him to build his line for only about $50,000 per mile.

A rival firm, the Milwaukee & Wawatosa Cable Railway, proposed to build from 4th and Wells Streets to North Avenue and thence west toward Wawatosa, but made no progress. The West Side Street Railway briefly showed interest in building a cable line west on Wells, but the Milwaukee City Railway, the dominant horsecar operator, felt the city was not large enough to generate traffic to warrant cable traction's huge investment.

Hinsey followed his acquisition of the State and 18th Street franchises with a really staggering success: On February 27, 1888, the council granted him a comprehensive franchise for a system of some 27 miles, granting him access into almost every part of the city. In addition to the routes west and north he had already secured, he received rights for lines south on Kinnickinnic Avenue, southwest on Lapham

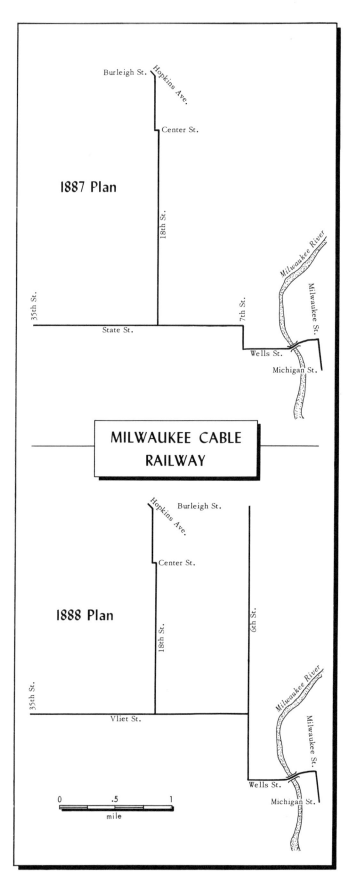

474

and 8th Streets, and northeast on Oakland Avenue. Other operators and many political observers were outraged at this grant, which included several routes previously denied Hinsey's rivals. Mayor Wallber opposed the franchise, stating that the company should show its good faith by building the State and 18th Street lines, but the council passed the franchise over his veto. Nothing was done to construct the larger system (which is not shown on the accompanying maps), and all subsequent discussion concerned building the original lines north and west.

The West Side Street Railway's plan to build an electric line on Wells Street, which it opened in 1890, caused Hinsey to revise his plans. Not wishing to run his line west on State, only two blocks north of Wells, he moved the projected line four blocks farther north to Vliet Street. This plus a new route north to the city limits on 6th Street were written into a franchise of June 1, 1888. For the first time, the franchise read only that cable traction should be used, without specific reference to the Rasmussen system. The 6th Street line would have included a grade of 10.75 per cent immediately north of Reservoir Street, for which a standard system would have been more appropriate than the Rasmussen method.

Whether any actual construction was undertaken is doubtful. Superintendent Hopkins of the Newark installation stated that work was under way in Milwaukee, and the SRJ reported in September 1888 that construction had been begun on the west line. The failure of the Rasmussen system in Newark, which was becoming successively more apparent as 1888 wore on, undoubtedly prevented any extensive construction. It is fairly certain that no sites for powerhouses were chosen.

Since no progress was being made by 1889, Hinsey's political power again proved the company's principal strength. A lesser man would probably have had

his franchise revoked for non-fulfilment, but Hinsey on October 14, 1889, secured a modification of his franchise, dropping the line west and routing his 18th Street line into the city via Vliet, 8th and Wells. More important, he secured the right to build the system as a pair of electric lines. After renaming the enterprise the Milwaukee Electric Railway, he quickly built the 6th Street line to Burleigh and the modified 18th Street line to North Avenue. Both became parts of the Milwaukee Street Railway, but were abandoned in the mid-1890s as redundant.

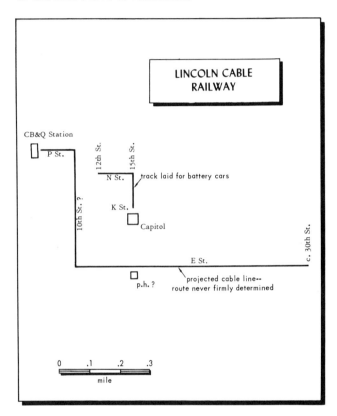

Lincoln, Nebraska

Population in 1890: 55,154

LINCOLN CABLE RAILWAY

The land boom which generated cable railways in the other Missouri Valley cities also gave rise to a project in Lincoln, though it aborted relatively early. John H. Ames of Lincoln conceived the line as a connection between the Burlington Station at 7th and P Streets and the mildly hilly residential area to the southeast of the city. He incorporated the Lincoln Cable Railway on May 3, 1887 and eight days later received a franchise giving him the choice of a large number of streets. His intention was to run east on P Street, south on one of the main streets through the central

The Milwaukee Electric Railway operated the projected 6th Street cable line with these small electrics from the St. Charles Car Company.

business district (of which 10th Street would probably have been the most attractive), and finally east on E Street for a total distance of about 2½ miles, bringing his line to a terminus in open country around the present intersection of 30th and E. The powerhouse was to be on E Street south of the capitol. Ames visited New York in July where he engaged W. H. Paine to design the line.

Partly because of difficulty in financing an enterprise as expensive as a cable line, Ames in October 1887 changed his project to a battery car line, and borrowed $200,000 in New York to build it. Taking advantage of the great breadth of his franchise, he changed his route to run through the business area north of the capitol. The company built less than a mile of track on N from 12th to 15th and on 15th from N to K before funds were exhausted. Nothing further was built, and the line never operated. It was absorbed into the Lincoln electric street railway system which was begun in 1891.

KNOWN FOREIGN INSTALLATIONS

DUNEDIN, NEW ZEALAND

Roslyn Tramway 1881-1951, 1.4 miles
Mornington Tramway 1883-1957, 1 mile
Maryhill extension 1885-1916, 1919-1955, .6 miles
Kaikorai Tramway 1900-1947, 1.17 miles
Mornington Borough Council, Elgin Road line, 1906-1910, .8 miles
3'-6", single-jaw and double-jaw side grips; Hallidie bottom grip on Roslyn line until 1903-1906

MELBOURNE, AUSTRALIA

Melbourne Tramway & Omnibus Co. 1885-1940, comprehensive system, 45.5 miles
4'-8½", single-jaw side grip

SYDNEY, AUSTRALIA

New South Wales Government Tramways
North Sydney line 1886-1900, 2 miles
King Street line 1894-1905, 2.75 miles
4'-8½", single-jaw side grip

LONDON, ENGLAND

Highgate Hill Cable Tramway 1884-1892, 1897-1909, 0.71 miles
3'-6", single-jaw side grip
Brixton Cable Tramway 1892-1909, 3.5 miles
4'-8½", Colam double-jaw side grip

BIRMINGHAM, ENGLAND

Birmingham Central Tramways Co. 1888-1911, 3 miles
3'-6", single-jaw side grip

MATLOCK, ENGLAND

Matlock Tramways Co., Ltd. 1893-1927, 0.62 miles
3'-6", Colam double-jaw side grip

GLASGOW, SCOTLAND

District Subway Co. 1897-1935, 6.6 miles
4'-0", single-jaw side grip

EDINBURGH, SCOTLAND

Edinburgh Northern Cable Tramways and successors 1888-1923, comprehensive system, 25.8 miles
4'-8½", Colam double-jaw side grip

DOUGLAS, ISLE OF MAN

Upper Douglas Cable Tramway 1896-1929, 1.62 miles
3'-0", Colam single-jaw side grip

PARIS, FRANCE

Tramway Funiculaire de Belleville 1891-1924, 2.044 KM
1 meter, double-jaw side grip

LISBON, PORTUGAL

Nova Companhia dos Ascensores Mecánicos de Lisboa
Estrêla line 1890-1912, 1.7 KM
Rua de Palma-Largo de Graça line 1891-1912, 1.05 KM
Companhia de Viação Urbana
Rossio – São Sebastião, 2.4 KM, 1899–early 20th Century
80 CM, bottom grip (?)

Note: The Kelburn Cable Tramway, Wellington, New Zealand, was a funicular using an endless cable to transmit power. The downbound car held the endless cable with a single-jaw side grip. The endless cable was stopped to halt the car at intermediate points; the cars did not go into partial release. The line was 3'-6", 746 yards long. This hybrid of funicular and endless-cable technology operated from 1902 until rebuilt with standard funicular technology in 1978-79.

Bibliography

Only general works of the cable period are listed here; source material and histories of individual lines are cited following the corporate histories in Part II.

BOOKS

J. Bucknall Smith, C. E., *A Treatise upon Cable or Rope Traction as Applied to the Working of Street and Other Railways* (London: Engineering, 1887). Second edition with additional material by George W. Hilton published by Owlswick Press, Philadelphia, 1977.

C. B. Fairchild, *Street Railways* (New York: Street Railway Publishing Co., 1892), Chapter II.

PAMPHLETS

C. P. Shaw, *Cable Railways vs. Horse Railroads* (New York, 1885)

John Stephenson Company, Ltd., *Motive Power for Streetcars* (New York, 1889).

Pacific Cable Railway Company, *The System of Wire-Cable Railways for Cities and Towns* (San Francisco, 1887). Reprinted by Glenwood Publishers, Felton, California, 1967. Earlier versions of this pamphlet are *The Traction Railway Company's System of Wire Rope Street Railways* (San Francisco, 1880), and *The Cable Railway Company's System of Traction Railways* (San Francisco, c. 1884).

A. H. Lighthall, *The Lighthall Cable Traction Tramway Company* (Washington, 1883).

American System of Traction Rope Railways operated by Independent Duplicate Cables (New York: American Cable Railway Company, 1888).

W. W. Hanscom, *Cable Railway Propulsion* (San Francisco, 1884).

Andrew Bryson, Jr., *The Return of Power in Electric and Cable Traction* (New York, 1889).

Henry Root, *Personal History and Reminiscences* (San Francisco, 1921).

ARTICLES

William H. Searles, "Cable Railways," *Journal of the Association of Engineering Societies,* VI (1886), 10-17.

Thomas C. Barr, "The Conditions Necessary to the Financial Success of Electricity as a Motive Power," in *Motive Power for Streetcars,* cited above.

R. J. McCarty, "The Economy of Street Railway Cables," SRJ, XI (1895), 377-380.

H. M. Kebby, "Construction and Operation of Cable and Electric Railways," SRJ, VII (1891), 237.

"Cable Railroads," M&SP, XLIII (1881), 145 ff.

"Cables and Electricity," M&SP, XLVII (1883), 270.

William D. Henry, "Conditions Necessary to the Financial Success of the Cable Power," SRJ, IV (1888), 307-309.

John Kilgour, "Horse and Cable Railways," SRJ, IV (1888), 327-328.

James A. Seddon, "Efficiency of Cable Roads," *Journal of the Association of Engineering Societies,* VI (1887), 141-155.

"Comparative Costs and Profits of Cable, Electric and Horse Railway Operation in New York City," SRJ, XIV (1898), 721-724.

Edward J. Lawless, "Cable Railway Practice," a series in SRG, Vol. III (1888).

W. N. Colam, "Cable Tramways," *Van Nostrand's Engineering Magazine,* XXXIII (1885), 97-104.

James Clifton Robinson, "Abridged Report on a Year's Progress of Cable Motive Power," *Proceedings of the American Street-Railway Association,* X (1891-92), 77-102.

"Origins and Development of Cable Railways: Biographies of Some of the Early Engineers," SRJ, XI (1895), 311-318.

ARTICLES *(Continued)*

Report of interview with Doane and Plimpton, SRJ, IV (1888), 135-136.

Interview with Asa Hovey, Kansas City *Times*, September 8, 1888.

NEWSPAPERS CONSULTED

San Francisco *Chronicle*
San Francisco *Evening Bulletin*
Daily Alta California (San Francisco)
Oakland *Tribune*
Los Angeles *Times*
San Diego *Union*
Portland *Oregonian*
Seattle *Telegraph*
Seattle *Daily Times*
Seattle *Post-Intelligencer*
Tacoma *News-Tribune*
Tacoma *Daily Ledger*
Spokane *Review*
Daily Intermountain (Butte)
Butte *Daily Miner*
Denver *Times*
Denver *Republican*
Rocky Mountain News (Denver)
Kansas City *Times*
Kansas City *Star*
Kansas City *Journal*
Wyandotte Herald (Kansas City, Kansas)
Omaha *World-Herald*
Omaha *Bee*
Sioux City *Journal*
St. Paul *Pioneer-Press*
Minneapolis *Journal*
Minneapolis *Tribune*
Chicago *Tribune*
Chicago *Daily Inter-Ocean*
Grand Rapids *Daily Eagle*
Daily Democrat (Grand Rapids)
Grand Rapids *Evening Leader*

Cleveland *Leader*
Cincinnati *Enquirer*
Cincinnati *Times-Star*
Pittsburgh *Post*
Pittsburgh *Press*
Pittsburgh *Times*
Philadelphia *Times*
Baltimore *Sun*
Washington *Post*
New York *Times*
New York *World*
New York *Herald*
New York *Tribune*
Brooklyn *Eagle*
Binghamton *Sun*
Providence *Journal*
Newark *Star*
Newark *Call*
Sentinel of Freedom (Newark)
St. Joseph *Daily Herald*
Lincoln *Daily News*
Daily State Democrat (Lincoln)
Nebraska State Journal (Lincoln)
Dallas *Times-Herald*
Dallas *Morning News*
Milwaukee *Sentinel*
Evening Wisconsin (Milwaukee)
Detroit *Evening News*

MANUSCRIPT SOURCES

Papers of J. B. Stone, American Steel & Wire Company collection, Manuscript Room, Harvard School of Business, Boston, call number DcC641-645.

Henry C. Collins, "The Cable Car Loses Its Grip: Born Thirty Years Too Late," unpublished MS in possession of its author, San Mateo, California.

Edgar M. Kahn, "Cable Railway Propulsion," unpublished MS in San Francisco Public Library, special collections.

Index

Street railways are listed under the cities in which they operated. Major companies are cross-indexed.